To Dad, who would have been proud

FROM MR SIN to MR BIG

A HISTORY OF AUSTRALIAN DRUG LAWS

desmond manderson

Melbourne
OXFORD UNIVERSITY PRESS
Oxford   Auckland   New York

OXFORD UNIVERSITY PRESS AUSTRALIA

Oxford   New York   Toronto
Delhi   Bombay   Calcutta   Madras   Karachi
Kuala Lumpur   Singapore   Hong Kong   Tokyo
Nairobi   Dar es Salaam   Cape Town
Melbourne   Auckland   Madrid

and associated companies in
Berlin   Ibadan

OXFORD is a trade mark of Oxford University Press

© Desmond Manderson 1993
First published 1993

This book is copyright. Apart from any fair dealing for the purposes of private study, research, criticism or review as permitted under the Copyright Act, no part may be reproduced, stored in a retrieval system, or transmitted, in any form or by any means, electronic, mechanical, photocopying, recording, or otherwise without prior written permission. Inquiries to be made to Oxford University Press.

Copying for educational purposes
Where copies of part or the whole of the book are made under section 53B or section 53D of the Act, the law requires that records of such copying be kept. In such cases the copyright owner is entitled to claim payment.

National Library of Australia
Cataloguing-in-Publication data:

Manderson, D. (Desmond).
   From Mr Sin to Mr Big.

ISBN 0 19 553531 6.

1. Drug abuse—Government policy—Australia. 2. Drug abuse—Australia.
3. Drug abuse—Social aspects—Australia. 4. Drug abuse—Australia—History.
5. Drugs—Australia. I. Title.

362.290994

Typeset in Malaysia by Syarikat Seng Teik Sdn. Bhd.
Printed in Hong Kong by Nordica
Published by Oxford University Press,
253 Normanby Road, South Melbourne, Australia

ACKNOWLEDGEMENTS

In the course of undertaking a task as large as this, one accrues many debts and is thankful for many kindnesses, small and large. My first interest in questions of drug policy came about when I began working in 1986 with Dr Val Brown as a legal researcher for a series of 'briefing papers' on the subject, which eventually turned into a book of which we were two of the authors. I will never forget her enthusiasm and support.

This project began as a much smaller publication funded by the Research Into Drug Abuse Program (RIDAP) of the National Campaign Against Drug Abuse (NCADA). Having completed that piece as part of my honours degree in history, it was suggested that I might be interested in working on a larger project on the history of drug laws in Australia. All I can say is that it seemed like a good idea at the time. RIDAP provided enough funds to enable me to devote myself full-time to the task for two-and-a-half years between 1987 and 1989. Many researchers spend their whole creative lives without ever being granted such a large stretch of time to concentrate on pure research. I feel immensely privileged and grateful that RIDAP took a punt on me. The staff of the Commonwealth Department of Community Services and Health involved with NCADA did not only provide me with a salary. I grew through the unwavering confidence placed in me, particularly by Dr Alf Leslie, then in charge of the programme.

While carrying out my research I was a Visiting Fellow in the Department of History at the Australian National University. There the Head of the Department, Ian Hancock, seemed to think it his duty to read the extremely verbose and deeply purple prose that I dumped on his desk at irregular intervals. I have benefited enormously from his kind and constructive criticism. Meanwhile I spent my time travelling to innumerable libraries and the government archives of the various States and the Commonwealth. I learnt a lot; mainly about how dreary such work is, and how underfunded and understaffed these facilities really are. To the many friends who put me up in their homes for days and weeks, and who put up, moreover, with my continual horror stories about documents lost, misfiled or burnt, and research enquiries thwarted: thank you.

In 1990 I continued to write part-time while the Faculty of Law at the Australian National University tolerated my part-time teaching presence. Tim Bonyhady, colleague and friend, provided me with immensely detailed comments on my draft, and many helpful conversations, from which I learnt a great deal about writing and editing. At this point the Australian National University, through the Editorial Committee of the ANU Press, provided some additional funding, which allowed the book to proceed in the way I preferred, and in particular allowed the inclusion of several pages of illustrations. I am very grateful for this assistance.

The rewriting and redrafting took place while I was based in Montréal, Canada, where members of the Faculty of Law were always interested and encouraging. Since then I have appreciated the professionalism of Peter Rose and Jo McMillan at Oxford University Press.

My father, who was always anxiously asking whether it was finished yet, has sadly not lived to see this day. But through it all, Mum and Dad, Lenore, Richard, and Roland, Ingrid McKenzie and many special friends have shown more faith in my ability to get it done than I often felt. They have made this book possible and worthwhile. My bad taste in puns I blame entirely on my family. That aside, any stylistic inelegancies, conceptual shoddiness, or factual errors that may have crept into the text are mine and mine alone.

Desmond Manderson
Montréal 1993

CONTENTS

ACKNOWLEDGEMENTS v

INTRODUCTION: IMAGE AND USAGE 1
    Poets and Other People
    Social Attitudes and Drug Laws
    One Hundred Years of Solicitude

1   A TENTACLE OF THE OCTOPUS 15
    The Chinese and the Afghan
    Introducing Mr Sin: Chinese Opium Smoking and Australians' Fears
    Voices of Protest
    Righteousness and Revenue: Political Responses up to 1893
    'They all go to the Chinaman': Aboriginal Opium Laws and the Chinese

2   THE CRUSADES 37
    Federation and Hesitation 1901–1905
    The Social Context: Health and the Law
    'The Chinese themselves': The Crusading Quong Tart
    Other Battles: Alcohol and Patent Medicines
    The Political Capitulation: Opium Prohibition 1905–1908

3   BAD HABITS 59
    The Expansion of Drug Laws and the Beginning of International Control
    'Funny Business in Bendigo': The Habit of Law-Making 1913–1920
    International Influences: The Habit of Conformity 1919–1931
    The Entrenchment of Policy

4 THE AGE OF THE EXPERT — 77

The New Priests
The Exclusion of 'Patent Medicines'
The Subordination of Pharmacy 1900–1920:
    Sovereignty
The New South Wales Pharmacy Board 1923–1934:
    Autonomy
New Rivalries

5 ILLNESS AND VICE — 93

'For Information': The Cocaine 'Crisis' 1923–1928
Vice: Legal Sovereignty and Illegal Use in the
    Late 1920s
Illness: Medical Sovereignty and Non-Medical Use in
    the Late 1920s
The Dichotomy of Drug Use: The 'British System' in
    Australia 1922–1939
The Dichotomy of Drug Use: The Case of Heroin
    1931–1936

6 CONVENTIONAL WISDOM — 115

The World at War
International Influence and the Expansion of
    Controlled Drugs: Pethidine 1946–1948
The Cold War
US and International Influences: The Prohibition
    of Heroin 1949–1955
Drug Use in the Late 1950s
The Single Convention on Narcotic Drugs 1961

7 THE BALANCE OF POWER — 139

The Beginnings of Change: NSW and Victorian
    Poisons Acts 1962–1966
The Changing Face of Illegal Drug Use
The Politicisation of Drugs from 1966
Bureaucratic Conflict and Invasion 1966–1969
The Changing Balance of Power

8   SHADOWS OF THE PAST — 155

Meta-Law in Australian Drug Reforms 1970–1972
The Politics of Cannabis 1970–1976
Cedar Bay
A New Political Consensus
The Age of Royal Commissions 1977–1980
A New Bureaucratic Consensus

9   A THOROUGHLY MODERN MELEE — 179

Introducing Mr Big: The Changing Face of Australians' Fears
A Split Personality?
Labor in Power 1983–1985
Dr Jekyll: Legislative Reform in South Australia 1984–1986
Mr Hyde: Legislative Reform in Queensland 1986

CONCLUSION: VOICES IN THE WILDERNESS? — 199

The Web of the Law
Clearing the Cobwebs

NOTES — 209

BIBLIOGRAPHY — 245

INDEX — 256

INTRODUCTION: IMAGE AND USAGE

'Drug' Laws in Nineteenth-Century Australia

Poets and Other People

It was a dark and stormy night. Marcus Clarke, Australia's most famous author, sat in his study crowded with furniture and knick-knacks, and began to write a short story. By his side a local doctor sat monitoring his health and behaviour. Medical supervision was by no means the norm at moments of literary endeavour in 1868, but this story was intended to be a scientific experiment. Clarke wanted to see what effect drug consumption would have upon his writing: 'Some time back, having read and heard of the effects produced by opium, I was tempted to try an experiment upon myself'.[1] Presumably he had read Thomas De Quincey's *Confessions of an English Opium Eater*,[2] and had heard the story of how Samuel Taylor Coleridge came to envisage *Xanadu* in an opium-induced dream.

But Clarke settled instead upon cannabis, 'of all narcotics, the most powerful', a drug which he considered would 'give extraordinary energy to the mind, inducing at the same time a mental ease and quietude'. The scene must have been amusing: the good doctor earnestly trying to combine the roles of physician, secretary and reporter—

9.15.—The drug is operating. His eyes are open, fixed and brilliant. He smiles occasionally. His hands lie by his side, and I was obliged to prop him up with pillows. Pulse at 83 ...

2.12.—The adjectives and metaphors are wonderfully expressive, and he seems to hit upon them at once, though he has told me that, in his normal state, he is much given to correction and amendation.

—the writer fascinated by his own mind:

I seemed to hear every colour on the pictures and walls as if it was a sound; and the noise made by the scratching of Dr—'s pen sounded like the roaring of a cataract ... I was dreaming all this time, but with a sort of inner consciousness that I was dreaming: for example, if I thought of a theatre, I found myself in one, knowing all the time that it was only a delusion.

The story that resulted, however, was hardly proof of the creative benefits of cannabis. It began as it went on, indulgent and melodramatic, taking its mood from the rainy evening outside:

A wild night!—a night when unholy things were abroad, Student Martialis! a night for Walpurgis revelry and witch meetings!—a fearsome night! [3]

Many other writers, of course, were habitual users of 'narcotics': De Quincey and Coleridge, Collins, Crabbe, and Keats. The Romantic poet whose laudanum or opium habit was a stimulus to the creative imagination or a balm to the soul is one of the most common images of opiate use in the last century.[4] In Australia, however, literary references to opium are few and far between. Marcus Clarke's experiment apart, the most sustained reference to drug use I have come across is by J. Fordel Henderson, who was born in Goulburn in 1879, and died in Suva in 1904 at the age of twenty-five. Henderson, alas, was no antipodean Coleridge, and his long autobiographical poem, 'The Opium Slave', merely demonstrates that the use of opium cannot compensate for a lack of talent.

> ...*The aftermath bitter as aloes!—The fast fleeting moments of pleasure*
> *Outweigh the fierce barbs so relentless, the knowledge of what might have been;*
> *I care not for good nor for evil! I live for the end as I measure,*
> *I know that the weakness is fleshly—but what of the sights I have seen?*
>
> *Beyond the smug looks of precentor with teachings of infinite beauty,*
> *Concealed from the eyes of the ranter, and hidden from all fellow-men,*
> *I shall lie down in peace and in leisure, my conscience ignoring its duty,*
> *And trace out the trend of my trances—in blood—with regret for a pen.*
>
> ...*O why should we cling to an earth-life—that is only a perilous bondage,*
> *When glimpses are given of countries, and wondrous sweet strange architecture,*
> *When all of the stones that are precious, when all of the leaves that are frondage,*
> *Combine in a beauty alluring, to lead us to higher perfecture?*[5]

In fact, in Australia, as in England and the United States, most opium use throughout the nineteenth century was neither romantic nor aberrant, but a function of its medical importance, which in this period was second to none. Until the twentieth century, opium strode the pharmacopoeia like a colossus. It is a narcotic (meaning that it induces sleep) and a nervous-system depressant—a sedative and an analgesic—and in the days when few diseases could really be 'cured', the relief of pain was all that medical science could offer. From Hippocrates and Plato to Oliver Wendell Holmes, its praises have been sung. 'Among the remedies which it has pleased almighty God to give man to relieve his sufferings,' wrote Thomas Sydenham in 1680, 'none is so universal and so efficacious as opium'. Opiates, the refined products of the opium poppy, included opium itself, laudanum (a mixture of opium and alcohol), morphine, a more concentrated form of the drug first derived in the 1830s, and heroin,[6] more powerful still and first sold by Bayer in 1898. The opiate family can be distinguished from cocaine, an alkaloid obtained from the leaves of the coca plant, which was commonly used as an anaesthetic until earlier this century; and from cannabis, the dried flowering tops of the hemp plant, which was rarely used for any purpose in Australia, and is not in truth a narcotic at all.

In England the use of opium by lower-class women to 'dope' into passivity children who had been entrusted into their care while their mothers went out to work in the factories has been well documented and gave rise to a considerable outcry in the mid-nineteenth century.[7] The Melbourne Chinese community, defending its own opium use in Australia in 1879, described this English practice in this way:

At this time, thousands of infants were being drugged to death in the manufacturing districts by women in whose charge they had been placed by their mothers, who were at work in the factories. At Ashton, the weekly sale of opiates for this purpose, by fifteen dealers, averaged six gallons, two quarts and one and a half pints. In Preston, twenty-one chemists sold, in a single week, £66 worth of Godfrey's cordial, childs' preserver, syrup of poppies and similar compounds.[8]

In this respect, Australian opium use seems not to have mirrored the English position, although the *Bulletin* in 1882 did report one case of a Woolhara woman who quietened her children with 'soothing syrup'. 'Then, when the bottle is gone, she sets about to look for another—or else buries the baby.'[9]

Opiates were taken amongst all classes to ease acute pain, chronic pain, and innumerable small sicknesses—sleeplessness, 'infants' complaints', and 'women's ailments' in particular—and for those whose pain was not physical, it calmed and soothed. Neither was its use mediated or controlled by medical supervision, which should not surprise. Doctors in Australia in the 1800s had far from the power and status they currently enjoy. The Melbourne *Age* in 1858 asked, 'Is medicine a device, or is it a science? ... Medicine never was, nor is it now, more than a pretence to a science'. It was, the editorial concluded, a case of 'the blind leading the blind'. As late as 1895, according to the *Bulletin*, little had changed:

Whatever strides surgery may have made, medicine proper is still little better than a poking in the dark, and not one layman in 10 000 has any suspicion of the frequency of the diagnostic and therapeutic blunders which the profession, for the sake of its collective repute, studiously endeavours to conceal.

Two years later the *Intercolonial Medical Journal of Australasia* bemoaned the fact that 'the medical profession, compared with others, does not yet occupy the social position and public importance that it ought.'[10]

Doctors in Australia were accordingly not in a position to control the kinds of potions people took, the reasons for which they were taken, or the sources from which they were obtained. Cures and treatments of questionable efficacy proliferated, advertised by the hundred in newspapers and later in magazines such as the *Bulletin*, while herbalism, homeopathy and other strains of 'alternative medicine' were not marginalised as they are today.[11]

Chemists and druggists were even greater rivals to the authority of doctors than 'irregular practitioners'. As T.S. Pensabene noted in *The Rise of the Medical Practitioner in Victoria*, the 1881 Census revealed 454 'registered medical practitioners', compared with 761 chemists, druggists and assistants (and thirty-five Chinese doctors, seven hydropathists, nine herbalists, nine medical galvanists, two medical magnetists, a medical botanist, a medical mesmerist, and sundry others). In sum, chemists and druggists totalled forty per cent of the medical labour force, midwives accounted for twenty-seven per cent, and regular practitioners for only twenty-three per cent. Chemists were entitled to give medical advice and to sell medicines without a prescription; they were cheap, quick and skilled at a time when doctors were not.[12] As the *Age* reported in 1876:

Nine-tenths of the population do not call in professional assistance at all. It is the chemist who is consulted in the majority of cases.[13]

During the nineteenth century, the pages of Australian newspapers and journals were littered with advertisements by chemists and druggists testifying to their rivalry with, rather than their subservience to, doctors. 'I had procured the best medical advice in the colony and England, but to no avail', testified one happy customer in the *Illustrated Sydney News* in 1868. 'I was induced to take a box of your Pills, and after taking a few doses, I am happy to say I feel my health wonderfully improved'.[14]

Legislation concerning chemists reflected their authority. In 1876 Pharmacy Boards were established in New South Wales and Victoria. These were not government-appointed bodies: they were chosen by, and represented, the chemists and druggists themselves. Clearly, they had considerable power, in the self-regulation of the profession and in administering and enforcing the Sale and Use of Poisons Acts of the colonies.[15] Such laws reflected not only the status of the profession, but the extent to which drugs and poisons were considered *their* domain rather than the domain of doctors. In contrast, each small step in the legislative protection of medicine was a struggle for recognition, fought vigorously by those within parliament and without who distrusted doctors and resented any attempt to co-opt the government in the entrenchment of their position. Pensabene tried to explain the disparity by arguing that chemists recognised that their 'function was subordinate to the medical practitioner',[16] yet his own evidence demonstrates that this was far from the truth.

In Australia, as in England, drugs and medicines were available from a wide variety of sources without constraint. In evidence before the United

Kingdom Select Committee on the Pharmacy Bill 1852, for example, doctors stated simply that it was 'impossible to prevent the sale of common drugs universally'; 'The public will buy drugs where they like and get medical advice where they like'. The prescription and sale of drugs by chemists without the authorisation of doctors—so-called 'counter practice'—while inimical to doctors' interests, was clearly 'carried on to a great extent by the great majority of chemists ... The chemists and druggists are the aggressors.' The Chairman of the Select Committee asked A.S. Taylor, Professor of Chemistry at Guy's Hospital, 'whether the dispensation of medical prescriptions is not a small proportion of the drugs sold throughout the country?'

I should think it was. I should think more dangerous drugs were sold separately; patent medicines, family medicines of that sort; probably the sale of those are much more numerous than the dispensing of medical prescriptions.[17]

Of these self-prescribed 'dangerous drugs', the products of the opium poppy were perhaps the most commonly used and sold: not only in medical prescriptions but in chemists' preparations, in bottles of laudanum, and in mass produced patent or proprietary medicines available from grocers, such as Ayer's Cherry Pectoral (which contained 2 grains acetate of morphine) or Godfrey's Cordial (which contained 3 fluid ounces tincture of opium).[18]

Social Attitudes and Drug Laws

In nineteenth-century Australia, opium was the preserve of neither the creative few nor the urban poor. It was freely available and freely used. Furthermore, perhaps partly as a consequence of the weakness of the medical profession, the line which is now seen to divide medical 'use' from nonmedical 'abuse' was not yet apparent. Many people who consumed opium undoubtedly did so out of habit. Indeed, temperance activists who would rather forfeit their lives than drink a nip of whisky, but who were addicted to opium, were the butt of many jokes. 'I believe the teetotallers have too little pleasure in this world, whatever they may hope for in the next,' said Godfrey Carter, a Member of the Victorian Legislative Assembly well known for his opposition to the temperance movement, in 1898,

and when I think that what little joy they have here at present is derived, to a great extent, from the use of morphia, chlorodyne, painkiller, and a variety of other preparations of opium, why should we prevent them from going to their chemists and getting these things?[19]

None the less, most people dependent on opium or cocaine had originally taken the drug for what they perceived to be 'health' reasons, whether it had been prescribed for them or, more typically, taken on their own initiative. Since patent medicines kept their ingredients secret, many users did not even realise that they were becoming addicted. If the pattern of Australian usage was similar to that which prevailed in Canada or the United States at the same time (about which more evidence is available), habitués came from all walks of life, but fell particularly within two classes. First, middle-class, middle-aged, White women who originally took opium to treat menstrual pains or simply as a balm to deal with the depression brought on by the constrictions and powerlessness of their lives (much as drugs like Valium were used in the 1950s and 1960s); and second, doctors and nurses, whose stressful work and easy access to morphine, especially, made them vulnerable to habituation.[20] The *Bulletin* in 1895 described the development of a cocaine habit by a Victorian doctor:

From time to time under special circumstances he ... had recourse to the drug, but only as it were medicinally ... Summoned ... to an urgent confinement case, the summons found him racked by lumbago, unable to move without extreme pain. He had to go. A syringe of cocaine with morphia enabled him five minutes after to set out on a two mile drive through a bitter cold night and a blinding snowstorm. Before starting out on his return, he repeated the dose.

'That,' concluded the *Bulletin* melodramatically, 'fixed the habit, and he was a cocainist'.[21]

As one reason for the consumption of opiates slowly became another, as treatment became habit and desire turned to need, no hard lines were drawn between 'good' use and 'bad'. A leader in the *Age* in 1892, commenting on the recent death of three doctors attributed to their use of morphine—perhaps from overdoses—concluded sanguinely, 'He seeks for ease, artificially procured, and to secure it may have to suffer the penalty of excess'.[22] For the *Age*, therefore, drug dependence, however much to be regretted, was still a matter of free choice. As one cynic put it, 'Well, why should we deprive these poor people of the privilege of killing themselves if they wish to do so?'[23] Opium dependence was perhaps a sad demonstration of people's weakness, but there was little to suggest that the intervention of the state was required.

Admittedly, some moral reformers and temperance activists were proclaiming the evils of opium and demanding regulation of its use as early as the 1870s. Yet, even for these people, the question of opiates was of secondary importance. A survey of leaders in the *Age* and the *Bulletin* from 1880 to 1900, for example, reveals a far greater number of articles devoted to alcohol abuse than to questions relating to opium. Moreover, especially in the *Age*, the character of the articles is quite different; those on alcohol advocated tougher laws, control or even prohibition, while those on opium generally rejected government regulation of its use and accused advocates of this approach of 'carrying astringency to the point of fanaticism'.[24]

Drug laws in the nineteenth century reflected a society in which drug use and abuse was seen as a continuum, and as a matter of individual choice, which required neither medical nor legal legitimation. Such drug control as there was came under the various colonies' Poisons Acts, slightly modified copies of the mother Act of the British parliament. The New South Wales and Victorian Sale and Use of Poisons Acts, for example, both enacted in 1876, listed a range of drugs and provided that, except in remote places, they could only be sold by a medical practitioner or chemist. The only limits upon their sale, however, were that the products should be clearly labelled 'Poison' and marked with the name of the product and the seller. There were no restrictions on who could buy these poisons or for what purpose they could be bought. Even these very limited provisions did not apply to medical prescriptions, homeopathic compounds, or patent medicines,[25] and the opiates and alcohol concealed in popular patent medicines could be sold by any grocer who felt inclined to share in the large profits they generated.

A few poisons, which were listed in the first part of the First Schedule to the Acts, were more rigorously controlled: the sale of these drugs required purchasers to state their 'name, place of abode and occupation and the purpose for which such poison is required or stated to be required', which was then to be recorded and signed by both buyer and seller. These poisons could not be sold

to any person who is under eighteen years of age or is unknown to the vendor unless the sale be made in the presence of some witness who is known to the vendor and to whom the purchaser is known ...[26]

Neither the effect nor the intention of these provisions, however, was to stop addiction or recreational drug use, but rather to aid in the tracing of poisoners and so, in the words of the preamble of the Acts, to prevent 'the commission of crime'. Drugs which were commonly used to carry out murder—arsenic, prussic acid, strychnine and ergot of rye—were included in the first part of the First Schedule; opium, opium preparations, and cocaine were not. As to these other drugs, the Preamble explained that 'fatal accidents occur by reason of the careless custody and use of such Poisons'.[27] The slight controls on these lesser poisons simply ensured that they were properly labelled, so that people would not be killed by consuming a poison in ignorance of its contents. If people knowingly wished to take opium, the law would not interfere.

Laudanum was listed in the first part of the First Schedule in New South Wales, but not in Victoria. Yet this did not reflect any concern about the habitual use of it, merely a difference in opinion as to how frequently it caused intentional or accidental death. Opinion was divided in the United Kingdom Select Committee on the Poisons Bill 1857, the model for the New South Wales and Victorian Acts. According to some witnesses, opium was 'one of the most common substances resorted to by secret poisoners' and, as already mentioned, was also implicated in the deaths of children.

Other witnesses argued that laudanum was so commonly used that it should not and could not be controlled. The difference between Victoria and New South Wales over the categorisation of laudanum simply reflected this divergence of views.[28]

Indeed, the Select Committee seemed concerned to protect the rights of habitual users. Lord Talbot de Malahide expressed concern during the hearings that if the provisions of the Poisons Bill were made too stringent, inconvenience would be given 'to persons of certain habits' for whom 'laudanum is a necessary of life'. Likewise, Lord Wensleydale asked a witness whether 'the improper use' of opium would be limited by requiring the signature of a householder for its purchase. The answer makes it quite apparent that neither Lord Wensleydale nor the witness saw the laudanum habit as 'improper use', for it was explained that Lord Wensleydale's proposal could not be carried out

unless there was a general certificate given ... to an opium drinker, which should last a considerable time. The certificate might state that such a person is in the habit of taking 100 drops of laudanum at a time; and the man should always go to a particular shop to buy it.[29]

One Hundred Years of Solicitude

Only one hundred years ago, legislative structures and social attitudes relating to 'drugs' were radically different from those now in place. Their use was left to individual choice, rather than being subject to strict medical control or even prohibited by law. The lines between medical and non-medical use, or between use and abuse, now so clear and bright, were indistinctly drawn. The addict was defined as neither diseased nor evil, and the label was not yet a way of pigeon-holing a whole person.

Indeed, even the use of the word 'drugs' is anachronistic. From time to time over the past one hundred years various substances, including opium, morphine, heroin, cocaine and cannabis, have been labelled 'illegal drugs', 'dangerous drugs', 'drugs of abuse', 'drugs of dependence', 'drugs of addiction', or just plain 'drugs'. This terminology has at best been no more than partially accurate and has frequently been used as a way of begging some central questions: why are some drugs banned totally, some partially and others not at all; why are some recreational drugs condemned and others condoned; what makes a 'drug' so special and so especially bad? Those who smoke tobacco or eat to excess are never punished, regardless of the harm they do to themselves or others; alcoholics are only punished for those dangerous or socially undesirable acts that affect others; but the user of illicit 'drugs' is punished simply for the act of using, or even of possessing, a particular substance, regardless of the social consequences of that act and regardless of whether or not it has caused harm or affected other people. This book explores the reasons why our laws have developed in this fashion. When, why and how did some 'drugs' become 'illegal'?

The use of the term 'drugs' to describe a particular group of chemicals does not, then, imply any inherent validity in the terminology. On the one hand, not all the substances commonly so called cause physical dependence—cannabis is one example. On the other hand, not all habit-forming substances are illegal, or even considered as 'drugs'—alcohol and tobacco spring to mind. Further, the amount of harm caused by the consumption of 'illegal drugs' is by no means clear. Undoubtedly, many (but not all) heroin users live lives of poverty and crime, and many die of hepatitis or AIDS through the use of contaminated needles, or from overdoses due to the unreliable purity of their supply. But a great deal of this suffering is attributable not to the drug itself, but to its illegality, which drives costs through the roof and users underground. In contrast, well over ninety-five per cent of drug-related deaths in Australia can be directly attributed to the use of legal drugs such as alcohol and tobacco.[30]

The phrase 'illicit drugs' is a legal not a medical categorisation. The abuse of alcohol presents a far more serious 'drug problem' than heroin does. In fact, it could be argued that my own concentration on opiates, cocaine and cannabis in this book merely perpetuates a false dichotomy that would be better discarded. But I have chosen to deal principally with these substances to demonstrate that the reasons why they have come to be treated separately and with special severity by the legal system have had little to do with concern over the health risks normally associated with them. I want to emphasise the other themes which have all played their part, separately and interactively, in the development of drug laws: racism, the rise of the medical profession, bureaucratic attitudes, the pressure of the international community, the emergence of a drug mythology, and political convenience.

One of the complexities I have sought to address in exploring these issues is that Australia operates under a federal system. The Commonwealth and every State and Territory has its own drug laws, always overlapping and sometimes contradictory. For the sake of clarity and manageability, my research has focused on the major laws that have moulded the legal framework in those jurisdictions that have had most to do with the development both of drug policy and the drug traffic. This book therefore concerns itself principally with the laws and policies of the Commonwealth government, and the governments of New South Wales, Victoria, and Queensland; of South Australia and the Australian Capital Territory to a lesser extent; and of Western Australia and Tasmania only in passing. My generalisations about drug laws 'throughout Australia' must be read in the light of these limitations. Again, the aspects of social history that I have studied have been limited, though important. Statistics and evidence about drug use itself, for example, have been of only minor interest to me. Instead, this is a legal history. I have chosen to explore the meaning and purpose of attitudes towards 'drugs' in Australia by considering what laws have been enacted on the subject, why, and with what effect. I hope to shed light on our complex, irrational legal system, and thus to shed light on ourselves.

At the same time, I have been careful to deal with much more than the words of the law and the political rhetoric that often accompanied them. Drug law and policy cannot be understood without reference to the popular pressures that influenced them, and, equally important, without evaluating the motives and agenda of bureaucracies, whose influence is often ignored but who were, at least until the 1960s, the single most important generative force in the development of Australian drug policy. At times, legislative policy has been influenced by particular groups or institutions, while on other occasions it has been a more general reflection of changing social values. There is no simple or over-arching reason for the development of drug laws in Australia. But there is one clear message: no matter what we are told, 'drug laws' have *not* been about health or addiction at all.[31] They have been an expression of bigotry, class, and deep-rooted social fears, a function of Australia's international subservience to other powers, and a field in which politicians and bureaucrats have sought power. Drugs have been the subject of our laws, but not their object.

In this book I do not deal specifically with what drug policy in Australia 'should' be. These are questions that readers must think about for themselves in the light of the historical and legal context. None the less, my values about drug policy have not, of course, been irrelevant. My aim in exploring the assumptions behind the emotional reaction that the word 'drugs' so often provokes, stems from my own belief that the legislative drug policy pursued in Australia has manifestly failed to reduce the harm associated with drug use and has, on the contrary, created a climate of fear and hatred that has been enormously destructive. My own values have not only influenced what I have written, but were also, to some extent, the reason that I thought a thorough examination of the history of drugs laws in Australia was an important and relevant project in the first place. Through this discussion of the history of drug legislation, I hope that fundamental assumptions about the inevitability, purposes and efficacy of restrictive drug legislation will be reconsidered.

This book is not just about drugs, however, but also about law as a phenomenon. Laws are beguiling things. The political expediencies that may have required their enactment are soon forgotten, the novelty of their form or content quickly fades. The stark statutory words alone remain, abstract and perfect, treated as eternal truths devoid of the social exigencies or political chicanery that gave birth to them. Legally, and in community attitudes generally, the fact of a law's existence is often its principal reason for continuing to exist. If a law is continually broken, far from its justice being called into question, the response is often to shore it up by making it still more severe. To break the law is seen as bad, wilful, and deserving of punishment *per se*. Continuing illegal behaviour is therefore taken as proof of the need for tougher laws. It is a vicious circle, each new law adding to the odium of the criminals and making further laws for their suppression more acceptable.

Drug laws have in this way developed and perpetuated social attitudes towards drug users. While the bifurcation between 'legal' and 'illegal' drugs was initially a legal construct, it has continued to affect how we think. Those who abuse the former frequently meet boredom, amusement, or perhaps disdain, but for those who use the latter, there awaits only hysteria and anger. Law has been not just a mirror of these social values, but an actor in their construction. This is a central argument of this book.

On the other hand, it is easy to assume, as writers in this area tend to do, that legislative form corresponds to social reality: that once a law is passed, people's behaviour changes accordingly. The question of whether laws and penalties, no matter how high, *can* substantially affect the consumption of or traffic in 'illegal drugs' lies at the heart of the current debate about the efficacy of drug laws, and is a question more properly addressed in a book on drug policy. Nevertheless, history teaches us important lessons here, too. Changing the law does not always change the world: certain practices continue regardless of the words of the law. Further, all laws have costs as well as benefits. The structure of drug control adopted in Australia has *caused* harm as well as having prevented it: to users, to the economy, and to social cohesion. The question is not whether, for example, the prohibition of cannabis or heroin has done any good, but whether it has done more good than harm.

People who have talked about the 'drug problem' over the past ten, twenty or one hundred years have been drenched too often in anxiety and concern, certain of the correctness of their position, and full of dogmatic answers. Their solutions to these complex problems now seem as simplistic and as all-encompassing as those old patent medicines that promised to cure everything from baldness to consumption. The 'war on drug abuse' is as much a nostrum promising a simple plan and a quick fix as were Ayers' Cherry Pectoral or Biles Beans for Biliousness. In exploring the sources of this facile and passionate righteousness, and in examining its effects, I am not merely motivated by curiosity or indulgence. Our laws and we ourselves are products of our past.

1

A TENTACLE OF THE OCTOPUS

*Opium and the Chinese
1857–1901*

The Chinese and the Afghan

The *Afghan* was a ship, but it was also, to many, a symbol—a symbol of the hordes of Chinese that they believed were bent on overrunning White Australia and destroying its way of life forever. It arrived in Australia in early 1888 along with three other ships containing a total of nearly 600 Chinese passengers. In Melbourne the Chinese people on board tried to disembark, but were refused permission to do so. The ship sailed on to Sydney but its passengers were again refused. There they waited, anchored off Circular Quay for weeks, hoping vainly for a change of heart. Parliament debated new laws to stop their immigration, and angry crowds lined the wharf, giving vent to their jaundiced view of yellow skin. On 3 May, while the Chinese Restriction Bill was being debated, no less a person than the Mayor of Sydney led an unruly procession from Town Hall through the city streets and into the precincts of Parliament House itself.[1]

The ship-bound passengers could do no more than observe this outpouring of anger from a distance, forbidden as they were to leave the tense and crowded ship. Some tried to make a break for it and swim to safety, but to no avail; like the man who was found by a young boy on the Quay shivering and exhausted, they were returned without delay to the *Afghan*.[2] Finally, defeated, it left, and eventually returned to Hong Kong. It was a Flying Chinaman, destined to wander the seas, never to find an Australian port in which to rest.

The actions of the governments of Victoria and New South Wales were clearly illegal. Under New South Wales law, for example, Chinese immigration was already limited and only one Chinese person was allowed to enter the colony for every one hundred tons of the ship on which they arrived and upon payment of a £10 'poll tax'. Certainly the ships held many more Chinese than this law would have allowed for, but the Collector of Customs improperly refused to accept the tax from *any* Chinese passenger. Moreover, Chinese people who were British subjects (such as those from Hong Kong) were exempt from the law (and any in that category should have been granted entry).[3] In addition, many of the Chinese had only been out of Australia temporarily and held naturalisation certificates issued by the Victorian government itself. On 19 May the Supreme Court of New South Wales ordered the release of some fifty passengers from the *Afghan* and another ship, but the cases of many others who were entitled to land were not even dealt with by the court; as to the Supreme Court order, the Collector was expressly instructed by the Colonial Secretary's Department to ignore it until the government gave its go ahead. Not only did this delay the release of the Chinese passengers, it also demonstrated the contempt for the law with which the government approached the whole episode.[4]

George Dibbs, leader of the opposition in New South Wales at the time, described the government's behaviour as 'unmanly, un-English, unpatriotic, unstatesmanlike, illegal and unconstitutional'. But the Premier, Sir Henry

Parkes, drew himself up to a rhetorical height:

I cast to the winds your permits of exemption; I care nothing about your cobwebs of technical law; I am obeying a law far superior to the law which issued these permits, namely, the law of the preservation of society in New South Wales.[5]

This 'superior law', in the form of the *Chinese Restriction and Regulation Act 1888* (NSW), was applied retrospectively to indemnify the government's illegal actions, increase the poll tax to £100 per head, and allow entry to only one Chinese per 300 tons. In other words, it prohibited Chinese immigration in all but name. The New South Wales government was not alone in its actions. Although the British government pleaded for restraint, the colonies gathered in June 1888 for an intercolonial conference on 'the Chinese question', and agreed to formulate uniform laws similar to the New South Wales Act.[6] Sir Henry Parkes, in a confidential letter to the Governor of New South Wales, Lord Carrington, noted that 'the question of Chinese Immigration has now a disturbing force peculiar to these Colonies ... The danger to the minds of the masses is now past modifying ...'[7] The *Chinese Restriction and Regulation Act 1888* (NSW) was, then, as George Dibbs said, 'a sudden spasm of fear and panic'.[8]

The history of the *Afghan* was merely one small incident in Australia's long history of racism directed at the Chinese. Fear of being overrun by the 'yellow peril' dated back to the early gold-rush years, when sizeable Chinese immigration to Australia began. Pockets of large Chinese populations were established at that time, and continued thereafter. The xenophobia that the mere presence of these people stirred up stemmed, in many cases, from a kind of fashionable social Darwinism—if only the strongest races survive, then to survive we must arm ourselves against pollution from other peoples. Thus, Sir Henry Parkes, in his second reading speech on the Chinese Restriction Bill 1888, urged members to

support us in this effort to terminate a moral and social pestilence and to preserve to ourselves and our children, unaltered and unspotted, the rights and privileges which we have received from our forefathers ... to preserve the soil of Australia that we may plant upon it the nucleus of a future nation stamped with a pure British type ...[9]

Underlying such emotionalism, however, were economic concerns which became more angry and increased in volume through the last twenty years of the century. The Chinese, it was said, worked long hours, seven days a week, when Australian unions had been fighting to reduce the hours of work. Further, most of the Chinese men who came to Australia did so to escape the poverty of China and to make some money for their families. They had no intention of staying permanently and left their wives and children at home. In consequence, they were able to live on less money than an

Australian labourer with a family to support. The Tasmanian Premier, Philip Fysh, made the point in a letter to Parkes in late 1887:

With you, I do not join in the outcry against the Chinese on the ground of their degraded character ... Generally, they must be regarded as a law-abiding, industrious class, whose presence would not only be tolerated, but courted, were it not that they are regarded by our labouring classes as undesirable competitors in the struggle for existence.[10]

As the *Bulletin*, whose masthead proudly proclaimed 'Australia for the White Man', stated in 1889:

The badness of the Chinaman, socially and morally, is the outcome of his low wages ... If Chinamen will tomorrow refuse to work for less wages, man for man, than Britons, and will refuse to work longer hours, the head and front of the objections to their presence will disappear.

For the *Bulletin*, the Chinese were 'jaundice-coloured apostles of unlimited competition'.[11]

The proponents of a 'White Australia', however, slid with ease from arguments of economic protectionism to visceral racism. The Chinese were painted as living squalidly and in filth, their habits depraved and their lives degraded. The absence of Chinese women was seen immediately as a threat to the honour and chastity of innocent European women and girls (and prostitution certainly flourished in the Chinatowns of large communities). That the Chinese men worked on Sundays was portrayed as an indication of the infiltration of paganism and devil-worship into god-fearing Australian society. In the slandering of the Chinese, almost anything went, as this extract from a tract written by someone who went by the ironic pseudonym 'Humanity' shows:

The Chinese amidst their evil surroundings, and their filthy and sinful abodes of sin and swinish devilry [will be] entered into by the servants of the Most High God! May the wayside scattering of the seed of holiness and truth take root in the hotbed of all unholy and unclean vices! ... It would never be believed that our Saxon and Norman girls could have sunk so low in crime as to consort with such a herd of Gorilla Devils ...[12]

Only slightly more moderate in tone, the *Bulletin* led the anti-Chinese crusade that culminated in the crisis of 1888. On 21 August 1886, its four-page feature on 'The Chinese in Australia' began as it meant to go on:

Disease, defilement, depravity, misery and crime—these are the indispensable adjuncts which make the Chinese camps and quarters loathsome to the senses and faculties of civilised nations. Whatever neighbourhood the Chinese choose for the curse of their presence forthwith begins to reek with the abominations which are forever associated with their vile habitations. Wherever the pig-tailed pagan herds on Australian soil, they introduce and practise vices the most detestable and damnable—vices that attack everything sacred in the system of European civilisation.

The article compared the 'repulsive' octopus, which it said grabbed unsuspecting victims in one of its many arms and sucked out their blood, with the 'Mongolian Octopus' or 'Devil-fish', which it maintained was similarly draining the life-blood of unsuspecting White Australia: 'Every one of these arms, each of these sensile suckers has its own class of victims or special mission of iniquity.' Central to the article was a giant double-page cartoon of a 'Chinaman' portrayed as a Mongolian Octopus, each tentacle entrapping a victim and labelled with what was seen to be a particular 'Chinese vice'. In the cartoon, the limb of 'smallpox [and] typhoid' is strangling two children; the arm of 'immorality' ensnares two blond-haired, Caucasian girls. 'Opium'—like 'bribery', 'customs robbery', 'cheap labour', and the gambling games of 'fan-tan' and 'pak-ah-pu'—was another of the many vices that it saw as contributing to the evil of the Chinese and, in the eyes of the *Bulletin*, rendered them sub-human.[13]

Introducing Mr Sin: Chinese Opium Smoking and Australians' Fears

Opium use by the Chinese was simply a part of this vast sweep of anti-Chinese sentiment, one tentacle of the octopus. The Chinese did not drink their opium, or take it in tablet form or subcutaneously as White Australians did; although occasionally chewed, it was the most invariable custom of the Chinese to smoke it, specially prepared in pipes, often in 'dens' fitted out for the purpose. Smoking was at once a private and absorbing reverie and a social activity. For the Chinese, opium functioned as a recreational drug, like alcohol or tobacco. Like any such drug, therefore, there were occasional users, regular users, abusers and addicts; there were houses in which the smoking of an opium pipe was regarded as a social courtesy, and others in which it was a serious business. Opium was, in short, as entrenched in the social life of the Chinese as ethyl alcohol is in that of Anglo-Australians.

From small beginnings on the Australian goldfields, the incidence of opium smoking increased enormously, reaching a peak in the 1880s. In 1857, when the governments of New South Wales and Victoria first imposed a duty upon the importation of opium, 328 pounds were imported into New South Wales, almost all of it destined for the 9000 Chinese resident in the colony. With opium assessed at 10 shillings per pound, the New South Wales government collected duties of just over £164.[14]

The imposition of an import duty can be seen as the first salvo in the drug war in Australia; already its early theme of anti-Chinese discrimination was evident. That year, a petition received by the New South Wales Legislative Assembly complained that

the Revenue of the Colony is principally derived from indirect taxation, to which the Chinese, from their habits and customs, contribute a small proportion.[15]

The reason that the duty was imposed was that it predominantly affected the Chinese. In an explanatory letter written to the Colonial Secretary of South Australia, the Victorian Under-Secretary wrote:

I am to intimate that the object of this Government in introducing the measure into Parliament was to put a certain restriction upon the consumption of the article by the Chinese Inhabitants of Victoria as well as to impose a Tax which would operate directly upon them ...[16]

The New South Wales Bill originally included as dutiable items goods mixed or saturated with any preparation or solution of opium. The Attorney-General's department wrote to the Collector of Customs, asking whether such a broad definition was necessary 'to prevent the evasion of the payment of duty upon opium intended to be smoked or chewed', or whether it would 'interfere with the importation, duty free, of medicines'. The Collector of Customs, J. Gibbes, decided that the provision should be narowed 'because I do not think it could be used for those purposes', and although Professor Smith advised the government that laudanum also 'may be drunk for the purpose of inducing the peculiar intoxication of opium', the provision was changed accordingly. It was therefore neither medicinal opium nor opium intoxication itself that was aimed at by the duty, but only opium which was smoked or prepared in such a form that it was able to be chewed. In Victoria, by contrast, where the effect of the Bill upon non-Chinese opium consumption was not considered, the broader construction of opium remained in the Act.

Despite the high rate of duty it attracted, the trade in 'prepared opium' (meaning 'opium suitable for smoking') was extremely lucrative. In 1885 Sun Mow Loong and other Chinese living in Palmerston (in the Northern Territory) applied for permission to start an opium farm, seeking a seven-year monopoly to compensate them for their trouble. Then in 1887 another firm offered the South Australian government £2000 more than any previous proposal had. The South Australian Minister of Education, attracted by the idea, called tenders, but nothing came of it.[17] The same year Sir Henry Parkes received a submission from two local entrepreneurs seeking 'the Sole right to import cooked or prepared Opium to the Colony of New South Wales for the use of Chinese' and offering to pay an increase of twenty-five per cent on the current duty for the privilege of becoming the

Government Opium Farmers of New South Wales. The submission noted that the previous year had seen the import of a staggering 37 368 pounds of opium.[18] These were the first arguments for the monopolisation of the opium trade in Australia, but by no means the last.

Following the Chinese Restriction Acts of the various colonies, the Chinese population declined, old immigrants returning home and few new ones arriving, and the importation of opium declined with it. In 1890, 20 178 pounds were imported into New South Wales, and 17 684 pounds into Victoria, of which not more than 400 pounds were for medicinal use. But per capita consumption was still extremely high. The census of 1891 indicates a Chinese population in New South Wales of 13 289 and in Victoria of 8489 (35 821 Australia-wide): consumption of opium by the Chinese was therefore something like one-and-a-half to two pounds per person per year. In 1902 the Chinese population in Australia had declined to 29 627, but New South Wales still imported 14 000 pounds of opium, Victoria 10 000 and Queensland, with a large Chinese population working on the canefields, 18 000 pounds. Perhaps only five per cent of this was imported for medicinal use, while the rest was intended to be sold to the Chinese community to be smoked.[19]

The prevalence of opium smoking within the Chinese community was high. Edmund Fosbery, the New South Wales Inspector-General of Police, reporting to Parliament in 1878, estimated that of 9616 Chinese in the colony, 4406 were 'opium smokers' (although the term was not defined). First-hand evidence from Chinese interpreters quoted in the *Report on the Condition of the Chinese Population in Victoria* in 1868, suggests that, if anything, Fosbery understated the position. Out of a population of 19 000 Chinese, the report concluded that fifty to ninety per cent smoked opium, around one-third of whom were 'confirmed smokers'. Neither was this the highest available estimate. In the gold-mining town of Ballarat, Victoria, the interpreter Abboo Mason said there were 800 Chinese and fifteen opium-shops. '90 Chinese out of 100 smoke opium. Out of the 90, 30 are confirmed smokers.'[20]

The smoking of opium was therefore the habit, at once both ubiquitous and unique, of an alien and distrusted minority. Many Chinese smoked opium: almost no Europeans did so. White Australians used different recreational drugs but their opiate dependence, on the other hand, was concealed by medical use. The purpose of consumption along with its mode and demography therefore distinguished 'their' opium use from 'ours'. Opium smoking was in all these ways able to be used as a weapon against the Chinese. It was seen as a 'Chinese vice' to be set apart, treated with calumny and obloquy, and finally outlawed.

Opium helped to reinforce the popular fiction of the 'dirty Chinese'. The mix of an unfamiliar odour, the crowded conditions of Chinese habitation, and Anglo-Australians' xenophobia, was a heady brew. Take, for example, one of the first government reports in Australia to deal with opium, the *Eleventh Report of the Sydney City & Suburban Sewage and Health Board*

(1876).²¹ Five of the members of the Board, Alderman Chapman, Doctors Read and Dansey, Mr Grundy and Mr Palmer, inspected the living conditions of some of the most poverty-stricken areas of Sydney, including Chinatown, touring at all hours of the day and night for fifty-one consecutive days. It was undoubtedly a difficult and unpleasant task which they carried out with courage and tenacity. Their reports are unsurprisingly emotional and at times it was clearly a struggle for them to continue.

The inspectors did not particularly concentrate on the Chinese. Many other slum areas were as dirty or dirtier. As New South Wales Chief Medical Officer, Dr Ashburton Thompson, insisted, 'The Sydney Chinese community are ... seldom quite so dirty, so indifferent to comfort and decency, or so squalid as some of our own poor often are'. But in dealing with the premises of the Chinese, the strange smell of opium, to which the Commissioners reacted on an aesthetic level, seemed to them to intensify the general lack of hygiene they found:

For the next forty-eight hours, and that of the previous night, the horrible sickly smell of opium smoking which pervades all the Chinese quarters seemed to adhere to us, to say nothing of the fear of infection, which is not a pleasant sensation.

The report speaks often of 'overcrowding ... and the bad ventilation of houses in Sydney'. In relation to the Chinese, however, it was opium that was blamed: the Commissioners asserted that the 'careful exclusion of light and fresh air' is 'one of the conditions necessary to the full enjoyment of opium'.²² For the poverty and 'strangeness' of Sydney's Chinatown, opium was brought to book.

Having been made to bear this sanitary and aesthetic burden, opium was then made to bear a moral one. Alderman Chapman and Dr Read understood that

the most revolting and immoral scenes are of frequent occurrence ... If half the stories we heard were true, it is more than time that this and other similar foul dens of Chinese depravity should be cleared of their occupants and thoroughly purged ... If these people ever wash themselves, they do it by stealth.

Cleanliness and godliness were thus neatly conflated. Indeed the Report included a special Appendix on Opium and Opium Smoking to 'give some idea of the prevalence of vice and depravity induced by this enslaving and degrading practice'.²³

Opium was seen as a pollutant, moral as well as physical; it was tainted by the environment of its consumption and by its connection with the Chinese themselves. The potency of these separate aesthetic revulsions—against dirtiness, the Chinese, and the smell of opium—was compounded by their mutual association, as can be seen from the description of an opium den contained in the *Bulletin's* 1886 feature on 'The Chinese in Australia':

Down from the fan-tan dens are stairs leading to lower and dirtier abodes: rooms darker and more greasy than anything on the ground floor: rooms where the legions of aggressive stinks peculiar to Chinamen seems ever to linger ... Yet the rooms are not naturally repulsive, nor would they be so when occupied by other tenants; but the Chinaman has defiled their walls with his filthy touch; he has vitiated what was once a reasonably pure atmosphere with his presence, and he has polluted the premises with his disgusting habits; and so it is that nought save suggestions of evil, incentives of disgust and associations of vice, now seems to move in the fetid atmosphere ... The very air of the alley is impregnated with the heavy odour of the drug.[24]

From being seen as a dirty habit in a dirty people, opium smoking came to be seen as an immoral habit in a hated people. It was a small step readily taken: from a symptom of depravity, opium became a cause of it; from a sign of evil, it became an active agent of it. Disentangling exactly what forms that evil was said to take is difficult, for the language used often lost clarity in the headlong drive for invective. Clearly, the physical harm suffered by Chinese opium smokers was merely a side issue. While the *Bulletin* described the 'shambling gait, glistening eyes, and trembling muscles' of an opium smoker, the purpose was to provoke disgust in the reader, not concern.[25]

Indeed, quite apart from the lurid descriptions given by the media and popular writers, evidence about the dangers of opium use were (and remain) melodramatic, anecdotal and uncertain. The addictive qualities of opiates were well known, and the first suggestions that addiction was a physical disease dated from the 1870s. Although the eminent doctor, Sir William Collins, writing at that time, declared that 'whoso betakes himself to the morphia syringe does so of his own naughtiness', from 1890 opium addiction began to take an established place in medical texts.[26] But beyond the *fact* of addiction, the actual harm caused by smoking opium was never made clear. Dr Thomas Scott, speaking in the Victorian parliament in 1893, insisted that 'only medical men know the unfortunate and terrible effects of the use of opium'. But his description of these medical effects would not have been out of place in the *Bulletin*:

Who has not seen the slave of opium—a creature tottering down the street, with sunken yellow eyes, closely contracted pupils, and his skin hanging over his bones like dirty yellow paper.[27]

The key words here are 'creature', 'dirty' and 'yellow'. The 'illness' of opium smoking was not far removed from the 'illness' of being inhuman, a 'filthy Chinaman'.

At the heart of the image of evil that developed about the Chinese and their opium use was the claim that women who smoked it either lost all sexual control or became so heavily drugged that they were unable to resist rape or seduction. The effect of opium was said to enable 'the criminal and sensual Chinese'[28] to have their perverted way with White women. Dependence or illness amongst the Chinese was irrelevant. It was the alleged sexual overtones of opium, and its use by White women, that mattered.

The great influx of Chinese to Australia was almost exclusively masculine: wives and families were left at home in China. The Chinese were consequently often involved sexually with non-Chinese women and were unable to be cauterised in a ghetto. European prostitutes were used by the Chinese, and a considerable number of European women married or lived with Chinese men in the Chinese quarters of Sydney and Melbourne and elsewhere. How could Europeans bring themselves to live with the Chinese?, asked xenophobic Australians. The thrall of opium provided a convenient answer. Opium became a symbol of sexual licence and an explanation for miscegenation. Of course, this was also grossly untrue, but never mind.

The *Bulletin*'s exposition of opium smoking in 'The Chinese in Australia' demonstrated this obsession, describing how the Chinese allegedly tricked women and girls into smoking opium. Sexual ruin was the 'only possible result when a lustful and unscrupulous Chinaman is one of the parties and an unsuspecting, though perhaps instinctively cautious girl, the other'.

One of the girls now kept in a den on the Rocks, says ... 'I went to — —' place when I was only about 16 because he used to give me presents. He then wanted me to smoke, but I never would, because the pipes looked so dirty. But one day he put a new pipe before me, and made it ready, and after the first whiff from it, he or any other man — — — — — —. I was completely at their mercy, but so help me God I was a good girl before that.'

'Shall the monsters of sensuality grapple the youth and innocence of Australia?' fulminated the *Bulletin*, warning that 'so long as the sensual Chinaman and innocent girls are permitted to come into contact, so long will the results be disastrous to the latter'.[29]

The same myth resurfaced again and again, told at times with pornographic alacrity—the innocent girl, the lustful Chinaman, trickery, the opium pipe, and sexual doom. 'Once the opium is administered to her', concluded one writer, 'all power to resist is swept away, and then the feast of lust, rape and the deadliest of all foul crimes ever committed, is fully enacted.'

A European girl lay as if under the soporific influence of hell, opium, or the Chinese drugs, nude, or nearly so; yes, dear reader, there she lay and on the same bed or couch, three adult and lascivious Chinamen lay around her; they were to me, so many fiends exulting o'er the deadened, inert, opiumed, drugged woman or girl aforesaid.[30]

Such bizarre descriptions suggest more about the phobias and fantasies of the writers than about the realities of opium use. Yet this literally incredible attribution of magical powers to a drug used in no less potent form regularly by many other Australians was frequently given official recognition: in parliamentary debates, in the *Report of the Sydney Sewage Board*, and a report of the New South Wales Select Committee on Common Lodging Houses (1876).[31] To take one example, the judgement of Richard Seymour, the 'Inspector of Nuisances' in Sydney, giving evidence to the Select Committee and, later, to the New South Wales *Royal Commission on Alleged Chinese Gambling and Immorality* (1892), was clearly clouded by his abhorrence of miscegenation and his need to 'explain' sexual relations between Chinese men and White women. The voyeuristic accounts of sexual relations he provided demonstrate his obsession with expunging the memory of 'a Chinaman [with] a girl on the table, with his trousers down and one of the girl's legs over his shoulder', or perhaps of 'a little red-headed girl there':

I said, 'we will try and wake her,' and I pinched her repeatedly on the legs and on the bottom, but she never stirred; and the other girl said, 'You can pinch there for the next few hours, for she is under the influence of opium ... '[32]

Opium for people like the Inspector of Nuisances was a way of explaining what he saw as a horrifying—but absorbing—perversion.

And so the Chinese opium smoker was seen as depraved and immoral: in his foul-smelling smoky 'dens', the sickly-sweet odour of opium seduced the weak, drove the pure away and led only the corrupt to ecstasy. Opium was a symbol and an agent of Chinese evil. The Chinese themselves remained conveniently abstract. They were not seen as individuals, but as 'hordes' of 'Chows' or 'Mongols' or 'Chinamen'. 'The Chinese in Australia' only once mentions Chinese people by name, and then only to list the two that the *Bulletin* wished to exempt from its general condemnation of 'the Mongolian devil-fish'.[33] But in an issue of the *Bulletin* that appeared at the height of the *Afghan* crisis, and which included a special supplement on the Chinese, there is a piece of fiction about the life of a man called Mr Sin Fat. His wife is a European woman who had been tempted by the lure of finery and hooked on opium years before. On the evil of 'the devil's drug' he grows prosperous, his dens 'reeking with the nauseating odour of opium and pollution and Chinamen, and always clouded with smoke'. In particular he rejoices in ensnaring 'girls of sixteen, decoyed in at the front door by the sheen of silk and the jingle of gold, and then left to percolate through that horrible den'. But one new victim turns out, unbeknown to Sin Fat, to be his wife's daughter. In a rage, Mrs Sin Fat demands he give up his protégée, and when he refuses, she stabs him to death with a pig sticker:

The girl hurried away, full of horror and fear, but saved, and her mother followed her at a distance.[34]

Here at last we have a face of evil, and a powerfully symbolic name: 'Fat' suggests bodily unhealthiness, while 'Sin' is a kind of moral unhealthiness. Indeed, as Sin Fat prospers and becomes more and more sinful, so too he gets fatter, until at last

> *he was fatter than fat, his obesity was phenomenal ... Layers of blubber bulged about his eyes ... and his mighty neck rolled almost on to his shoulders, and vibrated like jelly with every movement.*[35]

Fatness, like the odour of opium and of 'Chinamen', is presented as aesthetically revolting. Revulsion and evil are thus linked exactly as they were in Australian attitudes to opium. It too was 'fatty' (let us read: ugly or dirty) and this ugliness was taken to show that it was sinful. The one symbolised, proved and reinforced the other.

Moreover, as 'Fat' suggests bodily indulgence, 'Sin' suggests moral indulgence. Again, the former is evidence of the latter: obesity is the physical manifestation of an indulgence that is sinful and weak. It is a failure of moderation and a sign of excessive enjoyment of the pleasures of the senses. Opium smoking, too, was seen as evil because of its connotations of immoderateness and, as we have seen, sexuality. Opium smoking, like fatness, was a weakness of the flesh and a visible sign of the moral weakness within.

The name of Mr Sin Fat was not chosen lightly. It emphasised the parallel corporeal and incorporeal evil of Chinese opium use; it demonstrated the aesthetic and sensual basis of a more generalised hatred. Mr Sin may conveniently stand, therefore, as the archetypal Chinese opium smoker as seen through Australian eyes. Like so many others who have followed him as the embodiment of the evils of drug use, he was a fiction created by White Australians to pander to their prejudices.

Voices of Protest

> *Enough—enough—more 'by and by',*
> *but this may well suffice*
> *To contradict the wicked lie*
> *that we are full of vice.*

So wrote G.W. in The Humble Plea of the Poor Chinee!![36] The mythology of opium did not go unassailed. In 1884 the New South Wales Legislative Assembly commissioned a *Report upon Chinese Camps* by a police inspector and Quong Tart, a successful Chinese businessman. Yet although Quong Tart himself vigorously advocated the prohibition of opium, the Report categorically stated that the myth of sexual degradation was 'a fallacy and has nothing in truth to support it ... All the females themselves deny the allegation emphatically and smile at the credulity of any person believing such'. Likewise Victoria's official Chinese interpreter, Charles Powell Hodges, stated:

I give it an unqualified denial that opium is ever used for the purpose of seducing girls ... The statements in the press as to this have been so untrue and so malignant that on occasions I have had to keep out of the Chinese quarter till the storm of indignation has passed over.[37]

The New South Wales Royal Commission on Alleged Chinese Gambling and Immorality, which delivered its report in 1892, is a unique source on this question, for in the course of its investigations it interviewed several White women living in the Chinese quarter. Again and again it was suggested to these women that opium was used as a tool for their seduction, and that while under its influence they were unable to resist; just as insistently, the suggestions were denied.

[The Chairman, Mayor Manning:] Could any man take advantage of you in that state without you being conscious of it?
[Ellen:] No one in the world could.
What effect has it upon you? Does it render you unconscious? *No.*
.... And you say it never renders you unconscious? *No.*
Did it at first have that effect upon you?
No, never from the first.
Does it not excite the imagination? *No.*
Then what delight is to be got from it?
None at all; only when once you take to it you get the habit, and then you have to have it.
... Are you not in that state even partially unconscious? *Not at all.*
Does it not do so with others?
It never makes anyone unconscious.[38]

Similar questions were asked of all the other witnesses, but they too refused to be badgered. 'Is it a fact that opium-smoking will make you so unconscious that you do not know what people are doing to you?'—'It does not make you unconscious so that a man could do anything with you and you not know it?'—'You are quite sure about the effects of opium, that it could not by any means of using it bring about the state of unconsciousness I have described'—'Is it true that Chinamen decoy women [and] induce girls to smoke opium?'; the answers were in all cases clear and dismissive.[39]

The suggestion that they had been inveigled into unwanted sexual slavery by opium could not have been further from the truth. All the women who gave evidence had in fact been seduced by Australian men, exploited, mistreated and abandoned, unmarried. Cast out from respectable society, they were deemed worthy of nothing but prostitution. The Chinese, whether they married them or not, took them off the streets, protected them, and improved their living conditions. A woman named Hannah (none of the women were ever referred to by other than their first names), having recounted in resigned tones her abandonment by a man she sadly trusted, by her family and by society, concluded that 'the Chinese have been the best to me since I left my mother's home'; another woman called Adelaide 'could not wish for better treatment'. Against this evidence, the second-hand claims of witnesses like Seymour, who concluded that the women must be lying, appear unconvincing. Of his assertions Ellen said, 'It is only nonsense', and Pauline commented, 'Well, they might have been drinking. Opium would not do that'.[40]

The Commission was forced to conclude that 'there is no ground for suspicion that our alien population is now a danger to youthful virtue'.[41] What hypocrisy was brought to light! To the rhetorical question that underlay opposition to Chinese opium-smoking—why would any 'White woman' want to live with the Chinese?—came the answer: not because of the immorality of the Chinese, but because of that of 'White' society; not because of the evil of the accused, but through the guilt of the accusers.

Undoubtedly, the evidence of the Royal Commission notwithstanding, the sexual mythology of opium continued to hold fast in the minds of White Australians. It takes more than a few facts to make us abandon our cherished hates and fears. Moreover, on the dangers of opium-smoking in general, the Commission was far from sanguine. One evil, said the Commission,

is of momentous consideration, and curses nearly all the European women who associate with Chinamen. They become opium-smokers ... Their features were pinched and worn; when their time for smoking approached, they became restless and inclined to hysteria.[42]

As before, members of the Commission doggedly asked leading questions about the dangers of opium, and this time remained unrepentant despite the women's replies. Opium was said, without proof, to excite the imagination, induce dreams, destroy the appetite and render the smoker unfit for work, sluggish and lazy.[43] Quong Tart, in particular, once more serving the government as the representative of 'respectable' Chinese, was determined to make his point:

[Quong Tart:] Do you not think opium is a great evil?

[Ellen:] No, I do not think so. A woman who smokes opium has always got her senses about her, but a woman who drinks has not.

... Do you not consider opium-smoking a great evil?

[Ellen:] It is in one way, I suppose. It is right enough in another way.

... Do you not think that it is a very evil habit ...?

[Margaret:] Everyone to their fancy.

... *[Minnie:] It has no more effect upon me than an ordinary smoke.*

That is very strange. We have been told it has a very decided effect.[44]

Here, too, the heart of the problem was not the asserted effect that opium had on the Chinese, but the fear that it had spread to White women. Jessie Ackerman, a leader of the Women's Christian Temperance Union in the United States, and guest speaker at an anti-opium demonstration held in Sydney in 1894, made the point more clearly:

While in that terribly wicked city called San Francisco, a lady had said to her, 'We want you to see something of what opium is doing for our white people', and then, for the first time in her life, she visited an opium 'den'. She knew that countless thousands and thousands of people were addicted to it, but not till then was she aware that it ever touched the English-speaking or white people.[45]

Opposition to opium smoking in Australia, whether centred upon miscegenation or buttressed by this fear of contagion, continued to relate to racism. It was evil because of who and what it became associated with, and not for what it was or did.

Righteousness and Revenue: Political Responses up to 1893

Although Chinese opium smoking was reviled and feared, politicians were by no means unaware of the revenue it generated. By 1905, the duty on 'prepared opium' had risen to 30 shillings per pound. In contrast, no article of European consumption was taxed at a greater amount than 10 shillings. New South Wales collected £16 180 that year, the last in which the duty applied, Victoria £9438 and Queensland £24 831.[46] Governments therefore had a vested interest in the importation of opium; once begun, revenue raised is hard to do without.

The irony of the argument in support of its prohibition was lost on no one. Whose revenue were we to give up, asked the Sydney *Daily Telegraph* in 1884—and for whose sake?

It is very hard to tax the Chinese, but they are got at to the extent of £12 000 per annum through their love of opium. So far, then, as the Chinese are themselves concerned, we are asked to show our regard to their moral habits by surrendering £12 000 a year.[47]

Nevertheless, for most writers, the cost was worth it. As the *Telegraph* went on, opium should be banned not for the sake of the Chinese but to prevent the habit from spreading.

For governments, the matter seemed less straightforward. The first motion calling for a ban upon opium smoking in an Australian parliament was introduced into the Victorian Legislative Assembly in 1884. It was withdrawn principally because it was felt that prepared opium would simply be smuggled in. The only thing to shrink would be government coffers. At a meeting held in 1890, the Premiers of the various colonies concurred with this conclusion.[48]

Despite these difficulties, Opium Bills were again introduced into the Victorian parliament in 1891, 1892 and 1893, but all of them came to nought. The loss of revenue was not the only problem raised. In debate on the 1891 Bill, although everyone agreed that the smoking of opium should be 'put down', it was generally felt that the measure was 'altogether too extreme', full of absolute proscriptions and fierce penalties.[49] 'No person shall smoke opium' (promised the Bill), or grow it, or buy or sell or give away raw opium, or 'eat opium except when made up or compounded as a medicine'. The penalty for the most minor offence was a fine of at least £20.[50] In short, it was the kind of drug legislation that is today considered neither unusual nor harsh. But in 1891 it marked a radical departure. 'This was legislation run wild', cautioned Sir Bryan O'Loghlen, an ex-Premier of Victoria and staunch opponent of Federation: 'It would be a Draconian code, and would be a disgrace to the statute-book of the colony.' The Premier, James Munro, responded crossly to the criticism. 'It was absurd,' he said, 'to have a [small penalty] for the suppression of an evil which ruined men and women for life.' As opposition mounted, he castigated his critics: 'We will withdraw the Bill, and then you will be satisfied.'[51] He did and they were.

The Bill did not proceed beyond the first reading stage in 1892, but was again debated in 1893, and provides evidence for a hardening of attitudes towards opium smoking. More than in 1891, objections to the Bill centred not upon its purpose and design, but simply upon the question of revenue. It was this which eventually led to the Bill's defeat.[52] As the Victorian and New South Wales governments recognised in 1857 when they acted jointly to impose a duty on opium, if one colony alone were to prohibit it, it would simply be landed in the other colonies, to the benefit of their finances and the detriment of the prohibitor. When the Bill was before the House in Victoria, the Premier of New South Wales, George Dibbs, was reported as having expressed 'some degree of satisfaction as he believed the Bill would practically increase the revenue of New South Wales'.[53] It was a version of the prisoner's dilemma: it may have been in the interests of New South Wales and Victoria to jointly ban opium smoking—but not for either of them to do so if the other did not.

The Victorian Opium Bill of 1893 did not fail due to a lack of emotion or commitment on the part of honourable members, but, in large part, simply because there was no Australia-wide customs union. The majority of members supported the principle of prohibition; more than previously, indeed, their speeches peddled the melodramatic mythology of opium:

Those who have visited the gold-fields of Victoria have seen the Chinese camps and young girls—girls under age—who were once pure and virtuous, degraded so low that they were actually lower than the brute animals which surrounded them. This has been tolerated in Victoria. Go into Little Bourke-street. Go into the back slums of this city. Behold our young sisters there demoralised through the influences of this drug ...[54]

Such passionate condemnation was not entirely unanimous. L. L. Smith, MLA, in particular, insisted that the government's arguments might equally apply 'to a glass of beer or a glass of spirits ... Because some sot outside gets drunk, ergo the Premier of the colony must not take a glass of wine'. Opium smoking was to be banned, he concluded,

because a few ladies who have views of their own ... and a few ministers of religion ... waited upon the Premier and poured out their jeremiads before him.

But Smith was almost alone.[55] On his side, as for the majority, the temperature of the issue was rising, opinions were becoming intransigent, and debate was yielding its place to oratory. As the Melbourne *Age* commented, 'there seems to be no mean between the opponents of the drug and its friends'. While problems of revenue and pressure of other business buried the issue until the new century, dogmatism and passion continued to fester away below the surface, and the moral myths which made thinkable 'hysterical legislation of this kind', gained a tighter grip in the precincts of parliament and beyond, 'carrying astringency' as the *Age* said 'to the point of fanaticism'.[56]

'They all go to the Chinaman': Aboriginal Opium Laws and the Chinese

In fact, the first laws specifically to prohibit opium did not seem to deal with the Chinese use of it at all. The Queensland *Sale and Use of Poisons Act 1891* penalised

any person who supplies, or permits to be supplied, any opium to any aboriginal native of Australia or half-caste of that race ... except for medicinal purposes ...

South Australia, which administered the Northern Territory and also therefore had a large Aboriginal population, enacted a similar provision in *The Opium Act 1895*.[57] Neither provision prohibited the possession of the drug, but only its supply and then only to a small group of people.

Undoubtedly, opium smoking was something of a problem in those Aboriginal communities that had access to it. Significantly, both Queensland and the Northern Territory had large populations of Chinese, as well as of Aboriginal people. In 1877 the Palmer River goldfields in north Queensland, for example, had 17 000 Chinese and only 1400 Europeans; 7000 Chinese lived in the Northern Territory in 1887, compared with only 1000 Europeans.[58] Wages were frequently paid in opium in areas where nearby Chinese population centres made it available and it was, in addition, a common element of barter between the Chinese and Aboriginal groups themselves. Amongst Aboriginal people, the abuse of alcohol has long been both the cause and expression of despair. In areas with more Chinese than Europeans, the use of opium in similar ways is hardly surprising. The legislation enacted in Queensland and South Australia was a reflection of the paternalistic approach taken towards Aboriginal people in Australia. It is not surprising, then, that the paternalism of prohibitionist drug laws should first of all have been applied to them. The South Australian Opium Bill, for example, had originally proposed to prohibit the import of all opium except for medicinal purposes, but this the opposition defeated, arguing that:

[as with] the use of alcohol we had decided that there should be some restrictions in its supply to the aborigines who, Parliament considered, had not the same amount of personal restraint in this matter as Europeans ... [These] considerations ... did not apply to restrictions placed on Europeans and Chinese with reference to opium.

Although the question of the loss of revenue was also important, many members insisted that opium was less harmful than alcohol or tobacco, and in consequence only that part of the Bill dealing with the alleged particular 'problem' of Aborigines was passed.[59] Despite the enforcement of this Act, however (according to historian, Eric Rolls, up to twenty Aborigines per month were fined or gaoled), the opium trade in the Territory continued.[60]

The provisions of the 1891 Queensland Act likewise manifestly failed to stem the sale of opium to Aborigines. The Chief Protector of Aborigines, Archibald Meston, reported in 1897 that the law 'seems perfectly inoperative or abortive' and urged its complete overhaul.[61] The opium provisions of the *Aboriginals Protection and Restriction of the Sale of Opium Act*, enacted in that year, were much more thorough. The Act was the zenith of paternalism, a testament to turn-of-the-century White Australian thinking on 'the Aboriginal problem'. Under its authority, the sale of alcohol to Aboriginal people was prohibited, they were forced on to reserves far from their birthplaces, their children were taken from them to be brought up by churches and institutions, and even their marriage and employment was prohibited without express government authorisation. The Act embodied the belief that segregation was the answer to the problems being experienced by Aboriginal people. Segregation implied compulsory isolation from 'bad influences' and, accordingly, the Act enshrined a policy of absolute prohibition in relation to opium. In addition to the provision enacted in 1891, the new Act declared that opium not compounded for medicinal purposes could only be supplied or possessed by doctors, chemists or wholesale druggists.

The unlawful possession of opium and its supply to any person, Aboriginal or otherwise, was specifically penalised.⁶²

Although on its face the new Act applied to the non-medical use of opium by any person, it was still intended to apply only to Aborigines. First, it was located in an Act which dealt exclusively with them, and second, the administration of the law was partial. Both Meston and the Queensland Collector of Customs issued permits to sell opium to a large number of applicants—165 in 1898 alone—'from all quarters of south Queensland', and even provided blank permits for local police to distribute as they saw fit. These permits were granted almost always to Chinese people, for opium-smoking within their community. Although Chinese opium smoking was reviled and attempts to prohibit it had been made, this particular Act, despite its general terms, was exclusively concerned with opium use by Aborigines.⁶³

The issue of permits was completely unauthorised by the Act. 'In fact,' as the Under-Secretary of Justice explained later, 'the permits had no *legal* effect whatever, although no doubt they were an assurance that the Government would not strictly administer the law'. In 1900 the Protector of Northern Aborigines (the office of Chief Protector having been divided into two by the 1897 Act), Doctor Walter Roth, wrote that 'I fully realise the serious loss to the revenue (£35 000) were the opium clause of the Aboriginals Act to be strictly enforced, and I have accepted the situation accordingly'. None the less, he continued to complain vigorously, and, after the matter was drawn to the attention of the Commonwealth government when Roth gave evidence to the 1905 Royal Commission into Customs, and Excise Tariffs, the practice ceased.⁶⁴

The development of Aboriginal opium laws was a reflection of White Australian paternalism that viewed Aboriginal people as a 'special case'. But even here, the powerful role of anti-Chinese mythology cannot be ignored. In South Australia, opium use by the Chinese raised the spectre of sexual licence which obsessed the *Bulletin*, although on this occasion the victims were not 'innocent White girls' but innocent Black girls. 'The use of the drug,' argued the South Australian Attorney-General in his second reading speech, for example, 'work[ed] the everlasting ruin of the female aborigines ... lured from their happy wirlies to be the victims of Chinamen.' Beneath this solicitude, however, lay other concerns. The Attorney-General quoted with approval a petition from constituents in northern Australia, which stated, 'one time the Europeans used to find blacks useful, but now they cannot get them away from the Chinese camps'. The sale of opium by Chinese to Aborigines reinforced the reputation of the Chinese as unfair competitors in the labour market in areas in which Europeans, as I have already noted, were already a distinct minority. The prohibition of Aboriginal opium use was designed partly to protect their 'useful capacities'—for White employers.⁶⁵

Archibald Meston's staunch advocacy of opium prohibition, first as Chief Protector and later as Protector of Southern Aborigines, requires more careful analysis. The solution he advocated to the awful and complex problems of the Queensland Aboriginal population was enforced isolation. In one report, Meston commented that:

Opium has taken a strong hold on the Maryborough blacks and they require moving far from town with the least possible delay as they are a nuisance to the townspeople and a reproach to themselves.

The objections that the community itself was likely to raise were dismissed as 'sentimentalism ... deprived of tangible significance'. His report on the Aborigines of western Queensland came to the same categorical conclusion:

Opium and syphilis are destroying the aboriginals over the whole of western Queensland ... [and on the coast from Maryborough] to Cooktown. There is only one effective method of settling this opium habit ... and that is by absolute prohibition.
The Western blacks, like those of the coast, can only be saved from perishing, miserably and rapidly, by removing them to reserves created to secure their seclusion from contact with all other races.[66]

In this context, the threat of opium lay not only in the physical harm it wrought, but in the very fact of the racial contact it promoted. In 1901 Meston advocated the removal onto a reserve of a 'depraved half caste' who was living with a Chinese man. Typically, he showed little respect for the wishes of the individuals involved:

The Chinaman's offer to marry her, and the girl's willingness, ought not to be considered. She was an opium smoker, and as usual with Aboriginal and half-castes cohabiting with Chinamen, the medium of sales of opium to aboriginals ... I hold in utter abhorrence these marriages between Chinese and aboriginals, or whites and aboriginals.[67]

Meston abhorred, therefore, intermarriage in any context. His goal was the enforced isolation of all Aborigines from all pollutants—including not just opium but the Chinese people themselves.

Economic hostility to the Chinese, alluded to by the South Australian Attorney-General, was also an important factor in the workings of the Queensland Act. Dr Roth argued that the employment of Aborigines by the Chinese would lead to the spread of the opium habit. In 1898 he said: 'we do not consider it advisable as a general rule for any Chinese or coloured aliens to employ aboriginals: the temptation to supply opium is extreme'. Pressure to adopt and enforce this policy came from Queensland farmers in areas with high Chinese populations. A meeting of the Barron Valley Farmers and Progress Association (at Atherton) urged the government to forbid the employment of Blacks by 'Chinamen, Kanakas and Asiatics', allegedly because 'these are the only people who supply opium to the aboriginals'.[68]

While it was true that opium was sometimes used as a substitute for wages and as a medium of exchange, this practice was by no means limited to the Chinese.[69] More importantly, the farmers' objection to Chinese employment did not stem from any concern with Aboriginal welfare, as Roth discovered when he visited the Atherton area in September 1898. A man named Corbett, 'speaking for all the other farmers', complained that 'they could not get the blacks to work when they wanted them, while the Chinese', who farmed half of the surrounding land, 'could always get them, a fact which he accounted for by saying that the Celestial paid their Aboriginal employees in opium'. The solution seemed simple. As the local carpenter argued, 'the blacks should be taken from the Chinese and compelled to work for any Europeans who might require their services'.[70] Opium was, as ever, a scapegoat. The local White farmers, wanting cheap Black labour, could not understand why they would rather work for the Chinese. The use of opium was fastened upon as the only possible explanation for such a perverse choice.

The likely truth was that the Chinese treated the Aboriginal people with a modicum of respect. Roth reported the local police as saying that if the White population ceased starving and mistreating its Black employees, it could get as many workers as it wanted. But even the crudest kind of decency appears to have been beyond some of the locals. A man named Putt expressed his grievance with incredulity:

I have shot thirteen or fourteen niggers in this District and this is all the Government has done for me:—I can't get a ____ nigger when I want one. They all go to the Chinaman.[71]

Yet although Roth found that the Chinese were good employers, and did not pay their workers in opium, he none the less recommended the prohibition of Aboriginal employment by aliens. The long-term consequences of this policy are beyond the scope of this book. But one result of the early prohibition of opium smoking in the Northern Territory and Queensland is beyond question. In the waters off these jurisdictions, in Darwin and Cooktown, for example, opium smuggling into Australia began in earnest.

Men like Dr Roth were prepared to surrender the Aboriginal population to the tender mercies of men like Putt, simply because it was expedient to do so. In the deep undercurrent of distrust of the Chinese, and in government officials' willingness to give in to popular prejudice, the prohibition of Aboriginal opium use in Queensland and South Australia, far from being an exception, exhibited the same traits which characterised all the early history of Australia's attitude towards opium use. These traits were first legislated with respect to Aboriginal opium use because the supposedly benign paternalism of White Australia towards this country's first inhabitants was so deeply ingrained. But more far-reaching opium laws lay just around the corner.

THE CRUSADES

*The Campaign for Opium Prohibition
1901–1908*

Federation and Hesitation 1901–1905

The Federation of the Australian colonies on 1 January 1901 removed the force of the revenue-based arguments used against opium prohibition in the 1890s. The new Commonwealth government could not just enact any law it wanted: it had to be a law on a subject specified in the Constitution. Primary responsibility for drugs and health, for example, remained with the States. The Commonwealth was granted exclusive power, however, over the imposition of customs duties:

88. Uniform duties of customs shall be imposed within two years after the establishment of the Commonwealth ...
90. On the imposition of uniform duties of customs the power of the [Commonwealth] Parliament to impose duties of customs and of excise ... shall become exclusive.

These provisions have been of enormous significance in the development of drug laws in Australia, especially because almost all 'drugs' have been manufactured overseas and imported into Australia, and have therefore been subject to the control and supervision of the Commonwealth at the customs barrier. Under section 90 of the Constitution, the Commonwealth has exclusive power to prohibit the import of any goods absolutely, or to make their importation subject to any condition it chooses.[1]

The immediate consequence of the new Constitutional position was that governmental action to forego the revenue gained from opium was no longer subject to the interplay of State rivalries. To prohibit the import of opium would still cost a lot of money—the duty on 'opium suitable for smoking' in 1905, the last year it was collected, raised £65 960, of which one-quarter was kept by the Commonwealth and the rest distributed to the States[2]—but it could not be argued that a ban would be ineffective without interstate co-operation, for the States no longer had a say in the matter. Any law designed to prevent the actual smoking or other use of opium was still within the exclusive jurisdiction of the States. But if the Commonwealth decided to prohibit the *importation* of opium suitable for smoking, that decision would take effect Australia-wide.

Although Federation made the prohibition of importation easier to realise, it did not immediately lead to that result. The 'Chinese problem' was addressed by the Commonwealth more directly. To replace the various restriction and exclusion Acts enacted by the Colonies in 1888–89, the Commonwealth parliament in its first session passed the *Immigration Restriction Act 1901*.[3] This legislation enabled the institutionalisation of the 'White Australia' policy and effectively excluded Asian immigration until well after the Second World War.

'The opium question'—which is to say the question of the Chinese habit of smoking opium—was finally discussed as part of the meeting between the

State Premiers and the Prime Minister, Alfred Deakin, held in Hobart in 1905. It was not a victory for the anti-opium movement. As he and other government advisors had done in the past, the New South Wales Chief Medical Officer, Dr Ashburton Thompson, poured cold water on the heated claims of the anti-opium activists. The conference brief he prepared for the Premier of New South Wales, Joseph Carruthers, argued that specific laws relating to opium smoking should not be enacted:

1. The balance of evidence regarding opium in countries where it is commonly used by others than the sick ... is, in my opinion,
  (a) that at worst it is much less harmful than alcohol;
  (b) that although, like alcohol, it is sometimes abused, the result, as compared with the results of abuse of alcohol, are negligible;
  (c) that in countries where it appears (from the habit of using it) to be required it is, broadly speaking, not merely harmless but useful ...
3. It would be reasonable to restrict the sale of opium and its preparations or derivatives to druggists, who should sell it under the Regulations applicable to poisons (as they [already] do in this State).[4]

Carruthers accepted this view and reasoned at the conference that 'the charge of the European population using it is absolutely not sustained ... I think, altogether, it is one of the subjects we can very well leave alone'. Quoting the report of his own Inspector-General of Police, he pointed out that

there are only about 200 white smokers in the Commonwealth, and ... they are confined in nearly every case to the wives of Chinese, and to abandoned women of the lowest class. The habit is not on the increase.[5]

The conference resolution on the subject reflected this notable caution. While it unanimously agreed to joint action to prohibit 'opium dens and places used for promiscuous smoking' it did not propose the prohibition of either the importation or the sale and use of opium for smoking.

The discussion at the Hobart conference was a reaction to the campaign for the prohibition of opium smoking, waged intermittently but with steadily increasing vigour since 1873. The campaigners responded to the Premiers' indifference by redoubling their efforts. As inauspiciously as it had begun, 1905 was to be the climax and fulfilment of their endeavours. Bodies like the Public Morals Association (PMA), the Temperance Morals Committee of the Methodist Church, and the Anti-Opium League waited upon the State and Commonwealth governments, and 'monster meetings' in support of the 'Anti-Opium Crusade' were held throughout the country. The campaign was organised and determined. Petitions rained upon the Commonwealth parliament, from Brisbane, Broadmeadows and Bendigo, Camperdown, Kempsey and Cloncurry, Melbourne, Sydney and Adelaide, 'praying that further legislation be enacted to prevent the importation of opium for smoking purposes into the Commonwealth'. In all, 132 petitions were received, including five from Victoria each containing over 29 000 signatures, and one from New South Wales with more than 60 000 names. By comparison, no other subject prompted more than seven petitions in that year.[6]

Success came quickly. In the same year, Victoria prohibited the smoking of opium by any person, and the Commonwealth government prohibited its importation. South Australia amended its *Opium Act* to cover all persons, not just Aborigines. Three years later, the New South Wales government followed suit, by which time the members of the PMA in particular had become accomplished at letter-writing and petitioning.[7] Yet, as we have seen, the Prime Minister and State Premiers showed little interest in these reforms. Why did they change their tune so quickly? In order to explain the rapid and thorough success of the anti-opium campaign, it is important to understand the social context which made legislative prohibition an acceptable solution, the apparent support of the Chinese community, and the approach and strength of the European crusaders. It was within the framework of these influences that governments around Australia were effectively pressured into the construction of Australia's first prohibitionist drug laws.

The Social Context: Health and the Law

Perhaps in another time and place, hatred of the Chinese would not have led to the legislative proscription of opium smoking. But, in addition to its anti-Chinese sentiment, the anti-opium crusade appealed to the emerging values of Australian society. These values emphasised the ideals of physical health and purity in the future development of Australia, and put increasing faith in the power of the law to mould and enforce such ideals.

We live in a society in which almost everything we do is regulated by governments—licences to drive, to build, to own a dog or to sell flowers in the street. In relation to drug laws, ever more detailed regulation, increased police powers and stiffer penalties have extracted savage social costs and personal suffering with little evidence that such rabid law-making has done any good. Yet there remains in our society an innate faith in the efficacy of the law as an instrument of social change.

The power of legislative intervention was not always so readily accepted. Throughout the nineteenth century, *laissez-faire* philosophy had replaced the paternalism of the eighteenth century and dominated government philosophies in Australia as it did elsewhere. Adam Smith, Charles Darwin and Herbert Spencer were the prophets of the day. It was, economically and socially, survival of the fittest, and legislative non-intervention was a positive social good. In the fields of drug law, poisons, and health matters, the result was a notable lack of regulation. In the United States through the 1830s and 1840s, and in Great Britain in 1858, provisions that had restricted the practice of unlicensed medical practitioners in the paternalist era were systematically repealed. In the Australian colonies, various medical Acts enacted mid-century allowed for the registration of legally qualified practitioners, but gave them few privileges and certainly did not prevent medical practice by those who were unregistered.[8] In general, drug users, like trade and industry, were 'let to act' as they saw fit.

Every dogma has its day, but by the time of the Federation of the Australian colonies in 1901, that of legislative non-intervention was waning fast. A new era was waxing, in which legislation was seen as the cure to all ills. With a new country came a new spirit of hope; hope in the perfectibility of human society and in the ability of government and legislation to enforce social norms and, more, to change people's attitudes and behaviour. An ideology was developing which expected governmental supervision over all aspects of life. It is an ideology which has continued to grow in power and legitimacy to the present day. I am far from asserting that we would be better off with the *laissez-faire* dogmatism of the nineteenth century; only that our present attitude to law is inevitably as ideologically structured, as subjective and limited, as any.

This changing attitude to law, especially in areas connected with drugs and medicine, can be seen in the strong move towards increased health legislation around the turn of the century. Various Public Health Acts and Pure Food Acts gave greatly increased powers to the government and bureaucracy.[9] Speaking to the Victorian Pure Food Bill in 1905, some, like Mr Gaunson, who 'was indeed sorry that he had not been present to block the progress of this wretched Bill', remained unrepentant exponents of *laissez-faire*. But declarations of the changing times were far more typical:

> We know that John Bright and all the great school of thinkers with whom he was associated, objected to interference by central authorities. But the time has gone past for that objection.

Bill after Bill reflected the same opinions. In debate on the Inebriates (Amendment) Bill 1909 (NSW), which provided for the legal control and institutionalisation of 'the drunken poor', the leader of the Labor Party spoke of the new age dawning:

> In my experience of life I have met many individuals who have prayed to God that the state would save them, because they could not save themselves.

In the new age, the state would save us all.[10]

The anti-opium laws that were passed in the early years of the new century were part of this growing faith in the appropriateness and efficacy of legal control. In debate on the Victorian Opium Bill of 1891, much was made of its 'Draconian' and 'grandmotherly' nature, and the reluctance of parliamentarians to 'interfere in such matters' was an important reason for its defeat.[11] The legislators in 1905 displayed no such compunctions. Alfred

Conroy, Member for Werriwa in the Commonwealth House of Representatives, cautioned against the attitudes he saw embodied in the government's proposal to prohibit the importation of opium suitable for smoking:

> We are assuming that all we have to do is to pass an Act of Parliament when, hey presto, all sin and misery will disappear from the world. Honorable members, in spite of their experience as to the futility of laws for putting down the evil habits of the people are, nevertheless, ready to pass an Act for the prohibition of the opium traffic in the full belief that the evil will at once disappear.[12]

But his warning fell upon the deaf ears of neophytes. Faith in the infinite power of the law had taken root.

It was not only changing attitudes to law that led to an explosion in health legislation. There was in Australia from the late nineteenth century a developing ethos which condemned 'unhealthy' behaviour as unpatriotic and immoral. Australia was a bush nation, a country of men, tanned and strong, relying upon their physical prowess to create from the dust a fertile land. Sensuality and intellectualism were seen as dangers to the young Australia. Thus the Lamberts, adopting this approach in *The Science of Life* in 1883, cautioned their readers about the dangers that awaited young boys:

> A hearty unimaginative boy is not much to be feared, but a thoughtful, intellectual youth is endangered by his own mental capabilities. Activity, labour and manly fatigue are great essentials to youth.[13]

Aesthetics led to ruination; athletics, salvation.

Federation had also focused the minds of many upon what it meant to be an Australian; in a country with so little European history behind it, the answer seemed to lie not in an examination of the past but in a consideration of how to model the future. That discussion in turn was concerned to a considerable extent with the importance of physical health. Thus Dr John Cumpston, the first Commonwealth Director-General of Health, described himself as one 'who dream[s] of leading this young nation of ours to a paradise of physical perfection'.[14] The nation itself was to embody physicality, and the new administrative élite were to guide it.

Similarly, eugenics enjoyed an extraordinary amount of support in Australia: serious thought was given as to how government intervention could enhance the purity and quality of the race. An editorial in the *Sydney Morning Herald*, arising out of the debate on eugenics at a major 1914 medical congress held in London, declared that:

> we should adopt the same principles in breeding human beings as we successfully adopt in breeding sheep and cattle ... The ultimate object of eugenics must be some sort of racial selection.[15]

Undoubtedly, the paper, many doctors, and leading figures of the day (including Dr Cumpston) believed in using compulsory treatment and the force of law to improve humanity, as if it were a herd of merinos.

In its most extreme manifestations, State legislatures came close to fulfilling the dream of John Simeon Elkington (another leading health bureaucrat) that 'serious acceptance of a doctrine of national physical morality will cause preventable disease to be regarded as somebody's crime.'[16] The New South Wales *Venereal Disease Act 1918*, for example, provided for the compulsory treatment of syphilis, and prohibited either marriage or sexual intercourse by any person with a venereal disease, under penalty of a fine or imprisonment. 'I realize,' said the Premier, William Holman, 'that we are asking hon. members to vote for an entirely new conception of the duties of citizenship and of the obligation of the individual.'[17]

The emphasis on health as a desirable focus of legislative intervention led anti-opium rhetoric to be couched increasingly in terms of opium use as an 'illness'. As we have seen, the underlying hostility to opium smoking was racial. But an appeal to the health risks allegedly posed by the 'disease' of opium addiction made the brutality of absolute prohibition more acceptable. Undoubtedly the use of opium, like any drug, has health implications. No drug is harmless. But the health arguments were marshalled on the basis of the flimsiest anecdotal evidence, and for purposes quite unrelated to any genuine concern with the health of users. The appeal to health was a useful tool in the hands of anti-opium campaigners because it concealed—perhaps in the minds of the crusaders above all—its specific relationship to the Chinese, and served to legitimate and rationalise prejudice.

'The Chinese themselves': The Crusading Quong Tart

Who was there to defend the Chinese against the attacks upon opium smoking? Only the Chinese themselves. Yet, ironically, many of the leading anti-opium crusaders were Chinese. The Chinese Reform League, Quong Tart, Ah Ket and Reverend Cheong were central to the impetus and success of the movement. Quong Tart in particular campaigned assiduously from the 1880s on. In his *Report upon Chinese Camps in New South Wales*, commissioned by the Legislative Assembly in 1883, his opinions on the subject were clearly stated:

At the outset let me say that the fulcrum on which rests all vice, immorality and corruption with the Chinese is opium ... Of the great number who indulge in opium-smoking, fully nine-tenths admitted the necessity for reform, and declared their willingness to sign a petition calling upon the Government to stop the importation of opium into the colony in quantities beyond that which may be required for medicinal purposes.

Over the next twenty years, he made the same points time and time again, in his pamphlet *A Plea for the Abolition of the Importation of Opium*, as a member of the Royal Commission into Alleged Chinese Gambling and Immorality, and in various speeches and petitions.[18]

The influence of Quong Tart and other like-minded members of the Chinese community was profound. William Johnson, for example, a future Speaker of the House of Representatives and the man who nominated the Yass/Canberra region as the site of the capital of Australia, raised the opium question on several occasions in the Commonwealth parliament in 1905. In introducing a motion calling for the prohibition of the importation of opium suitable for smoking, Johnson was at pains to emphasise the Chinese connection:

One of the most satisfactory features of the agitation against the opium traffic is that the Chinese residents of Australia are joining in the crusade ... A great meeting was recently held in the Centennial Hall, Sydney, in which prominent Chinese merchants and other Chinese residents took a leading part.

In parliamentary debate, the comment that 'Chinamen themselves first proposed such a bill' was frequently used as an unanswerable argument for prohibition.[19]

What led Chinese people like Quong Tart to support a measure born and bred of European racism and paranoia? One reason relates to the history of opium use in China. Opium had been known for its medicinal properties for hundreds of years, and there had also been a small trade in opium for recreational purposes, which various edicts by the Chinese Emperor had failed to stop. But in the late eighteenth and early nineteenth centuries, Britain discovered that opium grown in India was a highly profitable cash crop that could be sold to the Chinese for precious silver. The East India Company, which knew a good thing when it saw it, began to push opium on the Chinese with exceptional vigour. By the reign of Queen Victoria, the opium trade had become for the British Empire a huge and vastly successful enterprise, and for the Chinese a disastrous drain on their economy. In 1839 the Emperor's specially appointed commissioner, Lin, prohibited the sale and use of opium, confiscated 2.6 million pounds of the drug that was lying in Canton harbour, and proceeded to destroy it all (which alone took twenty-three days to accomplish). Great Britain, far from applauding the move, declared war on China. Morality was no match for profit. The Opium War lasted for three years, and resulted in the ignominious defeat of the Chinese, a defeat which opened the country to trade, exploitation and virtual dismemberment by Western imperialism. By the end of the century, moreover, up to ten per cent of China's population may have been addicted to opium smoking. The opium habit was consequently seen by the Chinese as both a cursed legacy of Western intrusion and a symbol of China's powerlessness. As Chinese nationalism grew during the reform movement of the late 1890s, the humiliation and suffering that resulted from the Opium War fuelled the xenophobia of the time.[20]

For many Chinese abroad, in Australia and elsewhere, the campaign to eliminate opium smoking was in part an understandable expression of this nationalism; a desire no longer to be shackled to a grim and recent past. But there was much more to it than this. Consider Quong Tart, successful capitalist, friend of the famous, and the *Coeur de Lion* of Australia's anti-opium crusade.

Quong Tart was by all accounts a much-loved man. Born in 1850, he came to Australia when he was nine, living first among the Scottish settlers in the Braidwood region of New South Wales, and later in nearby Araluen. As his descendant and biographer, Edward Lea-Scarlett, wrote:

He could sing Scotch songs with singular pathos, recite Burns' poems with a genuine accent, play Scotch airs on the piano and jokingly alluded to himself as being a native of Aberdeen.

In Sydney through the 1880s and 1890s he developed a successful chain of tea rooms, which he claimed to be the first of their kind in Australia. It was, however, his personality that earned him fame and success. Indeed, his marriage to a European woman, Margaret Scarlett, far from inciting anger and outrage as might have been expected, was met with rejoicing not only by the Governor, Lord Carrington, who sent him a wedding gift, but even by the *Bulletin*. 'We have always declared,' it wrote, 'the dear girls used to go not for their tea, but their nice little Tart, and now he is married! Yum, yum.'[21]

Even at the height of the anti-Chinese campaign in New South Wales, the affection that was felt for him remained undiminished. In the second reading speech on the Influx of Chinese Restriction Bill in the New South Wales parliament, Sir John Salomons specifically exempted Quong Tart from his comments on the Chinese. When Tart protested to the Premier over the Bill, Henry Parkes explained that he was 'the only perfect specimen of his race'.[22]

In 1900 his premises in the Queen Victoria Building were burgled and he was assaulted. So aghast were the people of Sydney at the thought that anyone would dream of attacking Quong Tart that a testimonial dinner was held in the Town Hall, at which he was presented with a silver salver and a gift of 300 guineas, collected by public subscription. But Quong Tart was never the same again. When he died in July 1903, over 2000 people came to pay their respects.

Quong Tart was a philanthropist, famous for the free banquets he put on for those two kindred groups, local asylum inmates and MPs who had lost their seats in elections. He was the undisputed leader of the Chinese community, a fourth class Mandarin with a peacock feather, and unofficial Chinese Consul in Australia.[23] He was a capitalist and a crusader, deeply committed, like other 'leaders of the Chinese community', to the anti-opium campaign. And most of all, he was a devout middle-class believer in assimilation.

The fallacy in asserting that 'the Chinese themselves' desired the prohibition of opium smoking lay in the assumption that it was possible to speak of the Chinese as a homogeneous group. Quong Tart, in his 1884 report to the New South Wales Legislative Assembly on Chinese camps, claimed to speak for the nine-tenths of opium smokers who were 'willing ... to sign a petition calling upon the Government to stop the importation of opium'.[24] But these interviews with Chinese smokers took place as part of an official inquiry instituted following accusations about the immorality and uncleanliness of the Chinese. Intimidated by racism and hatred on the one hand, formality and authority on the other, forced to confess to an unacceptable habit on which Quong Tart's opinions were undoubtedly well known, it is hardly surprising that they should answer not honestly but 'correctly'.

Merchants and retailers like Quong Tart and Yee Hing spoke for the upper strata of Chinese society. Their concern was for the image of the capitalist middle class and not for the poor. In the 1884 petition he circulated following his report to the New South Wales Legislative Assembly, and in *A Plea for the Abolition of the Importation of Opium* (1887), Quong Tart in fact agreed that the Chinese were subject to 'habits of indolence ... gambling and criminal propensities ... scenes of grossest immorality'. But he defended his *own* class by blaming these problems upon opium, which he said was used exclusively by 'the very lowest orders of Chinese society':

Words cannot express how dreadfully hurt the respectable Chinese feel when things are said publicly against them, for the gentlemen who denounce make no allowance, but class all alike, although that is anything but fair, for no criminal case against the Chinese has ever come from any of the respectable business houses, large or small, but in every case originated in places where Opium is used.

Likewise, throughout the hearings of the 1892 Royal Commission into Alleged Chinese Gambling and Immorality, Quong Tart was at pains to defend 'respectable Chinese merchants'. The report of the Commission concluded that 'it is only fair to state that no traces of opium were discernible about the premises of the better class of merchants or cabinet-makers.'[25]

'Respectable Chinese' opposition to opium smoking was intended to enhance their reputation in White society, and therefore, in the long run, their economic security. Significantly, the Chinese Merchants' Defence Association was one of the prime organisations to lobby the New South Wales government for the prohibition of opium. Founded to improve the image of Chinese businesses, its members had decided in 1904 not to trade in opium any more, but then rescinded the decision when they realised that without legislative interference 'others might come along and gain by our loss'.[26]

According to a 1905 edition of the *Review of Reviews*, Yee Hing of the Chinese Reform League, who 'represented the firm which controls one-third of the opium trade in New South Wales ... said his firm was prepared to lose the business and the enormous profits that were made'. But this, too, was far from noble self-sacrifice. As he testified to the 1905 Royal Commission into Customs, and Excise Tariffs, opium smuggling was already rife. Legal importers, required to pay a hefty duty, were losing much of their business in any event. Yee Hing favoured prohibition only because he did not believe that 'fair competition [could] be established'.[27]

Further, opium was only a part of the large trade in Chinese imports, and although prohibition denied traders the profits of a marketable commodity, the long-term benefits of safeguarding their position in Australian society were more important. In his second reading speech on the Opium Bill 1905, the Victorian Attorney-General, John Davies, suggested that the merchants were willing to destroy their own stock, so intent were they upon ending the trade once and for all. The government, however, turned out to have been mistaken. 'The offer to destroy the opium was accompanied by the proposal that the Government should pay for it.'[28]

Chinese merchants' interest in opium prohibition was driven by a desire to safeguard their economic success by wiping out a habit seen as disreputable within the White community, and which reflected badly upon them. More generally, the Chinese middle-class sought assimilation into and acceptance by Australian society. In denying aspects of their life and culture which drew attention to their difference, they could thus protect their wealth and position. Quong Tart was an extreme example of the assimilated Chinese. President of the Braidwood Cricket Club and the New South Wales Lacrosse Association, he wanted most of all to be an English gentleman. It was a genuinely pathetic ambition for a kindly Chinese gentleman. He wanted the press cuttings that his wife had collected about him put into book form so his children could see that 'although their father was a Chinese, he could be creditably compared with thousands of European fathers'.[29]

The problem with opium, as far as Quong Tart was concerned, was that it was a Chinese custom that stood in the way of European assimilation. He hoped that, once opium had been prohibited, the Chinese

would completely reform with the assistance of the different Chinese clergy-men (Church of England, Wesleyan, Presbyterian and Roman Catholic), and become more attached to the European customs.[30]

They had only to exchange a junk of opium for a schooner of beer—or perhaps, for some of Quong Tart's fine imported teas—and all would be well.

Assimilation served the economic and social purposes of the successful Chinese. Anything that drew attention to the Chinese as a distinct group in Australia threatened them with a racial backlash. But what of the thousands of poor Chinese in Australia for whom Quong Tart and others did not speak, but whose habits they sought to suppress? Many of them had no intention of staying in Australia permanently; most lived in a congested, poverty-stricken environment; and all of them were subject to the racist attitudes and laws of a xenophobic society. What, then, did assimilation offer these people except the denial of the very cultural traditions and habits that gave continuity to their lives and solace to their loneliness? In poverty and the isolation of poverty, despised and rejected, the feeling of belonging to a community is a vital survival mechanism.

The 'lower class' Chinese targeted by opium crusaders like Quong Tart were hardly in a position to publicise their opinions. Nevertheless, the 1884 petition which Quong Tart said would be signed by 'nine tenths of opium smokers', gained the signatures of 768 local councillors and 2500 other Europeans, but only 500 Chinese out of a total Chinese population thirty times that number.[31] Naturally, the Chinese did not match the anti-opium campaigners petition for petition. They lacked commitment, money, organisation, language skills, and any knowledge of the workings of government. One solitary petition was addressed to the Victorian parliament in 1905 by a man who was apparently fit and 'had all his wits about him', saying 'that it was all nonsense about the evil effect of smoking opium'. The petition did not, however, comply with the proper formalities and was never officially presented.[32] But there is one other voice of dissent on the public record. In 1884, the *Bulletin* noted a response to Quong Tart's petition which, it will be recalled, blamed 'indolence, gambling [and] grossest immorality ... upon the use of opium by Chinese lower classes':

The following petition from poor Chinamen not so high up in the world as Mr (here there is a highly objectionable word) [wrote the Bulletin*]* QUONG TART, *humbly showeth*
(1) That your petitioners, having quite as lively an interest in the wellbeing of the community as Mr (the unmeaning adjective again occurs) QUONG TART *(who can enjoy many mild and fashionable dissipations denied to them, and whose feet appear to have outgrown his boots owing to the society of the sweet creatures who go to drink his tea and confide to him little secrets), trust you will not regard his 'feelings of alarm' at their use of opium ...*
(4) That your petitioners live in small houses because they like them, and because their fathers for the last four thousand years inhabited buildings of the same style of architecture ... The supposition that cutting off the opium supply would entice a better class of Chinese to NSW is purely visionary; for it is entirely wrong to say they do not use it. For these and many other reasons that could be brought forward, your petitioners trust that you will not entertain Mr QUONG TART's *proposal, and that you will convey to him your desire that in future he attend to selling his tea, and not shove his shovel in where there is no need. And your petitioners will ever pray.*[33]

I admit to many doubts as to the authenticity of this document. It is rather *Bulletin*-like and decidedly un-Chinese in its style. On the other hand, it flatly contradicts the *Bulletin*'s editorial line on opium, Quong Tart, and the Chinese, which makes it more credible. At the very least, the petition was probably an accurate description of the attitude of most Chinese opium smokers to prohibition. Moreover, it clearly recognised and reflected the class basis of Quong Tart's 'constituency'. Far from being the spokesman of working-class Chinese, it seems quite likely that Quong Tart was indeed considered a meddler who, in pursuing the economic and social aspirations of his own class, was prepared to throw poor Chinese to the wolves. They gave the Chinese middle class a bad press.

Other Battles: Alcohol and Patent Medicines

The early years of the twentieth century saw a climate ripe for those crusaders imbued with an unquenchable belief in health and the law. It would be a mistake, however, to think that opium smoking was the only object of their crusades. Many of the most vigorous anti-opium groups were temperance organisations whose activities were mainly focused on the prohibition of alcohol. Still other crusaders fought against the consumption of patent medicines, or tobacco, with equal passion. For Dr Samuel Knaggs, 'the pernicious habit of imbibing [immoderate] quantities of tea at each meal ... is as culpable and detrimental to health ... as the sensual indulgences of the inebriates' of all countries'.[34] The prohibition of opium was therefore a convenient sop to the pressure exerted for reform in many similar areas.

The question of alcohol and alcoholism drew the most zeal and passion from the crusaders and the most concerted attention from the community. The *Age* discussed long and hard the merits of the Göthenberg system, which if instituted would have resulted in the sale of liquor being placed exclusively in government hands. Meanwhile, in rough-and-ready weeklies like the *Bulletin* and the *Review of Reviews*, quack cures for drunkenness abounded, from Eucrasy, Anti-Dipso, and Langston's Vegetable Cure for Alcoholism, to Keeley's 'bichloride of gold', which even an editorial in the *Age* declared to be a successful treatment for the 'physical disease' of alcoholism.[35] In fact, many of these cures contained high concentrations of alcohol or morphine, and thus merely succeeded in replacing one addiction with another.

Some crusaders acted in pursuit of a lone and maverick obsession, such as E.W. Cole, founder of Cole's Book Arcade, who wrote and published *The Pound Pamphlet Word for Word*, dedicated to ridding the world of alcoholism and the use of patent medicines.[36] In general, however, the campaign for the prohibition of alcohol was the preserve of well-organised women's religious groups such as the Women's Christian Temperance Union, the Order of the Sons of Temperance, the International Order of Good Templars, the New South Wales Conference of Churches of Christ Temperance Committee, the Vaucluse Prohibition League, and so on. The energies of these and other similar organisations also led them to seek to expand the 'tempering' influence of women's virtue into the coarse masculine realm of public life. Ultimately, and in Australia and New Zealand before anywhere else, they achieved political enfranchisement.

The lobbying of the alcohol prohibitionists at times came surprisingly close to success. In Victoria a number of areas, including Camberwell, a suburb of Melbourne, voted for the abolition of liquor licences in their regions in accordance with the 'local option' provisions of the *Licensing Act 1906*.[37] In New South Wales pressure grew throughout the First World War for a vote on prohibition. To appease the temperance lobby in the run-up to the first post-war election, legislation was enacted which required a referendum to be held within eighteen months. 'The popular belief,' declared Reverend Hammond, 'is that Prohibition is coming'. It was not to be. To public uproar, the incoming Labor government of John Storey refused to hold the referendum. Reverend Hammond accused the government of 'flouting the law', the opposition was scathing, and the *Sydney Morning Herald* censorious, but the Labor Party, fearing a massive loss of jobs in what we would now call the 'hospitality industry', held firm. 'I am known to be as honest as the Premier himself', protested one speaker in the heat of debate. 'There is nothing very virtuous in that,' was the Premier's reply.[38]

Despite their eventual failure in Australia, the prohibition movement was a powerful moral and political influence, whose voice was heard long and loud. Queensland voted on alcohol prohibition in 1920 and New South Wales, finally, in 1928. In 1930 a vote on total prohibition took place in Victoria and was only defeated by 507 025 votes to 388 833.[39] In Western Australia a prohibition referendum took place as late as 1950, while in New Zealand a vote is still required to be held with every general election. In the United States, of course, the legislation of morality did indeed lead to the creation of a teetotalitarian state from 1918 to 1933.

Finally, however, the prohibitionists in Australia could not defeat the lethargy and indifference of governments or the power of vested interests involved in the production and sale of alcohol. The Labor Party was described as 'the political bulwark of the liquor trade'; the Liquor Trade Defence Union organised its own groups, such as the Freedom League, to counter the temperance unions, and held 'monster meetings' of its own.[40] Most importantly, alcohol was not seen as some peculiar foreign evil, but as the nation's drug of choice. The *Bulletin*, proud standard-bearer of Australian chauvinism, defended alcohol as the birthright of the White races:

Thus, while it would be absurd to attribute European progress to the use of alcohol, the fact that semi-barbarism, stagnation, and even regression characterise the lands where distilled and fermented liquor are almost unknown cannot be gainsaid ... Let us leave these dead seas of Eastern humanity—leave them to their sobriety and their barbarism.

'The fittest,' argued the *Bulletin*, cleverly evoking Charles Darwin against those who sought temperance legislation to protect the health and strength of the nation, 'are not always the careful, canny, prosperous, sober, mediocre bourgeoisie'.[41]

An ultimately more successful campaign was conducted by those concerned about the sale of 'patent medicines', ready-to-use drugs packaged and sold directly to the public through chemist shops and even grocers. Although I also use the popular term 'patent medicines', very few of them actually possessed a patent and they are more accurately described as 'proprietary drugs'. The leading knight templar in this war was undoubtedly Octavius Beale, patentee of the all-iron piano tuning system, founder of Beale's Pianos, one-time president of the Federated Chambers of Manufacture of Australia and of the Commonwealth Chamber of Commerce. Like E.W. Cole and Quong Tart, he was a capitalist entrepreneur with crusading instincts. Primarily concerned to maintain 'the White race' against the threats of decadence, contraception, and the 'yellow peril', his views first gained prominence when he was a Commissioner on the 1903 New South Wales Royal Commission into the Decline of the Birthrate, and later in his book, *Racial Decay*, authoritatively described as 'quite the oddest book ever published in a field where there are many competitors'.[42]

In 1905 Beale, driven by his concern with the use of drugs as agents of 'race suicide'—contraceptives and abortifacients—badgered Alfred Deakin to appoint him to inquire into Secret Drugs, Cures and Foods. The Prime Minister was initially reluctant but, in the face of Beale's insistence, he finally consented on the understanding that, although the project was given the official title of Royal Commission, it wasn't going to cost the Commonwealth government a penny. Deakin certainly got value for money. So lacking in restraint was the 400-page report on patent and proprietary medicines which Beale produced that the government, before its release, had to enact legislation protecting Royal Commissions from actions in defamation.[43]

Beale's criticisms of 'patent medicines' centred upon the secrecy which surrounded their ingredients and the dishonesty of their advertising. The 'secret' of many of the medicines he investigated proved to be nothing more than their high alcohol or opiate content. Whisko, 'a non-intoxicating stimulant', was 28.2 per cent alcohol, Pe-ru-na 28.5 per cent, and Warner's 35.7 per cent. Hostetters Stomach Bitters, at 44.3 per cent, was stronger than most spirits. Mrs Winslow's Soothing Syrup, Bonnington's Irish Moss, Ayers' Sarsaparilla and Godfrey's Cordial all contained opium; Ayers' Cherry Pectoral was morphine-based; and Cigares de Joy was a popular brand of marijuana cigarettes. His solution, however, was simply to expose the dangers of these medicines by forcing the manufacturers to state their formulae clearly on the label.[44] It was their secrecy that was of prime concern to him.

Beale was by no means sanguine about addiction to alcoholic and opiate-based drugs. He discussed the 'exposure of the young to demoralisation and even to debauchery by ... preparations of cocaine, of acetanilide, of sulfonal, and other synthetic depressants, of opium ... ' But his crusade was more general. Accordingly, although he congratulated the Commonwealth on the prohibition of opium smoking, and agreed that it was 'of racial importance in itself', he undoubtedly thought it of only minor significance.⁴⁵

Every page of Beale's report was branded with the zeal of the crusader, every line dripped moral outrage. As the trade journal, the *Chemist and Druggist of Australasia*, wryly commented in 1906, 'Mr Beale is terribly in earnest, and evidently industrious. He takes himself very seriously'.⁴⁶ He was a first-strike writer, not given to pacifism in the employment of adjectives. Evils were 'multifarious', practices 'pernicious' and 'rooted and grounded in greed', vices 'nameless and unnatural'. Much of the report consisted of the narration in his own emotional language of hearsay stories of depravity and tragedy, the layout designed in varying styles and sizes of print in order to excite the reader and emphasise particular points. In short, it looked rather like a 400-page advertisement for the kind of patent medicine he decried.

Throughout the report, too, Beale manifested the twentieth-century crusader's faith in the law as the ultimate instrument to preserve the health of the nation:

*It is said that 'you cannot make people moral by Act of Parliament.' But that is precisely what you can do, and it is the only way ... This doctrine of laisser-faire, of unrestraint, [is] in diametrical antithesis to the Christian philosophy, which we surely cannot be expected to ignore.*⁴⁷

Despite Beale's outcry against proprietary medicines' 'secret formulae', and those of other inquiries undertaken in the United States and the United Kingdom, the battle to institute controls over them was a difficult and drawn-out affair. The consumption of these medicines was, again, a common European indulgence and not an alien habit: Australia was the largest per capita consumer in the world at the turn of the century. In addition, advertisements for such products kept many newspapers afloat and created a powerful vested interest in the survival of the patent medicine industry. In 1913, Australia's stocks of proprietary drugs were estimated to be worth £3 125 000; manufacturers spent £160 000 annually on advertising.⁴⁸

Gradually, the secrecy surrounding proprietary drugs was destroyed, and with it their lure. Regulations under the *Commerce (Trade Description) Act 1905* (Cwlth) prohibited the import of medicines unless they contained a label stating 'a true description of the goods'. The States enacted similar provisions in various Pure Food Acts, which required products to display a label stating 'the quantity or proportion of any morphine, opium, cocaine, heroin ... cannabis indica ... or preparation of any such substances contained therein'.⁴⁹ The result of these provisions was to prevent the secret use of these drugs in 'patent medicines', and the accidental formation of a habit amongst users ignorant of what they were taking. But the regulation of these and other 'drugs' went far beyond the mere destruction of their secrecy. 'Drug' laws, as will be discussed in more detail later, dealt with the use and possession of these substances and not merely how they were labelled. Other laws, then, enacted for other reasons, went far beyond the mild disclosure provisions of the Pure Food Acts.

The provisions of these Acts, for their part, did not go so far as to require the disclosure of the 'trade secrets' of patent medicines. The miraculous ingredients that apparently made Liquizone 'liquid oxygen' at room temperature, and Pe-ru-na more medicinal than whiskey, were not required to be disclosed to sceptical governments and the credulous public. Between 1910 and 1927, four interstate departmental conferences, organised to agree on uniform food and drug laws, drafted model regulations based on a Western Australian provision requiring proprietary medicines to include on their labels a 'statement of the ingredients and their preparations ... unless exempted by the lodgement of the Formula with the Central Health Authority'.[50]

The power and influence of the proprietary medicine industry, however, was not yet spent. In Victoria, the passage of a disclosure law along these lines in 1924 was vigorously resisted by a wide coalition of chemists', manufacturers' and shopkeepers' groups as well as the Proprietary Articles Trade Association.[51] The regulation did not enter into force until 1929, and even then it was generally not observed. As late as 1932, The Honourable H.F. Richardson complained in the Legislative Council that the Minister for Health was upholding the law. 'I appeal to the Minister,' he said, 'to see that there are no further prosecutions'.[52] Victory on this question, therefore, came slowly and with difficulty.

The Political Capitulation: Opium Prohibition 1905–1908

As the passion of the crusaders of the early twentieth century broke like an ocean against the various rocks that ired them, only the Chinese opium smokers had no one to defend their interests—not even influential Chinese. In 1893 L.L. Smith wryly observed that:

No one proposes to interfere with the moderate smoker who enjoys his pipe, but we are going to interfere with the Chinamen because there is nobody to help them.[53]

In addition, the campaign against opium smoking was in tune with the growing faith in the legal enforceability of health, and tapped into deep undercurrents of sexual and racist fears. The crusading spirit was pacified by the line of least resistance.

On the initiative of the Prime Minister, Alfred Deakin, and despite the mood and recommendations of the Hobart conference held that year, the States agreed to share jointly the loss of revenue consequent on a Commonwealth ban, and on 30 December 1905, by Proclamation, the

Commonwealth Government declared that 'the importation of opium, suitable for smoking, shall be prohibited absolutely'.[54] While the Commonwealth could stop opium coming into the country—and prepared opium was almost without exception imported—the prohibition of the act of smoking itself was a State matter. These State laws were substantially the same in every case. Each generation has shored up that original structure according to the faith and whims of the time, but beneath the contemporary confusion and complexity, the basic principles of drug legislation have remained unchanged. The opium prohibition laws, in bald and attenuated form, established a structure and precedent which have not been questioned since:

1. *This Act may be cited as the Opium Smoking Prohibition Act 1905 ...*
2. *No person shall smoke opium.*
3. *No person shall sell or deal or traffic in opium in any form suitable for smoking.*
4. *No person shall prepare or manufacture opium in any form suitable for smoking.*
5. *No person shall have in his possession order or disposition opium in any form suitable for smoking.*[55]

These laws were unusual in two ways. First, they were unique in the unqualified nature and ferocity of their provisions, and second, they dealt with only one type of opium. In terms of the character of the provisions, it was not only the abuse, not even only the use of opium suitable for smoking, but even the mere possession of it, that was deemed criminal and subject to severe penalties. William Holman, representing the Labor Party in New South Wales at the time, was unconvinced:

I submit that it is a most dangerous principle for the House to introduce in its legislation, that the actual use of a drug of this kind by an adult ... should in itself be made an offence. [This] is not an act of humanitarianism, but an act of absolute brutality ... unprecedented, so far as I know, in legislation, except as regards the Acts in the sister states, which are purely experimental.[56]

Holman's concerns were not commonly shared. In New South Wales, the *Police Offences (Amendment) Act 1908* aroused the opposition of the Labor Party in particular, and was carried on the second reading with only forty-four votes to twenty-four. The Bill was, however, as the *Daily Telegraph* described it, 'a legislative drag-net[:] opium-using, gambling, and time-payment furniture dealing come within its ambit'. Opium occupied a small part of the Bill and was merely tangential to most criticism of it.[57] In Victoria and the Commonwealth, opposition to the prohibition of opium smoking was almost non-existent. In fact, the issue quickly became old hat. One member of the House of Representatives grew exasperated at the obsession with the subject displayed by William Johnson:

> Mr Page.—*Why should the honorable member inflict all these statements on the House, when the Government are going to prohibit the importation of opium?*
> Mr Johnson.—*I hope that they are.*
> Mr Page.—*They have said so, and therefore the honorable member is merely flogging a dead horse.*[58]

A few members raised cautious and prophetic voices of doubt. 'I venture to say', warned Alfred Conroy, 'that if we legislate on the lines proposed, the evil, so far from disappearing, will become ten times worse than ever.' The general attitude of politicians around the country, on the other hand, was that the provisions, although drastic, were necessary. As the federal Member for Melbourne Ports said, 'Honorable members have made up their minds on the subject, and nine out of ten in the community are in favour of prohibition'.[59]

In terms of the substance of the legislation, it was unusual because it dealt with one particular kind of opium. Neither the pernicious concealment of opiates in patent medicines, nor the common habit of laudanum-drinking, was penalised. It was only the importation of 'opium suitable for smoking' that was prohibited and only the smoking of opium that was outlawed. Likewise, the *Police Offences (Amendment) Act 1908* (NSW), defined opium exclusively as 'any preparation thereof in a form capable of being used for the purposes of smoking'.[60] Clearly, opium use by the Chinese was the sole concern of legislatures. As Joseph Bosisto, a druggist and so one of the Victorian Legislative Assembly's resident 'opium experts', had explained in 1893, parliament sought 'to restrict and regulate the importation, sale and use of Chinese opium ... We should not legislate for the other opium at all'.[61]

Behind this discrimination lay the familiar fears of White Australia. The parliamentary speeches of William Johnson, whose energy and passion was the driving force behind the government's action in 1905, were often in a lurid style that would not have been out of place in the *Bulletin:*

> *One case in Melbourne struck me as being particularly abhorrent, for on one opium couch, smoking from the one tray, was a shrivelled up, decrepit-looking old Oriental, resembling nothing so much as a revivified Egyptian mummy, and a young European woman of scarcely twenty, very scantily clothed.*

Fear of contagion was even more dominant than the theme of miscegenation in parliamentary debates. Of the Chinese themselves, it was conceded that it might be 'a devilish good job to let them all smoke opium until they were wiped out of existence'. But as Mr McCutcheon then interjected in debate on the Victorian Opium Smoking Prohibition Bill, that was not the issue, 'We want to protect white people'.[62]

Some, like Bosisto, who reasoned that 'the very slight proportion of morphine [in opium] has a greater effect upon the brain of a European than upon the brain of an Asiatic', needed to explain such discrimination. For most, rationalisation was unnecessary. It was enough simply to declare that 'we' were at risk. 'White men and White women' were to be isolated from any contact with the drug by the legislation; and if, as a result, 'the Chinkey will get deleterious opium', too bad. To quarantine the clean, you must make the dirty suffer.[63]

No one could doubt the sincerity of the crusaders or their political mouthpieces. Nor could anyone deny that they heard only what they wanted to hear—rumour, exaggeration, myth or untruth. What motivated these sea-green incorruptibles, these 'moral entrepreneurs', who set themselves up as the creators of a new society?[64] For a few, like Quong Tart, it was a need to belong and to be accepted. For many it was racism, and for many more a fear of sexuality. For some it was simply the fear of non-conformity. But in all cases, the motivation lay a great deal deeper than any concern merely with the dangers of drug use.

It was because these reformers were propelled by such deeply rooted urges that they became so passionate, so committed and so unable to distinguish truth from caricature. The *Bulletin* could speak about the seduction of White women through the use of opium, Quong Tart could claim that all the Chinese in Australia blamed filth and degradation upon its wiles, and some even argued that opium made the skin of the Chinese yellow. The facts were only secondary because opium smoking itself was merely a trigger for the expression of deeper motivations. And for the most part, there was no reason to question their hearsay hysteria.

For others, the images and evils of opium smoking had become an ingrained myth, beyond the realm of fact. The sensual Chinese, whose opium was a tentacle of the octopus grappling with the lives of innocent Whites, was as real as a nightmare, and as unshakeable. For people in the grip of myth, the prohibition of opium smoking was an attempt to outlaw phantoms.

Above all, however, the opium laws were a sop to popular pressure on a subject about which governments simply did not care. The States' opium prohibition Acts and the Commonwealth Opium Proclamation together made it illegal to smoke or even to possess opium suitable for smoking, or to sell, deal, traffic, prepare, manufacture, order, dispose of or import it. The senior members of government who guided these measures through parliament had access to all the reports and advice which made it clear that such laws constituted an unprecedented absolutism and a gross over-reaction. As Mr Beeby said of the *Police Offences (Amendment) Act 1908* (NSW):

We are merely satisfying the pharasaical conscience that some people in the community possess. [It is] merely an attempt to placate a section outside.[65]

But the Chinese did not matter and had no interest groups to protect them. Politicians were accordingly willing to succumb to pressure from activists and popular opinion. Draconian penalties placated those panic-stricken by the problem and gave the appearance of decisive action, while in fact impacting upon only a small and powerless subculture. It was the beginning of a pattern that would determine the development of drug laws in Australia for years to come.

Like all legal orthodoxies, however, once enacted it soon became assumed that the approach taken by the opium prohibition laws was both necessary and inevitable. Laws gain a permanence beyond their years, and their mere existence validates later laws built upon them. Yet the first modern 'drug' laws in Australia were not enacted for any reason to do with the qualities or dangers of opium itself. They were a function of hostility to the Chinese, and a fear of miscegenation and contagion; of the political powerlessness of the Chinese; of the emerging social values of the time; and of the influence, energy and scope of the temperance movement. They were a product of the noisy passion and determination of a few, and the compliant indifference of the rest.

3

BAD HABITS

*Bureaucratic Dynamics
in the Emergence of 'Drug' Laws
1908–1935*

The Expansion of Drug Laws and the Beginning of International Control

Quong Tart promised that the prohibition of opium smoking would 'stamp out the evil ... within twelve months', but he did not live to witness the naiveté of his prophecy.¹ As early as 1908, the Commonwealth Comptroller-General of Customs, H.N.P. Wollaston, stated in his report to the Commonwealth Parliament that 'it is very doubtful if such prohibition has lessened to any great extent the amount which is brought into Australia':

> Owing to total prohibition, the price of opium has risen enormously ... The Commonwealth gladly gave up about £60 000 revenue, with a view to the suppression of the evil, but the result has not been what was hoped for. What now appears to be the effect of total prohibition is that, while we have lost the duty, the opium is still imported pretty freely.

Nevertheless, he was sanguine about the future prospects for the suppression of opium smoking; not because of the operation of the Opium Proclamation, but because of the exclusory provisions of the *Immigration Act 1901*. Opium smoking was 'practically limited' to ageing Chinese people, he argued, 'who will ultimately die out, and their places will not be taken by others'.²

The operation of the prohibition laws continued to be presented as a problem affecting only the Chinese in the following years. It was the responsibility of the Commonwealth Department of Trade and Customs to prevent the illegal importation of prohibited or restricted goods into Australia. In relation to opium, their operations centred almost exclusively on smuggling by the Chinese in North Queensland and Northern Australia. Prosecutions at State and Commonwealth level reflected this priority for many years. In 1926, for example, there were 216 people prosecuted for offences concerning prepared opium, all of them Chinese, and only eleven convictions for other drug-related offences. In 1936, 124 people were prosecuted for drug offences, 121 of whom were Chinese; and 51 kilograms of opium suitable for smoking were confiscated.³

Not that Chinese opium use retained the public significance that it had achieved prior to 1905. From time to time, parliament witnessed outpourings of inelegant but fervid rhetoric. Newspapers in search of sensationalist stories reported on the moral and physical horrors of 'dope' and the growing army of evil addicts. But government policy-makers were not alarmed. As Australia's report to the League of Nations stated in 1921:

> The narcotic habit affects only a very small proportion of the population. The principal illicit traffic is in relation to Opium. The only nationality addicted to opium smoking to any extent is the Chinese.⁴

Fearful, however, that Chinese opium smokers were seeking to evade the effects of prohibition by switching from prepared opium to legal opiates, such as laudanum and morphine, the drugs to which restrictive controls applied gradually expanded. Indeed, the fact of illegality itself encouraged a shift from smuggling opium, which was bulky and mild, to the more concentrated forms of the drug, morphine and heroin, which were easier to smuggle and more profitable. The relative unimportance of 'the drug problem' did not therefore lead to legal stagnation. Rather, it meant that no one questioned this gradual expansion.

In addition, exactly because drug policy was not seen as particularly important, Australia was swayed by the enthusiastic pressure in favour of increased drug controls exerted by overseas countries. The move towards more restrictive drug policies did not occur in a vacuum; the eddies within each country were part also of world-wide currents.

At the Shanghai conference called to discuss the British opium trade with China in 1909, the United States was quick to seize the moral high ground. While the British argued that 'misunderstanding and misapprehension can only result from a vote in favour of prohibition in an unqualified form', United States delegate, Hamilton Wright, declared with typical righteousness that 'the American Delegation have adopted and cling to the principle of prohibition'. The United States' commitment to opium prohibition was not, however, purely a moral crusade. By championing the cause of the Chinese against the United Kingdom it sought to gain diplomatic kudos and Chinese trade. Arguably, the Harrison Act 1914 (US), which effectively prohibited both the import and use of opium and heroin in the United States, was an adjunct to this foreign policy, the principle purpose of its enactment being to secure its reputation as the vanguard of international drug prohibition.[5]

The conference held at The Hague three years later was far more all-encompassing. Forty-six countries (Great Britain representing all its colonies and self-governing dominions) discussed not only Chinese opium, but the international consumption of morphine, cocaine, cannabis, and a recently-marketed opiate called heroin. Hard political realities again lay behind the high-sounding rhetoric. Britain was determined to discuss cocaine and morphine to divert attention from its opium trade. Germany, fearful of international supervision over these drugs, of which it was the world's major manufacturer, and hoping to postpone the operation of the treaty forever, insisted that the convention should not come into effect until it had been ratified by every country present. But, contrary to Germany's expectations, this is precisely what transpired in 1919, when article 295 of the *Treaty of Versailles* stated that 'ratification of the present Treaty shall ... be deemed in all respects equivalent to the ratification of [the Hague] Convention'.[6] The dramatic expansion in the objects and subjects of international law at last achieved by the *Hague Convention* was thus an off-shoot of political gameplaying.

Australia became a party to the *Hague Convention* when Great Britain signed on its behalf in 1912, and again on signing the *Treaty of Versailles*. The Convention was not, however, specific in the obligations it set down, and its articles were by and large hortatory rather than compulsory. It required the enactment of laws for the 'gradual and effective suppression of the manufacture of, internal trade in, and use of' opium for smoking, and 'to confine to medical and legitimate purposes the manufacture, sale, and use' of medicinal opium, heroin, morphine and cocaine. But the form those laws was to take was left up to individual signatories, 'with due regard to the varying circumstances of each country'. Neither was it very clear exactly when drug use could be said to be 'legitimate'. Great Britain, for example, argued that the smoking of cannabis in India was culturally normal and therefore 'legitimate' although not 'medical'.[7]

The *Hague Convention* did not pass unnoticed in Australia. In 1913, the Prime Minister, Andrew Fisher, promised the British that State governments were being asked for their co-operation in the enactment of uniform legislation; that is, legislation that would be passed by the different State governments in identical terms. Indeed, a Draft Uniform Opium Bill was submitted to the States by Sir Robert Garran the following year. Uniformity, however, was a distant goal. A draft bill prepared by the New South Wales government, for example, was quietly pigeon-holed, 'pressure of government business' always ensuring that it was 'unable to be dealt with'. The Commonwealth Attorney-General's Department finally gave up asking about it after a decade of polite enquiries.[8]

None the less, in addition to the absolute prohibition on the smoking of opium, laws were formulated shortly after the signing of the *Hague Convention* which forbade the consumption of an expanding range of drugs, except on the authority of the medical profession. As early as 1913, Victoria regulated that cocaine, heroin, and morphine 'shall not be delivered (whether in pursuance of a sale or otherwise) except on the written prescription or order of a duly qualified medical practitioner' and, furthermore, forbade their distribution except by authorised persons, such as doctors or chemists. These regulations were reissued in 1917 and clearly constituted a radical change from the provisions of the Poisons Acts under which they were issued and which had remained substantially unaltered since the *Sale and Use of Poisons Act 1876*. Because regulations are subject to less parliamentary scrutiny than legislative amendments, the extent to which new policies can be carried out by regulation rather than by an amending Act is limited. Under the Act, regulations could only be made 'generally for carrying into effect the objects of this Part'; it was certainly arguable that such a radical expansion in controls over poison use was a departure from the Act and not simply a way of 'carrying into effect' its objects. The Registrar of the Pharmacy Board, C.L. Butchers, in fact commented that the new law, while 'nominally in effect', was probably invalid. Only in 1920 did the enactment of a new *Poisons Act* (Vic.) finally regularise the situation.[9]

The new Act further expanded the new regime of control: not only 'morphine, cocaine, ecgonine and diamorphine (commonly known as heroine

[sic]) and their respective salts, and medicinal opium' specifically, but 'any preparation, admixture, extract or other substance containing not less than one-fifth per centum of morphine or one-tenth per centum of ecgonine, cocaine, or diamorphine', became subject to the Act. This encompassed a wide range of previously uncontrolled preparations. By dealing with classes of drugs it was not necessary to mention every product which the Act sought to control; any medicine containing a potent quantity of opiates or cocaine was subject to the Act and therefore available only on a medical prescription. In addition, any new drug which, while not covered by this formulation, was 'likely to be productive if improperly used of ill effects substantially of the same character or nature as or analogous to those produced by morphine or cocaine', could be made subject to the provisions of the Act by proclamation (that is, without the Act having to be formally amended).[10]

Commonwealth law also expanded. In 1914 the opium prohibition originally proclaimed in 1905 was rewritten. As well as the absolute prohibition on the importation of 'opium suitable for smoking', it established conditions on the import of 'medicinal opium, morphine, cocaine and heroine [sic]', and preparations and compounds containing 0.1 per cent heroin, 0.2 per cent morphine or 0.1 per cent cocaine (the very formulation used in the *Hague Convention*). These conditions were designed to ensure that the substances would be sold only by the importer to druggists and doctors. In addition, the importer was required under clause 4(b) to make enquiries 'assuring himself that such goods are intended for medicinal use only'.[11]

Through the 1920s and 1930s, the list of restricted drugs grew steadily. By 1930 regulations under the *Poisons Act 1920* (Vic.) applied to morphine, cocaine, synthetic cocaine, ecgonine, methyl-ecgonine, benzoyl-ecgonine, heroin, benzoyl-morphine, dihydro-oxycodeinone, dihydro-codeinone, medicinal opium and Indian hemp. The complexity and detail of the legislation also increased in an attempt to leave no stone unregulated. The 1922 regulations enacted under the *Poisons Act* created a complex system of licences, authorisations and record-keeping, and penalised not only the illegal supply or sale of 'Dangerous Drugs', but simply their possession. Without a medical prescription in writing, only a specially authorised person (such as a chemist or doctor) could now even legally possess these drugs. Under the *Poisons Act 1925* (Vic.), 'possession without lawful authority' was subject to a fine of £100 or 12 months' imprisonment. Step by step, a regime had been implemented according to which the use of a wide range of drugs was either prescribed or proscribed. Other jurisdictions followed with similar laws later; New South Wales not until the enactment of the *Police Offences Amendment (Drugs) Act 1927* and the other States, in which illicit use was less common, later still.[12]

'Funny Business in Bendigo': The Habit of Law-Making 1913–1920

While the terms of the *Hague Convention* helped define the drugs to which restrictive controls began to apply, internal dynamics were even more important. Bureaucratic rather than political exigencies were a vital element in this process. Public servants are typically seen as impartial conveyers of the energy or vision of others, reflecting a social or political demand and obediently carrying it out, but their power and influence is much greater. They give flesh and meaning to the law and in the process affect both its substantive content and future development; they shape policy, and advocate, entrench and advance their own agendas. Furthermore, because the 'drug problem' was seen as minor, the policies developed by administrative bodies remained relatively autonomous of party-political considerations. Political insouciance served to enhance the power of the public service.

The Department of Trade and Customs, charged with the administration of the Commonwealth *Opium Proclamation* and its successors, was particularly important. It acted both to change the laws relating to the importation of various drugs for which it was constitutionally responsible, and to place pressure on State governments in other areas, such as the possession and supply of drugs. Unlike the moral entrepreneurs who had crusaded against Chinese opium use, or the international endeavours of the United States, its actions were not designed to generate public concern and create new legal structures. In this respect, the attitude of Australian policy-makers was in stark contrast to that of the United States Federal Bureau of Narcotics (FBN). Under its long-serving and zealous Commissioner, Harry Anslinger, and shaped by the international prohibitionist posturing of the United States government, the FBN ran campaigns designed to generate fear and paranoia about drug use, and became a world-wide pedlar of myths, rumours, and sometimes downright lies, about drugs and drug users.[13] The Commonwealth public service in particular treated the matter without undue hyperbole; on the other hand, the FBN believed that if truth was not stranger than fiction, then fiction would suffice.

The distinction was, in part, one of administrative structure. First, despite the legislative and administrative authority of the Department of Trade and Customs, the Department of Health was also an influential medical and policy adviser. But the Department of Health, formed in 1921 under the directorship of Dr John Cumpston, was assigned a role of advice without power. The Department had no laws to enforce: importation was dealt with by Customs, while health laws *per se* were a State responsibility. Removed from questions of law enforcement, it maintained that 'the drug problem' was medical and not criminal, and that the solution did not necessarily lie in more laws and tougher penalties. It was to some extent an outsider body that played devil's advocate. In contrast, the FBN was the sole federal agency in the United States responsible for both the development and enforcement of drug policy. No alternative voice tempered its faith in the efficacy of tough laws, or limited its ability (as the formulator of government policy) to realise the goals it had set (as an enforcement agency). It was as if the Commissioner of Police ran the Attorney-General's Department.

Second, drug interdiction was only a small part of the responsibilities of the Department of Trade and Customs. It was by no means dependent for its survival or growth on the public importance attached to drugs. On the other hand, if 'drugs' ceased to matter, so too did the FBN. The greater the menace apparently posed by drug use, the more vital appeared its fearless opponents in the FBN, and the more resources and status it accrued. While the FBN therefore had a vested interest in the promotion of more fear of and more laws about drugs, the Customs department did not.

In Australia, drug policies were not in the hands of panic-mongers. The complex system of prohibition and regulation that none the less developed reflected continuing bureaucratic concern with Chinese use of legal substitutes and, more generally, the assumption that drug laws were valid and effective simply because they existed. Laws beget laws and control creates the desire to control still more. The simple fact of the existence of a law justifies its continuation and entrenchment. And so, each time the hydra of drug use appeared, circumventing the law of the land, its head was slashed off. Moreover, just as the perception that non-medical drug use was a minor, alien problem increased bureaucratic power, it also encouraged this particular kind of legal development. Since drug laws were not an important issue, the *habit* of law-making was decisive. Legislative and administrative arrangements were put in place to close loopholes, and render the operation of the existing laws more efficient. This gradual accretion of laws proceeded without question: it was a habit that there seemed no demand and no good reason to change.

The development of *General Order 1020*, an internal document used by the Department of Trade and Customs to instruct officers in how to enforce the *Opium Proclamation 1914*, is a good example of the incremental and unthinking manner in which laws changed. Originally, while importers, in fulfilment of clause 4(b) of the Proclamation, were expected to record details of all opium sales, it was only the total weekly sales of morphine that had to be recorded. The sale by importers of unusually large quantities of opium, but not of morphine, had to be shown to be for 'perfectly legitimate ... *bona fide* medicinal purposes'. Then in 1915 the Queensland Collector of Customs reported that 'owing to the restrictions placed upon the importation of Opium, Morphia is being used to take its place' amongst 'a race becoming rarer on account of the "White Australia" laws'. The Commonwealth Comptroller-General of Customs, Stephen Mills, in response to the increasing use of morphia 'for improper purposes in lieu of opium', set about amending *General Order 1020*. Over a four-year period, the status of morphine was gradually subjected to the same requirements as opium. The loophole which the Chinese had taken advantage of 'with the evident intention of defeating the object of the Department', had been closed.[14]

As one head of the hydra was cut off others grew to take its place. In 1917, Mills warned that

in view of the limitation which has now been placed on the sale of

Morphine and its Salts, careful supervision is to be exercised to see that the sales of cocaine, heroine [sic] ... are not unduly increased.[15]

But by 1920, they too had been made subject to the same intrusive procedures.

The Department of Trade and Customs was engaged in increasing the breadth as well as the depth of its control. It saw its role as filling in the gaps left by 'very incomplete' State drug laws.[16] Thus, although the department's Constitutional responsibility was limited to the importation of drugs, the operation of clause 4(b) of the *Opium Proclamation* and *General Order 1020*, which interpreted it, allowed it to slip its constitutional leash. The obligations placed upon importers to ensure that drugs were purchased from them 'for medicinal use only' effectively co-opted importers in the supervision of drug retailers, over whom the Commonwealth had no legitimate control. If importers failed to co-operate, they risked losing their import licences. By means of this stratagem, the Customs department indirectly began to supervise the distribution and sale of drugs.

When doctors or chemists purchased from importers more than the 'normal' amount of a drug set out as a guideline in clause 5 of *General Order 1020*, the Customs department investigated. The use of unusually large amounts could be approved for 'medicinal purposes'. Alternatively, the department could impose conditions on the retailer to ensure that there was no diversion of supplies 'for improper use', or, if the retailer did not co-operate, instruct importers not to supply to that retailer at all.[17]

In 1921 one dentist, for example, sought to obtain twenty ounces of cocaine from an importing and wholesale druggist; he had, in the preceding three months, purchased a further twenty-four ounces. Under clause 5 of *General Order 1020*, 'normal' use was expected to be four ounces per annum. Dr Cumpston, who advised the Department of Trade and Customs, concluded that 'this dentist, working each day for 365 days, would only consume 20 ounces if he injected 100 patients every day'. Accordingly, the importers were instructed not to sell the dentist any drugs specified in the *Opium Proclamation 1914* 'without the approval first obtained of the Collector'. As the New South Wales Collector of Customs commented in 1919:

a system is gradually evolving by which this Department is assuming the responsibility for the control of local retail sales of the Drugs in question, and that in some cases pharmacists are actually sending their patients to the Customs House to press for further supplies of Morphine and Opium Preparations.[18]

In 1922, the Department of Trade and Customs proposed still further controls. *General Order 1020* controlled importers and those who purchased directly from them, but not pharmacists and doctors who received opiates or cocaine through local suppliers. The *Draft General Order 1020*, which was circulated for approval, proposed restrictions on the sale of proclaimed drugs by 'Wholesale and Manufacturing Chemists ... *not licensed as Importers*'. Furthermore, the undertaking that importers were required to extract from wholesalers as to the 'medicinal' purpose of their purchases, was now to be obtained by wholesalers from *their* purchasers. *Draft General Order 1020* would have extended Customs' control over drug use one level down in the chain of sale.[19]

Draft General Order 1020 would have involved the Department of Trade and Customs in drug control unrelated to the act of importation, which was the sole constitutional basis of their authority. In the opinion of the Commonwealth Crown Solicitor, Gordon Castle, from whom legal advice was sought, the draft was not a legal exercise of power under the Constitution or the *Customs Act 1901*. Yet for some departmental officers, the legality of their actions was a secondary concern. One advised the Comptroller-General that

notwithstanding the Crown Solicitor's opinion it is submitted that unless and until objection is raised by the non-licensed persons or firms the undertaking as per draft submitted by the Collector be adopted and required.[20]

While cooler heads prevailed, the Department had already begun to see its purpose as the control of drug consumption and not of importation. The bureaucratic expansionary instinct was taking hold.

The importance of preserving existing laws from being undermined by the Chinese lay behind this instinct, and this led the Department to even more blatant intrusions into areas beyond its authority. Under the *Opium Smoking Prohibition Act 1905* (Vic.), possession of 'opium in any form which though not suitable for smoking may yet be made suitable' required a permit. Permit-holders, principally chemists, had to keep detailed records of how much had been sold and to whom. According to the President of the Victorian Pharmacy Board, however, laudanum, unlike raw or medicinal opium, was already processed and therefore incapable of alteration into a form suitable for smoking. In consequence, it could be sold (and drunk) without restriction under Victorian law.[21]

Although the sale of laudanum was a question of the interpretation of State law and had nothing to do with the Commonwealth government at all, in 1920 the Acting Comptroller-General of Customs complained to the Victorian government that 'large quantities of Tincture of Opium [laudanum] have been sold indiscriminately to the Chinese, principally in Echuca, and that no account has been kept by any of the chemists'. The chemists argued that the laudanum was not being smoked, and the Pharmacy Board defended its interpretation that laudanum was not subject to the Act. Nevertheless, the Department of Customs' opinion of the meaning of the law prevailed over the Victorian government's own advisers. The Registrar of the Board lamely concluded that 'the Department of Customs has since advised that laudanum can be rendered suitable for smoking and steps have been taken to inform pharmacists of this decision'.[22]

A similar situation occurred in Bendigo, Victoria. The chemist under investigation conceded 'that there has been some funny business going on in Bendigo, and that the Chinese must have been receiving a great deal of it'. Again it was pointed out that the Chinese were drinking laudanum, not smoking it; the Victorian Crown Solicitor himself insisted that laudanum was not subject to the regime established by the *Opium Smoking Prohibition Act 1905* (Vic.), which had been re-enacted without change as Part IV of the *Poisons Act 1915* (Vic.). But the Customs Department remained unimpressed. Without evidence of his own and contrary to local and expert opinion, the officer in charge insisted that 'it was being evaporated by them for smoking purposes'. The pressure tactics worked. 'It is no use saying any more about it,' pleaded the hapless chemist, 'I will have the whole thing stopped and cut it out altogether.'[23]

The Commonwealth Customs department was therefore prepared to distort the meaning of the Act in order to prevent the non-medical use by the Chinese of any drug. In 1920, on the recommendation of Acting Comptroller-General, Percy Whitton, the Prime Minister, Billy Hughes, wrote to the Victorian Premier, Harry Lawson, urging the 'necessity of strengthening the control over the sale' of laudanum in view of its increasing use 'for unlawful purposes'. Yet the use of the word 'unlawful' was clearly misleading here, for the illegality arose only on the questionable approach taken by the Customs department, based not on the danger of the drug or its use, but simply on who was using it. It was the Chinese themselves who remained problematic, although in fact the enactment of the *Poisons Act 1920* (Vic.), which expanded the regime of control to cover all preparations containing 'one-fifth per centum of morphine' (including laudanum) obviated the necessity for any specific legislation on the subject.[24]

International Influences: The Habit of Conformity 1919–1931

As the Commonwealth bureaucracy imposed its vision of drug control on the States, so too did the international community impose its upon on the Commonwealth. In part, this subservience was long-standing. So recently a colony of the British Empire, Australia's dependency was not sloughed off overnight. Treaties and conventions entered into by self-governing dominions between the wars were ratified by the United Kingdom 'on their behalf'. According to the 1926 Imperial Conference, in the spheres of foreign policy and defence, 'the major share of responsibility rests now, and for some time must continue to rest, with His Majesty's Government in Great Britain'.[25] In matters of economics and trade, as in the realm of culture and the arts, the dominance of the colonial power remained undimmed. Imperialism, after all, does not stop as soon as the ink is dry on the constitution.

The States, Victoria in particular, were guided in the development of drug policy by the law of the United Kingdom. In 1933 the Victorian Premier, Dr Stanley Argyle, explained that 'it has been the policy of this State to follow the British system where practicable'. The Sixth Schedule, which listed those drugs considered 'narcotic or dangerous' for the purposes of the Poisons Acts, expanded in line with the 'custom' of successive governments 'to follow as closely as possible the British parliaments' amendments of the law'.[26]

The United Kingdom principally used its power to demand Common-wealth compliance with the emerging international norms of drug control. Over the years, differences between the policies of the United Kingdom and those advocated by the United States and the League of Nations began to appear increasingly important. In general, however, the old and the new loci of authority acted together to demand obedience from Australia.

Following the First World War, the League of Nations established an Advisory Committee on Traffic in Opium and Other Dangerous Drugs. At first the Committee seemed only a 'gentlemen's club' run by the very colonial powers which still dominated the drug trade, and made all the more genteel by the absence from the League and its organs of the United States. While technically pursuing a foreign policy of isolationism, the United States nevertheless continued to act as the noisy missionary of stricter drug controls. The enactment of the Harrison Act in 1914 and of the Eighteenth Amendment—alcohol prohibition—in 1918 confirmed many Americans' image of their country as the conscience of the world. This image was only enhanced by their status as a global outsider, unsullied by international politics and able freely to criticise and press for change.[27]

Acting as an irritant and proselytiser, the United States and Harry Anslinger's FBN observed carefully the work of the Advisory Committee and were deeply involved in the various conventions organised under the aegis of the League of Nations. In the process, the reality of League control came more and more to accord with the rhetoric that had been espoused since the *Hague Convention*. And with the increasing demands made upon nations by the world community Australia, with no strong opinions of its own, was disinclined to disagree.

In 1921 the League proposed a system to ensure closer government supervision of the trade in drugs covered by the Convention. Governments were expected to provide the Advisory Committee with an annual report recording total drug imports and exports. In addition, under the League's proposal, a company wishing to export, for example, heroin or morphine from England to Australia needed an express authorisation from both governments each time a consignment of the drug landed.[28] Under the Commonwealth *Opium Proclamation* on the other hand, importers were merely licensed by the Department of Trade and Customs for a twelve-month period. The department argued that this procedure provided 'quite a sufficient safeguard without a licence being required to cover each importation'. Unhappy with this policy, however, the British Secretary of the Home Office, Malcolm Delevingne, began to cut unilaterally the amount of morphine and opium exported to Australia. Despite two reassuring replies from Acting Comptroller-General, Percy Whitton, Delevingne stood firm and aggrieved suppliers began to complain. In September 1922 the Australian government 'agreed to give its adherence to the recommendations of the League of Nations', persuaded not by the merits of the scheme, but by the League's demands and Delevingne's intransigence.[29]

The 1925 *Geneva Convention* developed international drug controls in many ways. It enshrined the import–export scheme in international law. A Permanent Central Opium Board (PCOB) was established to receive annual statistics from signatories on drug consumption, and to provide details of each country's estimated import requirements for the following year. Parties to the treaty were specifically required to enact provisions for the licensing and record-keeping of manufacturers, importers, and sellers of drugs. Yet for all its detail, the treaty failed to please the United States, which argued that 'production, excessive production, must be recognised as the root of the evil', and proposed international control over the production of opiates and cocaine. But the British delegate, concerned to protect the profits of the pharmaceutical trade, decided that 'the only thing to do with the Scheme is to bury it'. Still clinging to its principles, the United States delegation stormed out.[30]

Despite this show of pique, the *Geneva Convention* was no paper tiger. It had a significant effect on Australian policy. First, ratification committed Australia to the import–export scheme and to the submission of an annual report, statistics and estimates to the League and PCOB. Second, it required the enactment of laws to 'limit exclusively to medical and scientific purposes the manufacture, import, sale, distribution, export and use of' medicinal opium, cocaine, morphine, Indian hemp and heroin.[31] This influence was crucial in ensuring the adoption by State governments in Australia of a legislative scheme of detailed regulation, prohibition and severe penalties. On a problem that did not matter very much, the Commonwealth was prepared to apply considerable pressure on the States to ensure uniformity with the developing international consensus.

In 1923, on the insistence of Stanley Bruce, the Prime Minister, the New South Wales parliamentary draftsman was instructed to prepare a draft Bill in conformity with the *Hague Convention*, because of the 'urgency of the problem from an international viewpoint'. The Victorian parliament had passed laws that conformed to international requirements some years earlier, but New South Wales had not. The file was headed 'Execution of the provisions of certain articles of the International Opium Convention 1912'. The hostility of the pharmacy profession to certain details of the Bill led to its defeat, but Australia's ratification of the *Geneva Convention* led to renewed Commonwealth pressure on New South Wales. An Act similar to the *Poisons Act 1920* (Vic.) was finally passed as the *Police Offences Amendment (Drugs) Act 1927*. The history of the New South Wales legislation is discussed in greater detail in Chapter 4. For the present, I wish to note that according to Captain Frank Chaffey, the Minster responsible for its enforcement a few years later, it was

placed on the statute book of this state as a result of recommendations of the International Conference held at the Hague in 1912, and Geneva in 1925 ... It will be seen, therefore, that the control aimed at is an international matter, and that the Police Offences Amendment (Drugs) Act of this State only part of the world-wide scheme.[32]

Specific provisions of the Act were also influenced by the terms of the Convention. While the New South Wales Pharmacy Board sought to exempt from the Act any preparations containing less than nine-tenths of a per cent of morphine, the Director-General relied heavily on the Convention to support a lower figure. Originally a compromise of three-tenths of a per cent was agreed to, but following a complaint from the Western Australian government, the Convention's figure of one-fifth of a per cent was included in the Act.[33]

The *Geneva Convention* also required the prohibition of the non-medical use of 'Indian hemp', or cannabis. Although frequently used by Mexicans in the United States, and called by them 'marijuana', it was virtually unheard of as such in Australia (although 'Cigares de Joy' were a brand of marijuana cigarettes openly and commonly sold over the counter in Australia until after the turn of the century). As late as 1938 *Smith's Weekly* reported the 'first appearance in Australia' of 'a Mexican drug that drives men and women to the wildest excesses ... distorts moral values and leads to degrading sexual extravagances'.[34] Nevertheless, unknown as it was, the Commonwealth in 1926 and Victoria in 1927 acted to control its use. The *Poisons Act 1927* (Vic.) included 'coca leaves, crude cocaine, Indian hemp, and resins obtained from Indian hemp' because 'new resolutions have comparatively recently been agreed upon by the International Opium Convention in 1925'.[35] In New South Wales, the Colonial Secretary's Department, the Pharmacy Board, and the acting Director-General of Public Health, all thought its inclusion as a drug subject to the *Police Offences Amendment (Drugs) Act 1927* difficult and unnecessary. Still, in the absence of any pressure to the contrary, the demand for international conformity won out. The Under-Secretary of the Colonial Secretary's Department concluded that 'the omission of that drug from the operation of the Act would possibly be of small moment', but

having been considered by the Conference as requiring to be included, it might perhaps be as well, if practicable, to bring it within the purview of the dangerous drugs laws.

It was added to the Act shortly thereafter, much to the perplexity of James McGirr, MLA:

Indian hemp, or cannabis indica, is a green substance which causes violent vomiting if swallowed by a person ... Some of this mixture was swallowed accidentally, and the next thing we knew was that the drug was placed in the first schedule as an addictable drug.[36]

One further provision of the Convention had a specific impact on Australian drug controls. Under article 10, the Health Committee of the League of Nations could request State parties to apply the terms of the Convention to a drug or drugs not specifically mentioned in the Convention if they were being used 'successfully ... to evade the existing system of control'. Countries which agreed to such a request were then bound to apply the terms of the Convention to it and treat it as a 'dangerous drug'.[37] In this way, the drugs covered by the Convention were gradually expanded in the same incremental fashion as they had been in Australia.

Thus in 1928 the Health Committee recommended that the Convention be applied to dilaudide and benzoyl-morphine. Although the Commonwealth government analyst concluded that there was no scientific evidence to suggest that dilaudide was 'liable to abuse', his opinion had been forgotten within a year. The Comptroller-General, Ernest Hall, in a memo advising the Commonwealth to consent to the operation of article 10, baldly stated that dilaudide was 'capable of producing harmful effects'. Shortly afterwards, the Health Committee submitted that the Convention should apply to all morphine esters (of which dilaudide was one) unless they were proven to be harmless. Again the Commonwealth obediently consented.[38]

Article 10 did not greatly effect State law prior to the Second World War. No new drug could be added to the list of 'dangerous drugs' without a government proclamation, and this took time and paperwork. The Commonwealth's *Opium Proclamation*, on the other hand, rewritten in 1928, applied not only to a list of specified drugs but to 'all new derivatives of morphine ... liable to similar abuse', without their having to be specified by proclamation at all. Drugs like dilaudide, eucodide and aceticone became subject to the import controls set down in the Proclamation the moment officials within the Customs department formed the opinion that they were in fact 'liable to similar abuse'. Until the law was changed in 1939, the Health Committee's recommendations were promptly implemented by the Commonwealth without either legislative amendment or additional proclamation, simply as a matter of statutory interpretation.[39]

Australia was blown along by the winds of international opinion without genuine commitment or thought. Despite a personal plea from the Secretary-General of the League, no delegation was sent to the 1931 *Geneva Convention*,[40] which created an enforceable scheme, long advocated by the United States, to regulate the manufacture and international distribution of drugs. Signatories were required to send to the PCOB an annual estimate, in advance, of 'the quantity necessary for use ... for medical and scientific needs' of so-called 'narcotic drugs'. The amount that a country was entitled to manufacture was limited to this quantity plus export orders placed in advance by importing countries; the amount that suppliers in a country like Australia could import was likewise limited by the government estimates submitted to the PCOB. Additional imports were only authorised upon the submission of 'supplementary estimates' or in 'exceptional circumstances'. Moreover, the treaty absolutely prohibited the export of heroin by private importers. Thereafter, its importation could only take place directly on a government to government level.[41]

The Department of Trade and Customs seemed mainly worried by the number of conferences which Australia would have to attend if it signed this important Convention. It was recommended that Australia should wait and see if the United Kingdom ratified, and if the Convention was likely to come into force, which required the ratification of twenty-five countries. The department was prepared to follow, but not to lead; to comply, but neither to support nor oppose.[42]

Following pressure from the British government relayed by Stanley Bruce, in London, to the Australian Prime Minister, Joseph Lyons, the Commonwealth agreed not to delay ratification.[43] But it tried to minimise its obligations by making a number of 'reservations' in the instrument of ratification; that is, the Commonwealth, in agreeing to be bound by the Convention, proposed to exclude itself from certain provisions. The Commonwealth stated, in the formal government order which authorised ratification, that it only had responsibility over import and export; other matters relating to the sale and use of drugs were subject to State law and consequently outside its jurisdiction. Further, although the Convention required Australia to 'create a special administration' for 'applying the provisions of the Convention' and 'regulating, supervising, and controlling the trade in drugs', the Commonwealth insisted that the existing structures of the Department of Trade and Customs were adequate. Even this minor show of independence was short-lived. Bruce telegrammed that the 'United Kingdom government would be seriously embarrassed to agree to our reservations having previously objected to less wide reservations by other countries'. In November 1933 the Commonwealth authorised ratification of the 1931 *Geneva Convention* for a second time—without reservation.[44]

The Conventions which bound Australia to the new regime of international drug control were just the tip of an iceberg of words. Letters and statements from the Secretary-General of the League, the Advisory Committee and the Permanent Board, as well as the annual reports submitted to the League and the proceedings of conferences and conventions, inundated and indoctrinated Australia. 'The infliction of severe penalties' was recommended; 'the exemplary penalties imposed upon traffickers in the United States of America ... noted with satisfaction'; 'the terrible consequences resulting from the use of dangerous drugs' recognised; and 'curiosity' about drugs was not to be 'aroused'.[45] This barrage enshrined and entrenched an international orthodoxy which the Commonwealth, without strong opinions of its own, was prepared to follow.

The Entrenchment of Policy

The habit of law-making and the habit of conformity advanced in tandem, propelled by the dynamics of the institutions of policy and enforcement themselves: their need to administer the law efficiently, the natural tendency of incremental growth, their belief that drugs still mainly affected aliens, and their acquiescence, therefore, to the dogmatic opinions of others. Paradoxically, the inexorable development of drug policy was driven by its relative unimportance, the lack of domestic or political controversy and the consequent influence of international and bureaucratic factors.

As the structure of modern drug laws thus took shape, each brick depending on those beneath it for support and validity, few remembered or even thought to question why they had ever been laid. So effective had the gradual process of entrenchment been that alternative approaches soon became unthinkable. What counted was the preservation of the laws already in place. If they were failing, the answer was simple—more of the same, as W. Beckett, the Victorian Minister of Public Health, made clear:

> When the penalty has been found to be ineffective there is only one thing to do, and that is to make the penalty for the offence [more] drastic ... [W]e cannot have provisions of too prohibitive a nature in connexion with these matters.[46]

Governments and administrators developed an aversion to even the thought of a change in approach. In 1925, the Comptroller-General of Customs, R. Oakley, wrote a memo concerning Chinese opium use. Since 'the prevention of smuggling ... is extremely difficult [and] opium running will continue while a market exists', Oakley suggested that a policy could be adopted similar to that of the Japanese in Formosa (Taiwan) in which opium was made legally available to addicts by a government-run monopoly. When the matter was raised with State Premiers by the Prime Minister, Stanley Bruce, their response was uniform and inflexible: drug use was a Chinese problem of minor importance and was under control. Joseph Lyons, Tasmanian Premier at the time, commented that 'as there are not many Asiatics in Tasmania, opium ... has not so far presented a problem here'. The Queensland Premier, William McCormack, was irritated that a change in policy could even be countenanced:

> The present system is working very well indeed. Quite possibly it could still be further improved by tightening up the administration of the present laws. I see no reason, however, for starting up such a doubtful, expensive and trouble-raising scheme.

Two years after his original memo, Oakley sheepishly agreed that 'no further action be taken'.[47]

Ten years later a similar proposal made by Dr Cook, the Chief Medical Officer of the Northern Territory, in relation to opium smoking by Chinese and Aborigines in the Territory, received even shorter shrift. For the Comptroller-General, Edward Abbott, and the Director-General, Dr John Cumpston, the 'unwelcome criticism' that such a change would attract from the international community was itself a decisive argument. It was the typical defence of orthodoxy against novelty: any change is unwelcome for the publicity it brings. Above all, the proposal was a nuisance. Handwritten on the bottom of one of Dr Cook's letters was this note:

As our case against Dr Cook's suggestion is not particularly strong the best course perhaps would be ['is' crossed out] to refrain from furnishing any further reply unless again approached by the Dept. of the Interior.[48]

Cook reminded the Commonwealth that opium prohibition, whose validity was so entrenched and assumed, was itself once an innovation. 'The proposed scheme,' he insisted,

could not, at worst, be attended by more unsatisfactory results than attend the present total prohibition ... 33 years of experience in the Territory has indicated that [we have] selected a method of control which has proved unsatisfactory.

But Abbott's final answer was a masterpiece of inertia:

The various States also have their difficulties in suppressing the traffic in dangerous drugs and in the view of this Department it would be very unwise for the Commonwealth to now suggest that the system which has been built up over the years is a failure in its own Territory.[49]

Whether the Commonwealth's system was in fact 'a failure' was, to the Comptroller-General, immaterial. Any reform which might lead to unrest or disquiet, regardless of its merits, was 'unwise'. A change in drug policy in Australia would have been inconvenient and embarrassing, and that was all that now seemed to matter.

4

THE AGE OF THE EXPERT

'Drug' Laws and Professional Rivalry

The New Priests

The previous chapter described the bureaucratic and international factors that led to the gradual expansion of 'drug' laws in Australia. As subtle as the process was and as inevitable as it seemed, much more needs to be said about the broader currents of Australian social and legal development to answer the difficult questions it poses. First, why was it, the absolute prohibition of smoking-opium aside, that those drugs whose use was believed to be open to similar abuse, could only be possessed under the authority of a medical prescription? In 1904, when it was suggested in Victoria that no one should be able to 'dispense or sell narcotic drugs ... unless upon the order or prescription of a legally qualified medical practitioner', the idea was quickly scotched. One member complained that 'if he had to go to a medical practitioner and pay a guinea for a prescription before he was able to buy a little chlorodyne, it would be rather severe'.[1] By 1920, that was exactly the position. Why was sole and conclusive authority given so readily to doctors?

Second, how did these drugs eventually so capture public and political attention that their connection with the Chinese became irrelevant to the cry for ever-tougher laws and ever-stricter penalties? How did the focus of laws shift from the 'evil Chinese' to 'evil drugs'? This chapter considers the first set of questions in the light of the steady rise to power of the medical profession. The second set of questions, although related, is discussed in the next chapter, which takes the development of Australian drug legislation up to the Second World War.

In the years following Federation, the image of the healthy, bronzed Aussie took hold in the public mind. It was, at the same time, an era which glorified science. Art, architecture, music, political theory—nothing remained untouched by this new-found faith in modern technology. In ages past, priests were called upon in times of plague or disaster. During the drought which swept New South Wales in the 1870s, the Governor, Hercules Robinson, authorised a 'Day of Humiliation and of Prayer for Rain' in a 'solemn appeal to the Divine Mercy', and when it broke there was a day of 'Special Thanksgiving to Almighty God for His Great Mercy'. Robinson even refused to attend a cricket match held on that day because 'although I have my own private opinion about the Proclamation, it appears to me I am bound in public to maintain it'.[2] In the twentieth century, people instead turned to science as an answer to all their problems. Patent medicines, ever alert to the best way to seduce the gullible and vulnerable, sought to bolster their claims to respectability by the use of pseudo-science. Dr Williams's Pink Pills for Pale People declared itself a 'patiently elaborated scientific cure'. Electricity and magnetism, in particular, were forces mysterious, incomprehensible and scientific enough to be conscripted as the cure to all illnesses: bottled, made up into pills, to be worn as an 'electric belt' courtesy of Dr McLaughlin, or used for the treatment of 'complex nerve diseases' at the resplendent Freeman and Wallace Electro-Medical and Surgical Institute in Melbourne.[3]

While the shallow deceptions of patent medicines passed, faith in the mysteries of science did not. It was therefore only natural that *medical* scientists should become esteemed above all others, for they combined the value of health with the promise of science. In the 1880s the Melbourne *Argus* regularly complained about the ethics and standards of doctors, but by 1903 it had apparently come to the conclusion that 'no discovery and no treatment can be of worth unless it emanates from a member of the medical guild'. But the converse was also true. Every new operation or discovery became further proof that the medical profession would save us from all that ailed us. Eyeball transplants, a thyroid transplant which made an 'idiot child' 'sane', the transplant of part of the brain of a still-born infant as a 'cure for drowsiness'—all these were reported with the same unquestioning enthusiasm. 'There are men and classes of men that stand above the common herd,' the *Argus* wrote in 1912, quoting Robert Louis Stevenson. '[T]he physician ... is the flower (such as it is) of our civilization.'[4]

Scientific medicine seemed limitless in its potential and unfaltering in its advance. The mantle of priesthood began to cloak its triumphs. 'The physician learns to handle patients ... to call out their trust and restrain their fears,' wrote the *Argus* in 1911, '[he is] a peculiar combination of scientist, priest and teacher.' An article on 'hospitals old and new' that appeared in 1932 was less explicit:

And now you have been swept away from all that, and your horizons consist of a white enamelled room with only the distant hum of the traffic ... You lie thinking of ... the operating theatre, that temple of absolute cleanliness and asepsis.[5]

But it is not only the proselytising fervour of the article, nor its reference to the surgical 'temple', that gives it a revivalist flavour. It is a paean to passivity. To be cured, as to be saved, requires total surrender into the hands of those who know better than us. The role of 'patient' and parishioner alike is to hope, to pray and to trust.

The technology of medicine provided a justification for the growing domination of the medical profession and the powerlessness of its subjects. If it was the age of health and the age of science, it was also the dawning of the age of the expert. The complex tools of scientific medicine, in particular, were best kept out of the hands of mere mortals. Knowledge was becoming the property of doctors alone, made all the more valuable by the exclusivity and secrecy with which it was held. Knowledge remains their power, and is a potent force in the structure of our values, our behaviour and our lives.[6]

The appropriation and systemisation of knowledge by a clique is a fundamental part of the development of any profession.[7] Through the early years of the twentieth century it was exactly this process that transformed the medical profession in Australia, previously distrusted, disorganised and weak, into one of the most powerful sectors of Australian society. 'The qualified medical man ... is the heir to all medical science,' concluded the *Argus* in

1932. 'He alone has the knowledge which renders him competent to diagnose disease and the skill which enables him to apply it.'[8] The medical expert became the sole person entitled to determine who was sick, how they should be treated, and by whom. Health was too important to be left to the public.

This astonishing growth in doctors' power is characterised, in Evan Willis's important book, *Medical Dominance*, by the achievement of professional autonomy, authority and sovereignty. Autonomy, meaning the right to self-regulate the manner in which the profession was carried on and by whom. Authority, meaning that other health-care providers, such as nurses and chemists, became subservient to doctors' control. Sovereignty, through the belief held in the wider society that only doctors could properly make decisions on medical treatment and health.[9]

The development of restrictive drug laws took place in this context of far-reaching social change. By legislating so that drugs such as heroin or cocaine could not be possessed or sold except on a doctor's prescription, the over-riding authority of doctors was established, and the sovereign ability of the general public to decide what drugs they wished to take, and why, was denied. The use of drugs became a subject upon which only doctors were fit to pass judgement. Although not directly pressured by the medical profession, the emergence of drug laws in Australia therefore served to enhance medical authority and sovereignty and was a natural consequence of the rise of the medical profession in Australia.

Those who lost as a result of this medical take-over were those previously involved in the distribution of drugs: grocers and proprietary medicine manufacturers on the one hand, and chemists on the other. Proprietary drugs had been readily available in grocery shops and through chemists, and chemists also sold opiates over the counter, as well as 'special' recipes of their own devising.

Willis identifies three tactics employed by the medical profession in its struggle for dominance against rival health-care groups. First, occupations like midwifery were subordinated in the hierarchy of medicine: midwives became answerable to and supervised by doctors. Second, the expertise of other groups, like dentists and optometrists, was acknowledged but limited. Within their conceded territory, these professions became independent, but their authority was clearly circumscribed. Third, the claims to legitimacy of chiropractors and homeopaths, for example, were rejected entirely and they found themselves excluded from the emerging division of medical labour.[10]

It will be argued that, on Willis's analysis, the drug laws that developed in Australia, and that in the main required a medical prescription for their possession and consumption, excluded grocers and proprietary drugs from the division of labour, and led to the subordination of chemists. The framework Willis proposes, however, explains medical power in terms of rivalry between professional groups. In the process, the position of the health-consumer is ignored. The rise of the medical profession, as well as changing professional relationships *inter se*, also profoundly altered the relationship of the 'person in the street' to health-care providers and products. Vertical as well as horizontal social relationships underwent substantial modification. Thus the lack of drug regulation in the nineteenth century reflected the public's right to *treat themselves*. For all the dishonesty and manipulation that surrounded them, patent medicines were an important part of that right because they were available from chemists' or grocers' shelves, without prescription, if and when the customer wanted them. Chemists' practice of 'prescribing' the drugs they stocked (so-called 'counter practice') also offended doctors, not only because it may have been useless or dangerous, but simply because it involved medication without medical supervision. It was a public liberty antithetical to medical sovereignty.

The Exclusion of 'Patent Medicines'

The campaign against 'patent medicines' was not merely driven by their manufacturers' mendacity, sensationalism and crass commercialism— although these qualities they certainly possessed in abundance. It was also part of the medicalisation of drug use, a shift in the philosophy of drug control from one of free choice to one of detailed regulation in the hands of the medical profession. Beale's Royal Commission on Secret Drugs, Cures, and Foods was above all concerned, as its title indicated, with the secrecy of patent medicines. His message was that people believed the fraudulent claims made about these drugs because they did not know what was really in them; the solution was to compel manufacturers to disclose their ingredients. As the Premier of New South Wales, Charles Wade, explained in his second reading speech on the Pure Food Bill, 1908, disclosure provisions aimed 'to protect the public from being deceived through ignorance'. The four interstate conferences on uniform food and drug laws held from 1910 to 1927, which attempted to establish agreement between jurisdictions as to the content and aims of regulation in these areas, continued this theme. The Queensland delegate to the 1913 conference explained that the object 'was really to have the effect of destroying the patent medicine trade, as it was not considered a legitimate trade'.[11] By destroying the shroud of secrecy which cloaked proprietary medicines, it was hoped to destroy their mystique and their popularity. People were suckered, and shysters succoured, by ignorance.

These disclosure provisions, which I discussed in Chapter 2, undermined the mystique of patent medicines, but at the same time the right of doctors to keep secret their illegible Latin prescriptions was carefully preserved. This hypocrisy drew some criticism in the days when *laissez-faire* still governed the terms of debate. Speaking on a proposal to amend the Victorian *Poisons Act* in 1898, one honourable member asked:

why should they throw upon the vendors of proprietary medicines alone the burden of saying in English what those medicines consisted ... of? (Mr Outtrim—'Make the doctors do the same.') Yes; make the doctors do the same.

In fact, protests by the trade journal *Chemist and Druggist of Australasia* eventually forced the withdrawal of the Bill, for it also required the disclosure of the content of pharmacists' compounds. Public knowledge also threatened the legitimacy of chemists. But in the long run, only doctors were able to preserve their secrecy. At every interstate food and drug conference, and in every law enacted to force the disclosure of the presence of certain drugs—such as opium, morphine, and cocaine—in medicines, 'a drug supplied by prescription or order signed by a legally qualified medical practitioner' and 'a mixture supplied by a registered pharmacist for immediate consumption on his premises' were specifically exempted.[12] Many other compounds and remedies sold by chemists did not fall into these categories. They became second-class medicines, not to be accorded the same status or privileges as a medical prescription.

This principle was confirmed between the 1910 and 1913 conferences at the Royal Commission on Uniform Standards for Foods and Drugs. Jointly appointed by the Commonwealth and every State of Australia, the Commissioner was none other than Dr Ashburton Thompson. He heard evidence from twenty pharmacists who insisted that they should not be 'required to declare the presence in any mixture devised and supplied by them of any drug of which declaration is required by notice on the label'. It would, they warned, 'give patients information which had better be withheld from them'. As M. Rushton of the Tasmanian Pharmacy Board opined:

I think it is very undesirable for the public generally to know what medicine they are taking ... The public, in increasing numbers I am sorry to say, are allocating these powers [to prescribe for themselves] to themselves.

Dr Thompson rejected the pharmacists' special pleading. The use of 'dangerous drugs' in their concoctions, like those in the creations of drug manufacturers, should be disclosed. Yet he agreed that public knowledge of drugs was dangerous. The difference was that he believed the privilege of secrecy should be granted only to doctors. Dr Thompson concluded that 'the presence of certain drugs in any medicine shall be declared on the label except ... when they have been dispensed in obedience to the order of a legally qualified medical practitioner.'[13]

Secrecy was desirable in relation to the prescription of drugs because secrecy enforced the mystique of doctors, the magic of medicine, and the ignorance of the public. On the other hand, information concerning the ingredients of non-prescribed drugs weakened their hold over the public and was part of the process of delegitimisation. Only doctors were to be trusted: not manufacturers, not even chemists, certainly not the people who were expected to swallow their medicine while remaining 'wisely ignorant and knowingly untaught'. The mysteries of drugs were to be protected by experts.

The Subordination of Pharmacy 1900–1920: Sovereignty

At the same time, the medical profession was engaged in a battle against pharmacy centred on exactly which profession should properly be acknowledged as society's drug 'experts'. As with proprietary manufacturers, the threat pharmacists posed was two-fold. First, they were in the nineteenth century important rivals to doctors in the distribution of drugs in Australia. Second, they did not stand in the same relation to their customers as doctors did to patients. Chemists were advisers, and while they helped people who came to them for treatment, they did not seek to substitute their own decision-making power. Their power implied the continuing sovereignty of the general population as well as challenging that of the medical profession.

The Pharmacy Boards of New South Wales and Victoria, and of the other States, were powerful guardians of the status of chemists. They advised the government on drugs and poisons, and administered all the Acts which dealt with these matters. In Victoria, for example, regulations controlling the licensing of poison dealers and the issuance of prescriptions, and detailing the conditions under which the drugs specified in the *Poisons Act* could be manufactured, sold, distributed, and possessed, could only be made 'on the recommendation of the Board'.[14] As these laws expanded to control more strictly the use of opiates and other drugs, this broad regulation-making power, enacted in 1876 with very different purposes in mind, came to affect not only chemists, but the whole community.

In both jurisdictions, the Boards were also responsible for the investigation and prosecution of offences. In 1904, the New South Wales Pharmacy Board prosecuted Chinese grocers for selling opium without a licence, for the first time in fifteen years, although the government had refused to give legal assistance to the Board. Even after the enactment of the *Police Offences Amendment (Drugs) Act 1927* (NSW), the Pharmacy Board's inspectors continued to act as an alternative police force.[15] Throughout this period the Boards, comprised of and chosen by chemists and druggists themselves, acted as administrators, legislators and enforcers of the State drug laws. Such a cosy confluence of interest seemed to concern no one. Drugs and poisons were, without question, within pharmacists' sphere of influence.

Pharmacists sought to extend their sovereignty over drugs and poisons. The old Sale and Use of Poisons Acts only allowed doctors, chemists, and a few licensees (in country towns without a chemist) to sell poisons. Although this gave them a monopoly over other shopkeepers, proprietary medicines were excluded from the operation of the Acts and could therefore be sold by grocers in competition with chemists.[16] This threat had exercised the minds of the pharmacy profession for many years and led to many calls by Pharmacy Boards around Australia for a change in the law. In 1902, when a new Poisons Bill was being debated in New South Wales, pressure exerted by the Pharmacy Board for the exception to be repealed was only defeated after a large campaign conducted by the New South Wales Retail Trades Association. Clearly, the exception was treated as a serious challenge to its members' livelihoods: a questionnaire was sent to shopkeepers and grocers all over the State, and the Retail Trades Association received 585 replies in one week. That of P.D. Murphy was typical: 'we consider the action of the Pharmacy Board most disgraceful as it is in our opinion a distinct move to create a Monopoly in the Sale of Patent Medicines.' Many others wrote more inventively and invectively.[17]

The ambitions of pharmacy went still further. Amendments proposed by the New South Wales Pharmacy Board in 1918, for example, would have eliminated the sale of drugs not only by grocers, but by doctors; in Victoria a similar proposal had been made by Joseph Bosisto, to protect chemists from 'the continual interference of the medical body', as far back as 1857.[18]

Yet, while attempting to secure a monopoly in the sale of drugs, pharmacists insisted on their right of 'counter practice' in competition with doctors. In evidence presented before the Royal Commission on Uniform Standards, the President of the New South Wales Pharmacy Board said:

I have yet to learn that any harm has been done to the public by legitimate pharmacists prescribing in minor ailments, or yet of a case where the pharmacist prescribing has led to a drug habit ... I do a very large dispensing business, but I would say that we have more calls for relief over the counter than we have for dispensed prescriptions.

Indeed, in the Supreme Court of Western Australia, Justice Hensman held that as long as the chemist was principally in the business of selling medicines and not medical treatment, it was perfectly proper in normal circumstances for them to give advice as to which medicine best suited the customer's needs.[19]

Chemists' right to dispense drugs independently of medical advice lay at the heart of their asserted sovereignty over drugs and created between chemist and consumer a non-medical therapeutic relationship. Already, however, the position of chemists was being undermined. Royal Commissioner, Dr Thompson, was scathingly dismissive:

Pharmacists have no right to prescribe other than that enjoyed by every citizen ... [T]he impropriety of seeking, and the danger in taking, medicines prescribed by persons who have some chemical knowledge of the nature of drugs, but no knowledge at all of the human body, is generally known.[20]

Despite the strong and universal evidence of pharmacists from around Australia, the Commission thus declared unequivocally that only doctors should have the power to authorise the possession and use of drugs.

State and Commonwealth disclosure laws like the Pure Food Acts were not as important as the emerging 'drug' laws in the resolution of these conflicts. These laws, as well as changing the terms on which the general public were entitled to possess and use preparations containing more than a certain percentage of opium, morphine, cocaine, heroin, and so on, profoundly affected the balance of power in the health division of labour. The laws provided that these substances could only be sold by authorised persons (including chemists and doctors) and only on prescription. This had two important consequences. First, such laws eliminated altogether the unrestricted sale of opiate-based proprietary medicines like Irish Moss or Cherry Pectoral. Only by advertising their merits directly to doctors or removing the ingredients included in the 'drug laws' could manufactured drugs survive. Many, of course, did not—and we are not worse off in the absence, for example, of 'non-intoxicating stimulants' and 'cures for alcoholism' composed principally of opium. Indeed, there was a powerful unity of interests between doctors and chemists on this question. Both were opposed to their liberal sale, doctors because they promoted self-medication and undermined their sovereignty, and chemists because they encouraged people to buy drugs in groceries.

Second, however, the sale without a doctor's prescription, for example, of opiate preparations like laudanum by chemists was prohibited. 'Counter prescription' of morphine or opium was no longer possible. The general public could only receive drugs covered by the regulations from a chemist if they were prescribed by a doctor. Control over the distribution of 'dangerous drugs' had passed from the hands of the public and of chemists into the hands of the medical profession. Drug use was no longer seen as a matter of individual choice. It was a medical issue, to be decided not *by* the public, but *for* them.

Evan Willis defines chemists as a 'limited' and not a 'subordinate' profession.[21] Pharmacists are admittedly independent and self-regulating within the functions they are allowed to perform, and this is the reason he categorises pharmacy has he does. Nevertheless, in relation to 'drug' laws, doctors were placed in a position of authority over chemists. Chemists became economically reliant on the medical profession, since none of these drugs could be sold without the approval of a doctor. Conversely, doctors' profits were guaranteed, for every sale of a dangerous drug required a medical prescription and a medical consultation. It was a one-sided relationship of domination and subordination in which the erstwhile rivals of the medical profession were made to collaborate in ensuring the financial viability of medical practitioners, and their own economic dependence.

The new subordination of pharmacy was clearly articulated in the second reading speech of the Victorian Pharmaceutical Chemists Bill 1920. Clause 2

puts in clearer language what is the principal function of a pharmaceutical chemist, viz.:—To dispense the prescriptions of medical practitioners, and to sell the drugs so ordered.[22]

In twenty years, a matter of great contention and importance had become so obvious that it merely had to be 'put in clearer language'. As with the history of drugs laws generally, a new relationship quickly became an age-old custom, and the sheen of novelty was replaced by the patina of tradition.

The New South Wales Pharmacy Board 1923–1934: Autonomy

As pharmacists' sovereignty over drug distribution declined, so too did their administrative power and autonomy. It will be recalled that the old Poisons Acts gave the profession of pharmacy, through the State Pharmacy Boards, particular power over the administration of 'drug' laws. Increasingly it became clear that pharmacists were not the only ones affected by drug laws; it was not simply a matter of self-regulation. As New South Wales Minister for Public Health, John Daniel Fitzgerald, said to a deputation of pharmacists in 1918, 'I am not taking sides in this matter, gentlemen, but you represent one interest and you have been given power over other interests'.[23]

The autonomous power of the States' Pharmacy Boards was made all the more precarious by the arrogance and incompetence they displayed in their administration of drug and poison legislation. A bitter dispute over whether a certain chemist was entitled to be registered by the New South Wales Pharmacy Board, for example, became the subject of a Select Committee of the Legislative Assembly in 1905, which concluded that the Board had acted with 'laxity and carelessness'. Others, including the first president of the Board, by then retired, accused them of being power-hungry and biased. The matter seriously hurt the reputation of the profession. The same year a Poisons Bill advanced by the Board was variously described as a 'Bill to enable the Pharmacy Board to rake in fees and fines', a 'Bill to make a close corporation of the dispensing business', and 'to swell their own importance, to create a large department, to pay very fair salaries to inspectors and clerks'. Mr Levien, speaking in the Legislative Assembly, expressed the sentiment of many when he declared tersely, 'The Board is a damned bad lot'.[24] The Bill passed the second reading, but was then dropped.

This was not an isolated incident. In Victoria the Board's government funding was at various times cancelled or delayed because the Board did not properly justify its activities and expenditure.[25] In New South Wales government funding to the Board ceased for a number of years in 1902, and was always contentious. Scandal and controversy gave the Pharmacy Boards a reputation for partiality in the exercise of their functions, and undermined their position as the natural authority over drugs and poisons. The history of the New South Wales Pharmacy Board from 1923 to 1934 is a good illustration. In New South Wales and Victoria the Board administered the Poisons Acts. In Victoria, however, when new sections dealing with 'narcotic and other substances' were enacted, final authority to issue licences for the manufacture, sale, possession and distribution of these drugs was taken from the profession. Although licences were to be granted 'on the recommendation of the Board', the Board was answerable to the Chief Secretary's Department.[26] New South Wales's delay in adopting similar legislation was largely due to the dogged determination of the pharmacy profession to keep absolute control of drug laws.[27]

The New South Wales Dangerous Drugs Bill 1923 proposed provisions similar to those of the *Poisons Act 1920* (Vic.), which prohibited the use of certain drugs except on prescription, and divested the Board of administrative control. The result was an avalanche of protest. The President of the Pharmaceutical Society called it an 'unwarrantable usurpation of [pharmacists'] rights to administer their own legislation', and insisted that 'the Dangerous Drugs Act *must* be administered by the Pharmacy Board, and by nobody else'.[28] It was their autonomy that was at stake.

Gregory McGirr, Labor politician and chemist who acted as the Board's champion in parliament, also saw the issue as an internal matter of professional self-regulation:

Is it a fact that the Medical Practitioner and the Registered Dentist and the Registered Veterinary Surgeon have been given full privilege of their respective professions? ...
Is it a fact also that the Registered Pharmacists are to have their hardly won rights taken away from them?

More than this, the Dangerous Drugs Bill was seen as a calculated insult. 'Is it a fact,' McGirr went on, 'that ... in return for [their] interest in the welfare of the public, the Pharmacy Board have been completely ignored by the Colonial Secretary's Department in the drafting of the Bill?' Is this, one can hear him fuming, all the thanks we get?[29]

In response to the outrage, the Bill was shelved until a compromise emerged from the byzantine recesses of the bureaucracy four years later. The new proposal brought New South Wales broadly into line with Victorian and Commonwealth policy on drug laws, restricting the possession of morphine, cocaine, heroin and opium to licensed persons or under a doctor's prescription, while continuing the absolute prohibition of opium smoking.[30] The reasons for its enactment at that time were complex: in addition to the international pressures which were brought to bear as a result of the 1925 *Geneva Convention*, there was a lot of sensationalist talk about the use of cocaine in Sydney, which forced political action to enact 'tougher' drug laws.

For pharmacists, the *Police Offences Amendment (Drugs) Act 1927* was a mixed blessing. On the one hand, it removed their right to sell opiates or cocaine without a prescription: in relation to those drugs at least, the days of counter practice were gone. On the other hand, the Pharmacy Board in effect continued to administer the Act through a system known as 'divided control'.[31] Further, Inspector Robinson, an employee of the Board who acted as its private investigator, was given police powers to investigate breaches of the Act on the Board's behalf. Once Inspector Robinson had made a recommendation on a matter, the Board and not the police then decided whether to prosecute.

The Pharmacy Board proved hopelessly ill-equipped to carry out the important tasks entrusted to it under the Act. Regulations drafted by the Board in 1927 were described by Dr Dick, the Director-General of Public Health, as 'confusing and difficult to follow'. It was indeed a clumsy document, which did not so much employ legal jargon as impersonate it. In 1929, an inquiry into the finances of the Board undertaken by the Colonial Secretary's Department disclosed an 'unsatisfactory—in fact a disquieting—condition', characterised by indebtedness, disorganisation, and questionable accounting practices. The Board prevented the investigation from being completed, and its Registrar 'precipitately resigned'.[32]

Relations between the Board and the Department were further strained following the creation in 1928 of a Drug Bureau within the New South Wales police force, which was charged with the task of investigating breaches of the 'Drugs Act'. The functions of the Bureau—Detective-Sergeants Wickham and Thompson, two desks and a typewriter—therefore overlapped with Inspector Robinson, who reported directly to the Pharmacy Board. The distrust was also personal. Robinson was not trusted because he was rumoured to have resigned from the police force some years earlier in order to avoid bribery allegations. The Board in response wanted to know why the police had therefore been so eager to recommend him for the job, apparently writing on his discharge papers 'Character—Excellent'. For these reasons, then, the police thought Robinson an amateur and a nuisance; the Board, for its part, thought that the licensing and record-keeping requirements demanded of chemists by the Act were technical matters that could only be properly investigated by the Board. The result was a complete lack of communication. Wickham and Thompson complained that the Board regularly withheld important information from them, while Robinson responded that it was the police who were uncooperative.[33]

Resentment did not just mount over specific instances. The *Police Offences Amendment (Drugs) Act 1927* controlled the issue of prescriptions by the medical profession, and the terms on which the general public could possess 'opium and other drugs'. Dr Dick had argued since 1923 that it was no longer appropriate to treat the Act as if it only concerned pharmacists. Throughout 1930 the Colonial Secretary's Department prepared amendments designed to remove the Board from the administration of the Act. But relations between the two bodies were at rock bottom. They communicated with each other more through the rumour-mill than the mailroom. The planned amendments were hidden from the Board and proceeded with in secrecy.[34]

The final crisis came in 1931. Wickham and Thompson accused Robinson of withholding evidence in a case involving the alleged illegal supply of cocaine by a chemist. This raised the thorny question of whether the Board could be trusted to investigate probable drug offences committed by pharmacists, a state of affairs which the Colonial Secretary's Department described as 'most irregular'. Forced to hold an inquiry into the conduct of its own officer, the Pharmacy Board's President, McKimm, tried to protect the Board's reputation by blaming the Drug Bureau. Acting with a cavalier lack of subtlety, and a strong but misguided sense of self-preservation, he concluded that the police were 'deserving of severe censure for making unfounded charges'. He added that 'there appears to be some underlying motive for the false charge made by Detective-Sergeants Wickham and Thompson.'[35]

Far from safeguarding the Pharmacy Board, these accusations served only to emphasise its partiality. A second inquiry, under Stipendiary Magistrate Gates, exonerated Wickham and Thompson and concluded that they had been denied natural justice. The report slated the behaviour of the Board, and recommended that administration of the Act 'should ... be limited solely to trusted officers of the Police Department'. The police powers given to the Registrar and Inspector Robinson were immediately revoked by the Colonial Secretary although, true to form, it took over two months for the Board to relinquish the appropriate documents of authority.[36]

The Colonial Secretary advised Cabinet in 1932 'that an error has been made in entrusting the administration of the law to the Pharmacy Board'. Accordingly, section 2 of the *Police Offences Amendment (Drugs) Act 1934* baldly declared that 'the Police Offences Amendment (Drugs) Act 1927 ... shall cease to be administered by the Pharmacy Board, and shall be administered by the Minister.' James McGirr, MLA, like his brother before him, took the Bill as a personal affront, 'an insult to the whole 1400 members of the profession'. 'Today, in return for their services,' he concluded, 'they are handed an insult by the Government.'[37]

New Rivalries

While the story of the New South Wales Pharmacy Board was more dramatic than the events that occurred in other States, the result was the same. Pharmacy's reign over drug and poison laws ended, whether with a bang or a whimper. The battle to prescribe and sell drugs independently of medical control was lost. In the lean and trying times of the depression, chemists' real rivals were no longer the medical profession, but shopkeepers, grocers, and department stores who competed with them in the areas of cosmetics, health goods and proprietary products.

The attitude of chemists to proprietary medicines had always been ambiguous. For some, like the President of the New South Wales Pharmaceutical Society speaking in 1881, patent medicines were 'a blight to the profession of Pharmacy, paralysing its energies and lowering it to a debased commercial existence', which undermined its status as a profession.

To many others, particularly the large discount chemist chains in New South Wales, pharmacy was above all a money-making venture; patent medicines offered consistent profits, enhanced by mass-marketing techniques and enormous advertising budgets. But for pharmacists, weakened by their subordination and in economically straitened circumstances, the question of the status of pharmacy became less important than the brute need to make a living. From the late 1920s these new priorities were reflected in the development of a wide range of products, from manufactured drugs to hot-water bottles and toothpaste, all of which were advertised as being available only through chemist shops (not by law, but because of contractual arrangements made with suppliers); in the formation of the Pharmacy Guild of Australia to promote and develop the commercial side of pharmacy; and in the success of organisations that gave advice to chemists on matters like window displays, promotion and advertising.[38]

In this period of stress and change, 'dangerous drug laws' such as those in force in Victoria from 1913, or in New South Wales after 1927, were not completely unwelcome. While they ensured the supremacy of the medical profession, they also *protected* the interests of chemists, providing that only authorised persons were entitled to sell and dispense 'dangerous drugs': not grocers or other shopkeepers, but only 'a medical practitioner, registered pharmacist, or registered veterinary surgeon, or an assistant'.[39]

In theory, the provision was a galling one for chemists, for while they were prevented from prescribing drugs, doctors were still entitled to dispense them. In 1928, James McGirr called on the government to have the regulation changed, a proposal which the Minister rejected tersely. It was a moment of fine political symbolism, for the supplicant had been a chemist, and the Minister, Dr Richard Arthur, was a medical practitioner.[40]

In practice, however, chemists faced little competition from doctors. While chemists accepted a status without authority or independence over drugs, in relation to which their role was simply to distribute them upon doctors' orders, they gained in return a long desired monopoly over their new rivals and a secure economic niche at a time when they might have been squeezed out of the market altogether. Subordinate survival was preferable to high-minded oblivion.[41]

In 1938, Mr Justice Browne held an inquiry into chemists' complaints about unfair competition from pharmacy chains like Washington Soul (later Soul Pattinson) and Boots, large scale commercial enterprises whose aggressive marketing threatened to put the old-style pharmacist out of business. Mr Justice Browne's message demonstrated brutally the extent to which the status of pharmacy had declined:

Pharmacists must realise, therefore, however distasteful the realisation may be, that, in the main, they are shopkeepers and must compete with shopkeepers ... The chemist must meet business competition as other business people do.[42]

Pharmacists' glory days were gone. The medical profession had beaten back the claims to sovereignty of two dangerous rivals, the sellers of proprietary drugs and pharmacists. And by prohibiting the sale without medical mediation of these drugs, it also prevented the general public from making their own decisions. Choice was denied them, knowledge was concealed from them. No longer could one simply buy morphine or cocaine packaged at a store or compounded by a chemist. The appropriation of drugs by medical experts meant that they could only be legitimately used in ways and for purposes defined by doctors, that is, solely in the treatment of sickness as determined by doctors. The consumer of drugs had disappeared, and only the patient remained.

5

ILLNESS AND VICE

*The Changing Fear of Drug Use
1922–1939*

Illness and Vice

'For Information': The Cocaine 'Crisis' 1923–1928

Cocaine, known at the time as 'snow' or 'dope', came to prominence in 1919 when newspapers reported its use by some returned soldiers. It soon became associated in Sydney and Melbourne with prostitutes and the underworld.[1] This non-medical use simultaneously undermined the sovereignty of the medical profession and the ability of the law to command obedience and respect. Its use without a prescription was contrary to regulations under the *Poisons Act* (Vic.); and in New South Wales, although no drug law except the prohibition of opium smoking was yet on the books, the Commonwealth's *Opium Proclamation* effectively filled the gap in the law. But the class and criminal milieu of these cocaine users already branded them as threats to the social order. The labelling of their drug use as evil was a mechanism by which they could be further marginalised: they were lawbreakers already, and cocaine was guilty by its association with them.

By 1923 the use of cocaine had attracted considerable attention. The Melbourne *Herald* could only express its concern for 'the world's greatest curse' in verse:

> *You hear their sobs in the depths of night,*
> *Their faces twitch in the ghastly light.*
> *All lost, all lost, and all dead to Hope.*
> *'Dope', they cry, 'Dope, dope, dope, dope!'*[2]

The poetic spirit of J. Fordel Henderson lived on.

In the New South Wales Legislative Assembly, Ernest McTiernan, who later became the longest-serving member of the High Court of Australia, demanded that New South Wales law be brought up to date with that of Victoria, condemning the 'moral depravity' of cocaine use and the 'profiteering' associated with its sale. While the influence of the Pharmacy Board there delayed the enactment of 'modern' drug laws for another four years, in Victoria the government responded by updating the *Poisons Act* in 1925, increasing penalties and introducing a new crime of possession, made subject to a maximum penalty of a £100 fine, or twelve months imprisonment, or both. 'The illegal use of cocaine [is] an extreme danger to the community,' declared Dr Stanley Argyle, the Premier and Chief Secretary. 'Why not shoot them?' interjected an Honourable Member. 'It might be desirable,' conceded the Premier, adding with some regret that 'it is not done in civilised countries'.[3]

Such fear and vilification was quite out of proportion to the severity of the problem. Police Constable O'Connell, giving evidence at trial in 1923, estimated that there were about a dozen cocaine users in Melbourne. But the threat they represented stemmed not from their numbers, or the harm they were causing, but from the fact that they were already criminals. According to O'Connell they were 'women of ill repute ... in the slum portions of the city'. Their drug use therefore reinforced their continuing rejection of authority. As Dr Argyle explained, these twelve fallen women constituted an 'extreme danger' precisely because 'many of our worst criminals are cocaine fiends'.[4]

This climate of fear led to historical amnesia. In 1923, the New South Wales Director of Public Health, Dr Dick, announced that

the abuse of narcotics such as cocaine, morphia and similiar drugs is one of the most serious evils of the present day. Previous to the world war, there were comparatively few persons addicted to these drugs.[5]

Both in its overstatement of the extent of drug abuse in 1923, and in its silence about nineteenth century European and Chinese opium use, this statement was misleading. But labelling each new crisis as 'unprecedented' enabled harsh laws to be readily justified. Moreover, the myth that non-prescribed drug use was a modern trend made it appear as even more of a deviance from established social norms. Original sin is with us always, but new and original sins are not to be borne.

In New South Wales, too, the cocaine scare was overstated. Even in the peak years of the 'snow' storm, 1928 and 1929, only twenty-eight and thirty-four cocaine offenders were prosecuted.[6] In 1926 and 1927, the police department made 'urgent representations ... with a view to legislation being passed which will effectively deal with this evil.' But the report by Inspector Mackay, which led the Police Commissioner to make those representations, was based on an interview with one Ethel Johnson, whose inside knowledge hardly suggested a crisis:

Miss Johnson, what is the extent of traffic in 'snow' amongst unfortunates in Sydney to your knowledge?
A. There are about 15 girls, I should say.

Q. How often do they indulge in that dope?
A. Every night ...

Q. How many do you know that are making their livelihood selling 'snow'?
A. About 10.

... Q. Would you say that the habit of taking this is on the increase?
A.   It is on the increase every day. Minnie Riley is very bad from the effects of dope at the present time.[7]

Fifteen women do not constitute an epidemic. It seems most likely that the ten traffickers to which she refers did not exclusively support themselves from cocaine, but made money from a number of other sources, including pimping, bookmaking, and running errands for 'underworld' heavies such as Tilly Devine and Kate Leigh. As in Victoria, a handful of women became a crisis.

The public service in fact seems to have treated cocaine more as a minor curiosity than a plague. So uncommon was the drug that the police forwarded to the relevant government department, simply 'for information', tiny paper sachets containing cocaine from several street arrests, carefully labelling each. The officials' reaction reflected their unconcern. The cocaine was not taken away and destroyed, or put in a safe place, or sent to analysts, or returned to the police. These are all ways in which public servants might deal with such a hot potato now. But some things about bureaucracies never change: when in doubt, goes an old public service motto, file it. So the parcels of the drug were carefully placed between pages of long-forgotten correspondence and the first drafts of obsolete regulations. There they remained, undisturbed for sixty years until I came across them one surprising afternoon while researching this book. As I sat there in the reading room of a State Archive, surreptitiously unfolding the little parcels and staring at the tiny pile of white powder in front of me, I felt a real rush—not from drug use, but from the excitement of discovery, and of somehow coming closer to the reality of the past. But I'm sure the excitement I felt as a historian was much greater than the excitement those who originally filed it and forgot it felt, their actions testimony to the dispassion and lukewarm interest with which cocaine was viewed by the bureaucracy at the time.[8]

The police and the public were not so complacent. As in Victoria, cocaine's criminal connections threatened the establishment. Inspector Mackay wrote that

certain undesirables—bludgers, thieves, etc.,—have been disposing of large quantities of dope, known as 'Snow' to women of the town and also to that class of young woman who nightly frequent City Cafes dancing, drinking, etc.[9]

Mackay's objections to the cocaine traffic, then, were aesthetic and emotional, not rational or medical. He wished to eliminate the people who used cocaine—the 'bludgers' who sold it and the 'women of the town' who bought it and spent their nights drinking in cafés—and not just its use.

Under public pressure over cocaine use, and influenced by Commonwealth ratification of the *Geneva Convention*, the New South Wales government finally acted in 1927. The *Police Offences Amendment (Drugs) Act 1927*, similar to earlier Victorian legislation and in line with the Commonwealth's treaty obligations, prohibited, except on prescription, the sale, use and possession of opiates and cocaine, and subjected offenders to a maximum penalty of £250 or twelve months' imprisonment. As Carlo Lazzarini, the Colonial Secretary in Jack Lang's New South Wales Labor government, said in his second reading speech, the Act was designed to prevent the use of cocaine, in particular, by 'women on the streets and drunken persons ... and human derelicts'. But the quality of evil was especially invested in drug sellers who had become known as 'traffickers'. 'Sale' was a word too neutral in its connotations; 'traffic' conjured up images of the slave trade or electoral bribery. The trafficker was, above all, portrayed as a criminal, 'a most despicable scoundrel, worse perhaps, than the murderer', whose drug operation was only part of his or her illegal conduct and bad reputation.[10]

Those arrested under the Act were mainly prostitutes. Detective-Sergeant Wickham reported that 'hundreds' of 'immoral women' were addicts. Although usually prosecuted for possession, these women were clearly involved in trafficking, too. At her trial in 1928, May Smith was said to be 'the most notorious retailer of cocaine in Sydney', while Lillian Sproule was the 'most persistent seller of cocaine in Sydney', and Edith Mitchell a 'notorious peddler and addict'. The association of the traffic in cocaine with criminal elements was hardly surprising. The demand for a drug does not cease just because that drug is made unlawful. If it cannot be supplied legally, then it will be obtained illegally, with all the economic and social costs that implies. 'Immorality and dope', as Wickham put it, went hand in hand. To many in Australia, this nexus merely afforded grounds for the suppression of both.[11]

Newspapers, too, saw criminality as central to the drug 'evil'. A long article on the 'drug habit' that appeared in the *Sydney Morning Herald* in 1928 referred to the 'tentacles of the octopus of dope': 'doped racehorses ... attacks of razor gangs ... volcanic outbursts of underworld hate culminating in gun duelling in main thoroughfares and back slum areas.'[12] This was word-association journalism. Drug traders were engaged in other criminal activity, and this milieu of lawlessness blackened beyond redemption all cocaine users.

Cocaine use generated hate and hysteria because of the type of user with which it was associated. Drug laws once again had precious little to do with the qualities and dangers of the drug itself: they were simply an excuse for the suppression, as the *Sunday Times* put it, of 'a convicted criminal, a man devoid of all decent instinct, and a most undesirable citizen'.[13] Cocaine users were criminals or undesirables in matters other than their drug use, and therefore their drug use was seen as bad in itself. Opium use had been criminalised because it was a habit identified with the hated Chinese, and cocaine because of its connection with the urban underclass.

Vice: Legal Sovereignty and Illegal Use in the Late 1920s

The legal structure that we have seen emerge through bureaucratic and international pressure and in the context of medical dominance was unique in its severity and comprehensiveness. It gave the medical profession absolute control over the opiates and cocaine, and made illegal all recreational and non-medical uses. It forbade not only non-medical use, but mere possession of drugs without authority. But these were not just *medical* laws. The use of other dangerous drugs, in stark contrast, was not subjected to medical control. The use of alcohol and tobacco in Australia, for example, continued to be legally permitted and culturally expected. Laws provided for the treatment of inebriates (but not tobacco addicts) without controlling use or possession.[14]

As the 'cocaine crisis' in New South Wales and Victoria showed, however, the use and the sale of a few specific 'drugs', although it reflected growing medical sovereignty over all drugs, continued to be branded as a special vice. The existence of laws making certain kinds of drug use illegal was itself a powerful force in calumniating users. The legislative framework, first in Victoria and the Commonwealth, then in New South Wales, therefore began to change the way drug use was viewed. This process was by no means straightforward. Lawyers too often assume that a change in the law changes people's values; historians, that the law merely documents values. Neither is correct: the interactions between the words of a statute and the thoughts in our minds are complex and shadowy.

Laws are texts, like the Bible or a limerick: what they are 'about' is not transparent and eternal, but open to varying interpretations over time. Regardless of the original purpose of the laws, the existence of drug laws *made* the non-medical use of prescribed drugs, whether by the Chinese or by prostitutes, criminal and wrong. Those who broke the law were stigmatised simply because they had broken the law; as penalties increased, so did the apparent wickedness of their behaviour. A great divide was created between drug use that was medically-supervised and legal, and therefore legitimate, on the one hand, and that which was non-medical and illegal, and therefore wrong, on the other. The phrase 'illegal drugs' itself brought forward feelings of fear and danger. The illegal status of drugs was, for many people, incontrovertible proof of their malignancy.

The introduction of a separate crime for the possession of a controlled drug demonstrated this, for its main effect was to make prosecution and conviction easier. Early Poisons Acts only penalised the illegal sale of drugs: the offence, moreover, was committed by the vendor and not the purchaser.[15] With the enactment of the *Poisons Act 1920* (Vic.), the emphasis began to change. Regulations passed under it, while only specifically prohibiting the unauthorised supply and procurement of the drugs in question, provided that 'no person shall manufacture sell *or possess* any dangerous drug ... unless these Regulations so permit'. Then in 1925 a new *Poisons Act* (Vic.) specifically prohibited unauthorised possession, subject to a penalty of £100 or twelve months' imprisonment, or both. According to the second reading speech, the purpose of the section was to simplify the conviction of drug 'couriers', who did not themselves sell or use the drugs they carried. Neither abuse, nor use, nor even an illegal sale, needed to be proven. The evil the law aimed at was simply the failure to convict people involved in non-medical use. In the process, users and mere possessors came to be seen as evil. By 1930 the whole structure of the regulations had altered. The first substantive provision of the regulations began 'no person shall be in possession of a dangerous drug unless he is duly authorised under these Regulations', and then went on to define authorised persons.[16] As well as giving pride of place to this offence, the regulations were set out with a new-found clarity, introducing the fundamental principle of drug control—the prohibition of possession—and built on that foundation. The illegality of possession had become central to the structure of drug control.

The crime of possession indicated that breaking the law was itself seen to be wrong. Such laws in fact failed to prevent the use of prohibited drugs; but then as now, users were in consequence merely seen as more wicked and deserving of even harsher penalties. Of the seven people convicted of crimes relating to cocaine in Victoria in 1926, only one was imprisoned (for fourteen days); in 1929, although the Colonial Secretary, Albert Bruntnell, complained about judicial leniency, fifteen of thirty-four prosecutions in New South Wales resulted in prison terms ranging from at least two months to one year, and thirteen out of nineteen in Victoria. 'If I had power,' Stipendiary Magistrate Perry commented to one defendant, 'I would send you away for five years.'[17]

Legislative changes also resulted from this spiral of fear and anger. Only a year after the enactment of the *Police Offences Amendment (Drugs) Act 1927* (NSW), the *Sydney Morning Herald* criticised the maximum penalty of £250 and called for 'gaol without the option of a fine'. By the middle of the year the Commonwealth Minister for Trade and Customs, Herbert Pratten, in what was to be his last official act before dying suddenly on his birthday, increased the maximum penalty for illegal cocaine importation to three years' imprisonment. In Victoria, too, 'narcotics' penalties under the *Poisons Act 1927* rose from a maximum of £100 or six months' imprisonment in 1920, to up to £500 or three years' imprisonment, or both, in 1927.[18]

Captain Frank Chaffey's second reading speech on the 1934 New South Wales Bill, sang a familiar tune. The Bill, he declared, 'increases the penalties imposed upon those who are so mean and contemptible as to grow wealthy at the expense of unfortunate victims of the drug habit.' Yet, while addicts were portrayed as innocent victims of the trade, the maximum penalty of £400 and/or two years' imprisonment could be imposed on anyone convicted of possession.[19] Behind the occasional solicitous words concerning mere users, the development of 'drug' laws reflected a desire to suppress and punish all drug users for their criminal and therefore evil behaviour.

As dramatically as the cocaine crisis had blown up, it declined. In 1931 there were only five prosecutions, and in 1933, as in 1926, only one.[20] Virulent police activity and sensationalist reporting had, in any event, always exaggerated the real extent of cocaine use. But the lasting legacy of the cocaine 'crisis' was the addition of more severe penalties and laws. Moreover, to the criminal environment in which drug use took place was added the criminality of its use *per se*. In this vicious circle, the laws enacted generated the very images of evil and lawlessness which justified further laws.

In this climate, the original attitudes behind Australian drug laws were conveniently forgotten. Under the headline 'Surprising Discovery', the *Sydney Morning Herald* in 1930 reported that the police had 'found a Chinese and a white girl smoking opium'. 'I would never have expected to find a girl like you,' said Sergeant Small.[21] It was if the fear and paranoia surrounding

Australia's first drug 'problem' had never occurred. Now there was a new crisis to fuss over.

Illness: Medical Sovereignty and Non-Medical Use in the Late 1920s

The meaning and purpose of a law does not remain static. Rather, it is transformed by social context and debate. We have seen how the laws themselves were part of this dynamic, and how they exacerbated hostility towards illegal use. But the psychology behind this hostility was not the same thing as the reasons given to justify it. In the context of medical sovereignty discussed in the previous chapter, laws, the original purpose of which had been to stop Chinese users slipping through loopholes, came to be read very differently. New reasons were found to justify them, reasons based not on race but on medicine. While the vice of illegal use, and especially of trafficking, continued to be important in influencing how people felt about illegal drugs, this emotional reaction was *justified* by a growing emphasis on the medical dangers of drug use. The image of Mr Sin was fading and in its place came Dr No; a complex new mythology which justified the suppression of 'drug' use not just because it was sinful but because it was 'non-medical', not only because it was wrong, but because it was dangerous. Medical paternalism legitimised public hatred.

Why, for example, did the laws limiting use to contexts authorised by a medical prescription apply only to a few specified drugs, such as morphine, heroin, or cocaine? Practically, the answer lay in bureaucratic and international exigencies. Rhetorically and retrospectively, emphasis was placed on their addictive qualities. This was a new development. The use of the phrase 'drug habit' dates only from 1887, but by the time of Octavius Beale's Royal Commission, the fact of habituation was seen to be an important consequence of drug use. The President of the New South Wales Pharmacy Board, William Short, declared 'the habit of taking by hypodermic injections of cocaine or morphine' to be 'the worst curse of our civilisation ... a hopeless and irredeemable slavery every time'. The answer he proposed was medical control: 'entire prohibition without a medical prescription.'[22]

As addiction became more of a problem, it also came to be seen as a disease. A similar change had occurred in relation to alcoholism. People like Captain F.W. Neitenstein, the New South Wales Comptroller General of Prisons, had insisted around the turn of the century that 'habitual drunkenness is a nervous disease', requiring treatment in 'properly-graded moral hospitals'. In New South Wales and elsewhere, new Inebriates Acts reflected this change and envisaged incarceration as a form of treatment and not of punishment. Not that the medical inmate was granted more power over his or her destiny than was the criminal. The definition of alcoholism as a disease deprived the sick of all power and freedom. It was 'a benevolent form of despotism'.[23] Whether the prisoners saw it in the same charitable light is another question.

The sensationalist drug literature which began to circulate in Australia demonstrated this two-fold emphasis: addiction was a major problem, and a medical one. In Earle Rowell's *Battling the Wolves of Society*, for example, myths about the evil Chinese were again peddled, but more emphasis was placed on 'the disease of drug addiction ... which is said to cause agony, insanity and death'.

The typical opium addict is a poorly developed, poorly nourished individual, with cold, clammy, yellow, parchmentlike skin, who sits apathetically ... His appetite grows less and less, and the habitué eats usually once, seldom twice a day.

Cocainists, too, were said to contract the 'addiction disease' although, in reality, the addictive qualities of cocaine are doubtful. But, according to Rowell, the cocaine addict sees 'huge slimy snakes crawl through cracks in the sidewalk, and prehistoric monsters, intent on his destruction, emerge from keyholes'. Unlike the 1890s, however, the drug fiend of the 1920s was 'sick'. Addiction, for Rowell, was 'much more and worse than a vice or habit'. Addicts were villains, but they were ill and could not help themselves. Even the New South Wales Minister of Health gave his official imprimatur to Rowell's conclusions. 'As a medical man,' he wrote in a foreword to the book, 'I can unhesitatingly endorse all that he has written regarding the effect of "dope" in its various forms upon the human system.'[24]

In the scientific wonderland of the twentieth century, to label something an illness is, far from a concession of defeat, a proclamation of victory. To call addiction an illness, however, is simply to create by definition a medical condition out of behaviour that had hitherto been described variously as immoral, or criminal, or harmless. One of the characteristics of medical dominance is that the profession defines for itself its sphere of influence. The treatment of illness is the domain of medical authority, but the medical profession alone determines what is an illness and what is not. Yet the consequences of this definition are social as well as medical: the way we behave towards the sick and the restrictions we impose upon them are profoundly different from our behaviour towards those we call healthy. To label something a disease, no less than to label it a crime, is a means of social control, a way of suppressing non-conformity and demanding obedience. The more that human dysfunction or non-conformity is categorised as 'illness', the greater will be the influence accorded to the medical profession. Were every behaviour that our society finds dangerous or disturbing or disruptive labelled an illness, were every thief and murderer sick and every pornographer mad, then we would have no need for priests or police. Wigs and cassocks would lie mouldering, the courts silent and the churches unattended; only the hospitals would be full to overflowing.[25]

Addiction is real. It causes physical changes and leads to physical consequences. Addicts' obsessions may lead them to ignore their health, and to run the risk of malnutrition or infection. But addiction itself, even to

Mr Sin: The archetypal opium seller is about to inveigle his wife's daughter into taking a puff. (*Bulletin*, 1888, National Library of Australia)

'The Chow and his Charmers': 'So long as the sensual Chinaman and innocent girls are permitted to come into contact,' wrote the Bulletin, 'so long will the results be disastrous to the latter.' (*Bulletin*, 1886, National Library of Australia)

This famous cartoon, 'The Mongolian Octopus-Grip on Australia', depicts the Chinese population as a 'repulsive octopus'. 'Every one of these arms ... has its own class of victims or special mission of iniquity.' (*Bulletin*, 1886, National Library of Australia)

The remarkable Quong Tart, tea-shop proprietor, anti-opium activist and ardent anglophile. (From *The Life of Quong Tart*, 1911, National Library of Australia)

Quong Tart, Mandarin, and Mrs Tart (Margaret Scarlett) in formal costume in their role as doyens of the Chinese community in Australia during the late nineteenth century. (From *The Life of Quong Tart*, 1911, National Library of Australia).

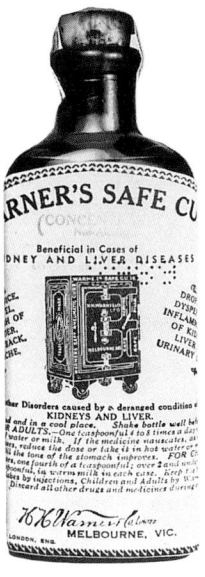

The patent medicines, of which Australians were the world's largest consumers, were not all they claimed to be. Thirty-six per cent of Warner's 'non-alcoholic' cure was pure alcohol. (National Library of Australia)

The popular Cigares de Joy, advertised as 'perfectly harmless ... pleasant to use and contain[ing] no substance capable of deranging the system', were marijuana cigarettes. (*Illustrated Australian News*, 1880, National Library of Australia)

Allen's Irish Moss, still widely sold, originally used opium as its soothing agent. (National Library of Australia)

Pineapple plantation labourers in North Queensland. In areas like this, which had a high Chinese population, White employers alleged that the Chinese were paying for Aboriginal labour with opium. (National Library of Australia)

Dr Walter Roth, Queensland's Protector of Northern Aborigines, whose protests against the lax administration of the Queensland Act prohibiting opium smoking finally led to their enforcement after 1905. (From *The Aboriginal Question in Queensland*, National Library of Australia)

Archibald Meston, Protector of Southern Aborigines, was a passionate believer in the enforced segregation of Aborigines from baleful modern influences such as opium. (From *The Aboriginal Question in Queensland*, National Library of Australia)

Octavius Beale, the Royal Commissioner into Secret Drugs, Cures and Foods (1907). This was the only government commission of inquiry ever paid for out of the pocket of the commissioner himself. (National Library of Australia)

The first Commonwealth Director-General of Health, Dr J.H.L. Cumpston (left), at Sandringham with family members around the time of his appointment in 1920. (National Library of Australia)

In August 1976, a commune at Cedar Bay was raided by Queensland police and customs officers. Under the pretext of searching for cannabis, food was doused with fuel, gardens destroyed, and children's clothing slashed - this photograph shows a family in the wreckage of their hut. (Australian Labor Party)

"Wait. It just came to me. My evidence is of **national importance.**"

In 1977, following the disappearance of anti-marijuana campaigner, Donald Mackay, three separate Royal Commissions into drugs and drug trafficking were operating in Australia. (Cartoon by George Molnar, *Sydney Morning Herald*, 1977)

The enactment by the South Australian Labor government of 'on the spot' fines for the possession of cannabis for personal use in 1986 seemed to some to be legalisation, thinly disguised. (Cartoon by Atchison, *Advertiser*, 1986)

Mr Big: The tailored suit, the jewellery, and the fistful of dollars all symbolise the image of evil represented by drug traffickers in contemporary Australia. (From *Drug Traffic*, 1980, design by Judy Hungerford)

heroin, does not make people sick. Some drugs are connected with certain illnesses. Alcohol can cause cirrhosis of the liver, and tobacco, lung cancer: addicts obviously consume more of these drugs and so increase their risk of contracting these diseases. But opiate use is not implicated with disease in this way.

Addiction has other, non-medical, consequences. Habitual consumers of heroin, morphine or opium, whether ageing Chinese or middle-class Whites who had originally taken the drugs for medicinal or quasi-medicinal purposes, often find themselves unable to moderate their behaviour as they might wish. They may abandon the world around them in favour of the introspective rituals of drug consumption. The problem of 'addiction' is, in this context, the mere fact of compulsive behaviour—of being 'out of control'—which reflects a social value and not a medical assessment. Yet the appropriation of the concept of addiction by the medical profession entrenched and legitimated the medicalisation of drugs, while concealing the non-medical values buried in the term. New reasons justified existing drug laws; reasons which spoke the language of medical power. By emphasising the medical dangers of controlled drugs, the prohibition upon 'non-medical use' was validated.

In addition, the concept of addiction affected non-medical users in two ways. First, by defining *all* users of illegal drugs as addicts, breaking the law itself became a sign of illness. Medical control was therefore entrenched whether morphine or cocaine was taken legitimately or not: the medical user had already acknowledged medical power, and the non-medical user was sick by definition, and was therefore an appropriate subject of medical intervention. Second, the labelling of illegal users as addicts explained their illegal behaviour in a way which did not challenge the justice of legal controls. Non-conformists were ill—their conduct was not a conscious decision to disobey the law, but a compulsion over which they had no control. Slowly but surely, the villain was becoming a victim.

Not that this changing emphasis led to a softening of the approach taken to drug users. Rather, it simply changed the rationalisations given in favour of more laws and harsher penalties. Lazzarini, in his second reading speech to the *Police Offences Amendment (Drugs) Act 1927*, explained that police needed to be able to deal with users 'in a very drastic way' because 'in a very short time they become addicts and human derelicts'. The opposition heartily agreed. Addicts, suffering 'one of the worst diseases ... that can possibly be placed upon mankind', were to be protected from themselves. 'We know that in this State to-day,' said James McGirr, 'addictable drugs are being obtained in every possible way.'[26] Legislative reform also began to reflect these changing concerns. By 1930, both New South Wales and Victoria had passed regulations under which doctors were prohibited from prescribing or administering a drug 'merely for the purposes of addiction'. Theoretically, addicted users could no longer feed their habits even if they were able to find a sympathetic doctor prepared regularly to prescribe the drug they needed.[27]

The *Poisons Act 1928* (Vic.) defined all prescription-only drugs as 'narcotics', implying that they were united by their medical and pharmacological nature as well as their legal status. The Act included both cocaine and cannabis, which are certainly not narcotics and the addictive qualities of which are at best open to doubt, but their categorisation using a medical term both legitimised their legal status and underscored that 'drug use' was a medical problem. In the then Federal Capital Territory (now the Australian Capital Territory), Part V of the *Poisons and Dangerous Drugs Ordinance 1933* dealt with 'any drug' listed in the Commonwealth *Gazette* 'the continual use of which is liable to induce the formation of the habit of addiction'.[28] Regardless of the many underlying attitudes and pressures that propelled the formation of drug laws in Australia, the medical concept of addiction was becoming the principal overt reason for their maintenance.

Neither the medicalisation nor the legal regulation of heroin, morphine, cocaine and so on were enough by themselves to affect the radical restructuring of drug laws and attitudes towards drugs that occurred in Australia between the wars. This restructuring acted synergetically to create a profound dichotomy in the way drugs were viewed: if prescribed, then legal and socially approved; if not, then condemned. The inconsistencies inherent in this approach were readily apparent: not all 'drugs of addiction' were addictive; not all 'narcotics' were narcotics; and other recreational and addictive drugs remained uncontrolled. But these logical problems were insignificant: the laws, once in place, personified both legal and medical sovereignty. To break the law and use drugs illegally, no matter what drug or what law was involved, signified a failure to 'follow doctors' orders' *and* a refusal to obey the law.

In the condemnation of those who traversed this division, sickness and evil were by no means antithetical. Charlie Woodward, for example, in his book *Peeps into Gaols, Police Courts, Opium Dens*, published by Australian Baptist Publishing in 1933, wrote about 'Opium Jack'. 'He lived to plan and plot for the destruction of young girls. He bartered with the Chinese for their bodies and souls.' The continuity with the old mythology of opium is striking, but this story was not about sexual licence. The message conveyed was that opium made people servants of the devil—'a fiend incarnate', Woodward wrote—with the desire and the power to barter for their very souls. The story ended with Opium Jack bedridden, 'seized with cancer'. Disease, then, served as both the result of Opium Jack's bedevilment and the means of divine retribution.[29] Similarly, Earle Rowell, while insisting that addiction was a disease, portrayed its most important consequences as moral rather than physical. 'Dope,' he wrote, 'stimulates the senses and pulls down that moral barrier.' 'The devastating power of narcotics,' according to Rowell, 'may truly be called the wrath of Satan.' For Woodward, drug addiction was an evil that made people sick; for Rowell, it was a sickness that made people evil.[30]

The phrases 'dope fiend', first used in 1896, and 'drug fiend', first used in 1925, suggest the mutuality of illness and vice, for 'fiend' implied uncontrolled and obsessive (addictive/ill) behaviour, and at the same time reverberated with its original meaning, 'an evil spirit' or 'a person of superhuman wickedness'. In the first Australian reference to 'drug fiends', Mr Prendergast, a Member of the Victorian Legislative Assembly, speaking on the Poisons Bill 1925 (Vic.), said 'their very natures have been changed'.[31] Drug fiends were sick, but it was an unnatural and devilish sickness.

Illegal drug users were seen as having been invaded by Satan and powerless to resist his sway. They were, in short, *possessed*. In this concept, disease and vice coalesced. Persons possessed, whether by addiction or evil spirits, do not choose to be infected and are not responsible for the symptoms that result. But they are incapable of saving themselves without help. The health of the powerless patient can only be restored by the authoritative intercession of the medical profession. The devil in a witch must be exorcised. New South Wales Commissioner of Police, James Mitchell, speaking in 1928, called 'the drug evil ... a canker at the heart of any community', and urged the enactment of laws 'protecting the addict against himself' with penalties such as ten years' imprisonment and the lash.[32] Jailing drug users, like burning witches, was not a punishment (cold comfort indeed!), but a necessary part of saving victims from a condition over which they had no control. The crime of possessing drugs was in this sense the crime of being possessed.

The Dichotomy of Drug Use: The 'British System' in Australia 1922–1939

In stark contrast to the medical and legal authority that jointly demonised the transgressors of drug laws, those who accepted the legal and medical boundaries that had been set in place met with support and reassurance. Even 'drug addicts' were able to continue their habit if they did so legally and under medical supervision. This is the issue to which I now turn.

As laws which prevented non-medical drug use developed around the world, an important question of interpretation arose. Was it legal for doctors to prescribe 'dangerous drugs' not for the treatment of disease, but simply to support the addicts on a steady dose of their drug of addiction—so called 'opiate maintenance,' the effect of which was not to 'cure' addiction but to avoid the difficult process of withdrawal. In the United States, the Harrison Act 1914, ostensibly a revenue-gathering measure, was soon used by the Treasury Department to enforce its belief that all addiction had to be stamped out. The prescription of heroin to slow down or prevent withdrawal symptoms was forbidden by regulation, and 'clinics' established after the passage of the Act to provide a legal source of drugs for users were forcibly closed. In 1919, when this decision was challenged in a string of court cases, the United States Supreme Court ruled that opiate maintenance was not a legitimate medical practice and therefore not permitted by the Act. Under Harry Anslinger, head of the FBN, this image of the addict as irredeemably degenerate strengthened and triumphed. Indeed, even though the Supreme Court overturned its previous decision in a case decided in 1925, Anslinger's FBN had the power and influence to ensure that this new ruling was routinely either ignored or misrepresented.[33]

In the United Kingdom, a similar dispute arose under the Dangerous Drugs Act 1920. The Rolleston Report (1926), established by and adopting the medical perspective of the United Kingdom's Department of Health, which appointed it, concluded that habitual drug use 'must be regarded as a manifestation of disease, and not as a mere form of vicious indulgence'. In contrast to the United States, the Report established the right of doctors to treat addicted patients any way they chose, including maintaining for them a regular supply of a drug of addiction. Addiction to heroin or morphine was not prohibited if the user's supply was authorised and supervised by a doctor. This practice survived virtually unchanged into the 1960s, and came to be known as 'the British system'.[34]

Although, as in Australia, the concepts of disease and vice mingled, the emphasis in these countries clearly differed. For all their similarities as agents of social control, treating people as sick is not the same thing as treating them as criminal. In the United States, the belief in the viciousness of addicts led to their persecution. In the United Kingdom, if only the label of 'sick' was accepted, addicts were protected by the medical profession and treated with compassion.

In Australia by 1930, as I have already observed, State regulations forbade the supply, administration or prescription of a drug 'merely for the purposes of addiction'. Nevertheless, while the *words* of this law implied a rejection of the disease model favoured in Britain, its interpretation by bureaucracies around the country significantly changed its apparent meaning. The 'maintenance' of a sizeable number of addicts continued as a settled policy requiring the connivance not only of State law enforcement agencies and Health departments, but also of the Commonwealth public service. Laws do not just exist in the abstract. They are enforced and given substance by organs of government. Neither is this interpretative function in any way neutral. In Australia, as occurred in relation to the very different history of the United States drug laws, bureaucracies made and remade laws by interpreting and putting them into effect, and they did so in response to their own exigencies and as a product of their own subjective perspectives.

While cocaine use by prostitutes and the 'underworld' attracted publicity and penalties, most drug addiction in Australia still conformed to nineteenth-century patterns. Apart from ageing Chinese opium smokers, drug addicts were middle-class, middle-aged, frequently doctors or other health-care professionals, and their habituation was most often the result of careless or lengthy therapeutic use. This demography continued with remarkably little change until, during, and well after, the Second World War. The different status of this kind of user was recognised even in the United States. In 1921, the President of the American Medical Association, Alexander Lambert, carefully distinguished the 'otherwise normal' middle-class morphine or cocaine addict, from the 'correctional case ... mental defective [or] social misfit'. Those from 'higher social ranks' could be cured, but members of 'the outlaw population' were to be punished.³⁵

The Commonwealth government's exclusive power over importation gave the federal bureaucracy a position of considerable influence in the formation of drug policy in Australia. This influence extended, as we have seen, to the retail and wholesale trade. In practice, the delivery by importers and wholesalers to chemists or doctors of unusually large amounts of morphine or heroin required the approval of the Customs Department, which, after the formation of the Commonwealth Department of Health in 1921, acted on the advice of the Director-General of Health, Dr Cumpston. Many applicants needed large quantities of prescribed drugs to treat serious illnesses. In one case, for example, the Collector of Customs complained that he had received an application for an amount of morphine 'unusually large even for a confirmed habitué ... sufficient to supply half a dozen morphia-fiends'. The fiend turned out to be a shire clerk with incurable rheumatism.³⁶

Nevertheless, many others sought morphine or heroin for the long-term 'maintenance' of their addiction. The Department of Health did not deal with these cases any differently. Supply was authorised as long as the user was being prescribed the drug by a medical practitioner and supplied by only one chemist. As explained in a Department of Health memorandum in relation to one early authorisation in 1922, 'the sudden withdrawal of the drug is likely to prejudicially effect [the] patient's health'. This case was typical. The original dosage of 240 grains (half an ounce) per month was doubled the following year, and continued at that level or higher for at least ten years more. Whatever the purpose of the original prescription, the patient was addicted to morphine. Yet no determined attempt was made to lessen the dose and no questions were raised.³⁷

Dr Cumpston occasionally expressed concern about the Department's policy. In 1929 he wondered 'whether the opium has produced,' in 'cases of opium habit ... from time to time referred to this Department,' a 'disturbance of moral character or social adjustment'. But the sanguine approach of the Commonwealth bureaucracy was again evident. Dr Cumpston concluded that 'in the cases which have so far come under observation, no such disturbance has been recorded'. Again in 1931, in response to the regulations prohibiting prescription 'merely for the purposes of addiction', although Dr Cumpston advised that in the case of 'a pure drug addict' efforts should be made to reduce the dosage, no attempt was made to enforce the instruction.³⁸

The essence of Commonwealth policy remained the institutionalisation and medicalisation of drug use. A departmental note on the relevant New South Wales regulation was explicit:

> *When the Regulations were framed the view was held ... that the position would be met by providing a means by which the 'addict' by becoming a 'patient' could obtain whatever quantity of the drug his medical adviser considered necessary for his requirements ...*³⁹

The level of addiction amongst legal users varied considerably; in the case of morphine, from a mere fifty grains to over one ounce (480 grains) per month. In the fiscal year 1934–35, thirty-six chemists and doctors in New South Wales alone were authorised to receive 'excess supplies' of 'habit-forming drugs', ranging from a small amount over the limit set down in *General Order 1020*, to 320 ounces of opium and twenty-eight additional ounces of morphine.[40] It is not clear how much of this excess was used simply to 'treat' addiction, but at a time when only a few Australians were addicted to 'dangerous drugs' of any kind, the Commonwealth approved the prescription of addictive drugs for the purpose of drug maintenance as a general practice. These people were not alienated fringe-dwellers or 'undesirable citizens'. They were of 'good reputation' and 'able to earn their own living'.[41] They were middle class, not only economically, but because they were integrated into the existing social system and accepted its constraints. They played by the rules and the rules rewarded them.

Of those few surviving files that detail specific cases, at least ten (over half) were doctors. Originally, addicted doctors were allowed to 'treat' themselves without interference. By 1932, however, the policy had changed. 'Medical drug addicts' were not allowed to continue in practice, and were no longer allowed to self-prescribe. Their addiction was to be supervised in the same way as all other cases considered by the Department. Later, Cumpston also recommended that the drugs being prescribed to them should be reduced at the rate of five per cent per month. This policy, too, was never enforced.[42]

Dr Q. Ercole seems to have been a typical example of a medical drug addict. He was an Italian immigrant who first took to morphine when ill during the First World War at Gallipoli. In 1935 he wrote to the Commonwealth Department of Health that:

I should say now that it is half habit and half necessity ... It is a serious point with me, that is to give up the habit portion of it, as my life is not long and I want to die as clean as I possibly can.

Cumpston originally recommended a gradual reduction of dosage, but by 1940 Ercole was taking no less. At times he attempted to cure himself, seeking advice, for example, from the National Psychological Institute (Inc.), which advised him that his morphine addiction was caused by the restless spirit of a previous occupant of his house who had committed suicide by overdose. In between these efforts, however, Dr Ercole practised those arts of deception which, in a less respectable addict, would have demonstrated incorrigibility and evil. On at least a couple of occasions he illegally obtained additional morphine from another chemist to supplement his legal dosage, and once he claimed to have lost half of his monthly entitlement and asked for more.[43] Yet, despite these lapses, no action was ever taken against him. Above all, his repentance and his willingness to try and keep within the boundaries of bureaucratic and medical control ensured that his legal supply of the drug continued.

Commonwealth policy was not without its critics. Influenced, perhaps, by the United States FBN, the Customs Department, in particular, saw all addiction as criminal. In a 1937 case it sought, against the wishes of her doctor, a reduction in the dosage prescribed to one addict. But the Department of Health defended its position by quoting, significantly, from the Rolleston Report:

The administration of morphine may be regarded as a legitimate medical treatment in the case, inter alia, of an addict who, while capable of leading a useful and fairly normal life so long as he takes a certain non-progressive quantity, usually small, of the drug, ceases to be able to do so when the regulation allowance is withdrawn.

In three other cases that year, the Department of Health likewise approved the prescription of heroin and morphine to applicants 'suffering from no disease except ... addiction'. The Department's position as an outsider body, advising on medical questions without the direct law enforcement responsibilities of the Department of Trade and Customs, ensured its unflinching and influential defence of the 'British system' in Australia.[44]

The 'respectable' users who were occasionally prosecuted in Australia were those who did not play the game. One couple sought to supplement their doctor's morphine prescriptions with forgery; another man was convicted twice for procuring heroin for his wife, who had become addicted during a long illness; a woman tried to forge the prescription of her doctor husband; and a doctor was prosecuted for failing to observe the record-keeping requirements of the 'Drugs Act'.[45] Many more addicts than these were legally supplied with heroin or morphine. Even as the development of tougher penalties and stricter controls was justified by reference to the evils of addiction, those who accepted that drug dependence was an illness requiring subservience to the medical profession and obedience to the law found sanctuary. Far from challenging medical and legal sovereignty, addiction on these terms in fact confirmed it.

The Dichotomy of Drug Use: The Case of Heroin 1931–1936

The maintenance of addicts highlighted a double standard. Unlike in Britain, the 'British system' in Australia remained largely secret. In answer to a 1936 League of Nations questionnaire, Victorian Senior Constable Brown stated that 'the use of cocaine is prevalent amongst [prostitutes] and the criminal class', while 'no member of the above professions [doctors, dentists, vets and chemists] is known as an addict of any drug.' The Tasmanian Premier, Albert Ogilvie, in answer to another survey the following year, declared that there were 'nil' addicts in the medical profession. Yet the surviving Commonwealth files record the cases of two Tasmanian doctors, including a surgeon at Hobart General Hospital.[46]

Public knowledge of the maintenance of addicts would undoubtedly have undermined the rhetorical war waged against drug criminals, and weakened the emerging and changing reasons used to justify strict drug controls. For what distinguished these users from those who were arrested was not the nature or purpose of their use or the fact of addiction, but simply the legal status of their conduct and the presence of medical supervision. The hypocrisy in the treatment of different categories of drug users and addicts, which first began with the enactment of the opium prohibition laws at the turn of the century, was entrenched. All medically prescribed drug use was accepted, while any use of 'illegal drugs' without medical control was a symptom of sickness and a sign of evil.

The use of habit-forming drugs did not decline with the enactment throughout Australia of a comprehensive regime of drug control. Australia had not taken the dangers of drug use to heart: it had merely compartmentalised them. The very clarity with which the line between proper and improper use was drawn validated authorised drug-taking exactly as it stigmatised that which was forbidden. Heroin use demonstrated this dichotomy. Although its control was central to Australia's drug policy, *medical* use flourished. Heroin was prescribed for the alleviation of chronic and acute pain, during the final stages of cancer, and to ease the pains of childbirth. It was available from chemists as an ingredient in cough suppressants and, as we have seen, addicts were allowed to have it under medical supervision. In 1931 Australia consumed 3.10 kilograms of heroin per one million persons, more in total than the United States, Canada or Germany and, per capita, behind only New Zealand. Australia consumed three times as much heroin per capita as the United Kingdom and twice as much cocaine.[47] Hitherto we had been world leaders in the popping of patent medicine pills; now we had moved on to other drugs.

The Commonwealth government viewed this extraordinary level of use with equanimity. But other countries saw heroin use differently. United States Treasury officials charged with the implementation of the Harrison Act 1914 effectively prohibited its use for any purpose whatsoever, and its importation was banned as early as 1924.[48] At the same time, and undoubtedly influenced by the United States, the Council of the League of Nations instructed the Secretary-General 'to ask the various Governments their views as to the possibility of a total suppression of the manufacture of heroin or of its limitation'.[49]

Despite a lack of international consensus, pressure from the League grew. The Conference called to formulate the 1931 *Geneva Convention*, citing 'the highly dangerous nature of diacetylmorphine [i.e. heroin] ... and the possibility in most, if not all, cases of replacing it by other drugs of a less dangerous character', recommended that governments 'examine ... the possibility of abolishing or restricting its use'. In addition, article 10 of the Convention placed special restrictions on the procedure for heroin importation. Meanwhile, a Committee of Experts was appointed to inquire into the prohibition of its manufacture. Under considerable pressure from the League, the Committee returned the conclusions it was supposed to: 'We feel that the dangerous nature of heroin from the social point of view overshadows its therapeutic importance ... [H]eroin can be entirely dispensed with.'[50]

The absolute prohibition of heroin was a different kind of proposal from those previously advocated by the League. For the first time since the prohibition on opium smoking, the passion of the international community threatened to lessen medical authority, which it had previously done so much to enhance. And while the development of an international regime of drug control had only entrenched the dividing line between medical/legal and non-medical/illegal use, on this occasion it was proposed to move the line. That which was already under medical control would now be illegal; that which was commonplace would now be prosecuted. While the New South Wales Premier agreed with the Committee's conclusion, the Western Australian and Victorian Premiers did not. The opinion of the Federal Council of the Australian branch of the British Medical Association (the peak body representing doctors in Australia) proved conclusive. Joseph Lyons, then Prime Minister, quoted it in his reply to the Secretary-General of the League in January 1935:

The Federal Council ... is not aware of any addiction as regards diacetylmorphine, and, in view of the definite usefulness of this drug in clinical practice, it is not in favour of the prohibition.

Nothing was done to change the law relating to heroin or to temper its consumption. By 1936 heroin use in Australia even outstripped that of New Zealand; Australians consumed fourteen per cent of the world's legally produced morphine and 7.5 per cent of its heroin.[51]

The Commonwealth's decision to swim against the current of international opinion was unusual, and demonstrated the power with which the distinction between 'good' and 'bad' drug use had already been etched. But the international community itself was not yet united on the issue. Recommendation 6 of the Final Act of the 1931 Conference only advocated the *'possibility'* of abolishing *or restricting'* the use of heroin. More importantly, Australia was not alone in its reluctance to act. In Britain, the use of heroin to treat disease and control addiction was never under threat. In most cases, the United Kingdom and the League of Nations had been united in their efforts to forge an unquestioning mettle out of malleable Australia. They had guided Australian policy in the same direction. On this occasion, however, they were in conflict. The Second World War was still to come; Singapore had not yet fallen and the English Channel seemed a greater moat against invasion than the Pacific. When the League of Nations, under the watchful eye of the United States, pulled one way and Great Britain another, Australia showed that it was still a loyal subject of the crown.

In other ways, however, Australia remained obedient to the international community. The 1936 *Geneva Convention for the Suppression of the Illicit Traffic in Dangerous Drugs* did little other than confirm the approach established by earlier treaties. Signatories agreed

to make the necessary legislative provisions for severely punishing, particularly by imprisonment or other penalties of deprivation of liberty ... the manufacture, conversion, extraction, preparation, possession, offering, offering for sale [and so on] ... of narcotic drugs.

In addition, the Convention dealt with extradition and the punishment of offences committed in other jurisdictions.[52]

The Commonwealth argued that the Convention was of little relevance to it because, unlike prior conventions, it dealt not with the importation and production of drugs but with their domestic manufacture, possession and sale. The Commonwealth, it was argued, did not have the constitutional authority to give effect to these matters: its power over drugs 'stopped at the customs barrier'. In Australia, health in general, and the internal control of drugs in particular, were by common consent the province of State governments. The decision of the High Court of Australia in *R. v. Burgess*, a case concerning international treaties and the Australian airline industry, also handed down in 1936, should have changed all that. Section 51(xxix) of Australia's Constitution expressly gives the Commonwealth parliament the power to make laws with respect to 'external affairs'. The meaning of this provision has long been a matter of debate. In *R. v. Burgess* Justices Evatt and McTiernan (and to some extent Chief Justice Latham) held that the Commonwealth parliament had power under section 51(xxix) to pass a law giving effect to the terms of any international convention signed by the Commonwealth, whatever its subject matter. Justices Dixon and Starke, taking a more limited view, thought that the Commonwealth could only enact legislation if the subject matter of the Convention was 'indisputably international in character'. But, although the case concerned air navigation, Justices Evatt and McTiernan specifically mentioned the 'suppression of traffic in drugs' as an illustration of international issues that could undoubtedly be legislated upon. Coming in the same year as the Convention 'for the suppression of the illicit traffic in dangerous drugs', these statements could hardly have been coincidental. Chief Justice Latham was even clearer:

No one would to-day be inclined to deny that the production and sale of recently invented narcotic drugs is a matter of international interest and concern.[53]

As the Attorney-General's Department concluded in 1938, 'it would certainly appear that Parliament is authorised to make laws to give effect to the Conventions in relation to dangerous drugs.'[54]

The fiction of Commonwealth powerlessness was maintained despite this clear advice, because the Commonwealth was not interested in expanding its involvement in the area and was prepared to use the Constitution as an excuse. Drugs mattered so little that the Commonwealth was not prepared to rock the boat. 'The authority for the sale and distribution of these drugs with in [sic] Australia is within the constitutional power of the States,' the Commonwealth Minister for Supply, Senator Henty, insisted as late as 1967.[55]

The deliberations of the Commonwealth bureaucracy as to whether to sign the treaty at all also reflected the fact that drug laws in Australia remained unimportant. The Comptroller-General, Edward Abbott, was 'not convinced that any great necessity exists for the conclusion of such a Convention so far as the Commonwealth is concerned.'

The illicit traffic in dangerous drugs in Australia cannot be regarded as extensive ... There is no pressing need, so far as this country is concerned, to strengthen the measures already provided.

State Premiers' replies to a questionnaire circulated by Abbott reflected the same complacency: in Western Australia drug addiction was 'considered to be very uncommon', in Victoria there was 'very little', while in Queensland it was 'unknown' and in South Australia, 'negligible'.[56]

As before, however, the bureaucracy was prepared to follow the international community with all the velleity of a eunuch. The enactment of domestic legislation to bring Australia into line with the terms of the Convention was deferred 'until the opportunity is afforded of considering cognate legislation of the Parliament of the United Kingdom'. And although the Convention was still thought to be unnecessary, a new Comptroller-General, H. Morris, advised in 1938 that Australia should ratify it simply because it was the Commonwealth's practice to support the activities of the League.[57]

The Commonwealth government did not ratify the 1936 Convention. Although the decision to do so had been made, the Second World War proved a serious distraction. Yet the same patterns of thought and behaviour—of lack of interest and obedience—were as evident in 1936 as before. Amidst the complex new reasons, rationalisations and attitudes relating to drug use that were shaping the development and interpretation of drug policy in Australia, some things remained constant: Australia had no need to think for itself, for the rest of the world thought for it.

CONVENTIONAL WISDOM

International Influence and US Power
1940–1961

The World at War

Following Robert Menzies's 'melancholy' announcement on 3 September 1939 that Great Britain was at war and that 'as a result' Australia was also at war, issues of drug policy understandably took a back seat. Despite the demise of the League of Nations as a result of the war, however, the international regime of drug control had become so powerful and accepted that it continued to function: the import–export licence system still operated; reports of smuggling enterprises thwarted and caches of illicit drugs uncovered were still circulated amongst interested parties;[1] and annual reports, statistics and estimates were dutifully supplied to the Permanent Central Opium Board.

At the beginning of the war, this caught the Australian government by surprise. It had ceased providing statistics to the Opium Board because it thought that was the policy of the United Kingdom. An angry telegram soon made it clear that the United Kingdom had been co-operating with the Board throughout, and Australia immediately changed its position 'in accordance with the lead in the matter given by the British authorities'.[2] In drug policy, as in the declaration of war, Australia in 1939 was still a dependency.

Australia's isolation, the conduct of the war, and Britain's inability to safeguard Australia's defence, however, began to alter our international relationships. It was becoming clear that Australia's future lay in the Pacific, not in the North Atlantic. An embassy was established in Washington in 1940, and in 1942 the Prime Minister, John Curtin, said what everybody already knew: the United States was now the 'keystone' of Australia's defence. It was the start of a power shift which extended far beyond questions of defence and geopolitics and which was, in the future, to re-orient every aspect of Australia's political, economic and cultural life.[3] Its genesis during the Second World War was perceptible in the sphere of drug policy as elsewhere.

The United Kingdom had always been more tolerant of the non-medical use of opium and cannabis in its colonies than had the United States. It had argued that the use of cannabis in India, while not 'medicinal', was, within that culture, 'legitimate' under the terms of the *Hague Convention*. While the 1925 *Geneva Convention* deleted the word 'legitimate' and only authorised drug use if it was 'medicinal or scientific', it did not unequivocally and immediately prohibit opium or cannabis smoking.[4] Much to the chagrin of the United States, the United Kingdom right up until the Second World War tolerated opium and cannabis smoking in Aden, Zanzibar, India, Burma and its Far Eastern territories, in some cases licensing users, and in others organising the trade as a government monopoly.

The United States used the war against the Japanese to further advance the cause of a prohibitionist drug policy. In 1943 it announced that it was determined to enforce the immediate and absolute suppression of opium smoking in all liberated territories, whether or not they had been British colonies prior to the Japanese invasion. Australia's position reflected how far the war had altered its loyalties. The federal Cabinet, briefed a month before the British response was made known, gave top priority to the need 'to operate with the US forces in the present struggle with a minimum of friction'. Consequently, although the pre-war position of the British government was well known, Cabinet opted to support the United States. Furthermore, while 'in ordinary circumstances the views of the United Kingdom Government would be sought', and, moreover, the issue concerned the policy to be enforced in British colonies, Cabinet's decision was taken 'without reference to the British Authorities'. So far had Australia already travelled into America's sphere of influence. Lacking support and powerless, in practice, to intervene, the British had no choice but to consent. In November that year the United Kingdom 'decided' that smoking monopolies would not be re-introduced in Far Eastern territories freed from Japanese domination.[5]

Domestic drug issues were of little importance during the war. Occasional noises were made about the sale of drugs and poisons by and to aliens, but nothing came of these rumblings of racism and fear.[6] The only issue of any concern was how best to safeguard the import of vital drugs into Australia. When Britain ceased exporting heroin to its enemies, Germany began the large-scale production of methadone, a synthetic substitute. The Australian government, fearful of some disruption in its own trade routes to Britain, tentatively explored the possibility of domestically manufacturing morphine for the first time. Commonwealth Scientific and Industrial Research (CS&IR, later CSIRO) accordingly began the experimental cultivation of the opium poppy in 1940, intending to produce a small amount of morphine for emergencies. But J.G. Starke, a lecturer at the University of Sydney's Law School (and future Professor of Law at the Australian National University), had bigger plans. As a lawyer in the Drug Traffic section of the League of Nations before the war, he had learnt about a method of manufacturing morphine from 'poppy straw', which was said to be unsuitable for conversion into opium suitable for smoking. In 1941, with the financial backing and involvement of the giant oil company, Golden Fleece, he proposed the cultivation of opium not as a wartime exigency, but as a long-term commercial venture. Various State and Commonwealth departments and committees prevaricated; on the one hand, the project was backed by a large and reputable manufacturer, but on the other, domestic cultivation was seen as a dangerous precedent. In the course of these deliberations, Starke became disillusioned with those who suspected him of only being involved in the venture for personal profit. He joined the Air Force and 'gave up being an idealist'; Golden Fleece decided to concentrate on selling petrol.[7] The suggestion of poppies for profit was an idea that as yet still aroused fear and cynicism.

Starke's ideas had not fallen on wholly fallow ground. The idea was taken up by CS&IR and in 1945 it declared itself ready to manufacture 5000 ounces of morphine. But not everyone was convinced that domestic production was a good idea. Both CS&IR and the Medical Equipment Control

Committee of the Commonwealth Department of Health decided in 1946 that self-sufficiency in morphine was not essential; twelve months later, however, they had changed their minds. The Department of Trade and Customs, on the other hand, true to its law-enforcement perspective and fearful of any possible diversion to the illegal trade, was consistent in its opposition to the cultivation of 'habit-forming drugs'. In fact, according to research undertaken by the pharmaceutical firm Drug Houses of Australia, the morphine extracted by the poppy straw method was not potent enough to be competitive. It therefore only requested permission to continue experiments designed to try to increase the morphine content of the poppy straw to an economic level. Accordingly, an area of about five acres in total was cultivated in all mainland States (except Queensland, where the climate was unsuitable) through the late 1940s and 1950s. The industry was not yet viable, but there seemed every possibility that Australia would one day be able to produce for itself some of the morphine and codeine that it consumed with such enthusiasm.[8]

International Influence and the Expansion of Controlled Drugs: Pethidine 1946–1948

The Second World War was only an interregnum in the steady growth of international drug controls and of the international drug bureaucracy. The functions entrusted to the League of Nations under the old Conventions were transferred to the United Nations (UN) in 1946. The UN in turn delegated these responsibilities to various subsidiary bodies. The Permanent Central Opium Board (PCOB), the members of which were now appointed by the Economic and Social Council of the UN (ECOSOC), continued to administer the 'estimate system' which, it will be recalled, controlled the import and export of dangerous drugs throughout the world. A Division of Narcotic Drugs (DND) was established within the UN Secretariat to perform administrative duties previously carried out by the Secretary-General of the League, such as collecting and circulating annual reports from parties to the Conventions. These reports dealt with matters including the annual consumption and manufacture of, and illegal and legal trade in, the drugs covered by the treaties signed by reporting nations. In addition, two advisory bodies were set up: a Commission on Narcotic Drugs (CND) (akin to the old Advisory Committee) advised ECOSOC on drug-related issues, and an Expert Committee on Addiction-producing Drugs was set up by the World Health Organisation (WHO) to advise the UN on medical aspects.[9]

Procedures set in place before the war continued. Until its functions were taken over by the WHO, the Health Committee established by the League of Nations continued to recommend, in accordance with the procedure laid down in article 10 of the 1925 *Geneva Convention*, that the terms of the Convention be applied to new and previously uncontrolled drugs and compounds. Spurred on by the 'recent impulse given particularly during the last war to the development of synthetic drugs', this process effected considerable legislative change around Australia.[10] As more drugs were developed and promoted or began to be used, fears of their addictive potential were aroused, and the holey dyke of drug control repeatedly patched. It was a juggernaut of incremental expansion with which Australia was well familiar.

Pethidine, a synthetic narcotic analgesic first issued by Roche in 1942 and similar in its action to morphine, was an early example. In 1945, after the United States FBN had expressed concern about its alleged habit-forming properties, the Health Committee, using its powers under article 10, recommended to State parties that pethidine be treated as a 'dangerous drug' under the provisions of the various international treaties. The Commonwealth Department of Trade and Customs immediately extended the provisions of the *Opium Proclamation* to include pethidine. Its importation into Australia was now subject, like morphine, heroin or cocaine, to the complicated guarantees extracted from importers and wholesalers designed to ensure the drug was only used for *bona fide* medicinal and scientific purposes.[11]

This was not the end of the matter. Complete compliance with the Health Committee's recommendation required that pethidine be treated as a narcotic under State law, too, to ensure strict controls over its sale, use and possession. Not for the first time, the opinions of the Commonwealth departments of Health and Customs differed. The acting Director-General of Health, A.J. Metcalfe, advised the Commonwealth in March 1946 that 'the majority of States are not in favour of the Health Committee's recommendation', citing the position at that time under New South Wales, Victorian and Western Australian law, where the drug was subject to less stringent controls than morphine or heroin. New South Wales was particularly adamant:

Exhaustive enquiries have failed to trace any addiction to this drug whatever. On the contrary it is found to be an excellent drug to overcome addiction to morphine.[12]

In early 1947 the Department of Trade and Customs asserted its authority, determined that Australia should fulfil its international commitments. The Department was, in this way, faithful to its origins and responsibilities, first, as a law enforcement body, and second, as the agency that dealt with the international community on these matters. Its responsibilities therefore governed its perspective, which was strongly committed to both prohibitionism and to international drug control. A formal request from the Prime Minister to State Premiers, couched in terms which emphasised Australia's obligations to the international community, led New South Wales and Western Australia to change their minds. The views of the States, however, were merely tools to be manipulated by the Customs Department as it suited them. Thus, although the Victorian government concluded that there was 'no evidence ... which would warrant listing this drug as a narcotic', Kennedy, the Comptroller-General of Customs, advised the Commonwealth that 'none of the States had any objection to the proposal'. Still the Commonwealth Department of Health argued that pethidine was not subject to abuse in Australia and was able to be adequately controlled without being classified as a narcotic, but Customs ignored its protests. In the face of such obstinacy, Metcalfe, while making it clear that he did not resile from his opinion, conceded defeat. 'There may be good and sufficient reasons, apart from the purely medical aspect, why such drugs should be listed as Dangerous Drugs in this country,' he noted pointedly.[13]

One by one the States proclaimed pethidine as subject to the same controls as the opiates. Only in New South Wales did the proposal continue to meet any opposition; ironically, the police in that State argued that there were 'no recorded instances of addiction to this drug', and the Director-General of Public Health supported the position of the Commonwealth Department of Trade and Customs. After something akin to a manhunt, Customs eventually uncovered a solitary case of pethidine addiction. Throughout 1947 a large amount of correspondence concerning this individual case took place between health officials, the Department of Customs and the New South Wales police, culminating in a letter from the Prime Minister, Ben Chifley, to the Premier of New South Wales, James McGirr, in November. Chifley warned that 'there may be other cases and that, in the public interest, every precaution should be taken to guard against the indiscriminate use of the drug.' In the face of the evidence of one lone addict, New South Wales caved in; pethidine was proclaimed as a dangerous drug under the *Police Offences Amendment (Drugs) Act 1927* (NSW) the following February.[14]

The institution of stricter controls over pethidine did not lessen its use. Total pethidine sales in Australia in 1951 were up sixty per cent on the previous year, although many factors contributed to this explosion. The coming into force of the *Pharmaceutical Benefits Act 1951* (Cwlth), was particularly important. Under this Act, the only analgesics for which government benefits were paid were 'dangerous drugs', including pethidine, thereby encouraging their prescription by doctors at the expense of unlisted analgesics such as aspirin.[15]

Neither did the proclamation of pethidine as a dangerous drug, and the institution of controls ostensibly designed to *prevent* its overuse, seem to halt the growth of addiction. Within a few years, pethidine was second only to morphine in terms of the number of dependent users recorded in Commonwealth statistics. As late as 1967, by which time cannabis use had increased markedly and accounted for sixty-one 'detected drug addicts' in Australia, there were fifty-eight morphine addicts noted in the Commonwealth government's Annual Report to the United Nations, compared with thirty-seven pethidine addicts. By contrast, there were only six recorded heroin and two cocaine users. Governments' faith in the ability of law and medicine to control drug use had once again proved ill-founded.[16]

The factors that led to the proclamation of pethidine around Australia were repeated time and again with other drugs through the late 1940s and

1950s. Heptalgin was another drug recommended for control as a narcotic by the Health Committee, although there was no evidence of use or addiction in Australia. Again, however, the moment two users were discovered all objections dissipated and the drug was promptly proclaimed, along with nine others like it. In most cases, there was not even any debate. As in the case of methadone, listed as a dangerous drug under State and Commonwealth law in 1948, the opinion of the Health Committee was in practice conclusive.[17]

The 1948 *Paris Protocol* entrenched this practice. Technically, the Health Committee could only recommend and advise governments. Under the Protocol, however, a declaration by the WHO that a new drug was 'liable to the same kind of abuse and productive of the same kind of harmful effects' as any drugs included in the 1931 *Geneva Convention* was binding, and the terms of the Convention thereafter automatically applied to it. Furthermore, while the WHO deliberated, the CND could decide to apply the Convention to such drugs provisionally. For parties to this Protocol, the categorisation of a new substance as a 'dangerous drug' was no longer their decision.[18] In reality, however, the Protocol was not a radical change: Australia had always conformed to the international community in any event.

By these means, the number of controlled drugs in Australia expanded steadily and without question. The original *Police Offences Amendment (Drugs) Act 1927* (NSW) controlled morphine, cocaine, ecgonine, heroin and their salts, opium, and preparations containing 0.2 per cent morphine or 0.1 per cent ecgonine, cocaine or heroin. By 1959, two proclamations before the war and fifteen after it had included an additional fifty-eight synthetics, derivatives and substitutes, as well as their salts and preparations. Part 1 of the Sixth Schedule to the Victorian *Poisons Act 1958*, arranged differently, listed seventy drugs plus their salts and preparations.[19]

The Cold War

While the *Paris Protocol* was only a slight change, the *Opium Protocol* of 1953 was more significant. Effective control of the cultivation of opium had long been a pet ambition of the United States, in keeping with its belief that the best way to stop drug addiction was to suppress the supply of drugs, not to try to modify the demand for them. The United States sought to establish an international opium monopoly that would restrict opium growing to a small number of countries, set production quotas and fix the price—a similar scheme, for the cultivation of opium, to that which had been established in 1931 with respect to its manufacture. But many countries were not enamoured of this suggestion, and in 1951 the CND concluded that 'present circumstances make the establishment of an international opium monopoly ... difficult for the time being'. The Protocol that finally emerged was a compromise. Cultivation was limited to seven traditional opium-growing countries, but no international monopoly was created. Further, over-production of opium was to be prevented not by the imposition of quotas but by the indirect means of restricting the stocks of opium able to be kept on hand by any country.[20]

Nevertheless, with the signing of the 1953 Protocol (ratified by twenty-seven countries including Australia) all stages in the legal opium trade from germination to consumption were now subject to international law. Symbolically, too, the 1953 Protocol, together with those of 1946 and 1948, reflected the triumph of prohibitionism on the international stage, and the increasing power of the United States to control the direction of policy. No longer hamstrung by an isolationist foreign policy, the United States was a vigorous member of the UN and all its agencies. Through the 1950s, the United States's shrill rhetoric about the evils of illegal drug use dominated the actions and statements of all the relevant international organisations as never before.

At the heart of this rhetoric sat Harry Anslinger, the formulator of, spokesman for, and personification of United States drug policy for over thirty years. He was a cop who started out enforcing alcohol prohibition in the roaring twenties and ended up enforcing drug prohibition into the swinging sixties. Anslinger became an expert simply by the constant and emphatic repetition of his opinions. His speeches and articles, often ignorant and frequently hateful, appeared in every major newspaper and relevant journal in the world. But during the 1950s, America's anti-drug campaign was accompanied and intensified by a twin paranoia which warped public debate in the United States for years: communism. The fear of 'drugs' and the fear of 'communism' had much in common. Both were 'pathogens', agents deemed responsible for everything bad. In both cases, the larger the lie, the more emotional and sweeping the language used to justify it; the more vague the accusation, the more successful it became in by-passing people's rationality and appealing directly to their visceral fears and needs. Senator Joe McCarthy was the front man, but behind him, working in tandem towards similar obsessive ends, were the those twin bureaucratic zealots of conformity, the FBI's J. Edgar Hoover and the FBN's Harry Anslinger.

The fear of drugs was used to justify anti-communist extremism and the fear of communism was used to justify anti-drug extremism. In congressional debates on the drastic legislation enacted in those years to suppress illegal drug use—the death penalty, for example, could be imposed in some cases—the drug trade was claimed to be part of a 'pattern of Communist narcotic aggression' and a 'Red China' conspiracy.[21] International drug control organisations were subjected to the same propaganda. From 1952 Anslinger, United States representative on the CND from its inception until 1957, and then again from 1962, regularly spoke of heroin trafficking as

a deliberate policy which was being followed by Communist China as a means of earning foreign exchange and of undermining the morale and health of the population of other countries.

The Chinese policy, which aimed to 'spread addiction', was contrasted with the policies endorsed by the United States and other 'free countries'.[22] The rhetoric of prohibitionism and anti-communism were intertwined.

In Australia, while our politics and culture drifted more and more into America's sphere of influence, the link between communism and drugs was never made, simply because the drug problem continued to be of only minor importance. There was no cold war on drugs in Australia. But the FBN's articles, pamphlets and reports were widely circulated and Anslinger was acknowledged to be the 'world recognised authority on the illicit drug traffic'.[23] Indeed, myths about the evil drug user and pusher, which the United States peddled around the world, were in fact all the more readily accepted in Australia because there was no local experience to compare with it and few local users to object to it. Australians were therefore indoctrinated with stories of communist heroin traffickers and depraved marijuana smokers for a generation before there was any significant illegal use of these drugs in Australia at all. It is not surprising that their appearance in the 1960s provoked anger and fear. Fairy-tales learnt as children can affect the thoughts of adults.

In particular, the attitude of Australians to cannabis was shaped by United States mythology. The very use of the name 'marijuana', in preference to cannabis or Indian hemp, or hashish or ganja, reflected the fact that in the United States it was associated with Mexicans, exactly as opium smoking had been associated with the Chinese in Australia in the 1890s. More specifically, Anslinger frequently claimed that cannabis was associated in some vague and unspeakable way with sexual perversion. In the 1930s, FBN pamphlets like 'Marijuana—Weed of Madness' were full of such suggestions. At the 1956 congressional hearings on the Narcotic Drugs Control Act (US), Anslinger agreed that marijuana was responsible for 'many of our most sadistic, terrible crimes in this Nation, such as sex slayings'.[24]

These stories first filtered into Australia before the war. In 1938, the Daily Telegraph in Sydney wrote about an 'evil drug ... blamed recently in America for many sex crimes'. *Smith's Weekly*, similarly relying on information obtained from the FBN, reported that

the [marijuana] addict becomes at times almost an uncontrollable sex-maniac, able to obtain satisfaction only from the most appalling of perversions and orgies.

The link soon became incontrovertible. A 1952 editorial in the *Australian Journal of Pharmacy*, which discussed the importance of pharmacy in modern life, pointed out that the chemist was entitled 'to hand out the "sex drug" so often referred to by some newspapers, with which he alone is familiar'. Everyone knew what the 'sex drug' was; it was not necessary even to mention it by name. The New South Wales Colonial Secretary's Department kept a file marked simply 'Sale of sex drugs. Press cuttings re'.[25]

In the light of this propaganda, laws against cannabis continued to be passed, although its use in Australia was almost unknown. In 1940, following a recommendation of the Health Committee, itself influenced by a United States memorandum concerning 'the alarming influence of addiction to Indian hemp on the development of criminality', the Commonwealth agreed to extend the import controls exercised over Indian hemp and its extract and tincture, to include also preparations made using it. Then in 1956 the Commonwealth absolutely prohibited the importation of cannabis into Australia: it was removed from the same schedule as morphine and placed with opium prepared for smoking.[26] At the time this was seen as a minor change because its use was so uncommon. Indeed, the first case in Australia of an illegal cannabis crop was heard only in 1957. A Queensland man was convicted of importing cannabis seeds, described in Sydney's *Truth* as 'the notorious sex drug, marijuana'. 'Greek migrant's sex drug fine' blazed the *Daily Telegraph's* headline.[27] Unusual as marijuana was, the mythology about the 'sex drug' flourished, an introduced plant putting down powerful roots in the domestic soil.

US and International Influences: The Prohibition of Heroin 1949–1955

Only once did the changes wrought by international opinion and growing United States authority meet any resistance within Australia. The issue led to the most important drug debate in Australia during the 1950s, which concerned the prohibition of heroin. The obsessive war on heroin engaged in by the United States and the FBN had, in time, borne fruit. In 1949 the WHO's Expert Committee on Drugs Liable to Produce Addiction declared that 'the disappearance of diacetylmorphine [heroin] from world markets could only be considered as a boon and a step in the right direction'; calls for its prohibition from other bodies, like ECOSOC and the CND, became more frequent and strident.[28]

Yet Australia's legal heroin consumption continued to rise. In Finland, consumption declined from 25.54 kilograms per one million people in 1946, to 4.49 kilograms per million in 1951. In the United Kingdom, another significant user, it averaged 2.22 kilograms throughout this period, while in New Zealand the figure fell to 2.06 kilograms. In Australia, on the other hand, the figure was 2.42 kilograms per million in 1946, 4.3 kilograms in 1949 and 5.25 kilograms, the highest in the world, in 1951. While elsewhere diacetylmorphine was being dispensed with, in Australia it was still being dispensed.[29]

In 1949 the PCOB discussed the 'alarming increase' in the use of heroin in a number of countries, singling out Finland, Italy, New Zealand, Sweden and Australia. The publication of consumption figures from 1946 to 1951 in a 'Special Issue Dealing with Heroin' of the United Nations' *Bulletin on Narcotics*, caused a further outcry. The matter was raised at the next meeting of the CND, and a letter from the Secretary of the PCOB to the Prime

Minister sought an explanation.[30]

In response, A.J. Metcalfe set out the Australian position in an explanatory statement issued by Australia's UN delegation in 1949, and another sent to the Expert Committee on Drugs in 1950:

> *The consumption of heroin in Australia is high by comparison with other countries but it does not follow that addiction is more common in this country than in any other ... Heroin is commonly used in Australia as an ingredient in cough mixtures ... The small permissible dose used for this purpose is unlikely to cause addiction but does cause increased national consumption.*

As Metcalfe indicated, in some States preparations containing heroin were only listed as 'dangerous drugs' if they contained more than 0.1 per cent heroin. Cough mixtures, other proprietary drugs and chemists' preparations with less than 0.1 per cent heroin therefore did not require a prescription and were available over the counter. It is doubtful, however, whether this anomaly alone could explain Australia's high level of consumption. In 1951 only seven out of the fifty-two kilograms of heroin imported into Australia were used in proprietary medicines.[31]

In Victoria regulations were amended in 1949 to prohibit the use of heroin in proprietary medicines, but this only applied to drugs manufactured in the State. The Pharmacy Board proposed uniform national action to list as 'dangerous drugs' all preparations containing any amount of heroin. In 1952 the Victorian government had the question listed for discussion at the Premiers' Conference. The response was underwhelming. Queensland and South Australia, which already controlled all heroin preparations, were not interested in national action, while New South Wales was 'satisfied with the existing control of the sale of heroin'. The question was removed from the agenda and Victoria was forced to act unilaterally.[32]

Certainly in 1952 no State, not even Victoria, proposed the total prohibition of heroin. The Director-General of Health in New South Wales said that 'Heroin ... is quite effectively controlled in this State and ... I see no justification to enforce absolute prohibition'; the Australian Federal Council of the British Medical Association (BMA)—which later became the Australian Medical Association, one of the most powerful lobby groups in the country—likewise insisted in September 1952 that there 'should be no curtailment of its availability'. This was not surprising. The addition of a substance to the list of dangerous drugs enhanced medical power. But heroin was already on that list, already exclusively controlled by doctors. It was frequently prescribed in childbirth, for the treatment of intractable pain, and in cases of terminal cancer, where its efficacy was and still is unparalleled; it is a much stronger pain-reliever than morphine and, unlike morphine, leaves the patient awake and alert. Prohibition would prevent these uses; it was a proposed drug law which, for the first time, was contrary to the interests of the medical profession. On the other hand, as Metcalfe stated in 1950, 'cases of addiction in Australia [were] rare'.³³ Why then should heroin be prohibited? Its use in Australia was not problematic.

The Commonwealth government, meanwhile, was typically sensitive to the 'embarrassment' being caused to its international reputation. A departmental 'Inquiry into Narcotic Control in Australia' was held by the Commonwealth's Senior Pharmacist, R. Cunningham, in 1952. Cunningham criticised the lack of uniform legislation on heroin in Australia, 'inadequate' drug inspections, and the fact that preparations containing less than 0.1 per cent heroin were not controlled in some States. Remedying these deficiencies did not require prohibition, but Cunningham was swayed by two factors. First, he was aware of the international pressure to which Australia was being subjected. Second, he was influenced by the myths of drug addiction propagated by the FBN. His assertion (in a memo later that year) that experts favoured the discontinuance of the use of heroin was based almost exclusively on a reading of United States sources. In the report of his inquiry, he stated that heroin addicts displayed 'an utter disregard for the conventions and morals of civilization'. Even were this the case, it is hard to see its relevance. The issue in Australia (as opposed to the United States) was not illegal addiction, which was insignificant, but whether heroin had a legitimate role in medical practice. But Cunningham, confusing the two, concluded that 'serious consideration be given to complete prohibition in medical practice'.³⁴

Public debate also confused the Australian issue with American fears. A member of the newly formed Victorian Drug Bureau was reported as saying that 'on a population basis Australia has the biggest illicit drug trade in the world', simply because the very high levels of drug importation 'could not have been used legitimately'. This was nonsense. No one had ever suggested, and the Commonwealth government consistently denied, that Australia's levels of drug consumption were a function of illegal use.³⁵

The Commonwealth acted quickly and unilaterally. In May 1953, claiming to have consulted various health authorities including the National Health and Medical Research Council (NH&MRC), the Commonwealth advised State Premiers that the importation of heroin was to be absolutely prohibited. In fact, consultation had been a sham. The NH&MRC refused to consent to the abolition of heroin and only agreed to seek further advice from the BMA and the Royal Australian Colleges of Surgeons, of Physicians, and of Obstetricians and Gynaecologists. But Metcalfe wrote to them directly, asking that they give 'sympathetic consideration' to prohibition. Put that way, the Federal Council of the BMA reneged on the opinion it had expressed only six months earlier and, after consulting with the Branch Councils of each State, indicated its acquiescence to the Commonwealth's position in March 1953. That was enough consultation for Metcalfe. He did not even wait for the other bodies to reply, but immediately wrote to the Comptroller-General of Customs asking him to prepare the relevant proclamation. The Royal Australian College of Physicians replied in early April and the Royal College of Obstetricians and Gynaecologists in May. Both bodies clearly believed that 'the use of heroin should not be prohibited', but Metcalfe was not interested. He wrote back to the Royal Australian College of Physicians thanking them for their letter, without letting them know that the Commonwealth had decided to act contrary to their advice, let alone that it had not even bothered to wait to hear their point of view before acting. The new proclamation went ahead regardless, and was gazetted on 25 June. Heroin, like opium prepared for smoking, could no longer be imported into Australia for any purpose. A month later the Royal Australian College of Surgeons replied to Metcalfe's letter, agreeing to the ban.[36] It was rather like opening the gate after the horse had bolted.

The letter to the States of May 1953, as well as notifying them of a change in Commonwealth law, sought uniform action on the part of State governments to prohibit the domestic manufacture of heroin immediately and, once the stocks of the drug that had been imported prior to the Commonwealth ban had run down, to prohibit its use and possession altogether. Without such complementary legislation the Commonwealth would have been placed in the ludicrous position of prohibiting the importation of a product that it was legal to possess and sell. As the letter explained, Commonwealth policy was a response to international opinion, and State co-operation was required to carry it out.

The publicity given to the decision once again emphasised the dangers of addiction and illegal use—issues irrelevant to the conditions of heroin use in Australia. The *Sydney Morning Herald*, for example, in an article which appeared in December 1954 headed 'Heroin Ban Will Aid NSW Fight Against Drug Addiction', reported that

Heroin, the most vicious drug of addiction known to man, will be banned in NSW ... The Act is expected radically to alter the statistics that, until recently, showed Australia to have the world's highest rate of heroin consumption.

Readers were thus led to believe that heroin was to be banned because of its use by addicts, and that Australia's high levels of heroin use reflected high levels of addiction.[37]

The Commonwealth's decisive action put maximum pressure on the States to bend with the wind. The *Poisons (Heroin) Act 1953* (Vic.), which prohibited the manufacture and preparation of heroin (but not its possession) in Victoria, was described as an 'interim measure', a 'gesture' to appease the Commonwealth Government. As the Victorian Minister of Health, W.P. Barry, explained:

It can be seen that in presenting this Bill, we, in Victoria, are observing the request of the Commonwealth Government and the United Nations Organization.[38]

By October 1953 all States had consented to the prohibition of manufacture either by agreeing not to grant any manufacturing licences, as in Queensland and South Australia, or by preparing specific legislation on the subject, as in the other States. New South Wales acted even more decisively. Its Director-General of Health, Dr H.J. Wallace, proved as easily convinced by the dogmatism of others as the Commonwealth had always been. Although he had stated in April 1952 that he could 'see no justification to enforce absolute prohibition', by June 1953 he had become 'strongly of the opinion that prohibition of [the] use or possession of heroin ... should be adopted'. The *Police Offences Amendment (Drugs) Act 1954* (NSW), made it an offence not only to manufacture but to prepare, sell, distribute, supply, deal, possess or use heroin for any purpose, with or without a medical prescription.[39] In New South Wales (and by similar legislation in Western Australia), heroin, like opium prepared for smoking, became an outlaw drug.

Only at this stage did any opposition from the medical profession emerge. In the United Kingdom, opposition to a similar regulation emerged just in time. Knighted surgeons and benighted patients alike wrote to the *Times* calling the ban variously 'foolish and immoral' and 'rather stupid'. The *Times* itself editorialised that heroin addiction in Britain, as in Australia, was 'an evil of microscopic proportions', and characterised those who still wished to use it, especially in the treatment of terminal illness, as 'law-abiding, stricken and suffering men and women'. Debate in the House of Lords was heated, Lord Jowitt calling the prohibition 'a grievous mistake', while Lord Haden-Guest, on the other hand, insisted, with all the compassion of his class, that 'there has been too much sob stuff about relief of pain'. Finally, however, the United Kingdom reversed its decision and allowed the medical prescription of heroin to continue.[40] The tradition established by the Rolleston Report continued.

In Australia the balance of power had changed. Australia no longer followed Great Britain's every step. Letters of complaint from doctors only began to appear in the newspapers over a year after the enactment of the *Police Offences Amendment (Drugs) Act 1954* (NSW). 'NSW Ban On Heroin May Cause Suffering' proclaimed the *Sydney Morning Herald*. The tabloids were rather more melodramatic: the *Daily Mirror* claimed that eighty per cent of doctors opposed 'the inhumane heroin ban'; and, according to the *Sun*:

in the opinion of an overwhelming majority of medical men ... the political decision was more than a major mistake. They claim it was a blunder that is causing indescribable agony.[41]

Those who had originally supported the ban simply because of Commonwealth pressure now found themselves under pressure from a different quarter. The New South Wales Director General of Health, Dr Wallace, explained that prohibition '*presumably* ... was a case of sacrificing the needs of the few for the good of the many'—as if he had had nothing to do with the New South Wales law. The Federal Council of the BMA, and its

Branch Councils, were accused of having decided the matter without consulting their constituents. A spokesman for the Northern Branch commented that 'the Government has only blindly followed the lead of the United States'. When, in 1956, the Federal Council held a plebiscite of doctors and State branches, only Western Australia expressed itself in favour of continuing the ban. The BMA again reversed its decision and the *Sydney Morning Herald*, although castigating it for being 'unduly tardy', applauded, concluding that the government had been over-influenced by the WHO and had not paid enough attention either to the lack of heroin addiction in Australia or to the opinion of the medical profession.[42]

In the face of medical opposition, the New South Wales and Commonwealth governments both agreed to 'consider modifying the ban on the drug heroin'.[43] But the protests had been too little, too late. In fact, at this stage the Commonwealth was never likely to renege on its policy of prohibition. On the one hand, Australia's international reputation was at stake and, on the other hand, the United States mythology of drug addiction had taken too firm a hold. Neither were State governments ever likely to take a stand on a subject on which they had, throughout, shown only a willingness to do as they were told.

Some States, which had been less hasty than New South Wales and Western Australia, were able to act more cautiously. In early 1955 South Australia enacted a law allowing for the proclamation of 'prohibited drugs', which it would be an offence to manufacture, sell or possess under any circumstances. This was clearly aimed at heroin, but in March 1956 the government 'decided to defer for the time being the matter of recommending the complete prohibition of the drug'. Queensland similarly prohibited the manufacture but not the possession of heroin.[44]

Victoria, which alone had proposed heroin law reform in 1952, in fact did more than any State to reverse the effect of the ban. The extremely vigorous protests of a number of institutions and doctors, including Sir William Refshauge, future Commonwealth Director-General of Health and at that time Medical Superintendent at the Royal Women's Hospital, had some effect. The doctors at the hospital were 'ropeable' at the ban, and while the Premier indicated that 'his hands were tied' in regard to the prohibition of manufacture, the legal status of the possession of heroin in Victoria was not altered. It could, as before, be legally possessed if it was medically prescribed. Furthermore, a substantial quantity of heroin was stockpiled by hospitals prior to the Commonwealth's import ban, and the government decided that it was 'not necessary at this juncture to impose any further ban upon the rather limited use to which heroin may be put in Victoria at present'. A number of major hospitals in Victoria continued to prescribe heroin in rare cases of intractable pain throughout the 1950s and 1960s.[45]

None the less, the prohibition upon importation and manufacture effectively prevented the legal use of heroin in Australia. Its occasional use in Victoria apart, even in States where it could still be legally prescribed, it was not legally obtainable. Under the pretext of wiping out illegal use, legal use had been suppressed. In the policy of absolute prohibition, and in the rhetoric about addiction and illegality which constituted its public face, Australia was being steadily drawn into the sphere of influence of the United States. But already the legislation was creating its own reality. The controversy surrounding its enactment was quickly forgotten and the myths of addiction seemed confirmed by the legislation which reflected them. By the time recreational heroin use began to develop in Australia a decade or so later, the status of heroin as a drug apart was well entrenched, and the status of heroin users as pariahs likewise assured.

Drug Use in the Late 1950s

The changes that we have seen, important as they were, did not alter the basic structure of legislation or the demography of drug use in Australia. Little seemed capable of stirring or redirecting the complex system of drug controls developed prior to the Second World War. Australia's commitment to the developing international framework of drug controls was absolute, although it carried out its responsibilities with little enthusiasm. The quarterly statistics submitted to the PCOB were often carelessly compiled: in the first quarter of 1952, for example, every single figure originally calculated by the Department of Trade and Customs proved wrong. A departmental officer complained the following year, 'the Permanent Central Opium Board has been pointing out discrepancies in Australian statistics with monotonous regularity'. Nothing improved. The 1954 statistical return was so badly put together that the government hastily withdrew and rewrote it.[46]

There was no motivation to resist international pressure either. Australia continued to do as it was told. In 1956, for example, Victoria limited the cultivation of narcotic plants 'at the request of the United Nations Organisation, made through the Commonwealth Government'. 'In other words,' said one speaker, 'there is no local problem, but it is desirable that the request of the organization be acceded to.'[47]

There seemed no reason to resile from the degree and nature of control that had recently emerged and hardened: the legislative structures—proscription and prescription, and heavy penalties—were settled policy; bureaucratic arrangements for the administration of State, Commonwealth and international law were established, detailed, and rarely altered. Regulations issued under the *Police Offences Amendment (Drugs) Act 1927* (NSW), for example, which dealt with such matters as licences and authorities to manufacture, distribute, possess and prescribe the drugs covered by the Act, although amended from time to time and new drugs added by proclamation, were not replaced, rewritten or reissued from 1935 to 1967.[48]

Commonwealth attempts at reform met with similar lethargy. The Commonwealth Director-General of Health proposed either the enactment of Commonwealth legislation to cover the field of dangerous drugs, or the development of uniform laws to be passed by the States, as early as 1949, a suggestion supported by Cunningham's inquiry in 1952. Nevertheless, although the NH&MRC developed a model Act and regulations that year, the States were not interested in adopting them. 'Only SA replied,' wrote one disgruntled official, 'The rest have no intention of doing anything unless continual pressure is applied.' Draft uniform poisons schedules were produced in 1955. Schedule 4 included 'prescription poisons' such as barbituric acid and chloral hydrate; schedule 8 was headed 'Drugs of Addiction' and was to include 'all those drugs listed under International Conventions as dangerous drugs, narcotics or drugs of addiction'. If every State adopted these schedules, a step towards uniformity would have been achieved. Still the States dragged their feet, each holding out for the number and structure of schedules most like their own, insisting that only the other States should change. They appointed sub-committees and advisory bodies of their own: the bureaucratic wheels rolled on inexorably.[49]

Behind the words of the law, patterns of drug use also continued relatively unchanged. The cocaine trade, which had improved the circulation of many a newspaper in the late 1920s, had subsided, or at least disappeared underground. Chinese opium smoking continued to dominate the work of law enforcement officials: occasional shipments of prepared opium were interdicted by Customs officers, and the opium dens of Dixon Street and Little Bourke Street were raided from time to time. In 1951, to take a typical year, the Customs officials made fifty-four seizures. Of those charged, all were Chinese except one retired nurse who was found dead, and three crewhands on ships in port at Sydney Harbour. The rest were either the Chinese crew of visiting ships, or local Chinese, who were almost always over fifty-five years old, some as old as eighty. The Chinese were persecuted and prosecuted for their habit as some of them had been for nigh on fifty years. But their numbers were ageing and dwindling. In 1961 George Toong, an eighty-nine-year-old Chinese market gardener, was fined £10 for smoking opium. It had been his habit for sixty-seven years, but he gave it up in shame. According to government records, by 1958 there were twenty-four 'known' Chinese opium users left in Victoria, and sixty-four in Queensland.[50]

During the 1950s, the number of convictions for illegal opiate and cocaine use, never high, stabilised at a low level. As the Commonwealth government noted in its 1955 Annual Report, provided in accordance with its obligations under the 1931 Convention, and again in virtually identical language the three succeeding years,

apart from opium and an occasional seizure of Indian Hemp, there is virtually no illicit trafficking or peddling in narcotic drugs in Australia except in respect of small quantities diverted from legitimate trade channels.

The Annual Report for 1957, for example, noted that only thirty-three people had been charged with illegal possession of drugs and only nine with offences connected with illegal trafficking. In New South Wales and Victoria an average of around seventy prosecutions for breaches of State drug laws were mounted annually.[51]

These were the law-breakers. As in the period before the war, many drug dependent persons continued to be routinely supplied with prescriptions to satisfy their drug addiction. The Comptroller-General of Customs, F.A. Meere, wrote to *National Geographic* in 1955 that

very few addicts other than opium addicts obtain their drugs from illicit sources. Most addicts to refined drugs obtain their supplies under medical supervision.

Numbers varied little from year to year. In the fiscal year 1957–58, forty-three such cases were noted in Victoria, forty-one in Queensland, twenty-nine in New South Wales, three in Tasmania and two in South Australia. Indeed, these statistics on 'known addicts' to 'narcotic drugs', taken from the Commonwealth's Annual Reports, dealt only with medically controlled and legally permitted addiction. Figures concerning Chinese opium use were given separately because, with its overtones of vice and non-medical use, this was clearly considered an exception to the norm of legal and medical control.[52]

The majority of these addicts were over fifty years old, and almost none were under thirty-five. As before, they were middle-class 'therapeutic addicts' whose drug use had begun as a result of extended treatment with morphine for an illness or chronic condition. Professions with access to drugs were over-represented: in the twenty-year period up to 1954, for example, out of a total of 204 people brought to the attention of the New South Wales police as drug addicts, there were thirty-two doctors, two chemists and forty nurses. The other States reflected a similar pattern of addiction into the 1960s. With the exception of Queensland, which claimed that no doctors were 'known addicts' (almost half its known addicts were listed as 'housewives'), over one-third of the drug addicts noted in the States' reports to the Commonwealth for inclusion in the Annual Reports were medical and allied professionals.[53]

The maintenance of 'normal', so-called 'therapeutic addicts' was not seriously challenged during the 1950s, but the extent to which it was institutionalised varied. The Commonwealth, through the Model Dangerous Drugs Act and Regulations drafted by the NH&MRC, and circulated to all States in 1954 and 1958, urged States to prohibit the supply of a 'dangerous drug' to a 'drug addict' except with express government approval. In practice, however, bureaucratic control was neither consistent nor comprehensive. The Commonwealth Department of Health continued, as the Attorney-General's Department had put it in 1938, 'to interest itself in such cases'. But the Department's constitutional position was 'not a strong one' and its involvement was therefore limited to ensuring that users were not supplied with excessive doses or by multiple suppliers.[54]

In New South Wales and Victoria, the question of prescribing drugs of addiction for the purpose of 'maintenance' was simply left to the discretion of the medical practitioner involved. The Premier of New South Wales explained in 1947 that 'there is no power that they shall institute disintoxication [sic] ... At best they may become stabilised on a certain dose.' Maintenance was not controlled by the government, but was left to doctors.[55]

In contrast to this *laissez-faire* approach, the prescription of narcotic drugs to addicted persons under South Australian and Queensland law required the approval of the State Health departments. Thus the Queensland Poisons Regulations specifically acknowledged and provided for 'treating a drug addict [with] rational supplies of any dangerous drug ... at [the Director-General's] discretion'.[56] In South Australia, only two or three cases at any one time were dealt with in this way, but in Queensland the maintenance of addiction was common and systematised, and addicts registered and monitored. Opiate maintenance was carried out under bureaucratic supervision and stamped with bureaucratic legitimacy.

This reflected in part the power of the Queensland health bureaucracy. The *Health Act 1937* (Qld), one section and six sub-sections long, had been the shortest and most incomplete 'drug Act' in the country. Until 1946, for example, medical practitioners did not have to account for any dangerous drugs obtained for self-administration. In the following twenty years, not only were various inconsistencies with the laws of other States remedied, but the Queensland Act became in many ways a model. By the late 1950s, when moves began to devise uniform Poisons Schedules which would be consistent from jurisdiction to jurisdiction, the schedules to the *Health Act* (Qld) were taken as the model.[57] This thoroughness was a function of the integration of drug policy and administration solely within one department. In Queensland, the Department of Health was in a position of unfettered authority. In contrast, New South Wales drug laws were administered by the Colonial Secretary, Commonwealth responsibilities were mainly handled by the Department of Customs, while in Victoria, administration was split between two bodies, the Pharmacy Board and the Department of Health. In each of these jurisdictions control was either divided, or exercised by a body not committed to health matters. While the New South Wales Director General of Public Health, H.G. Wallace, therefore believed that 'only when the restraints imposed by an institution are present can such treatment [maintenance] be satisfactorily given, the Health department in that State did not have the power to enforce its vision.[58]

The exclusive authority of the Queensland Department of Health led to the triumph of the medical model of addiction in that State, and the institutionalisation, more than anywhere else in Australia, of a system of drug maintenance which reflected medical and bureaucratic power. Elsewhere, there were sniping attacks on the legal maintenance of addiction. 'Addiction,' wrote one member of the Department of Trade and Customs, underlining it for effect, 'is not a medical need.'[59] Such criticism did not succeed in preventing medical practitioners from freely prescribing morphine, pethidine, and so on to their patients, but they did ensure that the system was not further legitimised. But in Queensland, with no counter-balance to medical authority, legal maintenance flourished and was institutionalised.

Even more remarkably, this institutionalisation extended beyond so-called 'therapeutic addicts'. Some time after the end of the Second World War, it was decided that the few ageing Chinese opium smokers left in the State should be incorporated within the framework of legal drug use. Since opium prepared for smoking was, of course, illegal to possess, use or import, these Chinese users were legally supplied with tincture of opium (laudanum) as a substitute. By 1955, there were thirty-four Australians of European descent receiving morphine, pethidine, or, in a few cases, methadone, under the control of the Queensland government, and sixty-eight Chinese, all over the age of fifty. By 1960, although the number was gradually declining, forty-seven of the Chinese still remained.[60]

This was a tolerance breathtaking, if not for its boldness, then for its rarity. The wheel had come full circle. There had been many Chinese in Queensland in the years before the operation of the 'White Australia' policy: their opium use had been important in the enactment of the first opium laws in Australia, and the focus of the interdiction activities of the Commonwealth Department of Trade and Customs between the wars. Now, having been hounded for over half a century, the Chinese were finally left in peace—not because of any new understanding of opium, but simply because they were no longer a threat. As the Comptroller-General of Customs had predicted in his 1908 report on opium, the elimination of opium smoking had been effected by the *Immigration Restriction Act* (Cwlth), and not the *Aboriginals Protection and Restriction of the Sale of Opium Act*. Sympathy for its last few victims was, after all, merely the prerogative of a gracious victor.

The actual effect of this policy on criminality is difficult to determine. But certainly the government attributed the very low levels of illegal drug use in Queensland to the maintenance programme legally available to all addicted persons. In the 1958 Annual Report submitted by the State to the Commonwealth, the Queensland Director-General of Health wrote that 'all addicts receive their supplies from licit sources ... and as a consequence, control presents no difficulties'. Written with typical self-confidence, the Department was not exaggerating. From 1956 to 1965, only two cases of trafficking in or illegal possession of dangerous drugs were prosecuted in Queensland—one involved a visiting Greek sailor in 1957 and the other was the result of a police raid of a party in 1963. In 1965 the Under Secretary of the Department of Health complained that despite the best efforts of the Criminal Investigation Branch to uncover an illicit traffic in narcotics, 'no information has been received, and no bona fide complaints made'.[61] Even by comparison with the low levels of illegality prevalent in Australia as a whole, the Queensland situation was remarkable.

In the 1990s a proposal for the legal supply of heroin to users is likely to be met with uncertainty at best and downright hostility at worst. Yet not so long ago the legal maintenance of opiate users under medical supervision was the norm, in Queensland and around Australia. Such a scheme is often called 'the British system', a phrase which suggests a safe distance in time and place from the Australian context and denies any parallel development here. But well into the 1960s 'the British system' was the Australian system.

The Single Convention on Narcotic Drugs 1961

The effect of the expansion of control to large numbers of new drugs, of the prohibition of heroin, and of the maintenance of addicts, was to confirm a deep division between legal, medical drug use and illegal, non-medical abuse. Drugs that fell on the wrong side of this division were now commonly known as 'narcotics'. The United Nations created a Division of Narcotic Drugs, and the Advisory Committee on the Traffic in Opium (outdated and unfashionable word) was replaced by the Commission on Narcotic Drugs. Not all 'dangerous drugs' were in fact narcotics, but the term implied there was a medical commonality which justified the similar legal treatment of this congeries of substances. In a similar spirit of circularity, delegates to the 1954 meeting of the CND argued that 'drug addiction' should be defined as 'the illicit use of substances covered by international treaties on narcotic drugs'.[62] 'Narcotic drugs' were anything defined as such; addiction was a function not of the nature or extent of use, but of its legal status.

As 'narcotics' became increasingly evil, non-'narcotics' became, by contrast, good and safe. Restrictions imposed on the sale of preparations containing aspirin, phenacetin and caffeine (APC), such as Bex tablets and Vincents' powders, were removed in Victoria in 1951 as they had been in New South Wales a few years previously. Although the addictive nature of APC powders was well known, the Victorian parliament was unconcerned. Mr Cook found it 'amusing' to hear members asserting that APCs were addictive, and most members agreed with Mr Barry that 'there is not much to be afraid of in an aspirin, an Aspro or an APC tablet'.[63]

As a cure-all for women who felt unwell or depressed, 'a Bex and a good lie down' was an Australian cultural tradition. It was a way to suppress women's feelings of alienation, an agency of their oppression, and an easy means of social control. Australians became the largest consumers of APC tablets and powders in the world—another chapter in our long history of extreme drug-taking—and in consequence had the highest incidence of renal disease in the world. Ready availability did not itself cause high levels of use. Rather, it was the attitude that lay behind this freedom: just as illegal drugs were unacceptable and bad, those that were legal to buy were considered to be good. 'Narcotic drugs' were seen to be the only drugs that were dangerous.

The 1950s were, in Australia, a time during which the status quo was entrenched. 'Dangerous drugs' were rarely on the public agenda. But as the 'peace against drugs' endured through cold war and prosperity, alternatives to the orthodoxy voiced by international organisations and the United States became increasingly unthinkable. The intolerant and inflexible attitude that characterised governments' response to burgeoning drug use in the 1960s was bred in the years of complacency that preceded it.

The international community and, increasingly, the United States, had been central to the development and reinforcement of this value system. In 1961 the signing of the *Single Convention on Narcotic Drugs* in New York epitomised the powerful international consensus behind those values and demonstrated the scope and detail of international drug control. Begun in 1949, it consolidated, replaced and substantially added to the nine prior international agreements concerning 'narcotic drugs'. The Convention established the International Narcotics Control Board (to replace the PCOB), the central role of which was, and remains, the administration of the estimates system, the setting of limits on licit world production of drugs covered by the treaty, and the enforcement of these limits. The CND, on the other hand, was a creature of the UN answerable to ECOSOC. It carried out, generally speaking, the role of policy formulation. In general, the Convention continued and still continues the structure of drug control established previously. Each party must provide to the Board annual estimates of and statistics relating to its drug requirements and use. Manufacture and importation by a country is to be kept 'within the limit of the relevant estimate', and every import and export requires a separate authorisation by the government of both countries involved. In accordance with the 1948 Protocol, the Convention may at any time be extended to any other substance upon the recommendation of the WHO and with the approval of the CND.[64]

The question of controls over production remained contentious. The *Single Convention* required an opium-producing country to notify the Board or ECOSOC of the amount to be produced, the production controls in place and 'the name of the country or countries to which it expects to export such opium', after which the relevant international body could approve of production or recommend against it. This was in many ways a weaker method of control than that established by the 1953 Protocol (which was never ratified by enough countries to bring it into effect). It allowed any country, including non-traditional producers, to produce opium as long as it first '[took] account of the prevailing world need for opium'. It did not apply to the manufacture of drugs from poppy straw at all. And it only allowed the Board or ECOSOC to 'recommend' against production. Accordingly, while many countries praised the Convention's 'flexibility', the United States declared that 'the entry into force of the 1953 Protocol would remove any reason for accepting the Single Convention'.[65]

Of course, the sight of the United States complaining about not getting its own way was by then familiar. On the whole the *Single Convention* established more detailed controls over the international and domestic drug trade than ever before. State parties had to 'require medical prescriptions for the supply or dispensation of drugs to individuals' and 'shall not permit the possession of drugs except under legal authority'. As in the 1936 Convention, which Australia never ratified, 'serious offences shall be liable to adequate punishment particularly by imprisonment or other penalties of deprivation of liberty'.[66]

Even more importantly, the Convention went further than ever in reflecting the United States's long-standing obsession with marijuana and heroin. Although the Convention did not absolutely prohibit heroin, it did place the drug in schedule IV. Most 'dangerous drugs' were included in schedule I. Schedules II and III listed a few drugs controlled slightly less rigorously. Schedule IV drugs, on the other hand, were subject to all the controls of the Convention, and in addition:

A Party shall adopt any special measures of control which in its opinion are necessary having regard to the particularly dangerous properties of a drug so included; and

A Party shall, if in its opinion the prevailing conditions in its country render it the most appropriate means of protecting the public health and welfare, prohibit the production, manufacture, export and import of, trade in, possession or use of any such drug ...

The only drugs in this schedule were ketobemidone, desomorphine, heroin, cannabis and cannabis resin.[67] Those who were to argue in years to come in favour of the medical use of heroin, the decriminalisation of cannabis, or even for a distinction to be made between the harmfulness of heroin and cannabis, now had the *Single Convention* to fight against. The particular evils of cannabis and heroin were enshrined.

Australia's signing of the Convention, and its ratification in 1967, tied Australia even more tightly to a system of control that had been steadily entrenched over many years. The *Single Convention* symbolised the orthodoxy that prevailed in the international community, the power that community exerted over Australian policy, and the strength of the United States within it. It was no mere pious expression of generalised platitudes and good intentions. It was the binding codification of Conventional wisdom.

This wisdom Australia adopted as its own. In contrast to the previous international agreements, Australia was actively involved in the development of the *Single Convention*; both State and Commonwealth governments considered the draft in detail, and a number of minor suggestions and changes were proposed by the Commonwealth. In particular, it successfully insisted that 'poppy straw should not be subject to controls as stringent as those applying to opium'.[68] From then on, Australian drug policy began to be developed not only in Geneva and New York, but in Canberra and Sydney. But domestic drug policy did not thereby break away from the norms of international law. Those norms had been too deeply embedded in our thinking for that. Conformity now no longer came from blind obedience but through deliberate choices, and the values that guided those choices had been firmly inculcated during the preceding years.

THE BALANCE OF POWER

*Political and Bureaucratic Rivalry
1962–1970*

The Beginnings of Change: NSW and Victorian Poisons Acts 1962–1966

The structure of drug laws stood, imposing, authoritative and unchallenged, begun in response to the prejudices of a different time, developed as an arm of medical power, and expanded under overseas influences. Few doubted the effectiveness of preventing harmful drug use by prescription, prohibition and penalties; few could even imagine an alternative. In fact, little illicit drug use tested the truth of these assumptions. Slowly, however, the static certainties of the past began to be undermined. Drug policy began to matter: politicians saw votes in it, bureaucracies saw power and prestige in its administration. Consensus was replaced by rivalry and as the profile of the debate was raised, the standard of debate was lowered.

The 1961 *Single Convention on Narcotic Drugs* stood as a symbol of the past, but also as a signpost to the future. The Commonwealth, influenced by the scope of its responsibilities under the Convention, immediately increased its involvement in State law. The National Health and Medical Research Council (NH&MRC), a Commonwealth institution, had been advocating since 1955 the adoption by the States of uniform poisons schedules in conformity with the system adopted by the Conventions and consistent from jurisdiction to jurisdiction. At the time, drugs listed in one schedule in one State (and therefore subject to certain controls and penalties) were often listed in a different schedule in another State (and subject to different controls). Now, the *Single Convention* gave a further impetus to reform. Faced with State laws which had been subject to only piecemeal reform over the years, the Commonwealth refused to ratify the Convention until the drug legislation of the States complied with it.

Victoria's Chief Health Officer, Kevin Brennan, conceded that the State's *Poisons Act* was 'disordered, outmoded and complex', while the President of the Victorian Pharmacy Board, Nigel Manning, described it as a relic of 'the horse and buggy days'. In 1962 Victoria thus became the first State to rewrite its Poisons Act. In 1960, New South Wales had agreed to adopt the uniform schedules and revise its legislation, but the defeat of the Labor government in 1965, after twenty-four years in power, delayed matters. None the less, the Bill introduced into parliament in 1966 was virtually identical to that drafted under the previous government, and was met with enthusiastic bipartisan support. 'I should have to be somewhat of a mental contortionist to indulge in such opposition [to the Bill],' said Labor's ex-Minister of Health, W. F. Sheehan, 'particularly since it has been so well and carefully drafted'. Drug policy clearly still remained the bailiwick of bureaucrats and not politicians.[1]

The general lines of these reforms were similar. The *Poisons Act 1962* (Vic.) and the *Poisons Act 1966* (NSW) adopted the NH&MRC's system of classification, schedule 4 being (in the words of the Victorian Act) 'substances ... restricted to medical, dental or veterinary prescription', while schedule 8, which included harsher penalties and specifically penalised unlawful possession, referred to addictive drugs 'including those so classified by the United Nations Organisation'. Unaltered since the turn of the century, the absolute prohibition on smoking opium, which forbade its possession by any person, was extended in both jurisdictions to include Indian hemp, and the penalty was increased from £250 or 12 months' imprisonment to up to £2000 or ten years' imprisonment or both (in New South Wales, $2000 and/or two years).²

In Victoria a new offence was created, under which 'every person who [illegally] prepares, manufactures, sells, or deals or traffics in' opium, Indian hemp or other drugs of addiction, was liable to a penalty of £2000 and/or ten years, as opposed to the penalty of £250 and/or twelve months for other offences such as the illegal possession of a drug of addiction. For the first time, the trafficker, whose evil had been central to the rhetoric about drug use since the 1920s, was singled out for special punishment. In New South Wales, on the other hand, a similar offence dealing specifically with drug trafficking applied to prepared opium, cannabis and 'prohibited drugs' (heroin)—all three absolutely prohibited in New South Wales—but not to drugs available only on a medical prescription. The maximum penalty provided for these offences was, moreover, no higher than the penalty for illegal possession. These distinctions and confusions made the New South Wales Act as difficult to follow as ever.³

Important changes also took place in the structure of administrative control. The Commonwealth government and the NH&MRC had recommended that 'narcotic drug administration ... be closely integrated into the Health Authority' of each State. In New South Wales, drug law had been administered as a police matter within the Colonial (later Chief) Secretary's Department since the enactment of the *Police Offences (Amendment) Act 1908* (NSW). Now the *Police Offences Amendment (Drugs) Act 1927–1954* (NSW) was repealed, and laws concerning 'drugs of addiction and prohibited drugs' were included within the New South Wales *Poisons Act* under the responsibility of the Minister of Health. The removal of opium from the *Poisons Act* in 1908 thus ended with its reincorporation in the Act of the same name almost sixty years later.⁴

The change also marked the final elimination of the New South Wales Pharmacy Board from the administration of the *Poisons Act*. The Department of Health had recommended the repeal of the *Police Offences Amendment (Drugs) Acts 1927–1954* (NSW) 'in order to adopt the proposed Uniform Poisons Schedules'. Cabinet likewise decided that it did not make sense to keep seven poison schedules in one Act, and schedule 8 elsewhere. But the inclusion of 'drugs of addiction' in the *Poisons Act 1966* (NSW) was used by the Health department to justify the removal of the Board's administrative functions in relation to other aspects of the Poisons Act, dating back to 1876.⁵ In 1934 it was decided that the Board's responsibilities for 'drug laws' should be taken away from it. It was now argued that the principle of 'unified control' required that the Department of Health manage the whole Act.

By adding to the Act an area of law from which the Pharmacy Board had already been removed, the Department of Health managed to take over the administration of the Act, despite the Board's protests and resentment. Its opposition to the change, which temporarily led to the withdrawal of the draft Act in 1962, was eventually ignored. The document submitted to Cabinet in 1963 by the Minister of Health, W. F. Sheehan (identical to the one submitted two years later by the new Liberal Minister, A.H. Jago), boldly asserted that 'the Pharmacy Board itself has suggested that this transfer should be made'.[6]

In Victoria, too, the Pharmacy Board's residual powers were taken over by the Victorian Department of Health. But the Victorian Pharmacy Board did not have the tradition of belligerence of its New South Wales counterpart, and went relatively quietly. The vestiges of an earlier era, when poisons laws were the private preserve of chemists, had been wiped out.[7]

What did these complex changes demonstrate? First, the growing influence of the Commonwealth over State policy and, in particular, its pressure for uniformity and institutionalisation. Despite the substantial reforms undertaken in New South Wales and Victoria, this pressure continued. In 1965 the Commonwealth wrote to every State government specifying the ways in which State legislation was seen to be inconsistent with the Convention, and emphasising in particular that each State's 'narcotic' or 'dangerous drug' schedule had to correspond with schedules I and IV of the *Single Convention*. Victoria's Senior Pharmacist, R.H. Borowski, bristled with irritation. 'Has the Commonwealth the power to take over the complete control of drugs of addiction in this State?' he fumed.[8]

Second, although Commonwealth influence and international law were important catalysts for reform, the States did not comply reluctantly. This represented a significant change from days gone by. The Departments of Health, in particular, seized enthusiastically the opportunities which these new trends offered to consolidate and increase their power at the expense of the pharmacy boards and police departments. Bureaucracies and politicians alike were beginning to see drug law and administration as a field of competition and power. The faint traceries of rivalry between Commonwealth and State governments, health and police departments, barely visible in the history of the new New South Wales and Victorian Poisons Acts, would soon be etched more clearly.

The Changing Face of Illegal Drug Use

The 1960s saw a rise in the consumption of prohibited drugs and drugs of addiction: the post-war baby-boomers were coming of age, restless and rebellious, resentful of authority and reckless of risk. New South Wales, with its large cosmopolitan capital on major Pacific and Asian trading routes, was the first State to begin to feel these changes. In 1960, for the first time, the New South Wales government's report to the Commonwealth for inclusion in the Annual Report by Australia to the CND noted some use of 'Indian hemp'. 'The parties concerned are invariably members of the theatrical world' and the problem 'has not reached a stage beyond control', it was noted. By 1966 New South Wales reported fifty-seven cannabis 'addicts', compared with twenty-four addicted to morphine, nine to pethidine, two to cocaine and three to heroin. These were not the ageing 'therapeutic addicts' of days gone by. The following year, the New South Wales government expressed concern about the use 'amongst young people' of amphetamines (247 charges were laid), barbiturates (171), cannabis (100) and LSD (66). Over ninety-three per cent of 'drug addicts' reported that year were thirty-four years old or less.[9]

We do not have to believe that these figures gave an accurate description of drug use in Australia to realise that both drug use and the way it was perceived were changing dramatically. The situation was further exacerbated with the arrival in Sydney in the late 1960s of large numbers of young, alienated United States soldiers on rest and recreational leave from service in the Vietnam War, who brought with them, attracted, consumed, sold, and gave away considerable quantities of cannabis and heroin. By any reckoning there was an explosion in the use of these substances and in related police activity. New South Wales police arrested nine people on charges relating to the use or possession of drugs of addiction or prohibited drugs in 1959, thirty-one in 1965, ninety-eight in 1966, and 1151 in 1972. Cannabis arrests alone rose almost 1000 per cent between 1966 and 1969.[10]

The situation elsewhere in Australia changed more slowly. In 1967 only eighty-six addicts (plus thirty-seven prepared-opium users) were recorded in all the other States combined. Sixty-one were 'therapeutic addicts', including nineteen medical and allied professionals and ten 'housewives'. Just over eighty-three per cent were over thirty-four years old. But within a few years, the trend established in New South Wales applied throughout Australia. By 1974 only 7.4 per cent of addicts reported in Victoria were over thirty-five years old. Even the way 'addicts' were categorised had changed. There were apparently no 'medical and allied professionals' addicted to dangerous drugs, and the categorisation 'housewife' had vanished altogether. The government instead now noted the number of 'students' and 'unemployed' people involved in drug use.[11]

The legal fiction that had operated so well to protect 'therapeutic addicts' was unable to cope with the changing demography of drug use. Morphine, pethidine, opium (and occasionally heroin) 'maintenance' had operated successfully in Australia because of the small number of people with which it had dealt. In most jurisdictions it had operated without direct government involvement and always without publicity. But increased drug use in the 1960s made the operation of a semi-secret treatment modality based on individual medical discretion impractical, and public awareness of drug use made treatment issues a matter of public debate. Pressure for the end of this ad hoc approach grew.

In Queensland in the 1940s the bureaucratic institutionalisation of maintenance had given it claims to legitimacy, but in the 1960s the appropriation of power from the medical profession by the organs of government in the other States made a marginal method of treatment much more visible. The new Poisons Acts enacted in New South Wales and Victoria brought the situation in those States broadly into line with Queensland and South Australian law, and with Commonwealth policy dating back to the NH&MRC's Model Dangerous Drugs Act. In New South Wales, for example, no drug of addiction could be prescribed for longer than two months, or to an addict for any length of time, without the authority of the Director-General on the advice of a Medical Committee.[12] The effect of these provisions around Australia was that the maintenance of any person by the prescription of a drug of addiction required the approval of State health departments.

Institutionalisation and increased use brought the system of maintenance out into the open. Maintenance might have continued, publicly accepted rather than covertly carried out. But various factors combined to make such an open scheme of legal drug use unworkable and unpopular. In the first place, neither heroin nor cannabis *could* be used in the medical maintenance of addiction since, like prepared opium, the Commonwealth prohibited their importation. In New South Wales the prescription of these drugs for any purpose was also illegal.[13] Furthermore, the medical profession argued that maintenance of addicts was a form of 'treatment' exactly because the drug was physically addictive and deprivation caused withdrawal symptoms. This approach was inapplicable and nonsensical in the case of cannabis.

Although legal maintenance in Australia had often extended beyond 'therapeutic addicts'—Chinese opium smokers were the clearest, but by no means the only, example—the fact that many users had *originally* taken their drug of addiction for medical purposes had always been an important part of the justification of the system. It proved that they were not to blame for their suffering. In addition, most legally maintained addicts in Australia had been middle class and middle aged: part of the system and subservient to it. Young cannabis and heroin users on the other hand were different. Their very youth at once branded them as potential rebels, with less of a stake in the capitalist system and external to the places of power. Their use was intentional and therefore an immediate affront to the rule of law; it was recreational and therefore a challenge to medical dominance over drugs. Their drug use challenged medico–legal drug control as the morphine-dependence of their parents never had.

As the legal addicts of the previous generation died out, young illegal drug users were not considered as candidates to replace them. Some legally maintained addicts remained in Victoria in 1968, but the following year the government reported that the forty-two permits issued to allow doctors to prescribe drugs of addiction 'were for use in the treatment of recognised medical diseases only'. In Queensland, which was still at that stage confident in the correctness of its policy, twenty-four legal addicts remained as late as 1972. But soon, throughout Australia, the policy of prescribed maintenance became a part of history more conveniently forgotten.[14]

The Politicisation of Drugs from 1966

The growth of illegal drug use effectively sidelined the disease model of addiction. The rhetoric about drug laws, which had always pretended that drug users were criminal and deviant, now began to correspond more closely with reality. In the crisis atmosphere that began to develop, the cyclic nature of this kind of public concern over drug use was forgotten. The cocaine scare of the 1920s was scarcely a memory, the anti-Chinese opium campaign completely forgotten; drugs were, once again, seen as an entirely new threat to society requiring drastic and immediate action. To be seen to be 'doing something about drugs' was an essential element of every political platform and a short-cut to popularity.

Thus in 1967 two urgency motions on 'drugs' were debated in the New South Wales parliament, the first since 1923. What caused this upsurge in public concern? Not only the extent of drug use, but its wilful nature and the youth of users also threatened many people. The young were said to be endangered, but it was the young themselves who were felt to be the danger. Certainly Clarence Earl, in moving one of the urgency motions, was principally concerned about the 'moral decay' and 'increase in vice' in 'many of our citizens within the under 23 age group'.[15] Jack Renshaw, leader of the opposition and former Labor Premier, moving the other, emphasised the 'present danger to the moral fibre of many young Australians'. The days of quiet and bipartisanship, however, were over. His proposal for the establishment of a Royal Commission was derided in a debate characterised by rancour and pettiness. 'I do not like to be interrupted in the middle of an insult,' complained the Liberal Premier, Robin Askin.[16]

Marijuana, in particular, became a focus for political anger and action. Australian's fear and ignorance of it, so thoroughly inculcated by overseas propaganda during the Menzies era, was now further provoked by the enormous increase in use. Several other factors also combined to generate the hatred many felt towards the drug. First, marijuana use challenged the validity of drug controls as a whole. Cannabis is not a 'safe drug'; evidence on the damage it may cause to the reproductive system of both males and females, in particular, is still being collected. But it is not a narcotic like heroin, or addictive like tobacco. Time and again the extreme dangers attributed to it have been shown to be wrong and, in retrospect, bizarre. In the 1960s high levels of use coupled with the relative weakness of the arguments used to defend its legal status, seemed to be the thin edge of the wedge. If cannabis law was being questioned, what would be next? The shrillness of anti-cannabis advocates was in direct proportion to the threat that its use posed to the perpetuation of the status quo.

Why else was cannabis included with heroin as a drug with 'particularly dangerous properties' in schedule IV of the *Single Convention*? Not because of its medical dangers, but because of the dangers it posed to the integrity of the legal system. Its relative harmlessness was its most 'dangerous property'. Why was an article questioning the reasons for the international prohibition of cannabis that appeared in the 1966 issue of the UN *Bulletin on Narcotics* the object of such vitriolic condemnation? Because cannabis was the weakest link in the international drug control regime. The CND's statements on cannabis over the years seemed designed principally to shore up the morale of the faithful. Having changed its yearly discussion of 'the problem of cannabis' to 'the question of cannabis' in 1959, the CND declared in 1966 that the problem was solved and the question answered. 'The subject could no longer appear on the agenda as the "question" of cannabis. There could be no question but that cannabis presented a danger to society.'[17]

In this climate of insecurity, it is not surprising that cannabis, which had been categorised as a 'dangerous drug' for many years and was proclaimed a prohibited import in 1956, was reclassified by the New South Wales government as a 'prohibited drug' like heroin, shortly after the enactment of the *Poisons Act 1966*.[18] This was an utterly pointless gesture. The only substantive change effected by the reclassification of cannabis was to prevent it being legally prescribed by doctors. But cannabis—unlike heroin prior to 1954—was not a commonly prescribed drug, nor was it ever used for the maintenance of addiction. The amendment therefore had no concrete effect. The sole purpose served by the government's action was to demonstrate its resolute belief that marijuana was a drug the evil and danger of which were on a par with heroin. This was a statement of its inflexible hostility.

Second, cannabis, more than any other 'illegal drug', challenged the power of the law. Users were not powerless addicts in need of medical treatment: they *chose* to smoke the drug and to break the law. And in that conscious illegality, they symbolically rejected society's right to require them to obey the legal system. In the development of Australian drug policy, each new law had emerged to shore up those that preceded it. The law was the law. But marijuana smoking challenged that attitude: it seemed to threaten the legal system as well as the drug-control system.

Third, and quite apart from these general implications, certain particular associations of marijuana itself seemed to condemn it to unique obloquy. In the 1930s, when White Americans feared a racial uprising by poor and oppressed Mexicans in the south-west of the United States, marijuana was said to 'remove the normal inhibitions of the individual' and unleash rage and violence. These alleged dangers, just like those associated with opium smoking in the past, were merely an expression of what the community feared about its users. In the 1960s marijuana became associated with a very different group of users: young, middle class, and White. The fears that it came to symbolise also altered to reflect the fear of change and radicalism that these users aroused. Far from promoting aggression, marijuana was said to result in 'dropping out, indolence, lowering of goals, alienation'. Its regular use was said to result in an 'amotivational syndrome'. At a joint Commonwealth/State Ministerial conference held in 1966, the Queensland Health Minister, S.D. Tooth, urged, against the advice of his department, that drug penalties should be increased because 'marijuana lead[s] to moral degradation, especially in Teenagers'. Four years later at a similar conference, the Western Australian Minister for Health argued that 'drugs is just the tip of the iceberg. Under it is promiscuous sex and permissiveness throughout the whole pattern of behaviour'.[19] Marijuana was a convenient scapegoat for youthful libertarianism, non-conformity and anti-materialism—a 'whole pattern of behaviour' that the establishment feared. It was indeed a 'sixties drug': what many people hated was not the drug, but the sixties.

Marijuana was not alone in generating these fears; LSD was another example. Lysergic acid diethylamide is a psychotropic or mood-altering chemical used for some psychiatric purposes because of its hallucinogenic effects. It was developed in the 1940s and began to appear in Australia at about the same time that £, s., and d. disappeared. It was seen as a young person's drug, taken for no other reason than 'fun and excitement'. The Beatles wrote a song about it; *Honi Soit*, the University of Sydney's magazine, published a recipe for its manufacture. Parliamentary debate likewise focused on its use by 'numerous youngsters' and 'university students—these wayward intellectuals feeling their way and wanting to be way out'.[20]

The CND's Committee on Drugs Not Yet Under International Control warned about the 'grave dangers of abuse' of LSD in 1966. Government reaction was immediate: the Commonwealth that year imposed strict controls on the importation of LSD and New South Wales classified it as a drug of addiction. In 1967 the New South Wales Poisons Regulations established a separate offence prohibiting the sale, supply, use, or possession of 'hallucinogenic substances', including LSD, except on the written authority of the Director of State Psychiatric Services, and Victoria made it an offence to prepare, manufacture, sell, deal or traffic, or possess a 'hallucinogenic drug' without authority. Detailed restrictions and conditions were also attached to its medical use. The creation of complex detailed legislative and regulatory control over LSD had taken only one year, and by 1969 every Australian jurisdiction had enacted similar controls and offences.[21]

I do not mean to suggest that LSD is a harmless drug: far from it. The reason that governments around Australia reacted so speedily to suppress its use, however, was not because of the harm it was causing, but because of the influential pressure exerted by the CND, and because of the people with whom it was associated and the connotations of vice that it suggested. As S.D. Tooth, the Queensland Health Minister, explained in 1969, the government had not acted to increase controls over barbiturates simply because 'barbiturates are not a problem to any great extent with teenagers'. It was abused by 'older people' and that made it different. LSD use may have been dangerous in itself, but more to the point it was a symbol of youth and rebellion which confronted medical and legal power.[22]

This was the new climate affecting the formulation of drug policy in Australia. The smell of fear was once again on the breeze, the demand for action was intense and reflexes were accordingly sharpened. Amphetamines, classified as 'restricted drugs' (schedule 4) under State law and according to the uniform poisons schedules of the NH&MRC, were also declared to be 'dangerous drugs' around Australia between 1967 and 1971.[23] Drugs were now becoming a politically prominent issue, and for the first time politicians were prepared to pursue Australian drug policy with energy.

The politicisation of the issue generated not just political interest, but rivalry and acrimony. In the competition for votes and power, drugs, like so many other things, started to become a party-political issue. Although both major political groups sensed that there was political capital to be made out of taking a law-enforcement line on drug issues, the conservative parties in particular tried to brand the Labor Party as opposed to strict legislative control. 'The pressure for legalization,' complained Country Party MHR, Bob Katter, 'came mainly from people with leftist leanings ... People who were outspoken on the Vietnam war and social issues also were outspoken on marijuana'.[24] The demise of the consensual approach to drug law that had characterised the pre-political era was to become even more prominent in years to come; but rivalry did not just occur between political parties. Competition between the levels of government soon emerged as an important factor in the new politics.

The Commonwealth had always hidden behind the supposed limits of its constitutional authority. In *R. v. Burgess*, the High Court held that the 'external affairs' power, section 51(xxix) of the Constitution, entitled the Commonwealth to enact as law the terms of those treaties entered into by Australia that were 'indisputably international in character', specifically including those relating to drug trafficking.[25] This decision was ignored. Thus, following the prohibition of the importation of heroin in 1954, the Commonwealth sought parallel State action to ban its manufacture because, according to Menzies, this matter was outside the Commonwealth's competence. Although the continual pressure applied to the States on matters ranging from jurisdictional uniformity to compliance with Australia's treaty obligations was a thankless task, the Commonwealth undoubtedly believed that any broader legislative involvement was more trouble than it was worth. Politically, too, drug policy, although increasingly significant, was not yet important enough to risk an altercation with the States over constitutional powers. Indeed, it is unlikely that anyone even thought to question the received wisdom that Commonwealth power on this issue was limited to the institution of import controls.

The ratification of the *Single Convention* and the growing political profile of drugs awakened Commonwealth ambition. In 1966, after a draft Act had already been prepared and agreed to by the Commonwealth government, State Premiers were informed that 'it is considered essential that the Commonwealth extend its legislation to cover control over all aspects of manufacture'. Angry at the Commonwealth's refusal even to consult with the States before embarking on this course of action, the Victorian Premier, Henry Bolte, complained to the Prime Minister, Harold Holt, that 'State powers cover the control of manufacture and distribution of narcotic drugs'. Bolte refused to send anyone from Victoria to a Commonwealth–State Conference on Narcotic Drugs Control organised by the Commonwealth that year as a protest against what was seen as Commonwealth intrusion, but to no avail. Suddenly, the Constitution was not an impediment to legislative action. The Customs representative, relying on section 51(xxix), said that the Premiers should be grateful that the Commonwealth was limiting itself to manufacture; it could 'if it so desired enact legislation in respect of all aspects of the convention'.[26]

According to its preamble, the purpose of the *Narcotic Drugs Act 1967* (Cwlth) was 'to regulate the Manufacture of ... Narcotic Drugs in accordance with the Single Convention on Narcotic Drugs, 1961', and the Convention itself was included in a schedule. In these ways, the Act was carefully designed to draw attention to the Commonwealth's external affairs power. The effect of the Act was to institute Commonwealth control over the manufacture of 'narcotic drugs'. Manufacturers now required a licence from the Minister and a permit from the Comptroller-General of Customs, as well as having to comply with State law on the subject. More than the terms of the Act, however, the mere involvement of the Commonwealth was significant. This was the first piece of Commonwealth legislation dealing with 'drugs' since the passage of the *Customs Act 1901* (Cwlth), and it had been enacted with a cavalier disregard for the sensibilities of the States. In fact, the actual terms of the Act were not communicated to State governments until one month after the Bill had been passed into law. In December 1967 Bolte wrote to the Prime Minister protesting that the *Narcotic Drugs Act* had been rushed through without consultation, and dealt with an area of traditional State responsibility. It was too late for such complaints. Drugs were front-page news and everyone, including the Commonwealth, was determined to be involved.[27]

Bureaucratic Conflict and Invasion 1966–1969

If the encroachment of Commonwealth legislative control alarmed State governments, the growing intrusion of the Commonwealth bureaucracy, and in particular the Department of Customs and Excise, filled State bureaucrats with horror. When drug control was an uncontroversial issue, co-operation between State and Commonwealth bureaucracies was routine. Now that it was a vital issue, rivalry between the various bureaucracies struggling for power over drug control administration and enforcement intensified. Relations between State and Commonwealth police forces and drug squads, between the Customs Department and the various State health departments, and even between the Customs Department and the Commonwealth Department of Health would never again be as easy as in the past. Too much was now at stake.

The 1966 inter-departmental Commonwealth–State Conference on Narcotic Drugs Control, chaired by the Department of Customs and Excise, resolved that 'a central Commonwealth authority' might usefully undertake a co-ordinating role 'down to supply by wholesalers'. But the department, eager to increase its own influence, misrepresented the resolution when it circulated its summary of the conference proceedings to the States. It reported that it had been agreed 'that the Department of Customs and Excise assume control over the dissemination of information on all inter-state transactions on narcotic drugs'. The actual resolution was neither so specific nor so far-reaching. This manipulation intensified the suspicion with which the Commonwealth and, in particular, the Department of Customs were already viewed by several States as a result of the events surrounding the enactment of the *Narcotic Drugs Act*. Victoria, which had boycotted the conference, resolved to attend future meetings of the Commonwealth–State Standing Committee on Control of Drugs of Dependence (put in place by the conference) simply to protect the Victorian bureaucracy against federal encroachment.[28]

The first meeting of the Standing Committee in December 1966 was chaired by the Department of Customs while each State sent representatives from their health departments, in every jurisdiction the relevant administrative body. As a result, two parallel conflicts emerged: State health departments distrusted the Commonwealth Department of Customs first because it was a federal body, and second because of its unrepentantly law enforcement and punishment-oriented perspective. Fearful of institutionalising a Commonwealth power base 'under a substantially non-medical administration', the department's attempts to have the Committee permanently constituted failed, and it remained only an *ad hoc* body.[29]

The question of ongoing administrative consultation was revived in 1968. In a careful attempt to ease tensions, the Prime Minister, John Gorton, wrote to State Premiers that he was 'aware that some State governments have had misgivings about the Commonwealth's role in the general field of drug control'. He reassured them that there was no intention 'to interfere in traditional areas of State responsibilities'. The States, and the Victorian government in particular, were still distrustful. A departmental briefing paper prepared for Victorian Health Minister, V.O. Dickie, suggested that the Department of Customs wanted to be as powerful as the United States FBN. Inter-governmental co-operation, the Minister was urged, 'should not be dictated by a Commonwealth Department which is not directly concerned with health':

There has been a definite attempt by officers of the Department of Customs and Excise to recite themselves into power in a field with a large medical and scientific content.[30]

None the less the first Commonwealth–State Ministers' Meeting on Drugs of Dependence was held in February 1969, and this in turn established the National Standing Control Committee on Drugs of Dependence (NSCCDD) to advise it. It was chaired by the Comptroller-General of Customs.

The continuing distrust of the Department of Customs and Excise was papered over. At a departmental meeting which was to report back to the Ministers' Meeting that year, the Comptroller-General of Customs proposed an exchange of officers between the Customs Department and State police forces. Such an exchange would in particular have facilitated the development of the inexperienced enforcement officers of the Department of Customs and Excise in their efforts to become Australia's principal drug-enforcement agency. But the mood of the meeting was hostile. According to the verbatim transcripts, only Victoria supported the proposal:

> The Chairman [the Comptroller-General] said that he was amazed at the negative reaction to the proposal ... In the circumstances, it seemed that he would be forced to report to Ministers that the Committee did not agree that any improvement was necessary.[31]

As it had done before, however, the Customs Department managed to sanitise its defeat. The summary of the meeting, which the department itself prepared, instead reported that 'with the exception of New South Wales and Queensland', the States had agreed to the proposal, although because the drug problem in Western Australia, South Australia and Tasmania was not very great, 'it is not necessary to implement such arrangements [in those States] at the present time'. By the time this summary had been considered at the next Ministers' Meeting, the truth had been distorted even further. Senator Scott, reporting the matter to parliament, said 'Ministers agreed in principle to exchange officers between the Customs Narcotic Bureau and the Police Drug Squads in each State. Such an exchange is already operating in Victoria'.[32]

The Changing Balance of Power

By the use of such stratagems, opposition to the institutionalisation of consultative bodies under Commonwealth supervision was deflected, and the Ministers' Meeting and NSCCDD became both the primary channel of inter-governmental communication, and an important vehicle for the formulation of uniform drug policies. Sir William Refshauge, Commonwealth Director-General of Health from 1960 to 1973, rarely went to meetings of the NSCCDD because 'it was of no interest to me ... Customs had the running. The Department of Customs and Excise had increasing power and authority over the whole area of drug laws; Sir William, to his later regret, feeling he could not fight it, preferred to ignore it.[33]

Other events were also enhancing both Customs' power and the narrowness of its perspective. The department's role as Australia's conduit to the international community on drug issues had ensured that the approaches espoused by the international community and the FBN were forcefully inculcated within the department. The lack of medical expertise within the Department of Customs and Excise, and the hostility between the it and the Department of Health, meant that any alternative to its law enforcement priorities was treated with suspicion. This perspective was further entrenched in 1970 when the narcotics operations of the department were hived off to a subordinate, independent body. This was Australia's own Federal Narcotics Bureau (FNB) which, like its United States counterpart, became solely responsible for the enforcement of Commonwealth drug laws and acted independently of both federal and State police. Far from being limited to controlling the importation of illegal substances, as its origins in the Customs Department might have suggested, the FNB was effectively a police force dealing with drug trafficking and smuggling. Like Anslinger's FBN, the Australian FNB, which grew from forty-three officers under its Director, Harvey Bates, to 233 officers under Commissioner Bates in 1979, had a vested interest in advocating those legal solutions which insisted that drug problems were problems of law enforcement. There was no place in a high-status quasi-police force for approaches which called for sympathy for criminals or cast doubt on the effectiveness of the criminal law.

At the same time, State health authorities were invited to take over responsibilities relating to the control of the legal narcotics trade. At first, these changes were only minor, but in 1974 Commonwealth control over the *legal* import and export of schedule 4 and 8 drugs (for medical purposes) was transferred from the Department of Customs and Excise to the Department of Health, and two years later the departmental power to grant and revoke manufacturing licences was also transferred. In this way, the legitimacy of Customs' power over the *illegal* narcotic trade was validated by its divestiture of what it distinguished as 'health matters'. By implication, illegal drug use had nothing to do with health. As Senator Scott, Commonwealth Minister for Customs and Excise, made clear as early as 1969, 'We are looking at illicit traffic in drugs and the health authorities are more concerned with licit traffic.'[34] The two perspectives which had, in the past, coalesced—illness and vice, public health and law enforcement—moved further and further apart.

As the balance of power changed, the Commonwealth Department of Health came to be seen by many politicians as a voice of dissent and a nuisance whose views were not to be trusted. In 1976, defending the Eastland committee report of the United States Congress, which strongly supported the United States's hard-line approach to cannabis, New South Wales MLA, Arthur Viney, had this to say:

The Health Commission of New South Wales had the audacity to produce as a critique ... the comments of a layman named Brecher, a propotist in the Consumers Union. Subsequently I ascertained through questions I asked that Mr Brecher's evidence had been brought forward by the Australian Department of Health. I have no faith in the competence of many advisers to the Crown in the Australian Department of Health.[35]

The atmosphere of animosity and resentment between the departments of Customs and Health was difficult to shake, but its origins did not so much lie in differences about the content of drug laws, but in who was to administer them. This was, in part, a consequence of the politicisation of drugs, for as drugs entered the realm of party politics, drug policy and drug law became more subservient to political influences than it had ever been. Political power was waxing, and waxing most emotional. The days in which drug policy decisions were made almost solely by the public service were over. Only administrative power remained, but the competition over who was to control it grew all the more fierce. Bureaucratic ambition stirred and bureaucratic rivalry developed as, for the first time, drugs became an important way to garner power and prestige.

The growing emphasis within the public service on administrative power had another subtle implication. Whereas the development of drug laws in the early years of the century reflected growing medical power, now doctors themselves found their freedom circumscribed by bureaucratic constraints. The legal medical maintenance of addicts was wiped out. Heroin and cannabis could not be prescribed at all, LSD and the amphetamines only with specific authorisation and in limited circumstances. A new phase was being entered. The use of 'dangerous drugs' was no longer just a medical matter. It had been appropriated by bureaucracies, systematised and institutionalised in response to their own complex latticework of ambitions and rivalries.

The delicate balance between illegal drug use as an illness and a vice was also changing in the same ways. Not only medical authority, but also the medical conceptualisation of addiction as a disease requiring treatment, were becoming less important than the character of drug use as a crime requiring punishment. The rhetoric about 'sick addicts' continued, but in reality, medicine was yielding its place to law, a change which the increasing suzerainty of Customs over Health served to accelerate.

While obsessed with administrative issues, neither federal nor State bureaucracies had any reason to question the general approach of drug legislation—not simply because it suited their own ambitions, but also because one of the central functions of any bureaucracy is to administer the status quo effectively. A great deal of energy within a department is focused on how to improve the operation of the entrenched legal structure and not to question whether it should exist at all. As Sir William Refshauge commented:

That's why I left the Department. I was beginning to see that happening in me. People would come to me with new ideas and I could see that I was not listening. I was losing my flexibility.[36]

More laws were developed, but they were more of the same. As with politicians, the habits of mind with which bureaucrats responded to the changing face of drug use remained rooted in the past. Australia in 1970 was a very different place from what it had been ten years earlier. Politicians and bureaucracies knew this to be so, but their knowledge had not led them to alter the direction of drug policy in Australia. It had merely increased their desire to be in charge of it.

SHADOWS OF THE PAST

*The Triumph of Meta-Law
1970–1980*

Meta-Law in Australian Drug Reforms 1970–1972

The *Convention on Psychotropic Substances 1971*, and the *Protocol Amending the Single Convention* signed the following year, the latest products of the international Convention factory, were a strange mixture. They acknowledged for the first time that the international drug control regime was not as successful as had been hoped. Both treaties referred expressly to the importance of the 'treatment, education, after-care, rehabilitation and social reintegration' of drug users, a jarring note of compassion. As the *Commentary* on the Protocol published by the United Nations explained, this reflected 'general acceptance of the view' that the Conventional system and its enforcement 'is not sufficient, and should not form the sole object of international co-operation'.[1]

The substantive terms of these treaties, however, were still dominated by the inflexible legal strategies characteristic of the Conventions since 1909. The 1971 Convention, sponsored by the International Narcotics Control Board (INCB), expanded the system of 'narcotic drug' control to include 'psychotropic substances' such as LSD, mescaline and psilocine, as well as requiring similar controls over amphetamines and barbituric acids. Detailed requirements were provided for the import and export, manufacture, prescription and keeping of records of all substances dealt with by the Convention. In addition, the INCB was given considerable powers to pressure parties which in its opinion were in breach of the Convention. It could 'ask for explanations from the Government', call upon it to take remedial measures, call the matter to the attention of other parties, publish a report dealing with it and, finally, 'recommend to [other] Parties that they stop the export, import, or both, of particular psychotropic substances from or to the country ... concerned'.[2]

The 1972 Protocol that amended the *Single Convention* further increased the authority of the INCB as the supreme international drug control bureaucracy. The Board was given the power 'to establish, communicate and publish its own estimates' if it believed the statistics supplied by a party were misleading. In addition, if the Board believed that a signatory's opium production was being substantially diverted to the illicit traffic, the Board was empowered to unilaterally reduce that country's estimates for the following year. Since other parties to the Convention were bound to comply with these estimates, the INCB was therefore given the power to control the flow of drugs into any country that, in its opinion, was failing to exercise satisfactory supervision over the production of opium.[3] The role of the INCB was expanded in other ways. It was enabled, on its own initiative, to call for consultation on a 'serious situation' or drug problem in a country, propose a study, suggest remedial measures, and recommend the provision of technical and financial assistance. The INCB was still largely dependent on international co-operation, but it was maturing into an influential body with wide-

157

ranging responsibilities and interests.[4]

While Australia's loyalty to the continuing internationalisation of drugs was unfaltering, the prompt ratification of these treaties had few domestic consequences. The Protocol did not require any enacting legislation as it dealt only with the international bureaucracy itself. The *Convention on Psychotropic Substances*, in contrast, dealt largely with matters traditionally within the jurisdiction of the States. When the Commonwealth finally enacted the *Psychotropic Substances Act 1976* (Cwlth), it respected this traditional division and did not provoke a battle as it had done in 1967. It was, in fact, the Commonwealth's refusal to invoke the external affairs power to 'enter the whole field' that provoked criticism from the opposition Labor Party.[5]

The reason that ratification was relatively unimportant was simply that Australian governments no longer had to be cajoled and pressured into legislative amendments; they had learnt their lessons well and were frequently in advance of the international community. In the case of amphetamines and barbiturates, for example, controls had been instituted well before the signing of the Convention. The Prime Minister, William McMahon, noted that 'existing Australian controls, both Commonwealth and State, are in many respects stricter than those envisaged under the Convention'.[6] The overwhelming power the drug control club had exercised in the formative years of Australian policy continued to guide and to haunt us.

On the domestic scene the illegal use of drugs, especially of heroin and cannabis, continued to increase steadily. In the face of this problem, the principles behind the legal structure remained untouched and unquestioned, while laws designed merely to better enforce that structure proliferated. Were drug laws failing to hold back the rising tide of illegal drug use? The answer was to make conviction easier and so to convict more people. Were the penalties imposed by the courts not serving to discourage illegal drug trafficking? The answer was to introduce higher penalties.

The incremental and circular nature of Australian drug policy, which was originally expressed by expanding the range of drugs to which the policy applied, was now expressed by expanding the controls which applied to those drugs. This phenomenon I call 'meta-law': that is, laws about laws, not laws about things. A meta-law does not alter what people can or cannot do: rather it aims at enforcing laws already in place. Laws which expand police powers simply make enforcement easier. Laws which make less onerous the proof needed to convict someone of a crime likewise do not change the fact that X is legal and Y is not: but the circumstances in which the courts will declare that a particular action falls into category Y and should therefore be punished, are expanded. Again, by increasing the penalty attached to a crime, governments hope to change behaviour not directly, but by the threat of greater punishment. These are examples of meta-law. They do not tell people what to do, but they do tell people not to break the law: you will be caught more often, convicted more easily, and punished more severely.

Thus, police powers of search and seizure gradually increased, specifically in relation to 'drug offences'. In South Australia the right to search premises or vessels and to stop, search and detain vehicles or persons without a warrant was granted to authorised police in 1970, and to all police in Queensland in 1971. In Victoria, the power to search without a warrant public places, vehicles and boats for the presence of poisons or deleterious substances, originally granted to 'authorised' police officers in 1967, was gradually expanded over the next four years until it applied to all police.[7]

By the very process of abstraction inherent in meta-legal solutions, underlying legal principles are concealed. What do you do if a building is unstable—do you study its foundations, or do you merely reinforce the scaffolding? The explosion of meta-laws in the last twenty years has been like so many flying buttresses, put in place first to steady the superstructure, and then to try and shore up the buttresses themselves. The outline of the edifice itself is almost invisible in the complex of struts which prop it up.

Don Chipp, crusading Minister for Customs and Excise from 1970 until 1972, was an influential exponent of meta-law. He was a young and aggressive Minister, a staunch advocate of increased resources and legislative powers for his department, a vigorous opponent of marijuana law reform and a voluble critic of judicial leniency in the infliction of penalties, which he incessantly proclaimed to be 'completely beyond [his] comprehension'. The distinction between the 'pusher' and the 'addict' was central to his rationale for increased law enforcement measures. 'People who are addicts are to be pitied,' he explained, 'and they should be treated.' 'The drug pusher who is not a user,' he said on the other hand, 'is an evil person who deserves no mercy.'[8]

The *Poisons (Amendment) Act 1970* (NSW), introduced by the Askin-led Liberal government, demonstrated the growing importance of the trafficker as the emotive target of meta-legal solutions. A.H. Jago, the New South Wales Minister for Health, introducing the Bill, explained that

lying at the core of the drug abuse problem is the pedlar. The pedlar is insidious and unscrupulous; without him there is no organised drug abuse problem.[9]

This was nonsense, both because most 'pedlars' are also users and because it assumes that there is no natural demand for the use of, for example, cannabis or heroin. But the image of the drug user as ill and not vicious had always threatened to undermine the punishment-oriented approach of governments. By distinguishing between user and trafficker this difficulty was avoided. Law enforcement measures could expand without criticism, focused in theory, if not in practice, upon evil drug traffickers. Once again, someone could be *blamed* for the continuing illegal use of drugs. The day of the evil drug fiend was over; that of the evil businessman was about to dawn.

The *Poisons (Amendment) Act 1970* (NSW) made it a separate offence to sell or deal in any 'drug of addiction', bringing New South Wales into line with other States. Now in every State drug trafficking constituted a separate offence. As recommended by the NSCCDD, an increased penalty of up to ten years' imprisonment was enacted for persons found guilty of the supply or sale of drugs. 'We need hard lines and not guide lines' the Commonwealth–State Ministers' Meeting held in April that year had declared. More importantly, any person found in possession of an amount in excess of what was termed a 'prescribed quantity' (for example, over twenty-five grams of cannabis or 0.5 grams of heroin) was 'deemed to have that drug or substance in his possession for supply or sale'. They then became subject to the higher penalty unless they could prove they were not traffickers. In South Australia, Queensland, and the Commonwealth, where similar laws were passed the following year, this amount was called a 'traffickable quantity'. The onus of proof was reversed and accused persons were required to prove their innocence.[10]

The *Customs Amendment Act No. 2 1971* (Cwlth) took a similar approach. Previously it had been an offence to be in possession of an illegal import. Now it became an offence to possess any narcotic 'reasonably suspected' of having been illegally imported. Even persons not involved in the act of importation were now guilty of a breach of Commonwealth law. Moreover, since the importation of heroin or cannabis was absolutely prohibited, any person found in possession of these substances would automatically fall foul of this provision—while actual proof of the act of illegal importation may not be available, it was *always* 'reasonable' to 'suspect' that they had been imported illegally. In effect although not in form it became a crime under Commonwealth law as well as under State legislation to possess schedule 8 drugs. The practice adopted by the Department of C'ustoms of referring cases to State police 'where direct evidence of importation was not available' was discontinued.[11]

As well as extending the authority of the department far beyond the customs barrier from which its constitutional authority derived, the Act was another meta-legal reform. Persons charged with possession were presumed guilty unless they could prove that the drugs they possessed had not been illegally imported. The prosecution did not have to show that the accused knew that the drugs in question had been illegally imported; the accused had to prove that they did not.[12] Rather than change the substantive law, this reversal of the traditional onus of proof, as in New South Wales, merely made it easier to obtain a conviction. Drug law, and in particular trafficking, was becoming a special case in which the normal principles of proof and normal levels of punishment did not apply.

The *Customs Amendment Act No. 2 1971* (Cwlth) was not supported whole-heartedly. Bill Hayden, a future leader of the Labor Party and, eventually, Governor-General of Australia, contended that 'criminalising has failed' and wondered if the control of drugs was 'a proper subject for police and prisons or is it a proper subject for medical authorities'.[13] More importantly, the Act ran counter to the tenor of the Senate Select Committee on Drug Trafficking and Drug Abuse that reported that year. Dominated by members of the Liberal Party, which was in government, the Committee had been instructed to report 'upon drug trafficking and drug abuse in Australia'. Such a broad topic, however, allowed it to deal not only with schedule 8 substances, but with 'all drugs capable of producing dependence', legal or illegal. Somewhat uncomfortably for the government, the Committee rejected the notion that illegal drug use was uniquely harmful or sinful, and it concluded that it was inappropriate to increase the penalties for illegal drug use.[14]

The creation of a parliamentary inquiry reflected growing community concern over 'the drug problem' which was in part generated by the politicisation of the drug issue itself. But politicians were not prepared to countenance opinions contrary to the received wisdom. Despite the Committee's recommendations, the *Customs Amendment Act (No. 2) 1971* (Cwlth) expanded both drug offences and penalties. Senator Turnbull, a member of the Committee, asked eighteen months later 'whether the Government has any intention of implementing anything' in the report. 'Even with a majority of Liberals on the Committee, no weight at all has been given to its report.'[15]

In general, the Act generated fervid support that brooked no opposition. Clearly, Don Chipp, the Minister responsible for the Act, was aware of its weaknesses. In late 1972, after visiting the United States and Europe, he concluded that 'the policing or law enforcement technique as practised in the United States particularly had failed'.[16] Yet as Minister for Customs and Excise he intensely pursued law enforcement strategies. His emotional reaction to the 'evil drug pusher' never allowed his critical faculties full rein. Instead, during his tenure, the interrelated trends that characterised legislative developments in the 1970s—towards meta-legal solutions and towards fierce condemnation of the trafficker—were given powerful and passionate impetus.

The Politics of Cannabis 1970–1976

Why was this law enforcement approach clung to with such tenacity even by those who knew its limitations? Three points related to the politicisation of drugs need to be made. First, illegal drug use in Australia created an emotionally-charged environment. Meta-law comforted a nervous public with the implicit assurance that those who broke the law were bad and worthy of punishment, and that 'the drug problem' *could* be beaten if only it was backed by enough resources and appropriately severe legislation. These attitudes, furthermore, resonated with the themes of drug policy followed in Australia for many years: of the incremental growth of legal controls; of demonology and scapegoating; of faith in the validity and efficacy of the law. Meta-law was easy and it was familiar.

Second, taking a tough line was politically advantageous. It was hard for politicians to ignore the popularity they gained by rhetorical support of meta-law and by noisy tirades against traffickers. But while this emotional pitch responded to public fears, it also perpetuated and intensified them. To be 'soft on drugs' came to look more and more like political suicide.

Third, the public and political attitude to drugs was not, as we have already seen, about public health at all. Here, then, we acknowledge why 'drugs' were such an emotional issue to begin with. In debate on the Poisons (Amendment Bill) 1970 (NSW), a government member made the approach of conservative politicians clear:

Permissiveness as a whole has many parts, including permitting homosexuality ... permitting sexual intercourse outside previously tolerated bounds; permitting easier divorce ... permitting attempted suicide; permitting euthanasia; and permitting soft, tolerant attitudes to the rearing and education of children and to discipline and authority generally.

One conservative speaker bemoaned the attendance of a member of the opposition at an anti-Vietnam War moratorium rally; another thought drugs were part of a communist conspiracy; the next complained that Mick Jagger and Marianne Faithfull were living together unmarried; and the next spoke about the dangers of pop festivals.[17] These apparently extraneous matters lay at the very heart of the opposition of these speakers to drug use.

In arguments about the dangers of marijuana, reference to the so-called 'amotivational syndrome' was common. According to this argument, marijuana use created laziness and disinterest. In this way, the rejection of materialism and alienation associated with young marijuana smokers was given a scientific aetiology—even though many young people who had never smoked marijuana had also rejected these values. The bottom line was, dope smokers are lazy. But by shrouding value judgements about the political and moral importance of work in pseudo-science, the actual underlying fears were both obscured and validated. As sociologist Joseph Himmelstein wrote, 'The amotivational syndrome ... was simply the counterculture writ small and turned into a psychiatric diagnosis.'[18]

The work of drug 'expert', Professor Hardin Jones, provided some of the most extreme examples of this technique. He was quoted at length in debate on the Poisons (Further Amendment) Bill 1977 (NSW):

The conditioned social responses, such as affection for parents and tolerance for their suggestions, are impaired ... The marijuana user does not want to be 'hassled'. Mild criticism or merely requesting that housekeeping chores be done may be interpreted as hassling ... The hypnotic effects of marijuana are, in my opinion, largely responsible for ... a yielding to homosexual advances, and overly generous compliance with unreasonable requests by friends ... The diurnal cycle of sleep and waking is largely inverted. The marijuana user stays up at night.[19]

What were his real objections? That 'drug users' were rebellious, that they did not listen to their parents, that they didn't do the dishes, that they spent too much time with their friends, that they stayed up late. These are familiar criticisms of the young, here *explained away* as symptoms of an illness. The rebellious behaviour itself was blamed on 'drugs' and discredited as sick, while the writer's own moral and political values were securely placed on a scientific pedestal.

Opposition to drug use reflected genuinely held political beliefs about a whole range of other social values and not just about the use of 'illegal drugs'. It is no wonder that a parliamentary inquiry, no matter how rational, failed to change anyone's mind. An inquiry about 'drugs' could not address the real and underlying fears which drug use aroused, or the political values it was seen to challenge.

Given these political implications, the Labor Party was particularly vulnerable to attack. Its 'softness' on drugs was seen as symptomatic of a general sympathy for social non-conformity, change and rebellion. As never before, drug policy became party-political. This was especially true in relation to marijuana. First, it was the drug of choice of the young; both the total number of users and its use proportionate to other drugs was dramatically on the rise in the early 1970s. In New South Wales, for example, fifty-seven cannabis users were convicted in 1966, and 365 in 1970 (forty per cent of total drug-related convictions). By 1977 the number had shot up to 4300 and (seventy-two per cent of convictions).[20] At the same time, sellers and users were discovering that cannabis is an easy plant to grow in Australia. Many users grew a couple of plants in their back gardens or in their roofs; some grew enough to sell to their friends and acquaintances; others began to take it on as a commercial venture. Especially in New South Wales, larger and larger crops were grown for distribution all over the country, carefully concealed from the prying eyes of the police. Marijuana was no longer commonly imported into Australia, although more concentrated versions of the drug were. It was cultivated on Australian soil, on a rapidly expanding scale and with increasing sophistication.

Second, doubts as to how dangerous cannabis really was made it the weak link in the drug control regime. As penalties relating to its possession and trafficking increased, so too did the chorus of criticism. Some argued that it was no more dangerous than tobacco and alcohol, and should be legalised. Still more spoke of 'decriminalisation', a word long enough to conceal a multitude of opinions: most commonly, it meant that users should be required to pay only a small fine—without the risk of a term of imprisonment—and that, if the penalty was paid, no criminal record should stigmatise the offender. Many others, who were not prepared to go so far, did not believe that the mere possession of marijuana deserved penalties as severe as those which attached to other schedule 8 drugs. They at least rejected the *Single Convention*'s assertion that heroin and cannabis were equally and especially dangerous,[21] and insisted that the punishment of offenders should reflect those distinctions. The drug control system, then, provoked controversy and opposition on the question of marijuana as in relation to nothing else.

Third, the Labor Party was more vulnerable to conservative attack on the question of marijuana law reform than on any other drug issue. In debates in the Commonwealth parliament from 1970 to 1972, Labor politicians, Dr Klugman, Dr Cass, Senator Cavanagh, Dr Everingham and Senator Wheeldon, all made their opinions on the need for legislative change clearly known.[22] All of them, then, were on the record as being 'soft on drugs'.

In this highly politicised climate, everything about the drug provoked controversy—even how it should be defined. In New South Wales, Victoria and South Australia, for example, Indian hemp was defined as 'the fresh or dried aerial parts of the plant known as Cannabis Sativa L'. The Chief Botanist of the Royal Botanic Gardens, Kew, however, advised that the genus 'cannabis' may include a number of slightly different species, of which 'sativa' is only one. In New South Wales in 1970, and in South Australia and Victoria later, the definition was revised to include 'any plant or part of a plant of the genus cannabis'.[23] The Commonwealth *Customs Amendment Act No. 2 1971*, on the other hand, defined 'cannabis plant' as 'a plant of the genus *Cannabis sativa*'. This was botanical nonsense. Although the definition claimed to be describing a genus, the words '*Cannabis sativa*' describe a species. The words 'genus' and 'sativa' cannot both be given effect to. While the High Court of Australia managed, unconvincingly, to avoid the problem when the section came up for interpretation in the case of *Yager v. Queen*, its decision was important mainly for the parliamentary ignorance it demonstrated.[24] Politicians' keenness to legislate against marijuana was not accompanied by even the most rudimentary knowledge.

The law in force in the Australian Capital Territory did not include a definition of cannabis.[25] After costs were awarded against the police in several cases, it was decided not to continue to prosecute users for mere possession until new legislation was passed. From 1973 until mid-1975, only one case of possession was prosecuted and the position in the Australian Capital Territory at that stage was therefore, in practice, one of decriminalisation. Matters then came to a head. The Australian Capital Territory at that time had no local government. It was administered federally by a Labor government, which, led by Gough Whitlam, had swept to power in December 1972 after twenty-three years in opposition. But the conservative forces showed no taste for opposition. By 1975 the government was being subjected to an intense campaign of destabilisation and was proving disorganised in response. This campaign centred on fear: fear of radical change, fear that the Labor Party was undermining the rule of law, fear of socialism and centralism.

Cannabis in Canberra was grist to the Liberal Party's mill. It aroused the fear of change that already characterised community concern about the drug; it represented centrist 'Canberra' going behind the backs of the States; and it hinted at a conspiracy to subvert the rule of law. Don Chipp accused Whitlam's government of acting with 'blackguardly impertinence' to effect legislative change in an 'underhanded and cavalier manner'. The image of deception which the government projected was hardly helped by the reply of the Attorney-General, Kep Enderby, who complained that the policy in the Australian Capital Territory 'would have gone unnoticed were it not for politicians like Mr Chipp trying ... to get their name in the papers'.[26]

Enderby's insouciance seemed only to confirm Chipp's charge, and a statement he made at the same time, which suggested that he wanted to introduce overriding Commonwealth legislation imposing uniform penalties for drug offences, including a significantly lesser penalty for cannabis use, caused a furore. 'Soft drug users will be fined an almost nominal $100' reported the *Australian* in an article headlined 'Govt will over-rule States on drug law'; the proposal was 'attacked as unconstitutional by three premiers' who vowed to 'fight [the] new drug laws in High Court'.[27] Hostility to cannabis use was therefore swept along in 1975 by fierce hostility towards the Whitlam government, coupled with arguments that related more to fears about 'States' rights' than to fear of drugs.

In 1975 a definition of cannabis was at last included in the Australian Capital Territory Ordinance. But at the same time, a new penalty provision was included:

the only penalty that may be imposed on a person convicted of an offence ... of having had in his possession a quantity of cannabis of less than 25 grams, is a fine not exceeding $100.[28]

While this did not constitute decriminalisation—offenders still had a criminal record—it was a significant amendment. For the first time in Australian history, the penalty for a drug-related offence had been substantially reduced. As well as reflecting the Labor Party's libertarian approach to individual morality and social conformity, and recognising the vast scale of cannabis use amongst normal young men and women, the law was in fact a function of the meta-legal approach, for as the image of the evil trafficker became more and more important, the crime of possession for personal use was de-emphasised. Mere possession, the punishment of which had been so important in the development of drug policy in Australia, was becoming a side issue.

On its face, however, the Ordinance ran counter to the dominant law enforcement perspective. The conservative parties mobilised, unable to stop the passage of the law in the Australian Capital Territory and fearful of Enderby's threat to introduce similar Commonwealth legislation. In Victoria, for example, the Minister for Health, Alan Scanlan, instructed the Chairman of the Mental Health Authority to prepare a paper 'indicating ... that marijuana impairs judgement [and] that in certain circumstances, marijuana becomes, with some users, a basis of experimentation'. These were forwarded to the Premier, Rupert Hamer, and described by Scanlan as 'reports by my officers setting out their views on the matters we discussed'.[29] Yet the reports were neither unsolicited nor impartial. They were prepared on the instruction of the Minister for the express purpose of reaching specific conclusions. No longer were the actions of politicians governed by the will of the bureaucracy; bureaucratic advice was now tailored to political order.

To alleviate States' fears, a NSCCDD working party was set up to examine penalties for drug offences. Although established during the tenure of the Whitlam government, it reported to the new Liberal government of Malcolm Fraser after the general election of December 1975. It did not advocate the adoption of the Australian Capital Territory law, but while it proposed a further increase in the maximum penalty for trafficking offences up to $100 000 and twenty-five years' imprisonment, it recommended that the penalty for trafficking in cannabis should not be increased. Malcolm Fraser stated that 'cannabis (at least in leaf form) is not as dangerous as heroin and should neither be placed in the same category as this drug nor attract as severe a penalty'.[30]

The Commonwealth amended the *Customs Act* accordingly. In Victoria, the *Poisons (Drugs of Addiction) Act 1976* introduced into Victorian law the concept of a traffickable quantity, such as that which had operated in New South Wales and the Commonwealth since 1970–71, and also established distinctly different levels of penalties for traffickers in marijuana (up to ten years or $4000 or both) and for any schedule 8 substance (up to fifteen years or $100 000 or both). To the meta-legal tactic of 'a really incredible penalty' for trafficking was added a two-tiered approach to punishment.[31]

Yet the political association between a 'hard line' on drugs and conservative politics made even this distinction—not a reform, but just a recommendation that the penalty not be further increased—contentious. In Queensland, Deputy Premier and Health Minister, Dr Llew Edwards, advised Cabinet to accept the Prime Minister's recommendation about cannabis, noting that 'there is strong evidence that its ill-effects are by no means as severe as that which occurs in the use of other dangerous drugs'. Edwards and the Department of Health, however, were rolled, and the Queensland government decided, instead, to increase maximum penalties for trafficking in *all* 'dangerous drugs' from $10 000 to $100 000 and from 10 years' to life imprisonment. The NSCCDD, the Prime Minister, the Health Minister and his department, were all ignored. The same year, an expert panel appointed by Dr Edwards reported to Cabinet 'that the present evidence gives no reason for believing that marijuana is a serious health hazard'. Cabinet refused to table the paper in parliament or to have it printed.[32]

Cedar Bay

The politicisation of drugs, and especially of marijuana, encouraged the adoption of tough law-enforcement strategies, and made other legal reforms difficult and partial. In Queensland, in particular, the Country Party's (later renamed the National Party) image as being 'tough on drugs' was a crucial element in its electoral support. The conservatism of the electorate as well as that of the government reinforced these values. In the far north of the State the conflict between the established residential population and the alternative lifestyle movement that was trying to make its home there was especially intense. 'Hippie-life worse than aboriginal. Pot-worshippers in humpies', screamed one headline from the Brisbane *Courier-Mail* in 1971, while in another article it condemned the use of marijuana by 'hippy or drop-out subculture youth'.[33] It was their membership in the subculture, not the fact that they smoked pot, that constituted the real objection.

The Cairns area was subjected to considerable police attention and community unrest in relation to 'hippie movements in North Queensland' in the following years. 'Over twelve hundred people are receiving unemployment benefits and a great number of them are drug users,' complained Anita Campden-Main, chairman of a steering committee that became the Cairns Drug Action Committee. In June 1974, for example, police and customs officials conducted a series of investigations over 300 miles of northern coastline, but only six arrests were made.[34]

On the morning of Sunday, 29 August 1976, the government acted with greater resolution. Twenty-two well-armed Queensland police, assisted by seven Commonwealth customs officers, a patrol boat, a customs launch and an RAAF helicopter, attacked the twenty inhabitants of Cedar Bay, near Cooktown, in the far north of the State. Up to one hundred marijuana plants worth about $20 000 were seized, making it unlikely that any 'trafficking' was going on beyond the people who lived there and their friends, and a number of arrests were made, mostly for vagrancy. According to the police, the primary purpose of the raid was to track down an alleged drug trafficker who had escaped from custody in Cairns and, in addition, to arrest any persons living on the commune found to be cultivating or in possession of cannabis. It was also wrongly alleged that the community was illegally encamped.[35]

Whatever the pretext, the real aim of the operation seems to have been to raze the commune to the ground. Houses were burnt; books, children's clothes and about four months' supply of food were doused in fuel and ruined; and a large amount of personal property was destroyed. Water tanks were filled full of holes and a hose cut to pieces. The main subsistence garden was destroyed and dozens of fruit trees were chopped down. One witness described the scene:

They began by searching us and our property, ripping all our food supplies apart with a knife and pouring shampoo all over them ... They proceeded to pour kerosene over our huts and clothes and set fire to them ... While these were burning they led us to the beach and handcuffed us to the trees.

Another commented that 'they were firing bullets everywhere and reminded me of cowboys ransacking a town'. Queensland Police Minister, Tom Newbery, claimed that 'many residents of the area were armed and fired shots when they fled into the jungle away from police'. Whether they were in fact armed is not clear; that they chose to run away scarcely comes as a surprise.[36]

Twelve people were charged. Four received terms of imprisonment for drug offences such as possession of marijuana seeds. The rest were charged with vagrancy and, although several of them claimed that their bank-books had been confiscated or torn up by the police in order to ensure that the vagrancy charge would stick, all pleaded guilty, fearful that if they did not bail would be opposed and they would be remanded in custody for another week.[37] Then, on 9 September, the convictions were set aside, not because of the handling of the raid, but because the Justice of the Peace who heard the cases had acted beyond his power. On the raid itself, the Queensland government remained unrepentant. The opposition's criticism of the police confronted those values of authority, conformity and obedience central to the government's philosophy. Senior government Minister, Russ Hinze, complained, 'The police are always in the wrong. You blokes always blame the police'. 'The Government will believe the police,' said the Premier, Joh Bjelke-Petersen.[38]

Illegal drug use was therefore crucial neither to the raid nor to the government's defence of it. It was a search-and-destroy mission directed against a lifestyle in relation to which marijuana use was only a symptom and a symbol. One police officer was reported to have said to one of those arrested that 'he wished I had run away [as] he would have shot me cause of being on dole'. That officer, at least, was not there to arrest drug traffickers, but to punish 'dole bludgers'. So too, Newbery emphasised that the inhabitants of the northern section of Cedar Bay were 'undesirable persons ... living in complete squalor. The stench of human excrement was over-powering'.[39]

Does all this sound familiar? A century earlier the Chinese had been characterised in exactly the same way, for the same purposes, and with a similar lack of proof. Marijuana smoking was associated with the residents of Cedar Bay just as opium smoking had been associated with the Chinese: as a rationalisation for oppression in fact rooted in less concrete fears. More shadows of the past. Still Australians feared and victimised people who were different. Still we used their drug use as an excuse for hating them, and as a means of explaining away their differences. Still we covered our prejudices with myths and demonology. Did White women live with the Chinese? Opium slaves. Did 'hippies' drop out and live on the dole? Prisoners of dope.

A New Political Consensus

Just as the rhetoric and paranoia of war defines pacifists as cowards and radicals as traitors, so the unfolding 'war against drugs' threatened to turn all those who did not support the orthodoxy into fellow-traffickers. In Queensland the Premier's Department prepared a 'special and urgent' briefing paper on 'marijuana, drugs and ALP' in 1979, which explored the political advantage that could be gained by the 'exploitation' of 'known sympathy within ALP for drug culture'. 'Is ALP on the take from the marijuana lobby to promote pot and drag its feet on effective policing?' the paper wondered and, later, 'Question: Is [legalisation] just another way of saying government was throwing in its cot [sic] with the drug criminals? Had [the Labor Party] been bought by criminal money?'.[40] The political risk of challenging the status quo was evident, the possibility of distortion and sensationalism endless.

Nevertheless, during the 1970s it was the policy of the Labor Party's Queensland branch 'to decriminalise the use and growing of marijuana for personal use'; the health committee of the Labor Party's New South Wales Central Executive recommended that marijuana be treated differently from the opiates; the Victorian Labor Party's spokesperson on health stated that State law enshrined 'a basic misunderstanding about cannabis or marijuana'.[41] This, however, was all in the wide open spaces of opposition. Once in government, the politicisation of drugs placed the Labor Party on the defensive: its failure to prosecute the 'war on drugs' would lose it many votes and gain it few. Political exigencies forced it to conform to meta-legal orthodoxy when in the narrow and cautious corridors of power. Thus, after three years of federal Labor government, the only change that advocates of reform could point to applied in an area of about 1000 square kilometres.

In New South Wales, Neville Wran's Labor government was elected in 1976 and immediately felt under pressure. In response to a memorandum from a bipartisan Joint Committee Upon Drugs which had recommended in March 1977 'that offences for the personal use of cannabis be no longer considered criminal offences', Neville Wran issued a definitive statement in which he claimed that 'certain fears have been deliberately generated amongst the community concerning the Government's intentions about the use of marijuana'. He announced that 'the Government does not intend to legalise the use of marijuana' and placed any 'material step towards dealing with offences involving the personal use of marijuana' in the distant future. Even the position in the Australian Capital Territory was described as an erosion of community standards.[42]

Supporting the status quo was politically safer than reform. The *Poisons (Further Amendment) Act 1977* (NSW) provided for a separate offence of cultivation of a 'prohibited plant' such as the opium poppy or cannabis, and increased all penalties for trafficking—to ten years and $25 000 for 'Indian hemp in leaf form', and to fifteen years and $50 000 otherwise. While this reform clearly distinguished between trafficking in cannabis and other drugs, as recommended by the Prime Minister the year before, the penalty for possession remained the same for both marijuana and other illegal drugs, and the penalty for trafficking in marijuana remained extremely severe. As the Labor Party proudly pointed out, the Victorian Liberal government's *Poisons (Drugs of Addiction) Act 1976* only provided a penalty of 10 years and $4000 for trafficking in marijuana.[43]

Still the opposition accused the government of being 'soft':

The Attorney-General smiled softly upon cannabis, and its user cults, much as if marijuana were a rose or a daffodil. A little more cautious, a little more the each-way bettor, the Premier likewise basically is a soft-liner.

The Labor Party was driven to ever greater heights in its attempts to deny its reputation as a party of reform. Neville Wran described 'drug traffickers and pedlars' as 'parasites' for whom 'no penalty was too great'. The opposition was accused of 'peddling' 'filthy lies' 'for their own selfish, miserable and unchristian political purposes'. Between June and September 1977, Wran's statement on cannabis was quoted verbatim in the parliament no less than four times.[44]

So effective had the conservative parties been in generating a fear of change that the Labor Party in government was forced to argue its policies according to criteria dictated by its opponents. All it could say was that it was a more effective administrator of the entrenched policies of prohibition and penalisation than the other side. The alternative was seen to be too politically risky.

The Age of Royal Commissions 1977–1980

Political speeches and police activity reassured few people. Year after year promises of victory in the 'war against drugs' remained unfulfilled, and its likelihood receded. Both the public and politicians sought answers: what was 'the drug problem'; who used illegal substances and why; should they be stopped and how? Alongside the extremism and enforced conformity that emerged from the years of political conflict, some influential reports dared to voice dissent.

The Senate Standing Committee on Social Welfare chaired by a Liberal Senator, Peter Baume, which began its inquiries in 1974 and tabled its report in 1977, was charged with the investigation of 'drug problems' arising from the use of alcohol, tobacco, analgesics and cannabis. Like the 1971 Senate report, to which to some extent it was a sequel, it was therefore determined to emphasise that the medical harm and legal status of drugs were not related. More than this, however, the Committee explored the myth-bound nature of the public's understanding of the 'drug problem', which it described in a memorable phrase as 'the drug problem problem'. The Committee saw the 'drug problem' as a cause for public concern—but also as a creation of it. Although the report particularly took to task the standard of public debate on drugs in Australia, its proposals for change proved no less discomfiting to the government. Specifically, in a recommendation subject to a strong dissent from two Senators, but nevertheless garnering bipartisan support, the Standing Committee recommended that the personal use of marijuana should 'not be defined in law as a crime ... the penalty [to] be solely pecuniary ... ' with 'no record of conviction ... used in subsequent proceedings'.[45] For the first time, an official report had recommended far-reaching change to the legal status of cannabis in Australia.

The South Australian Royal Commission into the Non-Medical Use of Drugs was a more comprehensive document and an even more thorough-going assault on orthodox wisdom. It was appointed in 1976 by Don Dunstan's Labor government, following a recommendation by the Labor Party's State conference that an inquiry be held into 'all aspects of marijuana' and pressure from the Liberal opposition for a more far-reaching inquiry. The leader of the opposition, Dr Tonkin, insisted that 'a full inquiry is urgently needed now—not at some time in the future'. Armed with extremely broad terms of reference, therefore, the three Royal Commissioners, under Professor Ronald Sackville, proceeded to question the whole basis of drug laws in Australia.[46]

Like the Senate reports before it, the methodology of the South Australian Royal Commission owed as much to the disciplines of philosophy and sociology as to law and medicine. The Commissioners were at pains to describe and puncture the elements of mythology and ideology which they saw as interfering with the development of a rational drug policy.[47] Aware of the need above all to dispel public ignorance and prejudice, the Commission instituted an innovative research programme and published several research and discussion papers. At last, in 1979, the Commission submitted its *Final Report*. In language at once elegant and precise, it attempted to reason from first principles the aims of drug policy and the best means of achieving those aims, assuming nothing and unencumbered by the shadows of the past.

Law enforcement strategies were consequently down-played. The 'reverse onus' provisions were criticised and their repeal urged. The enactment of abnormally high penalties was condemned. Even that shibboleth of orthodoxy, the crime of possession itself, was extensively criticised, although the Commission did not finally recommend its abandonment. More significant than its conclusions, however, was the fact that for the first time since its creation, the whole structure of drug control was opened up for debate. Why should someone be punished not because of anything they have done but merely because of what they possess? Does the crime of possession work? Even posing these questions was courageous.[48]

But if courage was a virtue, its conclusions on cannabis qualified it for sainthood. It recommended 'a partial prohibition model' under which 'cultivation for personal use, use in private and small-scale gratuitous distribution in private to adults would not be a criminal offence.'[49] This was not decriminalisation—it was a proposal for legalisation. Even more than the Senate Standing Committee's report, the Royal Commission assaulted orthodox wisdom.

Orthodox wisdom fought back. The report of the Senate Standing Committee was, predictably, shelved by the government. Debate was still proceeding in a dilatory fashion three years after it had been tabled, but, although ostensibly about the report, these debates made little mention of it at all.[50] The South Australian Royal Commission, on the other hand, could not just be ignored. Its attitude to cannabis had been foreshadowed by a 'discussion paper' published by the Commission well before the *Final Report* was issued. Regrettably, this attempt to prepare the electorate for its conclusions

171

backfired. Its proposals for cannabis reform dominated political debate and media coverage to the exclusion of all else, and the Commission's outspokenness on this one issue discredited it in the eyes of many people for whom, as we have seen, marijuana was a powerful symbol of deeper fears. Petitions of protest, signed by any number from twenty to 15 000 voters, flooded the parliament. The Liberal Party, which had originally demanded a full inquiry, accused the Commissioners of 'promoting a particular point of view' (as if Commissions shouldn't come to conclusions!), and called for its termination.[51] It was clearly trying to wind up an inquiry with which it disagreed.

The 'cannabis commission', as it was commonly called, was too controversial for the government's liking, too. Ill health forced Don Dunstan to retire and the newly installed Premier, Des Corcoran, announced that there would be no legislation reforming cannabis laws regardless of what the Commission said. The *Final Report* was laid on the table and ordered to be printed on 31 May 1979, but no Ministerial statement was ever made outlining the government's reaction to it, and its contents were never debated in the House.[52] Shortly afterwards, the Labor government was defeated at the polls and the work of the Royal Commission, tainted as a Labor initiative as well as for its conclusions, was condemned to gather dust on the shelves of the parliamentary library. Its history had demonstrated once again that political parties in Australia, whatever their complexion, were united in their support for a meta-legal orthodoxy which was familiar and politically safe.

It was the best of times; it was the worst of times; it was the age of credulity; it was the age of disbelief; it was, above all, the age of the Royal Commission. In part this was due to a genuine recognition that the problems of drug use were not going away, and that a more impartial evaluation of the issues was needed. But appointing a Royal Commission also gave governments, under pressure to 'do something' about drugs, an excuse for inactivity while also demonstrating their concern. On the other hand, the controversies surrounding the inquiries in the Senate and in South Australia were unwelcome to governments, which in general showed no interest in changing their way of thinking. By the late 1970s, Royal Commissions were no longer given such a free rein. They were subject to much more limited terms of reference, the purpose of which was to guide the inquiry in the directions preferred by governments; they were, in general, headed by men with a narrow and legalistic approach to the problems they were asked to address. Turgid in style and limited in scope, they became not tools for reevaluation, but a means of further entrenching and improving the functioning of the established legal order.

The work of the Senate Standing Committee and the South Australian Royal Commission provoked a direct reaction from the New South Wales Joint Committee of the Legislative Council and Legislative Assembly upon Drugs. Although a memorandum issued by it in 1977 had proposed a minor reform to cannabis law, its general tenor was extremely conservative. In its *Progress Report*, the Chairman, V. Durick, pointedly criticised the Senate

Standing Committee for dealing with alcohol and tobacco, but not the opiates. Furthermore, while previous reports had consciously tried to divest the debate on illegal drugs of emotion and exaggeration, the Joint Committee adopted a sensationalist tone. The traffic in heroin, for example, was said to constitute 'an insidious threat to Australian society which has been unsurpassed in the country's history', while the use of heroin was compared to myxomatosis in rabbits.[53]

Events soon overtook the Joint Committee. On 15 July 1977, shortly after the progress report was tabled, Donald Mackay, a leading anti-marijuana campaigner, disappeared from his home in Griffith, New South Wales. His presumed death at the hands of drug traffickers in a town with a large Italian community, which was said to be the centre of cannabis cultivation in Australia, brought together two deeply held fears; first, the fear of marijuana, and second, the fear of organised crime. The Wran government responded by establishing its own Royal Commission. Its terms of reference represented a significant change from previous reports. Legal drugs were explicitly excluded. The Commission was directed to report upon the identity of persons involved illegally in the cultivation, manufacture or supply of illegal drugs. Mr Justice Woodward, the Commissioner, was only to recommend changes in drug law and administration. This was to be no broad inquiry into questions of treatment, education or social policy. This was an inquiry directed towards the 'what', 'who', and 'how' of criminal drug activity, and not the 'why'. It gave priority to the evils of traffickers and the importance of law enforcement. True to its name, it was a Royal Commission into Drug Trafficking and not into drugs.[54]

The vast *Report* tabled two years later, almost 2500 pages in three volumes plus a *Further Report*, concentrated inordinately upon cannabis distribution networks in New South Wales—much of volume one and most of volume two. Alfred McCoy, whose book *Drug Traffic* appeared shortly afterwards, accused Woodward, with considerable justification, of hyper-sensitivity to criticism, self-importance, racism, 'pseudo-psychology, second-hand analysis and speculative enquiries' in his attempts to detect and prove 'Organized Criminal Activities within the Italian Community in Australia'.[55]

Where Senator Baume and Professor Sackville had queried the value of law enforcement strategies, Mr Justice Woodward sought only to improve them. As he emphasised, his terms of reference related not to medicine or sociology, but to 'the administration of the law'. He kept closely to this narrow brief. He was comfortable discussing inter-agency co-operation and the development of intelligence facilities, listening devices, sentencing principles, the forfeiture of assets and so on. Indeed on these issues, he was by no means supportive of all police demands for increased powers. But while Senator Baume and the South Australian Royal Commissioners had often found, during the course of their broad inquiries, that their most fundamental assumptions were being challenged and needed to be carefully reassessed, Mr Justice Woodward floundered, distinctly uncomfortable with such general questions.

The major problem is that this area of debate revolves around certain ethical or moral beliefs about drug use which differ from one group to another and are virtually irreconcilable.

By figuratively shrugging his shoulders, he tried to maintain the objectivity of his report. But in fact all he did was conceal and leave unexplored his own ethical principles. On the question of cannabis, for example, the Commission merely re-hashed a shopping list of arguments for and against legal reform. His own opinion, opposed to any significant change in its legal status, was presented as if it was the only reasonable stance to take unless a conclusive case for reform could be presented. And proposals for reform were rejected simply because they were not perfect solutions. No change was found to be a complete answer, so the Woodward Royal Commission advocated virtually no change.[56]

The method and emphasis of the Commission reflected exactly the metalegal approach. Issues which operated upon the legal system without altering its principles predominated. The evil image of the drug trafficker was shored up. Any analysis about the basis of drug control policy in Australia was avoided. The validity of the status quo was assumed but not discussed, and presented without context or justification, as if it were a kind of neutral policy without costs or dangers of its own. Unsurprisingly, Wran proclaimed the Commission 'the most refreshing, positive document about drug use, drug abuse, and drug peddling and trafficking thus far published in Australia'.[57]

Further reinforcement for the maintenance of the status quo in Australia came from the Australian Royal Commission of Inquiry into Drugs (ARCID), established by the Fraser government in late 1977 as a direct response, according to Senator Baume, to the radicalism of the Senate Standing Committee report tabled that year.[58] The Commissioner, Sir Edward Williams, was appointed by the governments of the Commonwealth and the States of Victoria, Queensland, Western Australia and Tasmania. At that time then, three separate Royal Commissions were operating simultaneously, one in South Australia, one in New South Wales, and one in every other Australian jurisdiction. Together, their reports alone totalled over 5000 pages. Their sheer volume demonstrated the prominence of drug issues in Australia, and the public's desire for answers and reassurance. But each Commission proved more orthodox in its analysis than the last.

Of the three, the ARCID was the most limited by its terms of reference. Mr Justice Williams was instructed to inquire into illegal drug importation and trafficking, illegal use, the extent to which such illegality was being pursued on an 'organised basis' and, finally, 'the adequacy of existing laws ... and of existing law enforcement'. Even more than the Woodward Royal Commission, ARCID was expected to assume that 'the drug problem' concerned only illegal drugs and was simply about trafficking, law enforcement and organised crime.[59]

These assumptions the Commission's report did not doubt. Consider the colour plates that adorned the preface. The first picture was of a single opium poppy, and the last of a cannabis plant. Between these photos of natural beauty lay maps of world drug production and traffic routes, and page upon page of clinical photographs—Buddha sticks alongside the dismantled radio in which they were hidden, sachets of heroin next to the objects in which they were concealed, and so on.[60] There were no people in these pictures, only objects: agents of corruption and places of secretion. For Mr Justice Williams, the 'drug problem' was not about people at all, but simply about law enforcement, about the prevention of illegal importation and distribution. And what of the only two living things in these pictures, so tastefully photographed? Our reaction to them is coloured by the images juxtaposed between them. *Papaver somniferum* and *cannabis sativa* seem to be presented like wanted posters, warning us to be on our guard. We may have begun by thinking that the opium poppy looked beautiful, but by the time we have reached the cannabis plant on the last page, we know better. Theirs is not the sweet beauty of innocence, but the cloying beauty of evil.

With his sympathies illustrated so vividly, Mr Justice Williams's emphasis on law enforcement, administration and the prevention of importation was predictable. The interim report he submitted to the Commonwealth on 19 September 1980 dealt in particular with the interrelationship of various enforcement agencies, and the functioning of the Federal Narcotics Bureau (FNB): this is a specific issue that I will discuss shortly. Likewise in the 'National Strategy' which he outlined in his final report, coastal surveillance, police co-operation and intelligence activities, powers of search and telephonic interception, inter-agency and interstate co-ordination were his central concerns. The drug legislation he proposed also focused on adequate police powers and institutional efficiency.[61] The drug problem was, to the ARCID, a question of the effective implementation of policy and not its formulation. If only the police did their job well enough, the problem would disappear.

When it came to fundamental issues of drug policy, the ARCID was all at sea. Like Mr Justice Woodward before him, Mr Justice Williams was unwilling to recommend any change unless the arguments were, to him, absolutely conclusive. The status quo emerged victorious by default. On cannabis, for example, his only concrete recommendation was that the convictions of persons under 21 years of age should be expunged after one year. Otherwise, he called for a ten year 'moratorium' in order to 'put aside polemics and to enter upon a period of balanced consideration of the issues of cannabis', during which period 'no relaxation of the present Australian prohibition on cannabis should be made'. A finer justification for inactivity could scarcely be imagined. Yet even this seemed too radical for governments. The Premiers' Conference held in June 1981 'deferred a decision on a recommendation of the ... Williams Report—that the laws relating to legalization of marijuana be considered in 1990.' In other words, the Premiers were not even prepared to decide to decide nothing for another ten years.[62]

Senator Don Chipp, who by now had left the Liberal Party to found the Australian Democrats, was one of ARCID's harshest critics. Remarkably, it was cannabis which excited Chipp's most scathing comments. Like Saul on the road to Damascus, Chipp had undergone a conversion since his days as Liberal Minister for Customs and Excise, although a change in his opinions had not changed his strident style. He described Williams's approach to cannabis as 'a gigantic cop-out, a disgraceful cop-out ... a pack of rubbish'. Beyond these insults, however, Chipp recognised that the central point of Williams's report was his concentration on law enforcement. 'There is nothing innovative in it. There is only an obsession—that is all I can call it—with cutting off the supply. It is like a fairyland.'[63]

Yet for exactly these reasons the government supported the thrust of the Commission. It had served its purpose. Debate on drug policy in Australia was safely entrenched in meta-law: the Ministerial Statement on ARCID discussed police co-operation and co-ordination, intelligence and information facilities, coastal surveillance and smuggling prevention, international initiatives; the Labor opposition responded on the same level. It delighted in quoting scandalous examples from Williams's report, such as that of the customs launch which broke down eighty-three times from Eden to Brisbane, or the customs houses in northern Australia—Australia's first line of defence against drug importation—which were only open during office hours. With some exceptions, it served both major political parties and governments around Australia to assume the validity of the structure of drug legislation in Australia and concentrate instead on point-scoring over administration and enforcement.[64]

A New Bureaucratic Consensus

The Commonwealth Department of Customs and Excise may have hoped to reinforce the political triumph of meta-law with its own triumph over rival bureaucracies. But long-standing rivalries coupled with its own ambition found the FNB isolated. It was viewed by State health departments as a police force playing with health issues, by State police forces as a bunch of bureaucrats playing at police work, and by almost all State bodies as a symbol of Commonwealth intrusiveness. Resentment grew in those bodies ideologically aligned with it as well as those to which it was ideologically opposed. In 1979 it was alleged that the Bureau had been infiltrated by persons involved in drug trafficking; circumstantial evidence linked an officer or officers of the FNB itself with the disappearance and murder of the two New Zealand drug couriers who made the allegations. Commissioner Bates tendered his resignation on 1 June and then withdrew it three days later. These matters raised fundamental questions about the 'quality, honesty and integrity' of the Bureau.[65]

Matters moved swiftly. In keeping with its law enforcement and administrative perspective, the ARCID investigated the 'notoriously poor' relationship of the FNB with other police forces. Its interim report excoriated the FNB mercilessly. The FNB's detectives and inspectors were inexperienced, yet claimed for themselves special expertise in the pursuit of drug traffickers, thus breeding 'an unjustified elitism'. They were viewed by other police agencies as ambitious, secretive, uncooperative and inefficient. Officers of the Bureau themselves described it as 'hopeless', 'completely incompetent', 'shocking', and 'the worst trained, worst disciplined and worst equipped law enforcement agency in Australia'. The very first recommendation of Williams's report was that the FNB be disbanded and that the Customs service in future confine its energies to 'the [customs] barrier' and not beyond.[66]

The execution of the FNB, like that of the New South Wales Pharmacy Board before it, was complete and sudden. Some, like Don Chipp, who had been so proud of the FNB when he had been Minister, still preferred to blame its demise on the jealousy and corruption of other police forces. But few had his faith and Williams's criticisms were supported, if support were needed, by equally scathing passages in the Woodward Royal Commission. The Bureau was dismantled, 'virtually overnight', on 8 November 1980.[67] Customs' power over the control of 'narcotic drugs', which had grown steadily since 1905 as it gradually slipped its constitutional leash and expanded its influence into all areas of drug law enforcement, thus expired. It had been the victim of over-ambition and rivalry.

The re-emergence of the Commonwealth Department of Health as the principal bureaucracy dealing with drugs of dependence, however, did not lead to a re-evaluation of the meta-legal priorities advocated by Customs. In the first place, politicians had replaced bureaucrats as the prime determinants of policy. In Queensland, we have already seen how the power and independence of the Department of Health was steadily eroded—from the end of legal maintenance to the Cabinet defeats of the Health Minister, Llew Edwards, the department's advice had become less and less important. On a federal level, a booklet on cannabis was prepared by the Commonwealth Department of Health in 1978. Its purpose was merely to marshal the arguments on both sides of the debate about the medical dangers and legal status of cannabis. But even this was too much for the Commonwealth–State Ministers' Meeting, which suppressed its circulation. Commonwealth Health Minister, Ralph Hunt, said:

I do not want to see, with our imprimatur upon it, a document which creates unnecessary confusion and gives arguments to people who are trying to push a cause with which the States do not agree.

The impartial opinions of the Department of Health were concealed from the public simply because they were said to be 'inconsistent' and full of 'lots of different pieces of information'. When bureaucratic advice refused to bend to the wishes of politicians, it was now routinely ignored.[68]

But the health bureaucracy had not just lost its sovereignty. It had also lost its character. The Commonwealth Department of Health had for many years been a small, professional, tightly knit department with high morale, dominated by doctors and committed to principles of health advancement. It was, as a number of past members of the department told me, a place with a sense of mission. Since the 1950s, as we have seen, both political influence and bureaucratic power led medical authority over drugs to be consistently undermined by bureaucratic constraints. At the same time, the Commonwealth Department of Health no longer allied itself so closely with the medical profession. During the 1970s the department became increasingly dominated by administrators with no particular commitment to health issues, whose expertise was bureaucratic, not medical. Legislation which had previously required that the Director-General be a medical graduate, was repealed. The position of Director-General became an administrative position like any other departmental secretary and the department likewise lost its unique identity.[69] As drug policy was demedicalised, so too was the Department of Health.

Once the Department of Health stopped approaching drug policy from its own special perspective, there seemed no reason for it to doubt the accepted wisdom. The natural bureaucratic tendency towards incremental growth and the better administration of the status quo took over. Indeed, the department's increased power following Custom's demise was itself an influential factor. It was no longer an outsider in the field of drug policy. The New South Wales and Victorian Departments of Health, no less than their Commonwealth counterparts, had in the past expressed some doubts about the merits of prohibitionist policy. By the late 1970s, however, they too had taken over responsibility for drug policy and administration. Within the mainstream more than ever before, State and Commonwealth health departments alike were finding the acceptance of meta-legal orthodoxy easy and convenient. They had, in short, been co-opted. It is not that power corrupts, but that the exercise of power gives no-one the time or the inclination to question its validity.

Those who still held fast to the old medical values of the department found themselves isolated. Dr Les Drew, the Commonwealth's Senior Medical Adviser on Drugs of Dependence and a Salvation Army officer with a proselytising spirit, found little sympathy or support within the department for his views. In 1980, for example, he wrote an article for the *Medical Journal of Australia* entitled 'Drugs: Time for Honest Debate', in which he argued that the distinction between legal and illegal drugs was irrational, that the 'current repressive approach' had not proven successful, and that 'a full exploration of ... costs, dangers and limitations' of new initiatives and alternatives was required. So alienated was Drew from those whom it was his job to advise, that he wrote under a pseudonym and was hauled over the coals when his authorship was discovered.[70] By 1980 Drew, whose views differed little from the department's approach under Directors-General Cumpston, Metcalfe, or Refshauge, felt impelled to behave like a media partizan to get his message across. Waxing political influence and waning medical power, health departments' own bureaucratisation and their co-option within the established system of drug control, had all led to a homogeneity of vision. Customs lost the battle, but their approach seemed to have won the war.

A THOROUGHLY MODERN MELEE

*Twin Policies of Containment
in Contemporary Australia*

Introducing Mr Big: The Changing Face of Australians' Fears

Increasingly detailed and Draconian legislation had failed to prevent rising levels of illegal drug use, addiction and conviction. Mr Justice Woodward calculated that there were 'approximately' 9257 regular heroin users in New South Wales in 1978. In Victoria, in 1979, 2563 cannabis offences were dealt with, and 580 involving heroin, a rise of 700 per cent in only four years.[1] Particularly in relation to marijuana, the courts were treated to an unending procession of young people facing the stigma of a criminal conviction. Poor or middle class, long-term unemployed or ambitious university students, many of them regretted not their actions, but their consequences.

The age of Royal Commissions had turned potential danger to the status quo into victory not by words, but by the silences between them. But they also reflected a subtle change in attitude. After the first opium laws had been enacted, drug use had been seen as a sin because it challenged the sanctity of the law. In later years, as the medical model of addiction gained favour, addicts came to be characterised as persons whose obsession robbed them of the power of intention. Their illegality was not their fault. For them, according to Woodward, 'the ability to choose to act wisely, or to modify behaviour, is limited or eliminated'. But traffickers were still seen as sinful; their illegal behaviour was a choice and they were therefore responsible for their actions. Thus ARCID recommended the enactment of two separate pieces of legislation in order 'to reflect the distinction between criminal exploitation of drug abuse and the social plight of the individual drug user'. The proposed Drugs of Dependence Act punished minor offences including possession and use. It accepted that users were sick and in need of help; penalties were relatively slight, and the emphasis was placed on treatment and community services. The proposed Drug Trafficking Act was designed to facilitate the detection and punishment of trafficking. It assumed that the drug problem was a question of law enforcement requiring stiff penalties, broad search powers, and complicated provisions for the forfeiture of assets.[2] Illness and vice were treated in isolation as if the problems they addressed were unrelated.

As drug use escalated, trafficking became more profitable and, consequently, better organised. Where originally importation, cultivation and distribution had been undertaken on a largely *ad hoc* basis by people who were mostly users themselves, it was now increasingly well co-ordinated. Individual growers (of cannabis) and smugglers (of heroin) continued to exist, of course, but they now shared the market with carefully organised business ventures, some structured with the complexity of a large corporation. The organism of community concern was likewise in transition. The Woodward Commission, and its *Further Report* in particular, concentrated specifically upon organised trafficking. Mr Justice Williams, too, saw organised crime and not drug use itself as the main enemy, warning that:

the illegal importation and the illegal production and illegal trafficking in drugs are engaged in both directly and indirectly by persons who engage on an organised basis in other illegal activities both related and not related to drugs.[3]

On the one hand, 'organised criminals' were the epitome of the old (and often false) image of the trafficker as a mercenary preying upon the weakness of others, for they had no involvement in drugs except as a profit-making venture. But, on the other hand, organised crime is feared because of the way in which it institutionalises criminality. This has nothing to do with drugs and everything to do with our concern that law-breakers may become a powerful force in our society, influencing and corrupting governments and effecting legal change outside of the democratic process. It is the notion of a conspiracy to subvert the law, which organisation implies, that raises concern. Furthermore, the evil consequence of organised crime is rarely contended to be the suffering which the drugs cause. Rather, it is the wealth and success of the criminals themselves which stirs up frustration and ire. Organised crime breaks the law and gets away with it. It exists for profit, and is profitable. This implies that violence and corruption, if comprehensive enough, may be rewarded.

This new focus on organisation and profit made the drug problem more than ever into a question of law enforcement. Drug legislation was seen as a means to combat economic crime perpetrated by wealthy trafficking institutions, and not as either a moral or medical imperative. The user, the addict, and the pedlar were all of little importance. In 1979, the federal Liberal government enacted amendments to the *Customs Act*. Provision was made for body cavity searches in certain circumstances, and the use of listening devices for the purpose of narcotics enquiries, even in the offices of lawyers known to represent suspected drug traffickers. In line with the recommendation of the NSCCDD, a new sentencing concept was introduced, that of a 'commercial quantity' of narcotic drugs, corresponding as a rule to an amount one thousand times the 'traffickable quantity'. Persons convicted of an offence in relation to a 'commercial' quantity became liable to a maximum penalty of imprisonment for life (the court was required to impose a gaol term and not simply a fine). A person convicted of a second offence in relation to a 'traffickable' quantity was likewise liable to life imprisonment. In contrast, the maximum penalty for a first traffickable offence was twenty-five years' imprisonment and/or $100 000 or, in the case of cannabis, ten years' imprisonment and/or $4000. Those for whom the drug traffic was not just business, but big business, were clearly being singled out for special treatment.[4]

The Act also established a system for the 'recovery of pecuniary penalties for dealings in narcotic goods'. While provision had always existed for the forfeiture of assets which were the proceeds of crime, it was difficult to prove that a particular asset had in fact been purchased by 'drug money'. In 1979, a new process was introduced. Under section 243B, the court decides if a person has 'engaged in prescribed narcotic dealings' and then assesses 'the value of the benefits derived' thereby. The defendant is then subject to a 'pecuniary penalty' equal to that value and payable out of *all* of the defendant's property, however acquired. Furthermore, since an action under this section is not technically a criminal matter, the prosecution only has to prove on the balance of probabilities that 'prescribed dealings' took place.[5] Accordingly, it is quite possible for a person acquitted of a criminal offence against the *Customs Act* (which requires proof beyond a reasonable doubt), nevertheless to be required to pay a vast fine.

These provisions aroused hostility on both sides of the House. Former Liberal Prime Minister, William McMahon, declared himself 'dumbfounded' and 'bewildered' by the system of pecuniary penalties. He and Tasmanian MHR, Michael Hodgman, particularly concerned by the effect of the provisions relating to listening devices on the long-standing doctrine of legal professional privilege (according to which nothing said by a client to their lawyer in confidence can used as evidence in court), crossed the floor. The government was unmoved. The relevant Minister, Wal Fife, said:

The Government recognises that these provisions contain harsh elements. No apology is made for that fact. It is part of an upgrading of the war against drug trafficking.

This was how the war was to be waged. The presumption of innocence, the burden of proof and the doctrine of privilege were all expendable. Yet even those opposed to the Bill did not disagree. Both McMahon and Hodgman were concerned about the use of listening devices in lawyers' offices to aid in the prosecution of other offences, such as 'murder' or 'homosexuality'. Their complaint was that the 'exceptional law' put in place was not 'restricted totally to narcotics and drug traffickers'.[6]

Extremism was not a new feature of drug laws, but users and pushers had been toppled from their plinth in the pantheon of evil. 'Commercial' penalties and complex forfeiture provisions were clearly addressed to those for whom the drug trade was big business. They were aimed at taking the profit out of drugs not just as a means of slowing the supply of illegal drugs to users, but because the profitability of the trade was itself the central evil.

In 1980 Alfred McCoy's book *Drug Traffic* was published, subtitled 'Narcotics and Organised Crime in Australia'. The two were almost synonymous by this stage. The illustration on the cover was the hand of a man dressed in a pin-stripe suit clutching a wad of money.[7] The new images associated with drugs more and more related to business. People spoke of 'Mr Big'. According to Victorian MLA, M.T. Williams, speaking in the Victorian parliament, the drug trade was controlled by 'multi-million dollar financiers' who were 'wicked men' and 'evil monsters'. 'Drug abuse is not an alternative lifestyle,' he continued, 'it is a vehicle for organised crime to control this country.' Tom Roper, the Victorian Minister of Health, in the second reading speech on the Drugs Poisons and Controlled Substances Bill 1983, also insisted that 'the new dimension of drug abuse was its promotion for profit, the involvement of organised crime'.[8] In these ways, then, illegal drug use was no longer seen as an evil in its own right.

There was no Mr Big: no one person or group of persons in charge of drug smuggling in Australia. But the image conjured up by this fiction, which stood at the apex of drug trafficking in Australia, was a potent new symbol of evil: he was a businessman whose wickedness stemmed from his respectability, his power and his wealth. Mr Sin, the symbol of the Chinese drug fiend, was also vilified for making a profit out of the misery of others, but his evil had been apparent in his fetid premises and bloated body. The evil of Mr Big, however, lurked beneath the surface, and its very concealment made it still more feared. The eponymous Mr Sin was replaced by the anonymous Mr Big. And while Mr Sin was hated for what he did to his victims, Mr Big was hated for the wealth he accrued and for his respectability and apparent immunity to prosecution. The drug trade was not a question of health or morality, but of economics and power.

The flurry of Commissions continued, ever more limited in scope and reflecting these perspectives. In 1981 and 1982, the collapse of the Nugan Hand bank and its associations with the drug trafficking syndicate of Terence Clark became questions of great political controversy. The 1983 report of the Royal Commission of Inquiry into Drug Trafficking, under Mr Justice Donald Stewart, was a paper chase into the complex financial interests of the Clark group and Nugan Hand. It was an impressive exercise in economic detection, but it was a dry, legalistic and economic document totally devoid of social content or social context. The Royal Commission on the Activities of the Federated Ship Painters and Dockers Union (under Frank Costigan, QC), set up shortly after the Stewart Royal Commission, was an inquiry into organised criminal activities in many areas; it too demonstrated that drug trafficking was seen as merely one aspect of a broader problem.[9]

A Split Personality?

The distinction between users and big-time traffickers, which the focus on Mr Big entrenched, made little sense, for the two are inextricably linked. It is naive to think that if only the activities of traffickers could be restricted, demand for the use of cannabis or heroin would disappear. There is a real demand for these drugs arising from the complex social and personal reasons for their use; and while there is a demand, there will be people prepared to take the risk of supplying. It is also unrealistic to expect that we can ever intercept more than a small percentage of the total volume of drugs smuggled into this country, no matter how harsh the laws or how powerful the police.

The use of and traffic in drugs are connected in other ways, too. On the one hand, if drug use itself were not prohibited, the drug trade would no longer be either a magnet for organised crime or as profitable to those involved. On the other hand, both the illegality and evil of trafficking are predicated upon the illegality of possession and consumption. Trafficking is illegal because it entices illegal possession; it is seen as evil at least partly for the same reason. Laws against trafficking historically developed as a means towards the more effective prevention of the crimes of possession and use. They were, in other words, tools in the suppression of the use of drugs. Ironically, the situation was now reversed. The suppression of drug use was mattering less and less. Governments, meanwhile, did not stop to consider whether the focus on trafficking was an effective way of reducing either drug use or crime.

The emphasis on Mr Big as an evil in his own right allowed a less severe approach to drug users by removing them from the centrality of drug laws. The harsh penalties imposed on marijuana smokers and other users of drugs could be softened without undermining 'the war on drugs'. The dichotomy between 'illness' and 'vice', to which I have frequently had recourse in explaining public attitudes to drug use, no longer held. While legislation focused on the 'Mr Bigs' of trafficking, drug users themselves were seen as neither patients to be treated nor villains to be harried. They were, to a large extent, seen as secondary: by-products or victims of the traffickers' business.

Every State in Australia rewrote drug legislation during the 1980s. The *Drugs, Poisons and Controlled Substances Act 1981* (Vic.), enacted in the last months of the long-lasting Liberal government in that State, was typical of those that followed. It was in every respect a thoroughly modern drug law, vastly complex—135 sections long and accompanied by over one thousand separate regulations—and comprehensive—schedule 8 now included 122 items, ranging from amphetamines, cannabis, cocaine, heroin, methadone, morphine, and pethidine, to every analogue, synthetic and derivative yet devised. In addition, schedule 7, which dealt with 'dangerous' and 'special' poisons subject to particular controls, included, along with cyanide and strychnine, LSD, mescaline, psilocybin and other hallucinogens. The content of the Act as a whole, however, was unsurprising. 'The key to the drug problem,' said W.A. Borthwick, Minister of Health, 'is the availability of drugs and the main object of this bill is to make it less attractive to traffic in drugs'. A person found guilty of trafficking in a 'drug of dependence' could be sentenced to twenty-five years' imprisonment and, in addition, a fine of up to $250 000 (accompanied by the familiar provision that possession above the prescribed amount was treated as trafficking unless the defendant could prove the contrary). 'Trafficking drugs of dependence is such a heinous offence,' explained the Minister, 'that the courts should not have an option of imposing a fine in lieu of a gaol sentence.'[10]

Some small alterations were made to the harsh edges of the law. Part X of the Bill established a Drug Rehabilitation and Research Fund to receive all moneys obtained from 'fines penalties and forfeitures'. Money obtained from traffickers was to be used for treatment facilities, research, and community education. On cannabis, however, the Act was equivocal. It was categorised as a 'narcotic plant', cultivation of which carried a maximum penalty of ten years' imprisonment or $100 000, or both. But cannabis was not defined as a 'drug of dependence' and, consequently, the maximum penalty for trafficking in it, while still severe (ten years or $100 000, or both), was somewhat less than that which applied to other drugs.[11] Those who designed the Act perhaps recognised that the sale of cannabis to a willing buyer was not as exploitative as the sale of heroin to an addict, and that many marijuana 'traffickers' were in fact only performing a service to their friends. In this way the Act acknowledged, if only to a limited degree, a clear distinction between cannabis and other illegal substances.

Upon the election of the Victorian Labor government in 1983, substantial amendments were prepared. The *Drugs Poisons and Controlled Substances (Amendment) Act 1983* (Vic.) showed that the new Ministry, like other Labor governments around the country, was prepared to lessen the excesses of drug policy, but not to question its fundamentals. The Act introduced an even heavier penalty for trafficking in a 'commercial quantity' of a drug and introduced in addition to fines and imprisonment a system of 'pecuniary penalties' similar to that which operated under section 243 of the Commonwealth *Customs Act*. In contrast, the amended Act lessened the penalties applicable to 'users or addicts' and other 'minor offenders'. The cultivation of marijuana 'not committed for any purpose related to trafficking' became liable to a maximum penalty of only $2000 or one year's imprisonment, or both (previously $100 000/ten years); possession of a 'drug of dependence' not for trafficking, $3000 or one year's imprisonment (previously $5000/two years); and use of a drug of dependence other than cannabis, $3000 or one year's imprisonment (previously $5000/two years). Furthermore, possession or use of a 'small quantity' of cannabis (less than fifty grams) became liable to a penalty of no more than $500. In this way, in Victoria at least, the most criticised aspects of drug policy were ameliorated.[12]

The reforms that emerged in other jurisdictions were similarly driven in apparently contradictory directions. First, meta-law directed at the economic profitability of trafficking expanded. By 1989 every State in Australia had enacted maximum penalties of, typically, twenty-five years' imprisonment and in addition, and not as an alternative, a $250 000 fine for the trafficking of a 'commercial quantity' of a drug.[13] In some jurisdictions the same offence attracted penalties of $500 000 or life imprisonment. Furthermore, provisions in all jurisdictions deemed a person in possession of more than a specified amount of illegal drugs guilty of the more serious trafficking offences unless they could prove their innocence. South Australia and Queensland, while their forfeiture provisions were not as severe as those enacted by Victoria or the Commonwealth, provided that where the profits of drug trafficking could not be traced to specific property or investments liable to forfeiture, the offender could still be required to pay an amount equal to that profit, out of all their assets whether legally acquired or not.[14] In those circumstances, the maximum fine levied on trafficking offences became irrelevent. Forfeiture provisions were a system of punishment directly proportional to profit and capable of imposing unlimited fines.

Meta-law directed at drug traffickers progressed in other ways, too. Internal body searches and the use of listening devices were allowed in some jurisdictions. Commonwealth legislation concerning telephonic interception, police powers, and the forfeiture and tracing of assets, greatly multiplied.[15] Around Australia, police powers of search and entry were gradually expanded and included the right to search people, vehicles and (in some States and some circumstances) premises without a warrant.[16]

Second, as the mere use and possession of drugs became a side-issue, more and more laws actually softened the effect of prohibitionist drug policy upon users themselves. In some jurisdictions, laws were enacted to encourage the treatment of drug users as an alternative to their imprisonment. In both South Australia and the Australian Capital Territory, the court, on the advice of an assessment panel, may order the treatment of an offender, with their consent, in which case the court may decide not to record a conviction in the case.[17] But while these laws were to some extent a reflection of the medical model of addiction that we have seen ebb and flow over the previous century, they were, even more, a demonstration that laws directed at possession and use were seen as unimportant. Thus, just as penalties for large-scale trafficking increased, penalties for the mere possession of small amounts of illegal drugs actually decreased. Marijuana laws in particular, the focus of such widespread civil disobedience and social criticism, began to change. In the Australian Capital Territory, a penalty of only $100 had applied to the possession of under twenty-five grams of marijuana since 1975 (a similar penalty in the 1989 Ordinance also applied to the cultivation for personal use of less than five cannabis plants). A $500 maximum penalty was introduced in Victoria in 1983 and in South Australia the following year.[18] In every jurisdiction in Australia, moreover, marijuana trafficking attracted a lesser penalty than trafficking in other illegal drugs. Clearly these changes were substantial. They seemed to be an admission that marijuana smoking could not be outlawed. But at the same time, they fell carefully short of decriminalisation. The principle of illegality was studiously protected, while the effect of prohibition was undermined.

The political emphasis on Mr Big, while it permitted the enactment of these reforms, also ensured that criticism of drug policy in Australia was contained within manageable limits. Possession and use were still criminal offences, with all the implications this had for the high cost of the drug, the alienation of users, the environment and subculture of use, the social consequences of conviction, and the way drug use was perceived in society. But pressure for a comprehensive reconsideration of these issues was able to be dissipated by careful compromises and minor amendments exactly because drug users themselves no longer mattered. On the other hand, emphasis on 'the drug trade' shored up the legitimacy of drug legislation by directing public attention to an area of unquestioned evil. The new consensus on the importance of meta-law, which had developed in the late 1970s, held firm, backed by political rhetoric which became more impassioned as penalties grew higher. Terry Sheahan, the New South Wales Labor Attorney-General, introducing the Drug Misuse and Trafficking Bill 1985, said of 'greedy ... drug entrepreneurs' that they would be given 'no quarter':

they will be hunted down with sophisticated weaponry; when caught they will be vigorously prosecuted; when convicted they will be stripped of their ill-gotten gains; when sentenced they will face the most severe penalties that the Courts can impose.[19]

In every State, drug trafficking became a step-motherhood issue, universally agreed to be bad but nevertheless repeatedly trotted out for advantage. Few thought to question this attitude. Few wondered if the causes of the increasing involvement of organised crime lay any deeper than the size of the penalties that those convicted faced. The emotional response everyone felt towards the Mr Bigs of this world drew attention away from the weaknesses of the structure of drug legislation itself and towards its populist façade.

Labor in Power 1983–1985

Labor governments, as well as conservative ones, generally supported these principles. There was nothing radical in the *Drugs Poisons and Controlled Substances (Amendment) Act 1983* (Vic.); the *Drug Misuse and Trafficking Act 1985*, introduced by the New South Wales Labor government, was in fact harsher than the laws it replaced and restructured. Although it introduced a complex gradation of penalties that distinguished between the moral position of the user and the large-scale trafficker, providing different maximum penalties for the cultivation, manufacture or supply of a 'small quantity', a traffickable quantity, an 'indictable quantity', or a 'commercial quantity' of a prohibited drug or plant, no distinction was made between the traffic or possession of cannabis and other drugs except where the amount concerned was an 'indictable' or 'commercial' quantity. In contrast to the position in Victoria and South Australia, the penalty for the possession of any quantity of cannabis was still up to $2000 and/or two years' imprisonment and, for 'commercial' trafficking in the drug, $500 000 and/or twenty years' imprisonment. The only difference was that commercial traffickers in other drugs could be imprisoned for life.[20]

Take also the federal Labor Party which, while in opposition, had not been uncritical of orthodox drug policy. Dr Neal Blewett, for example, a South Australian philosophy lecturer and member of the Council of Civil Liberties, was a strong advocate of marijuana law reform in the 1960s. Ten years later, Professor Blewett presented an influential paper to the South Australian Royal Commission, and another to the Williams Royal Commission. After the election of the federal Labor government in 1983, Dr Blewett became Minister for Health, a position he held until 1990.

The Trojan horse proved, however, low on horsepower. Shortly after his appointment, Dr Blewett let slip his opinion on cannabis in a television interview. The resultant furore demonstrated to him that a candid politician would soon be out of a job. His opinion threatened to alienate him not only from many people in the community, but from many of his more conservative Labor colleagues, too. Choosing to save his energy for 'more important health issues', he ran dead on the question of cannabis. It must be said that by defusing the cannabis issue, State policies on the issue have been allowed to develop without interference, and these policies have in some jurisdictions led to significantly lower penalties for marijuana use and possession. Marijuana smokers in general risk nothing like the persecution or punishment they encountered fifteen years earlier, and for this credit must be given to the policy of gradual non-confrontational change adopted by politicians like Dr Blewett.[21] None the less, this approach has made any complete reform of cannabis laws less and less likely. Political and social pressure for reform has faded away and the matter has been taken off the agenda—yet the possession of marijuana remains illegal. The integrity of the structure and principles of drug legislation have been maintained unimpaired, and a confrontation, which at one point challenged the assumptions behind the whole system of drug control, has dwindled to nothing.

Meanwhile, the war against Mr Big continued apace. In 1984, responding to public concern about the influence of organised crime especially in relation to the drug trade, the government established the National Crime Authority (NCA). The purpose of the NCA was to ensure that the inquiries begun by Justice Stewart and Frank Costigan did not die out; it was, in effect, to be a standing Royal Commission on organised crime, chaired first by Justice Stewart himself, whose previous report had marked him as a man cut out for just such a law-enforcement oriented task.[22] Since then the NCA has operated in a blaze of secrecy. Undoubtedly, its first priority has been the investigation of the relationship between organised crime and drug trafficking. The resources allocated to it, its broad powers and its covert operations have emphasised still further that the 'war against drugs' must now be waged with sophisticated equipment and unique powers of investigation and enforcement. The establishment of other bodies like the New South Wales State Drug Crime Commission and the Australian Bureau of Criminal Intelligence, have similarly enforced the belief that the 'drug problem' is all about the efforts of elite police to track down high-rolling Mr Bigs.

In the run-up to the 1984 federal election, the then Prime Minister, Bob Hawke, cried on national television when asked about the heroin addiction of his daughter. It was a natural outburst of personal anguish that would have been understood by all those close to people with problems of drug dependency. It was also a powerful symbol, first, of the extent to which illegal drug use had affected everyone in Australia, no matter what their position, and second, of the fear and anguish that such use aroused. It was a very private, very public act which expressed the importance of the issue in Australian society, and the emotionalism surrounding it.

The concrete result of Bob Hawke's tears was the Special Premiers'

Conference on Drugs held in April 1985, out of which emerged the National Campaign Against Drug Abuse (NCADA). Despite the hackneyed use of war-like metaphors, the informational materials produced by the NCADA have consistently dealt with both legal and illegal drugs equivalently. Further, the programme has led to increased funds for a variety of research, educational and community-based resources: to a considerable extent, it has acted upon the Premiers' recognition 'that drug abuse is a complex problem and that there are no simple or quick solutions'.[23] It would be remiss of me not to mention that a large proportion of the funding for my own research came from the NCADA.

None the less, the NCADA reflected the overall approach of the Labor Party in the 1980s. Despite a more sympathetic approach to users, the legal structure of drug policy was not re-evaluated. The Conference agreed that 'existing controls on cannabis are to be maintained', and

that it was essential that government efforts to combat drug trafficking and to prevent supplies of hard drugs coming into the country be intensified. Particular attention will be paid to those who control, direct and finance such activities.[24]

This commitment has been realised both in the allocation of Commonwealth funds to these purposes, and in legislation enacted by the Commonwealth relating to telephone interception, the confiscation of assets, the powers of the NCA, and so on. As in other jurisdictions around Australia, the Commonwealth government accompanied a more understanding approach to 'mere' users with increased severity against traffickers.

Dr Jekyll: Legislative Reform in South Australia 1984–1986

Labor and Liberal parties alike adopted dichotomous policies, savagely increasing some penalties and reducing others, but to a considerable extent both aspects served much the same purpose: containment. Criticism of the law-enforcement approach to the problems of drug use was quietened by the introduction of some reforms, while the growing—and popular—emphasis upon large-scale drug trafficking focused attention away from a general examination of the legal principles of prohibition and punishment. The structure of drug laws was thus shored up in two contrasting but interrelated ways. The result was a curious cocktail of tyranny and liberality, the exact mix of which varied from jurisidiction to jurisdiction. Two examples stand out as representing the extremes of drug policy in Australia. In isolation they seem inconsistent but they were merely clearer expositions of the two approaches struggling to co-exist. In South Australia, Dr Jekyll emerged victorious. In Queensland, Mr Hyde held sway.

The *Controlled Substances Act 1984*, introduced by the South Australian

Labor government of John Bannon, replaced and clarified the *Narcotic and Psychotropic Drugs Act 1934*, which had been described by South Australian Chief Justice, John Bray, as a 'repatched patchwork quilt'. It was a reform similar to that enacted in Victoria. New penalties were introduced for large-scale trafficking and forfeiture laws were expanded; the possession, use, or cultivation for personal use of a small quantity of cannabis, in contrast, was only to be subject to a $500 fine. While the Liberal opposition protested that this was 'the thin edge of the wedge', the amendment itself was in keeping with the trend in other jurisdictions. The South Australian Minister for Health, Dr John Cornwall, who at the June 1983 State convention of the Labor Party had led the debate on a resolution calling for the decriminalisation of marijuana and 'carried the day', was likewise at pains to acknowledge that 'the great majority of South Australians are not prepared to accept decriminalisation of marijuana'. 'This is a modest amendment only,' he said. 'I personally do not propose to take it any further at this time.'[25]

In other ways, however, the *Controlled Substances Act 1984* went significantly further than any other State legislation in reforming the drug-control system. A person charged with possession of a drug of dependence (other than cannabis), is referred under the Act to an assessment panel, which can ask them to enter into a written undertaking designed to help their treatment, education, rehabilitation, or addressed to 'any other matters [to] assist that person to overcome any personal problems that may tend to lead ... to the misuse of drugs'. In return, the assessment panel can stop the prosecution from proceeding. At the same time, the interests of the defendant are protected. The accused may refuse to be assessed or to give any undertaking and may choose to go to court instead; neither is it assumed that they are 'sick' and in need of treatment, but only that they may have 'personal problems'.[26] The withdrawal of an authoritarian legal system is not necessarily accompanied by authoritarian medical control.

Persons charged with a 'simple possession offence' were no longer expected to end up in court; on the contrary, they could *only* be charged with the express authorisation of the assessment panel whose priority was the welfare of the user and not the enforcement of the law. Recall that the illegality of possession and use was the basic principle upon which the whole edifice of drug control policy in Australia had been erected. Now it had virtually been sidelined. Yet the government was not prepare to reconsider the crimes of possession or use themselves, or the effect of the legal structure upon users or the drug trade in general. Rather, it attempted to avoid the consequences of legislative prohibition without amending the prohibition itself. The opposition protested that

> *where a breach of the law is alleged against an adult offender he should be dealt with by the ordinary courts of the land. To do otherwise is to erode the criminal justice system.*

'We are dealing with criminal matters,' insisted another speaker.[27] For the

Liberal Party, then, the law was the law. But the government agreed: the law's meaning was undermined, but its words remained.

Despite his parliamentary statements, Dr Cornwall and other prominent members of the Labor Party, including the ex-Premier and patron of the National Organisation for the Reform of Marijuana Laws, Don Dunstan, had no intention of leaving the laws relating to cannabis as they stood.[28] This mainstream support for reform, coupled perhaps with the long-term influence of the report of the South Australian Royal Commission, enabled more radical changes to take place. Notwithstanding the Special Premiers' Conference statement in favour of cannabis prohibition, to which the Premier had consented, further reform was introduced in 1986. The Controlled Substances Act Amendment Bill proposed several amendments to the Act, including an increase in the fine payable by a person convicted of possession of over one hundred grams of cannabis for the purpose of sale, from $4000 to $50 000. Hidden in the Bill, however, was a new scheme for the 'expiation of simple cannabis offences'. Possession and cultivation of a small amount of cannabis, which previously attracted a maximum penalty of $500, could, under the proposed amendment, be 'expiated' by the payment of a fee of $50 or $150 (depending on the amount involved). As in the case of parking fines, the expiation fee, if paid, would not be dealt with by a court, would not constitute an admission of guilt and would not amount to a criminal conviction. It was a proposal for decriminalisation, however much the government tried to deny it.[29]

The Labor Party allowed a free vote on the Bill and in consequence, it was opposed by some members of the Labor Party as well as all the Liberal Members. Debate was lengthy and acrimonious. Following criticism that the Bill would have allowed the smoking of marijuana in a public place '[by] Paul McCartney, Boy George and other rock stars ... in front of 40 000 to 50 000 young South Australians' it was hastily redrawn, but attacks that Dr Cornwall characterised as 'carping, cavilling and negative' continued. All the old arguments were rehearsed: 'Anyone else,' said one speaker, 'who commits an offence ... has a black mark against his or her name'. The deputy leader of the opposition complained that it was 'the conformists who do *not* ... throw aside all the mores that have helped keep the community together, who pick up the tab for the social misfits'. Above all, cannabis use still symbolised, for many people, social non-conformity and legal disobedience.[30]

Essentially, debate on the clause illustrated two different attitudes to the validity and function of law. Dr Cornwall, for example, insisted 'we must never glibly believe that the legislative solution will solve all our problems'. For him, the fundamental point was that the prohibition of cannabis had failed. On the other hand, K.T. Griffin, who led the debate for the opposition, argued that legalisation would make marijuana use acceptable and that its prohibition had prevented many people from trying the drug because, as he said, 'there are a lot of persons who obey laws even though they do not accept that the law is a good law'.[31] To those opposed to the Bill, the health arguments against marijuana were conclusive; to its proponents, the question was not about how people should behave, but how the law affected their behaviour. To the opposition, changing the law changed reality; to those in favour of the Bill, changing the law only acknowledged reality.

The Bill passed through the second reading despite passionate opposition and few signs of government support—only two government Members spoke in favour of the scheme in the Legislative Assembly, and Dr Cornwall alone in the Legislative Council. In the committee stage of the Bill's passage through the Legislative Assembly, the new expiation scheme, clause 8, was voted on separately, and four members of the Labor Party voted against it, including Lynn Arnold, the Minister for State Development and Technology (and future State Premier). In a moment of high drama, the Chairman of Committees, Mr Ferguson, announced the result of the vote:

There are 22 Ayes and 22 Noes. There being an equality of votes, I will give my casting vote for the Ayes.
Honourable members: Shame! Shame!
The Chairman: The question therefore passes in the affirmative.

The vote on the third reading was less close, many government members finding that although they opposed clause 8, they were not prepared to vote against the Bill as a whole. Showing tactical astuteness, the government had included several other unobjectionable amendments along with the expiation scheme: by twenty-four votes to eighteen, the Controlled Substances Act Amendment Bill was passed on 29 October 1986.[32]

A week later, the Liberal Party retaliated. The Controlled Substances Act Amendment Bill (No. 2), which they introduced, did one thing only: it repealed the expiation scheme. It was simply designed to force those members of the Labor Party who had refused to vote against the original Bill *as a whole* to take a definite stand. In a sniping spirit, and in an atmosphere of rowdy emotionalism, the vote on the second reading was taken. Again the vote was tied, twenty-one apiece, and the Speaker, John Trainer, was required to cast a deciding vote.

The Speaker: ... This measure being, in effect, the reconsideration of a question previously decided, and the Chair being free to exercise a personal conscience vote and to support the status quo, I cast my vote with the Noes. The question is not agreed to.

The Speaker therefore relied on the parliamentary convention that the presiding officer should not vote to change the law; it was a principle that the Chairman of Committees in debate on the previous Bill seemed to have overlooked. Still, the result stood and the Bill was defeated. Section 45a of the *Controlled Substances Act* remained on the books. The Labor government, not very convincingly, insisted that the expiation scheme did not amount to decriminalisation. Dr Cornwall argued that not just the sale but the possession of cannabis remained illegal; only the penalties had altered. But these arguments fooled no one. If the expiation fee was paid, none of the consequences of illegality would follow: no conviction, no criminal record, no court appearance.[33] Legislation had been passed which significantly lessened the control exercised over the use of a drug or poison in an Australian jurisdiction.

The South Australian amendment was the most radical change to cannabis laws yet undertaken in Australia. It seemed a rejection of the 'illness' and 'vice' models of drug control as applied to cannabis. The *Single Convention*'s insistence that cannabis was 'particularly dangerous' was ignored, as it had been to a lesser extent in other jurisdictions. But the *Controlled Substances (Amendment) Act 1986* was not a rejection of prohibition. It was merely an extension of the ambivalent nature of drug legislation throughout Australia in the 1980s. Penalties for the manufacture, production, sale or supply of all drugs of dependence and prohibited substances, *including* cannabis, were substantially increased by the amendment. In South Australia, seizures of over 300 grams of heroin could result in a penalty of $500 000 and life imprisonment; in New South Wales and Victoria a similiar penalty only applied to amounts in excess of one kilogram. Dr Cornwall boasted that the Bill enacted 'penalties for trafficking and trading to the highest level in mainstream Australia'.[34]

The Bill carried to an extreme the distinction between users and sellers that applied in every jurisdiction. One speaker said the government was 'having a bit each way', 'punishing more severely the Mr Bigs ... but soften[ing] up considerably on the users.'[35] Yet this was exactly the process underway throughout Australia. Comprehensive reform of 'drug' laws or cannabis laws was not undertaken. It is often argued that cannabis is bad because smokers buy the drug from illegal sources and are therefore exposed to criminal drug dealers. On this reasoning, the *illegality* of cannabis acts as a 'stepping stone' to heroin, rather than the drug itself. But the *Controlled Substances (Amendment) Act* did not solve this problem. Penalties for the sale of cannabis were in fact increased. Marijuana smokers in South Australia must still mix with law-breakers and drug-dealers in order to obtain the drug; they are now protected from the law, but their environment remains the same.

Although Lynn Arnold feared that decriminalisation would 'move the frontier of debate' and open up the 'plausible arguments' concerning legalised heroin,[36] the opposite may be the case. The use of certain drugs, even of cannabis, remained illegal, and their special status and imagery in the public mind was undisturbed. Cannabis, moreover, was set up as a special case with the consequence that the parallels between the operation of cannabis laws and the workings of other drug laws are more likely to be ignored than explored. The Dr Jekyll approach taken in South Australia suggests how amelioratory legislation may take the pressure off any critical reappraisal of the fundamentals of drug policy in Australia.

Mr Hyde: Legislative Reform in Queensland 1986

At the same time as cannabis reform took place in South Australia, the arch-conservative National Party administration of Sir Joh Bjelke-Petersen in Queensland enacted the toughest drug legislation ever seen in Australia. Its law-and-order approach to drugs was both politically expedient and, as we have seen, a genuine expression of conservative values in which illegal drug use was hated for what it symbolised, and with whom it was associated. The *Liquor Acts and Other Acts Amendment Act 1985* (Qld) illustrated the extreme lengths to which this approach could be taken. It provided that a liquor licence would be forfeited if

the licensed premises have been the resort of prostitutes, drug dealers, sexual perverts or deviants, child molesters or of persons under the surveillance of the police.[37]

If publicans served 'drug dealers' or 'deviants' in their bars, they would lose their licences. Drug sellers, people whose sexuality was not 'normal' (including, presumably, homosexuals), people the police thought trouble-makers (for whatever reason), were not necessarily guilty of any criminal conduct—certainly not by their presence in a bar—but they were all to be hounded out of 'decent' society. Not just their illegal behaviour, but they themselves, were condemned.

These modern outlaws were not defined. Who is a 'pervert' or a 'deviant'? What is a 'drug' and when does a user 'deal'? When is a premises a 'resort'? These questions seemed so self-evident to the Queensland government as not to require definition. 'We' are normal—'they' are not. *We know who They are*, said the Act; 'their' difference was a mark of identification and a crime in itself. The *Liquor Acts and Other Acts Amendment Act 1985* demonstrated an obsession with conformity and obedience of which the government's hatred of illegal drug use was merely an aspect and a symptom.

The essential 'otherness' of drug users likewise led to the enactment of the *Drugs Misuse Act 1986* (Qld), introduced by the Minister for Police, Bill Gunn. The Queensland Department of Health had lost its power; drugs were now a police matter. Warrantless searches, internal and body cavity searches, the use of listening devices, wide-ranging provisions dealing with the forfeiture of property and the confiscation of assets: in these respects, the Act was thorough, but not substantially different from other jurisdictions.[38] The Act, however, went further. It established two schedules. Schedule 1 listed heroin, cocaine, lysergide (LSD), and phencyclidine. Schedule 2 included over 130 other drugs, including barbiturates, amphetamines, hallucinogens, opiates and cannabis.

Schedule 2 also included bufotenine, the name invented to describe the acrid distillation of *Bufo marinus*, the giant cane toad. Since its introduction into the cane-fields of Queensland earlier in the century, the cane toad has proven to be one of the great biological disasters to befall this continent. Poisonous, ravenous, and prolific, it advances inexorably across the continent, causing extensive damage to crops and threatening many native species with extinction. Apparently this menacing toad, which otherwise seems unstoppable, can be boiled up and drunk with hallucinogenic results; I've even heard of hardy northerners squeezing its poison into their beers. I'm not sure how much credence to give to these stories; actual evidence of this kind of 'buphoria' seems scant, and the practice, by all accounts, is too revolting to be worth the trouble. None the less, so determined was the government to prevent the use of legal substitutes to evade the prohibition of recreational drug use that bufotenine was quickly included in the Queensland drug schedule and in corresponding schedules in other jurisdictions.[39] From 4-Cyano-2-Dimethylamino-4,4-Diphenylbutane and tetrahydro-cannibinol on the one hand, to mushrooms and poisonous toads on the other, drug legislation continued to be updated. Once again the hydra was decapitated. The obsessive determination of the legislature to enforce the law has been matched only by human ingenuity and the infinite diversity of the natural world.

The story of the cane toad demonstrates in miniature the approach of the *Drugs Misuse Act*: the law was the law, and no attempt to circumvent it would be tolerated. The medical model was rejected and the law enforcement model endorsed with a vengeance. The effectiveness of the law was assumed, if only legislation was comprehensive enough and penalties harsh enough.

In addition to offences relating to supply, cultivation, possession and so on, the Act created a new offence of 'carr[ying] on the business of unlawfully trafficking in a dangerous drug'. The *business* of supply, then, was the new focus of the law. 'Trafficking', on the other hand, is nowhere defined. Just like 'sexual perverts and deviants', 'we' all know what a trafficker looks like.[40] The penalty for these offences varied depending on the schedule in which the drug was listed and the quantity involved. For the most serious offences a new penalty was created: in addition to a penalty of up to $500 000 and the application of forfeiture provisions, 'imprisonment with hard labour for life which cannot be mitigated or varied by a court'. This was not a maximum penalty: the judge had no choice but to impose this sentence, which applied to serious offences concerning schedule 1 drugs, including 'trafficking', supply of any quantity to a minor, and possession of either a 'commercial' quantity or a 'traffickable' quantity, unless the offender was a 'drug dependent person'. In fact, although I have used the terms 'commercial' and 'traffickable', these words were not used in the Act. The quantity which I have called 'commercial' was only one tenth the amount needed to constitute a commercial quantity in other jurisdictions.[41]

Any other conviction relating to schedule 1 drugs, including mere possession of heroin or cocaine, subjected the offender to a maximum (but not mandatory) penalty of life imprisonment and/or $500 000: in Victoria, the same offender could only receive up to one year's imprisonment and/or $3000, in New South Wales, two years' imprisonment and/or $2000, while in South Australia they would probably not be convicted at all. Even a parent who discovered heroin in their house and did not report their child to the police was liable to a penalty of up to fifteen years' imprisonment. And penalties relating to schedule 2 drugs, while not so extreme, were still harsher than those applying elsewhere in Australia. Possession or cultivation of a small quantity for personal use was not treated as a special case; neither was cannabis. All attracted penalties far in excess of those applicable in other jurisdictions.[42]

The treatment provisions of the Act also reflected its philosophy. The court could order the compulsory treatment of any offender who is 'a drug dependent person'. The implication behind the section was that all drug dependent persons needed to be treated, whether they agreed or not. It is hard to view the effect of these provisions, which authorised the indefinite hospitalisation of a person without their consent, against their will, as anything other than an insidious form of punishment. Furthermore, the *Health Act* (Qld), which the new Act replaced, had provided that the detention of a first offender for treatment was 'deemed not to be a conviction'. Somewhat like the approach taken in South Australia, the dependent user was in this way not labelled as criminal. The *Drugs Misuse Act* deleted the provision.[43] In South Australia, of course, no dependent user could be treated without their consent.

In debate on the Bill, government speakers saw drug use as a symptom of a general disrespect for authority. 'Law is a duty,' said Mr Cahill. 'Standards, once the object of attainment, are now despised. The reluctance to accept society is massive; and drug statistics tell their dreadful tale.'[44] It would be easy, then, to characterise the *Drugs Misuse Act* as the kind of ham-fisted extremism typical of a Queensland government that will long be remembered for its intolerance and its corruption. Or to see it as an anachronism, a last cry of defiance from the disciples of Harry Anslinger. But this would only be part of the story.

Those who opposed the Bill did not object to its severity outright. The Liberal Party, in opposition at the time, supported the thrust of the Bill with little hesitation. Liberal leader Angus Innes said:

it is worth a try to throw the book at offenders in an attempt to strike terror into the hearts of the little people because, if they are knocked out of the system, the Mr Bigs are exposed ...

Although he thought that the Bill was 'something radically different', the government's approach was in keeping with the trend around Australia. The overwhelming concern with large-scale trafficking made the enactment of any laws, no matter how extreme, acceptable.[45]

Terry Mackenroth, leading the debate for the Labor Party, also agreed 'with the government's stated intent ... to deal with the Mr Bigs of the drug trade', and merely charged that the Nationals were not willing 'to go all out to stop this insidious drug trade'. So powerful had rhetoric about 'Mr Big' and organised crime become that the Labor Party, although it expressed some reservations, supported the Bill through the second-reading stage. Again, in relation to the penalty of mandatory life imprisonment introduced by the government for 'trafficking' offences, all three parties engaged in competition to see who was toughest. The Labor Party argued that a 'life sentence' was normally paroled after about twelve years, and proposed instead a penalty of twenty-five years. The Liberal Party favoured not only mandatory life imprisonment, but a mandatory non-parole period set by the court. All were keen to prove their determination to 'get the big boys'.[46]

The severity of the *Drugs Misuse Act* was supported in large measure by opposition parties because it was extreme, but not abnormal. It was part of the Australia-wide focus on the business of trafficking. Mr Big was the new image of evil in Australian society, and in his name anything could be justified. To voice doubt, even in the face of laws as brutal as those enacted in Queensland, was a grave political risk. The difference was that in other jurisdictions severity was enforced selectively and 'mere users' treated more gently. Users and traffickers were distinguished. Throughout Australia the popular aspects of drug policy, with its focus on cardboard cut-out 'Mr Bigs', garnered general support for the continuation of law-enforcement strategies, while ameliatory policies softened the wounds inflicted on those who seemed unfortunately, unaccountably, to be caught in the crossfire. In South Australia in particular, amelioration softened the implications of prohibition without questioning its fundamentals. In Queensland, on the other hand, there was no such subtlety. The *Drugs Misuse Act* was an extreme implementation of Australian drug policy. But it was a caricature, not an aberration. It epitomised, in exaggerated fashion, one of the two tactics by which criticism of drug policy was contained and diverted.

CONCLUSION:

VOICES IN THE WILDERNESS?

Conclusion

The Web of the Law

From Mr Sin to Mr Big, the history of Australian drug laws has seen the interplay of a variety of complex forces. History is a process, not a moment; over the past one hundred years, many overlapping strands and themes have woven together, coming to prominence and fading from the scene. The fear of drugs has grown from a moral concern about use, to a medical concern about addiction, to an economic and political concern about 'the drug trade'. Drug users themselves have variously been pictured as evil fiends to be outlawed, as sick and pitiable slaves to be 'treated', and as insignificant side issues. The crime of possession has moved from a daring innovation, to a crucial orthodoxy, to an unimportant one. And the main focus of political intervention has also changed, from opium smoking, to cocaine sniffing, to marijuana smoking and the injection of heroin.

The language of the law has changed, too. 'Opium' laws became 'dangerous drug' laws, which became 'narcotics', which became 'drugs of dependence'. Even in those few words, we are reminded of whole histories: fear of the Chinese, the influence of the United States, and concern with addiction.

The vast legislative framework which has developed has reflected these shifting priorities and images. But drug laws, while mirroring our view of the powerless, have been etched by the powerful. And the location of power has itself changed many times in the past one hundred years. Drug laws were first enunciated by White Australians and then in the voice of the medical profession; medical hegemony over drugs was itself gradually undermined by bureaucratisation; while over the last thirty years bureaucratic influence has in turn been weakened by politics. The international system of drug control has been a parallel and counter-balancing authority to these domestic trends, reaching its zenith in the period of bureaucratic dominance. In some ways it has declined in importance since then, although the patterns of thought it etched deep in the Australian psyche have not weakened with time.

Accompanying these ebbs and flows have been many lesser currents that have, none the less, left their own marks on specific laws, jurisdictions, and times: the decline of pharmacy and of patent medicines, the expansion and contraction of power of the Commonwealth Department of Customs, the changing face of health bureaucracies, Australia's changing relationship to the Mother Country and Uncle Sam, the steady expansion in the number and range of controlled drugs, and the changing status of cannabis from novelty item to imported mythology to home-grown crisis. The balance of power between State and Commonwealth governments, police and health authorities, has been another important sub-theme; likewise we may recall the breakdown of the long-standing political consensus on drugs, and the development, in the last couple of decades, of a new consensus based on the principles of meta-law.

In these ways, there has not been a single 'history' of 'drug' laws in Australia. Many shifting factors have acted together to get us where we are today. In this book I have discussed some of these, although I am sure I have ignored or failed to discover many more. Each factor has been subject to its own dynamics, and all have interacted in a complex and unpredictable fashion. History is not a line: it is a web in four dimensions.

Nevertheless, certain patterns have emerged that have changed surprisingly little since the opium prohibition laws. The flexibility and tolerance with which 'drug' use was viewed in the 1800s has gone: the division between 'legal' and 'illegal', 'medical' and 'non-medical' use is now so entrenched that the phrase 'drug abuse' is frequently used to mean *only* illegal non-medical use—and *any* illegal non-medical use. While the distinction between illegal 'drugs' and other substances has grown more profound, fear over their use remains, out of all proportion to the actual harm they cause. This fear, which has led so many people to describe drug use as 'the wrath of Satan', a 'cancer', or as 'undermining the very fabric of society', has not abated. Indeed, if anything, the current focus on organised crime has only exacerbated the atmosphere of crisis which has been whipped up so often in the past century.

More than this, however, attitudes to both 'drugs' and 'law' have shown a sometimes striking resilience over the years. From opium smoking to cannabis smoking, the condemnation of a particular drug use has concealed other concerns: from Mr Sin to Mr Big, we have outlawed phantoms and demons. Drug laws have developed out of prejudice, ignorance, and fear; from inertia at home and subservience abroad; through the interplay of professional, bureaucratic, political and international rivalries. The legal and social bifurcation that has developed between some drugs, the use of which is restricted or prohibited and censured, and others, equally harmful but more freely available, has not derived from their medical or chemical qualities. Drug laws have had precious little to do with drugs or health.

Even more consistently, the construction of drug laws has evinced an unbending attitude towards the legal system itself. Politicians, bureaucrats and many others have all assumed that the law is worthy of preservation because it is the law. The legal system has been buttressed by ever more complex provisions and fearsome penalties, each building upon and presupposing the validity of those that went before. The steady accretion of drug controls in the 1920s, the steady expansion of the number of drugs under control in the 1950s, and the steady escalation of penalties in the 1970s, all bear testimony to this process.

At the beginning of the twentieth century, science and law promised to usher in an age of certainty and rationality. The disciples of Newton conceived of the universe as a clockwork robot whose behaviour was orderly and predictable. But science has shattered its own illusions. The theories of relativity proved that everything depends on your point of view. Quantum mechanics recognised that the old rules simply do not always apply. Now chaos theory declares that disorder, far from being an aberration, is part of the natural state of the universe. In our attitudes to law as to the rest of our lives, however, the desire for certainty has not abated. We continue to assume, on the one hand, that laws develop logically, for just and apparent purposes, and, on the other, that they are capable of effectively achieving the goals set for them. The drug-control system has demonstrated this faith and these assumptions over and over again, accompanied by a steadfast refusal to analyse the real purpose or effects of the legislative structure. Notions of relativity, uncertainty, and chaos have not tainted it with doubt.

The legislative structure which has developed out of these patterns, some fluid, some static, has become so vast as to seem almost immovable. During 1991 I was involved, to a minor extent, with the preparation of a feasibility study which considered the possibility of making opiates legally available in the Australian Capital Territory to some users on a trial basis. Perhaps heroin; perhaps only to drug dependent persons; perhaps only as an experiment. Hardly a radical change, yet immediately I was struck by the legal obstacles to such a move. Australia's treaty obligations branded heroin a 'particularly dangerous' drug and expected parties to absolutely prohibit its possession. The international community likewise vigorously opposed any undermining of the prohibitionist model. The importation of heroin is absolutely prohibited under Commonwealth law; even if it were not, it could not be imported without the Commonwealth government notifying the International Narcotic Control Board (INCB) of a change to Australia's 'estimates', which would be unlikely to be viewed with favour.[1]

Neither could heroin be legally manufactured in most jurisdictions. In Victoria, provisions do exist for the legal manufacture of heroin upon the granting, by the Minister, of a special licence. In the early 1980s, Australia's Health Ministers decided to allow the legal use of heroin in the treatment of terminal illness and plans were made for its manufacture by a company in Victoria. But the plan did not proceed and no licence was ever issued. Even if the Australian Capital Territory could come to an agreement with the Victorian government, once the cargo crossed into New South Wales, where heroin is a 'prohibited drug', its transportation would constitute illegal possession, and probably illegal supply subject to a penalty of up to fifteen years' imprisonment. And what of the law in the Australian Capital Territory, where provision is made for the supply of methadone under prescription, but heroin itself is a 'prohibited substance' that cannot be manufactured, supplied or possessed except for limited 'research' or 'educational' purposes?[2] A web is made of many strands, but they knit together with awesome strength.

Clearing the Cobwebs

It is easy to despair about the possibility of any change, or even any rational debate about the purposes and effects of drug policy. But, as we have seen, things do change, albeit slowly. The approach to drug 'abuse' taken by the Queensland National Party government has proved too extreme and politically partisan to survive the electoral defeat of the government. In the complete rewriting of the *Liquor Act* (Qld), completed in 1992, the infamous provision relating to 'drug traffickers, sexual perverts or deviants, child molesters' and so on has been eliminated, replaced by far more general provisions dealing with the cancellation of liquor licences. The *Drugs Misuse Act* (Qld)—although it still includes some of the stiffest penalties in Australia, and still fails to provide a lesser maximum penalty for the possession or sale of cannabis—no longer requires judges to impose life sentences for some offences. The *Drugs Misuse Act Amendment Act 1990* passed by the Labor government of Wayne Goss, while keeping the structure of the Act unchanged, reduces the relevant penalties from maximum or mandatory life imprisonment, to maximum penalties from fifteen to twenty-five years depending on the offence.[3]

Meanwhile, in 1992 the Australian Capital Territory became the second Australian jurisdiction to decriminalise the possession or cultivation of a small quantity of cannabis (less than twenty-five grams or five plants) with the passage of a Bill introduced by Independent MLA, Michael Moore. Although the Bill in its final form imposes greater penalties ($100) for lesser quantities (twenty-five grams as opposed to up to one hundred grams) than those originally introduced, and the police in the Australian Capital Territory have long appeared to turn a blind eye to minor cannabis offences, the legislative change is still significant.[4] We might interpret this measure as a continuation of the trend begun in the Australian Capital Territory in 1975 and South Australia in 1986, or as an aberration, or as the start of a radical new direction in drug policy. One thing is clear: change continues to take place.

The last few years have also seen a significant increase in general criticism of Australia's drug-control system. 'Heroin: Why don't we just legalise it?', asked the *Bulletin* in a 1988 issue, the cover of which blared 'Can we afford not to say YES to heroin', while a century earlier it had seen opium as a tentacle of the 'Mongolian octopus'. The National Secretary of the Australian Federal Police Association, the retired Victorian Assistant Police Commissioner, the Law Council of New South Wales, and the New South Wales Bar Association have all called for sweeping alterations to the current prohibitionist model, including among their suggestions the legal provision of heroin to addicts and a complete rethinking of the role of the criminal law in personal drug use. The latest parliamentary report to deal with the subject, *Drugs, Crime and Society*, issued by the Parliamentary Joint Committee on the National Crime Authority in 1989, likewise trenchantly criticised the current approach of governments, condemned governments' preoccupation with the enactment of harsh penalties and with measures designed to suppress the *supply* of illegal drugs, and emphasised instead the costs of prohibition to drugs users, to the court system, and to society. The report concluded without dissent that Australia's policy of prohibition has in fact prevented the development of any effective controls on either the sale or use of illegal drugs.[5] Senator Peter Baume, amongst others, has spoken with more and more conviction as the years have passed. In one of his last parliamentary speeches on the subject, before retiring to take up an appointment as

Conclusion

Professor of Community Medicine at the University of New South Wales, he said:

Our strategies seek to prevent the production of certain designated illegal substances, and fail to do so; they seek to prevent the importation of substances, and fail to do so; they seek to prevent the distribution of substances, and fail to do so; they seek to prevent the sale and use of substances, and fail to do so.[6]

The pronouncements of the international community do not carry the weight they used to, either. Australia's independence in this respect has been growing ever since drugs began to 'matter'. In general it has not led to any conflict between domestic and international policies, but there have been exceptions. Building on the pioneering work of J.G. Starke and CSIRO, Australia has been successfully producing morphine in Tasmania, by the poppy-straw method, for local and international sale, since 1971. By 1983 Australia had become one of the four major world suppliers of raw materials for the production of opiates, producing the equivalent of thirty-nine tonnes of morphine annually—more poppy-straw concentrate than that produced by the rest of the world combined. Morphine produced by the poppy-straw method is not subject to detailed international supervision, and although the INCB and the Economic and Social Council of the UN have frequently urged 'new producers' to limit their production 'to meet mainly their domestic requirements' in the face of a 'vast [world] oversupply of opiates', the Commonwealth government has stood firm. In 1985 it specifically rejected the INCB's position and declared the Australian government's determination to continue to compete aggressively in the world market.[7]

No opposition to the power and authority of the UN, however, has been as public as that prompted by the adoption at a UN conference of the *Convention Against Illicit Traffic in Narcotic Drugs and Psychotropic Substances.* The Convention emphasised the importance of law enforcement strategies in the war against Mr Big. It contained provisions relating to the commission of offences by 'an organised criminal group', to the confiscation of assets and to international co-operation concerning search, seizure, extradition and so on. While not radically changing international law, it reflected the new Conventional wisdom that the 'drug problem' was about the 'links between illicit traffic and other related organised criminal activities'.[8]

The Convention has been severely criticised. Retired Federal Court Judge, Russell Fox, QC, in particular, has lobbied intensively against Australia's ratification of the treaty, arguing that it would further entrench a 'prohibitionist and penal' approach and 'put our policies on important matters beyond recall'. In response, the government has been forced to defend the treaty not by arguing the merits of law enforcement but by denying that ratification would commit Australia to any specific legal or policy strategy at all. So powerful has opposition been, however, that the Convention has not yet been ratified.[9]

Drug orthodoxy, therefore, is not now unquestioned. In part, this has been the result of the growth of organised crime and drug trafficking, which all the majesty of the law has proved manifestly incapable of preventing. The very fact that 'the drug problem' has become, as we have seen, a question of economics and power—rather than of morality—has, perhaps, allowed more radical options to be considered. On the one hand, organised crime is seen to threaten the integrity of the whole of the legal and political system, and so the stakes are high enough to countenance radical reforms. On the other hand, the removal of drug use itself from the centre of public concern may mean that legalisation or decriminalisation are no longer the impossible options they once were. The focus on 'the drug problem' as an economic one, which served to constrain drug reform in the 1980s, may yet allow an accelerated pace of reform in the years to come.

The spread of AIDS among users of illegal intravenous drugs has given a further impetus to demands for radical change. Illegality breeds secrecy, secrecy causes uncleanliness, and dirty needles kill. The personal costs of the prohibition of heroin to the health of drug users are now more apparent than ever, and many people who would not otherwise have done so have found themselves advocating a variety of radical solutions including the legal supply of heroin to addicts, or at least the legal supply of clean needles. Faced with a genuine human crisis rather than merely a rhetorical one, moreover, Commonwealth and State government policies have been notable for their restraint and practicality.[10] With this new emphasis on practical solutions directed to the health of users, the protection of the integrity of the legal structure may be becoming less important. Once something is defined as a health problem and not a legal one, the framework of the legal system no longer controls how solutions are formulated. The condition of illegality in which users currently consume heroin may be changing from a fundamental and unalterable principle, to merely one variable in an analysis directed simply at the minimisation of harm. With this pragmatic approach in place, anything is possible.

There are some indications that these attitudes may already be having an effect. In the Australian Capital Territory, for example, it is now specifically provided that the supply of syringes for the administration of a drug of dependence or prohibited substance is not a crime if it is done by an approved health worker and 'the supply of the syringe might assist in preventing the spread of disease'.[11] A similar provision can be found even in the Queensland legislation. The AIDS virus, then, is leading to legislation which permits previously illegal acts in the cause of advancing the health of users. Possession and use still remain illegal, but their meaning has been still further undermined.

These dynamics are only now working themselves out; the extent and direction of change will not be apparent for some time. In the meantime, I am not a seer or a prophet, but a lawyer and a historian. I do not wish to engage in prediction. At the same time, in my discussion of the past, I have tried not to let my own opinions about drug policy intrude too much into my historical analysis. Of course, neutrality is a fiction, and my own values have been clearly apparent. But anyone interested in options for drug control policies can and should turn to any number of books written by people far more qualified than I. One thing is apparent. 'Drugs' is a subject which people approach with many erroneous preconceptions, and a little knowledge can change people's opinions profoundly. Both Peter Baume and Peter Cleeland, chairmen of influential parliamentary committees on the subject, have stressed to me how much their thinking began to change when they first started to read and to listen.[12]

The mythology, preconceptions, and rhetorical excess surrounding 'drugs' in Australia did not emerge overnight. They are a product of our past. History, then, is a vital step in clearing our minds and starting afresh. No debate on drug policy can proceed rationally until we know where we have come from and why. I have hoped to show why and how laws have grown in this country, and I have dared to criticise some of the assumptions that people make—that laws have developed with specific and rational purposes in mind, that the reason for a law's enactment is the same thing as the reasons given for it, and that laws are effective tools in changing people's behaviour. Of course, laws are not without effect: clearly, they have influenced the way in which generations of policy-makers have approached the problems of drug use. Laws have operated most powerfully as influences on how we see the world and as limits on what we think is possible. They have not been nearly so effective as blunt instruments to make people do as they are told. We must always be conscious of the origin and the limits of laws. There are real problems associated with the use of any mind-altering substance (illegal or not): not legal problems, just problems. Poverty, sickness, alienation, despair, powerlessness. Drug use is only a symptom and an aspect of these problems. From Mr Sin to Mr Big, laws seem to have been far more effective in concealing them than in solving them.

NOTES

Abbreviations

AA	Australian Archives (ACT)
AONSW	Archive Office of New South Wales
ARCID	Australian Royal Commission of Inquiry into Drugs (Hon. Justice Williams, Commissioner), *Report*, AGPS, Canberra: 1980
CPD	*Commonwealth Parliamentary Debates*
NSWPD	*New South Wales Parliamentary Debates*
NSWRC	Royal Commission into Drug Trafficking (Justice Woodward, Commissioner), *Report*, Joint Volumes of Papers, 2nd Session, 1979–80, vol. III and 3rd Session 1980–81, vol. II, Sydney: 1980–81
NSWRCC	NSW Legislative Assembly, Royal Commission on Alleged Chinese Gambling and Immorality (Mayor Manning, Chairman), Government Printer, Sydney: 1892
PROV	Public Record Office of Victoria
QSA	Queensland State Archives
QPD	*Queensland Parliamentary Debates*
SAPD	*South Australian Parliamentary Debates*
SARC	Royal Commission into the Non-Medical Use of Drugs (Prof. Ronald Sackville, Chairman), Government Printer, Adelaide: 1978–79
SMH	*Sydney Morning Herald*
VPD	*Victorian Parliamentary Debates*

Introduction: Image and Usage

1 Marcus Clarke, 'Cannabis Indica', *Colonial Monthly* 1 (new series) (1868): 454–68, 454.

2 Thomas De Quincey, *Confessions of an English Opium Eater*, London: 1821.

3 *Ibid.*, 455, 458–9, 460.

4 See Alethea Hayter, *Opium and the Romantic Imagination*, London: 1968, esp.19–26 and 67–81.

5 J. Fordel Henderson, *The Opium Slave and Other Verses*, Brisbane: 1913, 3–6.

6 Diacetylmorphine was originally spelt 'heroine', although over time the final 'e' has been dropped. I will, except when quoting directly from other sources, stick

to the modern version.

7   Virginia Berridge and Griffith Edwards, *Opium and the People*, London: 1981, 30–52. See also Terry Parsinnen, *Secret Passions, Secret Remedies*, Philadelphia: 1983; Terry Parsinnen, 'Opium and the People', *Medical History* 26 (1982): 458–62; Virginia Berridge, 'Secret Passions, Secret Remedies...', *Medical History* 29 (1985): 210–17. See also Select Committee on Sale of Poisons Bill, *Report with Proceedings, Minutes of Evidence and Index*: 1857 (294 Session II), Vol. XII in *British Parliamentary Papers, Health—Food and Drugs 2,* Shannon: 1969, 102.

8   L. Kong Meng, C.H. Cheong, Louis Ah Mouy (eds), *The Chinese Question in Australia*, Melbourne: 1879, 14.

9   *Bulletin*, Sydney: 1882.

10 *Age*, Melbourne: 20 April 1858, 4; *Bulletin*: 6 July 1895, 27; *Intercolonial Medical Journal of Australasia* (1897): 327. See generally T.S. Pensabene, *The Rise of the Medical Practitioner in Victoria*, Canberra: 1980; Evan Willis, *Medical Dominance*, Sydney: 1983.

11 See for example debate on the Medical Practitioners Bill (Vic.), in *Victorian Hansard, Session 1857–8, Vol. 3*, 490.

12 Pensabene, 7, 6–15.

13 *Age*: 2 October 1876, 2.

14 *Illustrated Sydney News*, Sydney: 31 October 1868, 79.

15 *Pharmacy Act 1876* (Vic.), 40 Vic. No. 558, ss. 5 & 6; *Sale and Use of Poisons Act 1876* (NSW), 40 Vic. No. 9, s. 9. In New South Wales, the Board was not composed of chemists only until 1897 when the position was brought into line with that of Victoria: *Pharmacy Act 1897* (NSW), 61 Vic. No. 7, ss. 1 & 2. (Although the way in which Acts of Parliament are cited varies slightly between jurisdictions, and over time, I have, for the sake of clarity, cited all Acts consistently according to AGPS recommended style.)

16 Pensabene, 126 and *passim* 121–32. See also Gregory Haines, *The Grains and Threepenn'orth of Pharmacy*, Kilmore: 1976, esp. 58–63; but, for a contrary view, see *A Centennial History of the Pharmaceutical Society of Queensland* [no details]: 1980, 2.

17 Drs Wilson, Brodie, Webster and Marshall-Hall, and Prof. A.S. Taylor in Select Committee on Pharmacy Bill, *Report with Minutes of Evidence and Index*: 1852 (387), Vol. XIII in *British Parliamentary Papers, Health—Food and Drugs 1 (1852–55)*, Shannon: 1969, 13, 45, 156, 145 and *passim*. See also Select Committee on the Sale of Poisons Bill in *British Parliamentary Papers, Health—Food and Drugs 2*; and Select Committee on Chemists and Druggists Bill, *Special Report with Proceedings, Minutes of Evidence and Appendix*: 1865 (381), Vol. XII in ibid.

18 E.W. Cole, *The Pound Pamphlet Word for Word*, Melbourne: [no date], 106–11.

19 Mr Carter in *VPD, Session 1898, Vol. 90*, 2989.

20 David Courtwright, *Dark Paradise*, Cambridge, Mass.: 1982, 1–8, 36–48. See also Berridge & Edwards and Parsinnen; Robert Solomon & Michael Green, 'The First Century: The History of Non-Medical Opiate Use and Control Policies in Canada', *University of Western Ontario Law Review* 20 (1982): 307.

21 *Bulletin*: 28 December 1895, 28.

22 *Age*: 11 March 1892, 4.
23 Mr Carter in *VPD, Session 1898, Vol. 90*, 2989.
24 Mitchell Library, *Index to the Bulletin 1880–1895, 1896–1898, 1880–1901*, Sydney; Mitchell Library, *Index for 'Age' 1892–1899*, Sydney; *Bulletin*, Sydney: 1880–1901; *Age*, Melbourne: 1892–1899 esp. 27 October 1893.
25 *Sale and Use of Poisons Act 1876* (Vic.), 40 Vic. No. 559, ss. 3, 4, 6 & 13; *Sale and Use of Poisons Act 1876* (NSW), 40 Vic. No. 9, ss. 7, 11, 18.
26 *Sale and Use of Poisons Act 1876* (Vic.), ss. 5 & 8; *Sale and Use of Poisons Act 1876* (NSW), ss. 2 & 3.
27 *Ibid.*, Preamble; see also Mr Cumming, MLA, in *VPD, Session 1876, Vol. 25*, 1810.
28 Evidence of J. Abrahams, S.J. Birch, Prof. A.S. Taylor in Select Committee on the Sale of Poisons Bill in *British Parliamentary Papers, Health—Food and Drugs* 2, 44, 64, 102, 44–8.
29 Lord de Malahide, Lord Wensleydale and Herapath in *ibid.*, 102.
30 For a discussion of drug use and mortality, see V. Brown, D. Manderson, *et al., Our Daily Fix*, Canberra: 1986, 72–86.
31 J. Himmelstein, 'Drug Politics Theory: Analysis and Critique', *Journal of Drug Issues* 8 (1978): 37–52, 40–7. See also John Helmer, *Drugs and Minority Oppression*, New York: 1975 and R. Bonnie & C. Whitebread, *The Marijuana Conviction*, Charlottesville: 1974.

1 A Tentacle of the Octopus

1 AONSW, Colonial Secretary Special Bundle: Chinese 1888, 4/884.1.
2 *Ibid.*
3 *Influx of Chinese Restriction Act 1881* (NSW), 45 Vic. No. 11, ss. 4, 5 & 10. See also, for example (Vic.) 45 Vic. No. 723; (Qld) 47 Vic. No. 13.
4 AONSW, Colonial Secretary Special Bundle: Chinese 1888, 4/884.1. For a detailed discussion of the history of the events alluded to, see Eric Rolls, *Sojourners*, St Lucia: 1992, 464–504.
5 *NSWPD, Session 1887–8, 51 & 52 Vic. Vol. 32*, 4787, 4795.
6 *Chinese Restriction and Regulation Act 1888* (NSW), 52 Vict. No. 4, s. 2; NSW Legislative Council, *Conference on the Chinese Question*, Sydney: 1888, 5–6. See also (SA) 51 & 52 Vic. No. 439; (Vic.) 52 Vic. No. 1005; (WA) 53 Vic. No. 3; (Qld) 53 Vic. No. 22.
7 Letter to Lord Carrington, 8 June 1888, in Sir Henry Parkes, Correspondence Vol. 6, Sydney (ML A876): 142–4.
8 George Dibbs in *NSWPD, Session 1887–8, 51 & 52 Vic. Vol. 33*, 4897.
9 Dibbs paraphrasing Sir Henry Parkes, in *NSWPD, Session 1887–8, 51 & 52 Vic. Vol. 33*, 4789, 4793.
10 Philip Fysh, 25 November 1887, in AONSW, Colonial Secretary Special Bundle: Chinese 1888, 4/884.1.
11 *Bulletin*, Sydney: 12 January 1889, 5; 10 March 1888, 5.
12 'Humanity', *Sketches of Chinese Character*, Castlemaine: 1878, 3–4.

13 *Bulletin*, Sydney: 21 August 1886, 11–14; Phil May, 'The Mongolian Octopus Grip on Australia' in *ibid.*, 12–13. See also *Bulletin*, Sydney: Supplement to 14 April 1888.
14 NSW Legislative Council, *Votes and Proceedings 1858, Vol. 3*, 305, 320.
15 *Ibid.*, 299.
16 J. Moore for the Colonial Secretary, 13 August 1857, in AONSW, Attorney-General Special Bundles 1836–76: Vols 1 & 2, 9/2697 A & B, 627–8, 613–19. See *Opium Duties Act 1857* (Vic.) 21 Vic. No. 7; (NSW) 21 Vic. No. 1.
17 Rolls, 403.
18 J. Farrell and W. Heancham to the NSW government, August 1887, in Sir Henry Parkes, Correspondence Vol. 20, Sydney (ML A899): 242–4.
19 See Quong Tart, *A Plea for the Abolition of the Importation of Opium*, Sydney: 1887 (ML 178.82 B2), 11 and Alfred McCoy, *Drug Traffic*, Sydney: 1980, 72; NSW Census of 1891; *CPD, 1905, V Edw. VII Vol. 26*, 1773 & 1777.
20 Inspector-General Edmund Fosbery, 'Chinese, Information Respecting', in NSW Legislative Assembly, *Votes and Proceedings 1878*; W. Young, *Report on the Conditions of the Chinese Population in Victoria*, Melbourne: 1868 in Ian McLaren, *The Chinese in Victoria: Official Reports and Documents*, Melbourne: 1985, 33–58.
21 Sydney City & Suburban Sewage and Health Board, *Eleventh Progress Report* in NSW Legislative Assembly, *Votes and Proceedings 1875–6, Vol. V.*, 535–661.
22 *Ibid.*, 660, 568–9, 560, 603.
23 *Ibid.*, 546, 568–9.
24 'The Chinese in Australia', *Bulletin*, Sydney: 21 August 1886, 11–14.
25 *Ibid.*, 15.
26 Terry Parsinnen & K. Kerner, 'Development of the Disease Model of Drug Addiction in Britain', *Medical History* 24 (1980): 275–96, 283–4.
27 Dr Scott in VPD, *Session 1893, Vol. 73*, 2640.
28 'The Chinese Invasion of Australia', *Bulletin*, Sydney: 4 September 1886, 4.
29 *Bulletin*, Sydney: 21 August 1886, 11–14.
30 'Humanity', 4.
31 See, for example, Mr Abbott in *NSWPD, Session 1892–3, 56 Vic. Vol. 64*, 5128; Mr Johnson in *CPD, 1905, V Edw. VII Vol. XXVI*, 1768; Sydney City & Suburban Sewage and Health Board, 546, 661; Rev. Peter le Rennetel in NSWRCC, 171; NSW Legislative Assembly, *Report from the Select Committee on Common Lodging Houses* in *Votes & Proceedings 1875–6, Vol. VI*, 859, 864.
32 NSW Legislative Assembly, *Report from the Select Committee on Common Lodging Houses*, 859; NSWRCC, 437–8.
33 *Bulletin*, Sydney: 21 August 1886, 14.
34 'Mr and Mrs Sin Fat', *Bulletin*, Sydney: 14 April 1888, 8–9, 9.
35 *Ibid.*, 8.
36 G.W., The Humble Plea of the Poor Chinee!!, Sydney: [no date] (ML Q301.451/23).
37 NSW Legislative Assembly, *Report upon Chinese Camps*, 661; Factories Act

Inquiry Board, *Second Progress Report* in McLaren, 91.
38 NSWRCC, 387, 399, 401.
39 *Ibid.*, 405 (to Margaret), 413–14 (to Pauline) and 452 (to Maud).
40 *Ibid.*, 382, 384, 401, 414. See also the evidence of Rev. Peter le Rennetel, 171–3, and Mrs Sims, Matron of the Church Home, 439 & 442.
41 *Ibid., Report*, 21.
42 *Ibid.*
43 *Ibid.*, 395, 399–402, 418.
44 *Ibid.*, 388, 401, 405, 409.
45 *Official Report of Anti-Opium Demonstration*, Sydney: 1894, 2.
46 *CPD, 1905, V Edw. VII Vol. XXVI*, 1773.
47 'No More Opium', *Daily Telegraph*, Sydney: 7 January 1884, 4; see also 'The Chinese Question', *Bulletin*, Sydney: 1 May 1880, 1.
48 *VPD, Session 1884, Vol. 45*, 288-291; *VPD, Session 1890, Vol. 65*, 2374.
49 F.S. Dobson in *VPD, Session 1891, Vol. 68*, 2978.
50 Opium Bill 1891 (Vic.), cll. 13, 14, 17 & 18 in *ibid.*, 2800.
51 Sir Bryan O'Loghlen in *ibid.*, 2802; James Munro in *ibid.*, 2796, 2798.
52 In addition to general considerations of revenue, the 1893 Bill made it an offence to grow opium, which would have taken away the livelihood of a number of farmers in western Victoria engaged in growing opium poppies to serve the medical market: see Capt. Taylor in *VPD, Session 1893, Vol. 73*, 2652; see also, for example, L.L. Smith, 2635 and Mr Staughton, 2642–4.
53 John Valc in *Official Report of Anti-Opium Demonstration*, 9.
54 Mr McLellan in *VPD, Session 1893, Vol. 73*, 2650. See also, for example, Premier Patterson, Mr Bosisto, Dr Scott and Mr Graves, 2631–3, 2637–9, 2640–1, 2649–50.
55 *Ibid.*, 2633–7; but see Mr Staughton, McKenzie and Harris in *ibid.*, 2642–4, 2645–8.
56 *Age*, Melbourne: 27 October 1893, 4; L.L. Smith in *VPD, Session 1893, Vol. 73*, 2634.
57 *Sale and Use of Poisons Act 1891* (Qld), 55 Vic. No. 31, s. 13; *The Opium Act 1895* (SA), 58 & 59 Vic. No. 644, s. 3.
58 A.T. Yarwood & M.J. Knowling, *Race Relations in Australia*, North Ryde: 1982, 176, 185.
59 Mr Ash in *SAPD 1895*, 3025, and general debate 3021–44.
60 Rolls, 405.
61 Meston, 6 August 1897, in QSA, Colonial Secretary's Office: COL 140 Special Batches—Aborigines.
62 *Aboriginals Protection and Restriction of the Sale of Opium Act 1897* (Qld), 61 Vic. No. 17, ss. 3, 20–2.
63 Dr Walter Roth in Royal Commission into Customs, & Excise Tariffs, *Report and Minutes of Evidence*, Sydney: 1906, 432; A. Meston, 14 April 1898 in QSA, Colonial Secretary's Office: COL 140 Special Batches—Aborigines.

64 Under Secretary, 16 January 1909, in QSA, Premier's Department In-letters: PRE/A 1914-1956 Opium Convention; Dr Roth, 7 September 1900, in QSA, Home Secretary's Office General Correspondence: COL/143 Special Batches—Aborigines 1896–1902; Royal Commission into Customs, & Excise Tariffs, *Report and Minutes of Evidence*, Sydney: 1906, 432.

65 *SAPD, 1895*, 3021, 3021–3.

66 A. Meston, January 1897, in QSA, Colonial Secretary's Office: COL 140 Special Batches—Aborigines; Report on Western Aborigines, 16 June 1897, in QSA, Colonial Secretary's Office: COL 144 Special Batches—Aborigines 1899–1903. See also his Report in *Queensland Parliamentary Papers 1896*, 13.

67 A. Meston, 14 September 1901, in QSA, Home Secretary's Office General Correspondence: COL/145 Special Batches—Aborigines 1900–1902.

68 Dr Roth, 16 September 1898; Barron Valley Farmers and Progress Association, 19 April 1898, in QSA, Colonial Secretary's Office: COL 142 Special Batches—Aborigines.

69 See Protector of Aborigines, Mackay, in A. Meston's 1900 Report, in *ibid*.

70 Quoted in report by Dr Roth, 20 September 1898, in *ibid*.

71 *Ibid*.

2 The Crusades

1 *Constitution of the Commonwealth* (enacted by Commonwealth of Australia Constitution Act 1900 (UK), 63 & 64 Vic. ch. 12, s. 9); see *Customs Act 1901* (Cwlth), No. 6 of 1901, ss. 50, 52(g), 56.

2 Commonwealth Bureau of Census and Statistics, *Official Yearbook of the Commonwealth of Australia 1901–1908, No. 2*, Melbourne: 1909, 808.

3 *Chinese Restriction and Regulation Act 1888* (NSW), and cognate legislation in other colonies; *Immigration Restriction Act 1901* (Cwlth), No. 17, 1901.

4 Dr J. Ashburton Thompson, 25 January 1905, in AONSW, Attorney-General Special Bundle: Proposed Amendments to Police Offences Act 1904–08, 5/7745.2.

5 *Ibid.*; although some individual police reports submitted in the lead-up to the conference were not so sanguine.

6 AONSW, Attorney-General Special Bundle: Proposed Amendments to Police Offences Act 1904–08, *5/7745.2; CPD, 1905, V Edw. VII Vols XXV–XXVII.*

7 *Commonwealth of Australia Gazette No. 64*, 30 December 1905; *Opium Smoking Prohibition Act 1905* (Vic.), 5 Edw. VII No. 2003; *Opium Act Amendment Act 1905* (SA), 5 Edw. VII No. 890; *Police Offences Amendment Act 1908* (NSW), 8 Edw. VII ch. 12.

8 J.L. Berlant, *Profession and Monopoly*, Berkeley: 1975, 148–61; Paul Starr, *The Social Transformation of American Medicine*, New York: 1982, 30–59; T.S. Pensabene, *The Rise of the Medical Practitioner in Victoria*, Canberra: 1980, 121–4; *Medical Act 1862 & 1865* (Vic.), 25 Vic. No. 158 & 28 Vic. No. 262; *Medical Witnesses Act 1838* (NSW), 1 Vic. No. 3 and 2 Vic. No. 22; *Medical Witnesses Amendment Act 1845* (NSW), 9 Vic. No. 12; *Medical Practitioners Act 1855* (NSW), 19 Vic. No. 17.

9   See, for example, *Public Health Act 1902* (NSW), 2 Edw. VII. No. 30; *Pure Food Act 1908* (NSW), 8 Edw. VII. No. 31; *Pure Food Act 1905* (Vic.), 5 Edw. VII No. 2010.

10 *VPD, Session 1905, Vol. 111*, 2290, 2146; Mr McGowan in *NSWPD, Session 1909, Ser. 2 Vol. 33*, 687.

11 *VPD, Session 1891, Vol. 68*, 2800, 2802, 3408.

12 Conroy in *CPD, 1905, V Edw. VII Vol. XXVI*, 1779.

13 Lima & Samuel Lambert, *The Science of Life*, Melbourne: 1883 in David Walker, 'Continence for a Nation', *Labour History* 48 (1985): 1–14, 9.

14 Dr J. Cumpston in *Medical Journal of Australia*, 4 September 1920, 223 in Michael Roe, 'The Establishment of the Australian Department of Health: Its Background and Significance', *Historical Studies* 17 (1976–77): 176–92, 186.

15 *SMH*: 13 February 1914, 8.

16 Roe, 188.

17 *Venereal Diseases Act 1918* (NSW), Geo. V No. 46; Holman in *NSWPD, Session 1918, 9 Geo. V, Ser. 2 Vol. 74*, 3291.

18 NSW Legislative Assembly, *Report upon Chinese Camps*, Sydney: 1884; NSWRCC, *Report*, 21–2; Quong Tart, *A Plea for the Abolition of the Importation of Opium*, Sydney: 1887; Margaret Scarlett (Mrs Quong Tart), *The Life of Quong Tart*, Sydney: 1911, 46–9.

19 William Johnson in *CPD, 1905 V Edw. VII, Vol. XXVI*, 1769-72; Mr Zox in *VPD, Session 1891, Vol. 68*, 2793. See also Premier Patterson in *VPD, Session 1893, Vol. 73*, 2632; Mr Mackey in *VPD, Session 1905, Vol. 111*, 2122; Mr Hughes in *NSWPD, 2nd Session 1908 8 Edw. VII, Ser. 2 Vol. 31*, 2361.

20 See, for example, Frederic Wakeman, *The Fall of Imperial China*, New York: 1975, 125–42; Chang Hsin-Pao, *Commissioner Lin and the Opium War*, Cambridge, Mass.: 1954; A. Waley, *The Opium War Through Chinese Eyes*, London: 1958. See also Eric Rolls, *Sojourners*, St Lucia: 1992, 384–90.

21 *Australian Town and Country Journal*, Sydney: 29 October 1902, 24; *Bulletin*, Sydney: 18 October 1886. See the hagiographies of his wife, Margaret Scarlett, *The Life of Quong Tart*, Sydney: 1911, and a later descendant, E.J. Lea-Scarlett, Quong Tart: A Study in Assimilation, Sydney: 1968 (ML MSS. 1669).

22 Sir John Salomons in Scarlett, 15.

23 A letter written by consular officials in Sydney and another by leading political figures including Edmund Barton, Reid, Salomons, Stephen A.C.J. and Dibbs, urging his official appointment as consul, was sent to George Morrison to be conveyed to the Chinese government: George Morrison, Papers, Vol. 47, Correspondence 1903 (ML MSS. 312).

24 NSW Legislative Assembly, *Report upon Chinese Camps*, 665.

25 Petition for the abolition of opium, 5 April 1887, in Quong Tart, 6–7 & 5; NSWRCC, *Report*, 22; see also 77–101, 131. See also L. Kong Meng, Rev. C. Cheong, L. Ah Mouy (eds), *The Chinese Question in Australia*, Melbourne: 1879, 16.

26 AONSW, Attorney-General Special Bundle: Proposed Amendments to Police Offences Act 1904–1908, 5/7745.2.

27 *Review of Reviews*, Sydney: 20 June 1905, 560; Royal Commission into Customs, & Excise Tariffs, *Report*, Sydney: 1906, 430.
28 Mr Balfour in *VPD, Session 1905, Vol. 111*, 2400; see also Davies and Mr Evans, *ibid*, 2400–01.
29 Scarlett, Introduction. For a similar discussion of assimilation, see Neil Boyd, 'The Origins of Canadian Narcotics Legislation', *Dalhousie Law Journal* 8 (1984): 102–36, 115–19.
30 Quong Tart, 5.
31 *Official Report of the Anti-Opium Demonstration*, Sydney: 1894, 7.
32 *VPD, Session 1905, Vol. 111*, 2851.
33 *Bulletin*, Sydney: 15 December 1883, 4.
34 Samuel T. Knaggs, *Tea Poisoning*, Sydney: 1874, 5–6.
35 *Age*, Melbourne: 9 December 1893, 8. See almost any edition of the *Bulletin*, from 1890–1910; Peter Phillips, *Kill or Cure*, Richmond, Vic.: 1978.
36 See E. W. Cole, *The Pound Pamphlet Word for Word*, Melbourne: [no date].
37 *Licensing Act 1906* (Vic.), 6 Edw. VII No. 2068; see also *Liquor Act 1912* (NSW), No. 42 1912; *Liquor (Local Option) Amendment Act 1913* (NSW), No. 5 1913.
38 *Liquor Referendum Act 1916* (NSW), No. 10 1916; *Liquor (Amendment) Act 1919* (NSW), No. 42 1919; Rev. Hammond, 29 August 1919 and William Holman, 13 August 1919, in AONSW, Premier's Department Special Bundle 1914–22: Prohibition, 7/5929; *SMH*, 12 January 1921; *Daily Telegraph*, Sydney: 2 February 1921; Storey in *NSWPD, Session 1920, 11 Geo. V. 2nd Ser. Vol. 82*, 3790; see also 3788 *et seq*.
39 See *Argus*, Melbourne: 29 March 1930, 19–20, 31; 31 March 1930, 1.
40 *SMH*, 12 January 1921; AONSW, Premier's Department Special Bundle 1914–22: Prohibition, 7/5929.
41 'The Cursed Drink' and ' "The Cursed Drink"—Again', *Bulletin*, Sydney: 8 & 15 October 1887, 4 & 4.
42 Octavius Beale, *Racial Decay*, Sydney: 1910; *Australian Dictionary of Biography Vol. 7, 1891–1939*, Melbourne: 1979, 225.
43 AA: Prime Minister's Department CA 12; CRS A2 Correspondence Files 1904–20, 1909/3562, Report on Secret Drugs by Mr O.C. Beale; *Parliamentary Papers Act 1908* (Cwlth); Royal Commission on Secret Drugs, Cures & Foods (Octavius Beale, Commissioner), *Report, Vol. 1*, Melbourne: 1907.
44 *Ibid.*, 123, 426–31.
45 *Ibid.*, 89–98, 364.
46 Octavius Beale to Alfred Deakin, 9 April 1908, and *Chemist and Druggist of Australasia*, Melbourne: 1 August 1906, 198.
47 Royal Commission on Secret Drugs, Cures & Foods, 26, 418.
48 Royal Commission on Uniform Standards for Foods and Drugs in the States of the Commonwealth of Australia (Dr J. Ashburton Thompson, Commissioner), *Report*, Sydney: 1913, xxiii. See also British Medical Association, *Secret Remedies*, London: 1909 & 1912; Adams in *Collier's Weekly*: 14 October 1905 *et seq*.

49 *Commerce (Trade Descriptions) Act 1905* (Cwlth), No. 17, 1905 ss. 7, 9 & 15; Commerce Regulations 1913 (Cwlth), S.R. 1913, No. 347, r. 7; *Pure Food Act 1908* (NSW), 8 Edw. VII ch. 31, s. 5(k); see also r. 56 and *Pure Food Act 1905* (Vic.), 5 Edw. VII No. 2010.

50 Commonwealth & States of Australia, Report of the Interstate Departmental Conference on Uniform Standards for Foods and Drugs, Sydney: 1910, 1913, 1923, 1927.

51 PROV, VA 860 Chief Secretary's Office, VPRS 3992, Inwards Registered Correspondence Part III, box 2286, 24/11254.

52 *VPD, Session 1932, Vol. 190*, 2736. See also *VPD, Session 1927, Vol. 173*, 953–6; *VPD, Session 1929 Vol. 180*, 2122–4.

53 *VPD, Session 1893, Vol. 73*, 2634.

54 *Commonwealth of Australia Gazette No. 64*, 30 December 1905. See *Customs Act 1901* (Cwlth), No. 6 1901, ss. 50, 52(g) & 56.

55 *Opium Smoking Prohibition Act 1905* (Vic.), 5 Edw. VII No. 2003. See also *Police Offences (Amendment) Act 1908* (NSW) 8 Edw. VII ch. 12, Part VI:
> 18. For the purposes of this Part, 'opium' includes any preparation thereof in a form capable of being used for the purposes of smoking.
> 19. (1) No person shall—
> (a) unless the holder of a certificate to deal in poisons, issued under the provisions of the Poisons Act 1902, or any Act amending the same, sell or have in his possession, opium;
> (b) smoke opium;
> (c) keep open, manage, or assist in keeping open or managing, any house, room, or place used for the purpose of opium smoking.
> (d) being the owner or lessee of any house, room, or place, knowingly permit such house, room or place to be used for the purpose of opium smoking.

56 *NSWPD, 2nd Session 1908, 8 Edw. VII, Ser. 2 Vol. 31*, 1677–9. See also Storey and Dooley, *ibid.*, 707, 1716.

57 *Daily Telegraph*, Sydney: 15 October 1908.

58 *CPD, 1905, V Edw. VII Vol. XXVI*, 1774.

59 Mr Conroy and Mr Mauger in *ibid.*, 1778, 1775. See the second reading speech of Attorney-General Charles Wade, *NSWPD, 2nd Session 1908, 8 Edw. VII Ser. 2 Vol. 31*, 1614, or of Mr Mackey, *VPD, Session 1905, Vol. 111*, 2122.

60 *Police Offences (Amendment) Act 1908* (NSW) 8 Edw. VII ch. 12, s.18.

61 Joseph Bosisto in *VPD, Session 1893, Vol. 73*, 2637.

62 William Johnson in *CPD, 1905, 5 Edw. VII Vol. XXVI*, 1768; Mr Gaunson and Mr McCutcheon in *VPD, Session 1905, Vol. 111*, 2124.

63 Joseph Bosisto in *VPD, Session 1893, Vol. 73*, 2639; Mr Smith in *VPD, Session 1905, Vol. 111*, 2125; Dr Scott in *VPD, Session 1893, Vol. 73*, 2640. See also the second reading speech by Mr Mackey and the reply by Mr Prendergast in *VPD, Session 1905, Vol. 111*, 2122–3; the second reading speech by Charles Wade in *NSWPD, 2nd Session 1908, 8 Edw. VII Ser. 2 Vol. 30*, 1614–15; question and answer by Johnson and Alfred Deakin in *CPD, 1904, IV Edw. VII, Vol. XVIII*, 761 and Johnson in *CPD, 1905, V Edw. VII, Vol. XXVI*, 1768.

64 See Howard Becker, *Outsiders*, New York: 1963; Troy Duster, *The Legislation of Morality*, New York: 1970; Joseph Gusfield, *Symbolic Crusade*, Urbana: 1963; Brian Johnson, 'Righteousness Before Revenue: The Forgotten Moral Crusade Against the Indo-Chinese Opium Trade', *Journal of Drug Issues* 5 (1975): 304–26.

65 Mr Beeby in *NSWPD, 2nd Session 1908, 8 Edw. VII Ser. 2 Vol. 31*, 1690–1.

3 Bad Habits

1 Quong Tart in *Official Report of Anti-Opium Demonstration*, Sydney: 1894, 5.

2 Australia, Parliament, *Opium: Report by the Comptroller-General of Customs*, Parl. Paper 1907–8 vol. 2, Sydney: 1908, 1917.

3 *Report by the Government of the Commonwealth of Australia for the Calendar Year 1926*, in AA: Department of Trade and Customs, CA 10; CP 46/3 Papers Relating to Opium Traffic 1925–1933; Report by the Government of the Commonwealth of Australia for the Calendar Year 1936 in AA: Department of Health, CA 17; CRS A1928 Correspondence Files (1921–1949), 610/3 League of Nations—Consumption of Drugs (1936–8). For files on smuggling see generally AA: Department of Trade and Customs, CA 10; CP 46/2 & 46/3.

4 *Report by the Government of the Commonwealth of Australia for the Calendar Year 1921*, in AA: Department of External Affairs (II), CA 18; CRS A981 Correspondence Files 1927–42, League of Nations 46 Old Pt. 1.

5 *International Opium Commission I*, Shanghai: 1909, 61–2, 48 and Final Resolution 3 in Peter Lowes, *The Genesis of International Narcotics Control*, Geneva: 1966, 141–3; K. Bruun, L. Pan, I. Rexed, *The Gentlemen's Club: International Control of Drugs and Alcohol*, Chicago: 1975; David Musto, *The American Disease*, London: 1973, 4–51; John Lonie, *A Social History of Drug Control in Australia* (Royal Commission into the Non-Medical Use of Drugs, South Australia (Prof. Ronald Sackville, Chairman), Research Paper 8), Adelaide: 1979, 38–45; Harrison Narcotic Law 1914, Title 26, USC (USA).

6 Lowes, 173–97; *Opium Convention Signed at the Hague, 23 January 1912; Treaty of Peace Signed at Versailles, 28 June 1919*, article 295.

7 *Opium Convention signed at the Hague, 23 January 1912*, articles 1, 6 & 9.

8 Prime Minister Andrew Fisher, 20 June 1913, and other communications 1913–23 in AONSW, Chief Secretary Special Bundle: Police Offences (Drugs Acts) Amendment 1928–34, 5/5415.

9 *Poisons Act 1890* (Vic.), 54 Vic. No. 1125, s. 13; *Poisons Act 1915* (Vic.), 6 Geo. V No. 2707, s. 12(d); Poisons Act, Additional Regulation (Vic.), *Gazette*, 2 July 1913, 2768–9, consolidated in Poisons Regulations (Vic.), *Gazette No. 89*, 30 May 1917, 1585 *et seq.*, r.17; *Poisons Act 1920* (Vic.), 11 Geo. V No. 3113, 2nd Sch. & s. 10(2); see PROV, VA 860 Chief Secretary's Office, VPRS 3992 Inwards Registered Correspondence Part III, 1919/4146 Amendments to Medical Act 1915 Part III.

10 *Poisons Act 1920* (Vic.), 11 Geo. V No. 3113, 2nd Sch. & s. 10(2). See also *Police Offences Amendment (Drugs) Act 1927* (NSW), Geo. V No. 7, s. 18(2)(a) & (c).

11 *Opium Proclamation 1914, Commonwealth of Australia Gazette No. 71*, 12 September 1914, clauses 2, 4(b).

Notes

12 Dangerous Drugs Regulations 1922 (Vic.), *Gazette No. 102*, 6 September 1922, 2410–12, esp. rr. 4, 5 and 10; *Poisons Act 1925* (Vic.), 16 Geo. V No. 3401, s. 6; *Poisons Act 1927* (Vic.), 18 Geo. V No. 3542, s. 24; Dangerous Drugs Regulations 1930 (Vic.), *Gazette No. 12*, 413 *et seq.*, r. 5.; PROV, VA 695 Department of Public Health 1890–1943, VPRS 6345 Central Administration General Correspondence Files 1920–1981, 804/4 Proclamations Amending Schedules; and see *Police Offences Amendment (Drugs) Act 1927* (NSW), Geo. V No. 7.

13 See, for example, William Eldridge, *Narcotics and the Law*, Chicago: 1962; Alfred Lindesmith, *The Addict and the Law*, New York: 1965; Musto; John Helmer, *Drugs and Minority Oppression*, New York: 1975; R. Bonnie and C. Whitebread, *The Marijuana Conviction*, Charlottesville: 1974; Donald Dickson, 'Bureaucracy and Morality: an Organisational Perspective on a Moral Crusade', *Social Problems* 16 (1968): 143–56.

14 *General Order 1020*(3), (5) & (6); Collector of Customs Queensland, 12, 7 & 16 October 1915; Comptroller-General Stephen Mills, 22 October 1915; *General Order 1020* by Order A'377 & A'385, in AA: CA 10 Department of Trade and Customs; CRS A425 Correspondence Files 1935–56, 40/5008 Drugs—Control of Habit-Forming and Dangerous Drugs—Morphia, Opium etc. Papers 1907–1926.

15 Comptroller-General Stephen Mills, 4 April 1917, in *ibid.*

16 *Ibid.*

17 *Ibid.*

18 Examining Officer Wright, 15 April 1921; Dr J. Cumpston, 4 May 1921; see also 4 April 1921 and 12 October 1921; all in AA: CA10; CRS A425 Correspondence Files 1935-1956, 43/3535; Collector of Customs NSW, 7 January 1919, in AA: CA10; CRS A425 Correspondence Files 1935–1956, 40/5008.

19 AA: CA10; CRS A425 Correspondence Files 1935–1956, 43/3535. Italics added.

20 Crown Solicitor Gordon Castle, 15 February 1922; Inspector Smith, 11 March 1922; in *ibid.*

21 Shillinglaw, 17 May 1906 in PROV, VA 860 Chief Secretary's Office, VPRS 3992, Inwards Registered Correspondence Part III, 06/2094 *Opium Permits; Opium Smoking Prohibition Act 1905* (Vic.), 5 Edw. VII No. 2003, ss. 6 & 7.

22 Acting Comptroller-General Oakley, undated; Registrar C.L. Butchers, 29 April 1920; Under-Secretary of Victorian Department of Health; in PROV, VA 860, VPRS 3992, Inwards Registered Correspondence Part III, 20/2952 Sale of Opium.

23 Interviews with Mr London & Mr Butler, no date; opinion of Crown Solicitor, 16 July 1920; in PROV, VA 860, VPRS 3992 Inwards Registered Correspondence Part III, 20/6895 Sale of Opium.

24 Percy Whitton, 4 August 1920, in AA: CA 10; CRS A425 Correspondence Files 1935–56, 40/5008; *Poisons Act 1920* (Vic.), 11 Geo. V No. 3113.

25 *Imperial Conference 1926—Summary of Proceedings*, Canberra: 1927, 17.

26 Premier Stanley Argyle, 27 June 1933, in AA: CA 18; CRS A981 Correspondence Files 1927–1942, League of Nations Opium 37; Registrar of

the Pharmacy Board, C. Butcher, 3 October 1933, in PROV, VA 695, VPRS 6345 Central Administration General Correspondence Files 1920–1981, 804/1 Poisons Regulations.

27 For an example of how international drug prohibition was seen as an American invention and a matter of American pride, see Ellen La Motte, *The Ethics of Opium*, New York: 1924, 173–5.

28 Advisory Committee on the Traffic in Opium, *Report on the Control of the Importation and Exportation of Opium*, Opium Committee 147.1., 21 July 1923; Secretary-General Eric Drummond, 6 July 1921 & 30 May 1922; in AA: CRS A425 Correspondence Files 1935–56, 40/5008.

29 Minute, 23 November 1921, 30 December 1921, May 1922, 15 September 1922; letters, 6 April 1922, 21 April 1922 and 28 April 1922; Governor-General to Lord Milner, Secretary of State for the Colonies (UK), 8 June 1921, cables from London High Commission to Prime Minister William Morris Hughes, 19 December 1921 & 21 April 1922; other undated correspondence; in *ibid*.

30 La Motte, 11; Inglis, 161–70; *International Convention Adopted by the Second Opium Conference (League of Nations), and Protocol Relating Thereto, Signed at Geneva, 19 February 1925*, articles 12–18, 19–22, 5–6.

31 *Ibid.*, articles 12–18 (esp. 12–13), 21, 22 & 5.

32 See letter from the Prime Minister, William Hughes, 8 February 1923; Director-General of Public Health, 14 March 1923; in AONSW, Chief Secretary Special Bundle: Police Offences (Drugs Acts) Amendment 1928–34, 5/5415; Captain Chaffey in *NSWPD, Session 1933–1934, 23 Geo. V Ser. 2 Vol. 138*.

33 Comments to External Affairs Department from New South Wales government, 25 February 1927 & [no date], Western Australian government, 24 February 1927, Victorian government, 31 March 1927, in AA : CA 18; CRS A981 Correspondence Files 1927–42, League of Nations Opium 25; AONSW, Chief Secretary Special Bundle: Police Offences (Drugs Act) Amendments 1928–34, 5/5415.

34 *Smith's Weekly*, Sydney: 23 April 1938, in AA: CA 10; CP 723/1 Papers Relating to Narcotic Drugs 1929–1959. Illicit Traffic Seizures—Newspaper Articles Thereon.

35 Opium Proclamation 1926, *Commonwealth of Australia Gazette No. 115*, 25 November 1926; *Poisons Act 1927* (Vic.), 18 Geo. V No. 3542, s. 24; Victorian Chief Secretary Prendergast in *VPD, Session 1927, Vol. 174*, 1808.

36 Under-Secretary E. Harkness, 18 July 1927; see also acting Director-General of Public Health Sydney Morris, 20 July 1927 and Pharmacy Board, 28 July 1927; in AONSW, Chief Secretary Special Bundle: Police Offences (Drugs Act) Amendments 1928–34, 5/5413; James McGirr in NSWPD, *Session 1934–5, 24 Geo. V Vol. 141*, 2914–15.

37 *International Convention Adopted by the Second Opium Conference (League of Nations), and Protocol Relating Thereto, Signed at Geneva, 19 February 1925*, article 10.

38 Health Committee recommendations, 4 July 1928, 11 May 1929; Government Analyst, 3 April 1929; Comptroller-General Ernest Hall, 11 July 1929; all in AA: CA 10; CRS A425 Correspondence Files, 58/23167 Narcotic Drugs—

Extension of Control to New Drugs 1928–1949.

39　*Commonwealth of Australia Gazette, No. 32*, 5 April 1928.

40　Secretary-General, 25 October 1930; Deputy Comptroller-General E. Abbott, 18 February 1931; Comptroller-General E. Hall, 12 May 1931; in AA: CA 18; CRS A981 Correspondence Files 1927–42, League of Nations Opium 30; *Convention for Limiting the Manufacture and Regulating the Distribution of Narcotic Drugs, and Protocol of Signature; Geneva 13 July 1931*.

41　*Ibid.*, articles 2, 5(2), 6, 12, 14 (concerning manufacture and distribution), 10(1) & 10(2) (concerning heroin).

42　Acting Comptroller-General M. Synan, 25 August 1932; Comptroller-General E. Hall, 8 December 1932; in AA: CA 18; CRS A981 Correspondence Files 1927–1942, League of Nations Opium 30.

43　Prime Minister Joseph Lyons to Minister without Portfolio (London), Stanley Bruce, 10 October 1932; Bruce to Lyons, 14 October 1932; in *ibid*.

44　*Convention for Limiting the Manufacture and Regulating the Distribution of Narcotic Drugs, and Protocol of Signature; Geneva 13 July 1931*, article 15; Order by Governor-General-in-Council, 29 March 1933; see also E. Hall to Secretary, Department of External Affairs, 10 March 1933, Cabinet paper 15 March 1933; Stanley Bruce [no date], and Order by Governor-General-in-Council, 10 November 1933; in AA: CA 18; CRS A981 Correspondence Files 1927–1942, League of Nations Opium 30.

45　Secretary-General Eric Drummond 17 January 1924; *Resolutions Adopted by the Assembly, Traffic in Opium and Other Dangerous Drugs*, both in AA: CA 10; CRS A425, Correspondence Files 1935–56, 40/5008; *Report to the Council on the Work of the Advisory Committee in Opium and Other Dangerous Drugs*, in AA: CA 18; CRS A981 Correspondence Files 1927–1942, League of Nations Opium Old 1 Pt. 1; AA: CA 18; CRS A981 Correspondence Files 1927–1942, League of Nations 46 Old Pt. 1.

46　W. Beckett in VPD, *Session 1930, Vol. 184*, 4507.

47　Memo from Comptroller-General Oakley, 22 September 1925; Prime Minister, Stanley Bruce, to State Premiers, 30 September 1925; Joseph Lyons to Prime Minister, 19 October 1925; McCormack to Prime Minister, 14 June 1926; R. Oakley, 18 October 1927; in AA : CA10; CRS A425 Correspondence Files, 36/290 Drugs Opium—Prevention of Smuggling: Action by States; Licensing of Addicts in Northern Territory. On this subject, see also Lonie, 78–9.

48　Dr Cook, 5 August 1935; memoranda by Comptroller-General E. Abbott and Director-General Dr. J. Cumpston [no date]; 'MS' or 'MG', 7 January 1936; in *ibid*.

49　Dr Cook, 22 November 1935; E. Abbott [no date]; in *ibid*.

4 *The Age of the Expert*

1　Mr Watt and Mr Mackinnon in *VPD, Session 1904 Vol. 108*, 1889, 1890.

2　AONSW, Colonial Secretary Special Bundle: Prayers for Rain 4/814.2.

3　*Dr. Williams' Pink Pills for Pale People*, Sydney: 1898? See Peter Phillips, *Kill or*

Cure, Melbourne: 1978.
4   *Argus*, Melbourne: 7 February 1903, 14; 19 February 1912, 6; 28 March 1912, 7; 9 April 1912, 5; 17 August 1912, 18. See T.S. Pensabene, *The Rise of the Medical Practitioner in Victoria*, Canberra: 1980, 26–7, 37–48.
5   *Ibid.*, 16 September 1911, 18; 7 May 1932, 11.
6   See Michel Foucault, *The Birth of the Clinic*, London: 1973; Ivan Illich, *Medical Nemesis*, London: 1975; M. Larson, 'The Production of Expertise and the Constitution of Expert Power' in T.L. Haskell, *The Authority of Experts*, Bloomington: 1984, 28–80; V. Navarro, *Medicine Under Capitalism*, New York: 1976, 104–26.
7   See note 6 above; see also Eliot Friedson, *Professional Dominance*, Chicago: 1970; Terence Johnson, *Professions and Power*, London: 1972; Paul Starr, *The Social Transformation of American Medicine*, New York: 1982; Evan Willis, *Medical Dominance*, Sydney: 1983.
8   *Argus*, Melbourne: 15 January 1932, 7.
9   Willis, 1–24. See also Starr, 3–29.
10 *Ibid.*, 92–202.
11 Royal Commission on Secret Drugs, Cures & Foods (Octavius Beale, Commissioner), *Report, Vol. 1*, Melbourne: 1907; Premier Charles Wade in *NSWPD, 2nd Session 1908, 8 Edw. VII Ser. 2 Vol. 31*, 2418; Report of Proceedings in *Second Conference on Uniform Standards for Foods and Drugs*, Sydney: 1913, 18.
12 Mr Higgins in *VPD, Session 1898, Vol. 90, 3067–8; Chemist & Druggist of Australasia*, Melbourne: 1 August 1899; Commonwealth & States of Australia, *Conference[s] on Uniform Standards for Foods and Drugs, Sydney:* items 70–1 (1910 & 1913), items 72–3 (1923 & 1927); *Pure Food Act 1905* (Vic.), 5 Edw. VII No. 2010; *Pure Food Act 1908* (NSW), 8 Edw. VII ch. 31, ss. 5(k), 13(1).
13 Dr Ashburton Thompson and M. Rushton, in Royal Commission on Uniform Standards for Foods and Drugs in the States of the Commonwealth of Australia (Dr J. Ashburton Thompson, Commissioner), *Report*, Sydney: 1913, xxv–vi, 76.
14 *Sale and Use of Poisons Act 1876* (NSW), 40 Vic. No. 9; see *Sale and Use of Poisons Act 1876* (Vic.), 40 Vic. No. 559, s. 12; *Poisons Act 1915* (Vic.), 6 Geo. V No. 2707, s. 12; *Poisons Act 1920* (Vic.), 11 Geo. V No. 3113, s. 10.
15 See also Alfred McCoy, *Drug Traffic*, Sydney: 1980, 74–92.
16 *Sale and Use of Poisons Act 1876* (Vic.), 40 Vic. No. 559, ss. 4 & 13; *Sale and Use of Poisons Act 1876* (NSW), 40 Vic. No. 9, ss. 11 & 7; *Poisons Act 1902* (NSW), 2 Edw. VII No. 65, s. 5. In Victoria, the original reference to 'patent or proprietary medicines' was altered in 1915 to 'patent medicines', a narrower class: *Poisons Act 1915* (Vic.), 6 Geo. V No. 2707, s. 16.
17 PROV, VA1349, VPRS 1774 Correspondence Files 1880–1965, unit 11 Correspondence Files 1901–7; see also PROV, VA 1349, VPRS 3620 Pharmacy Board Annual Reports 1880–1977, esp. 1897, 1898, 1915; AONSW, Colonial Secretary Special Bundle: Re Sale of Patent Medicines by Grocers and Storekeepers 1901, 4/955.4.
18 AONSW, Colonial Secretary Special Bundle: Poisons Bill 1916–30, 5/5398;

J. Bosisto, quoted in H.V. Feehan, 'Personalities, Professions and Poisons', *Victorian Historical Journal* 48 (1977): 161–78, 167.

19 Royal Commission on Uniform Standards for Foods and Drugs in the States of the Commonwealth of Australia, 41–3; *Bingeham v. Stevens* in PROV, VA 1349 Pharmacy Board of Victoria 1876+, VPRS 1867 Legal Opinions 1877–1959.

20 *Ibid.*, xxv.

21 Willis, 125; see 203.

22 Hon. A. Hicks and Major Baird in *VPD, Session 1920, Vol. 155*, 1173 & 1704.

23 19 February 1918 in AONSW, Colonial Secretary Special Bundle: Poisons Bill 1916–30, 5/5398.

24 Report from the Select Committee on the Refusal of the Pharmacy Board to Register Mr Walter Trafford, in *NSW Legislative Assembly Votes and Proceedings 1905, Vol. 3*, 3; Mr Perry & Mr Levien in *NSWPD, Session 1905, V Edw. VII, Ser. 2 Vol. 20*, 3243–7 & 3259.

25 See *VPD, Session 1907, Vol. 118*, 2438; PROV, VA 1349, VPRS 1774 Correspondence Files 1880–1965, unit 14.

26 *Poisons Act 1920* (Vic.), 11 Geo. V No. 3113, s. 11.

27 See McCoy, 87–92.

28 President of the Pharmaceutical Society, McKimm, 30 March 1925, in AONSW, Chief Secretary Special Bundle: Police Offences [Drug Acts] Amendments 1928–34, 5/5414. See 'History of "drugs" legislation in NSW', in AONSW, Chief Secretary Special Bundle: Police Offences Amendment (Drugs) Bill and Related Papers 1924–34, 3/2376.2.

29 Questions on notice by Gregory McGirr to Oakes, answered 18 December 1923, in AONSW, Chief Secretary Special Bundle, Police Offences [Drug Acts] Amendments, 1928–34, 5/5415.

30 *Police Offences Ammendment (Drugs) Act 1927* (NSW), Geo. V No. 7, ss. 18(2) & 19.

31 Memorandum, 3 February 1927, in AONSW, Chief Secretary Special Bundle: Police Offences Amendments 1928–34, 5/5413.

32 *Ibid.*, Under-Secretary of the Colonial Secretary's Department, E. Harkness [no date] and 13 November 1929, in AONSW, Chief Secretary Special Bundle: Police Offences [Drug Acts] Amendments 1928–34, 5/5414; see generally the report by Wurth & Anderson in *ibid*.

33 Report by Wickham & Thompson to Superintendent, Criminal Investigation Branch, 24 August 1931; President of the Pharmacy Board, McKimm, to Colonial Secretary, 14 August 1931; in AONSW, Chief Secretary Special Bundle: Police Offences Amendments 1928–34, 5/5413.

34 19 October 1926, in AONSW, Chief Secretary Special Bundle: Police Offences Amendment (Drugs) Bill and Related Papers 1924–34, 3/2376.2; AONSW, Chief Secretary Special Bundle: Police Offences Amendments 1928–34, 5/5413.

35 Under-Secretary Harkness, 28 February 1930; Inquiry by McKimm, April–May 1931; in *ibid*.

36 Inquiry by Mr Gates, SM, 28 July 1931; McKimm to Colonial Secretary's

Department, 14 August 1931; Report by Detective Sergeants Wickham and Thompson, 24 August 1931; in *ibid*.

37   Ministerial brief, 5 April 1932; in *ibid.; Police Offences Amendment (Drugs) Act 1934* (NSW), No. 16 1934, s. 2; *NSWPD, Session 1934–5, 24 Geo. V, Ser. 2 Vol. 141*, 2913, 2918–2919.

38   See Gregory Haines, *The Grains and Threepenn'orth of Pharmacy*, Kilmore: 1976, 74–5, 150–1; *A Centennial History of the Pharmaceutical Society of Queensland*, 21–5; P. Sekuless, *The First 50 Years: An Historical Review of the Pharmacy Guild of Australia 1928–78*, Canberra: 1978, 4–21; McCoy, 48–52.

39   Police Offences Amendment (Drugs) Act 1927, Regulations (NSW), *Supplement to Government Gazette No. 120*, 30 August 1927, r. 18(2). See also *Poisons Act 1920* (Vic.), 11 Geo. V No. 3112, s. 10(1)(b); Dangerous Drugs Regulations 1922 (Vic.), *Gazette No. 102*, 6 September 1922, 2410–12, r. 3(a).

40   *NSWPD, Session 1928, 18 Geo. V, Ser. 2 Vol. 113*, 515.

41   See Haines, 97–145.

42   Mr Justice Browne, 'Report of the Industrial Commission of New South Wales on ... Pharmacy Chain Stores', in *NSW Parliamentary Papers, 1938–40, Vol. VIII*, 513 & 519.

5   Illness and Vice

1   Alfred McCoy, *Drug Traffic*, Sydney: 1980, 117–40.

2   *Herald*, Melbourne: 16 March 1923.

3   Ernest McTiernan in *NSWPD, Session 1923, 14 Geo. V, 2nd Ser. Vol. 92*, 1264–5; *Poisons Act 1925* (Vic.), 16 Geo. V No. 3401, s. 5; Dr Argyle in *VPD, Session 1925, Vol. 169*, 115.

4   *Argus*, Melbourne: 30 May 1923, 9; 21 July 1923, 25; 6 March 1925, 15; Dr Argyle in *VPD, Session 1925, Vol. 169*, 115.

5   Press release by Dr Dick, 14 April 1923, in AONSW, Chief Secretary Special Bundle: Police Offences (Drugs Acts) Amendment 1928–34, 5/5415.

6   AA: CA 7 Department of External Affairs (II); CRS A981 Correspondence Files 1927–42, League of Nations 46 Old Pt. 1.

7   Inspector Mackay, 23 June 1926, in AONSW, Chief Secretary Special Bundle: Police Offences (Drugs Acts) Ammendment 1928–34, 5/5415.

8   Naturally I have kept the details of the whereabouts of this file vague. I hope its contents will remain there for another sixty years.

9   Inspector Mackay, 16 June 1926, in AONSW, Chief Secretary Special Bundle: Police Offences (Drugs Acts) Amendment 1928–34, 5/5415.

10   McCoy, 117–40; Carlo Lazzarini and Mr Arkins in *NSWPD, 2nd Session 1926, 17 Geo. V, 2nd Ser. Vol. 108*, 1144, 1150 and *passim*.

11   *SMH*: 8 August, 1929, 13; 11 May 1928, 6; 26 September 1928, 12; 19 June 1929; 1 May 1930, 8. See also 19 January 1929, 22; 8 August 1929,13; 30 November 1929, 19; 2 August 1930, 10.

12   *Ibid*.: 14 April 1928, 18.

13   *Sunday Times*, Sydney: 1 March 1926.

14 See, for example, *Inebriates Act 1912* (NSW), 3 Geo. V, No. 24.
15 *Poisons Act 1915* (Vic.), 6 Geo. V No. 2797, s. 9(1). See also *Sale and Use of Poisons Act 1876* (Vic.), 40 Vic. No. 559; *Sale and Use of Poisons Act 1876* (NSW), 40 Vic. No. 9; *Poisons Act 1902* (NSW), 2 Edw. VII No. 65.
16 Dangerous Drugs Regulations 1922 (Vic.), *Gazette No. 102*, 6 September 1922, 2410–12, rr. 3, 4 & 10; *Poisons Act 1925* (Vic.), 16 Geo. V No. 3401, s. 6; Dr Argyle in *VPD, Session 1925*, Vol. 169, 115; Dangerous Drugs Regulations 1930 (Vic.), *Gazette No. 12*, 31 January 1930, 413 *et seq.*, r.6.
17 AA: CA 7; CRS A981 Correspondence Files 1927–42, League of Nations 46 Old Pt. 1; Albert Bruntnell, 3 May 1928 in AONSW, Chief Secretary Special Bundle: Police Offences (Drugs Acts) Amendment 1928–34, 5/5413; *SMH*: 6 January 1934, 14; 17 July 1930, 8.
18 *SMH*: 10 April 1928, 12: 8 May 1928; *Poisons Act 1920* (Vic.), 11 Geo. V No. 3103, s. 12; *Poisons Act 1927* (Vic.), 18 Geo. V No. 3541, s. 27.
19 Captain Chaffey in *NSWPD, Session 1934–5, 24 Geo. V. Ser. 2 Vol. 141*, 2906–10. See also *Police Offences Amendment (Drugs) Act 1934* (NSW), No. 16, 1934, s. 2(2)(d).
20 AA: CA 7; CRS A981 Correspondence Files 1927–1942, League of Nations 46 Old Pt. 1.
21 *SMH*: 12 May 1930, 12; see also 13 May 1930, 8; 23 March 1935, 12f.
22 First supplement to the *Oxford English Dictionary*, Oxford: 1933, 309; William Short, in Royal Commission on Secret Drugs, Cures & Foods (Octavius Beale, Commissioner), *Report, Vol. 1*, Melbourne: 1907, 234.
23 Minute, 29 January 1906 and *Comptroller-General of Prisons Report 1905*, in AONSW, Attorney-General Special Bundle: Working of, And Amendments to, Inebriates Act 5/7751.1; *Inebriates Act 1912* (NSW), 3 Geo. V, No. 24; Mr Prendergast in *VPD, Session 1904, Vol. 108*, 1764.
24 Earle Rowell, *Battling the Wolves of Society: The Narcotics Evil*, Warbuton, Vic.: 1929, 9–23 (see also 41), 29–32, 38, 3. This book was originally written and published in the United States, but its printing in Australia showed its significance.
25 Eliot Friedson, *Profession of Medicine*, New York: 1970, 185–6, 205–26; Thomas Szasz, *The Myth of Mental Illness*, New York: 1961, 44–5; See also, for example, Paul Wilson & John Braithwaite (eds), *Two Faces of Deviance*, St Lucia: 1978; Ivan Illich, *Medical Nemesis*, London: 1974; Susan Sontag, *Illness as Metaphor*, New York: 1988.
26 Messrs Lazzarini, Arkins & McGirr, in *NSWPD, 2nd Session 1926, 17 Geo. V, Ser. 2 Vol. 108*, 1144–6, 1148–50.
27 Police Offences Amendment (Drugs) Act 1927, Regulations (NSW), *Supplement to Government Gazette No. 120*, 30 August 1927, r.22; Dangerous Drugs Regulations 1930 (Vic.), *Gazette No. 12*, 413 *et seq.*, r.16. A less clear regulation aimed at the same problem was to be found in Dangerous Drugs Regulations 1922 (Vic.), r. 6(a).
28 *Poisons and Dangerous Drugs Ordinance 1933* (FCT).
29 Charlie Woodward, *Peeps into Gaols, Police Courts, Opium Dens*, Sydney: 1933, 35.
30 Rowell, 49 & 94.
31 *VPD, Session 1925, Vol. 169, 506; Oxford English Dictionary and Supplement to*

the *Oxford English Dictionary*, Vol. 1, Oxford: 1980, entries for 'Fiend'. The word 'fiend' in this context is said to be 'applied with jocular hyperbole to a person or agency causing mischief'. This is an error. While other uses of fiend clearly suggest only constant and obsessive conduct (as in 'a fresh-air fiend'), 'drug fiend' has other overtones, which are far from jocular.

32 NSW Police Commissioner James Mitchell in *SMH*: 11 April 1928, 15.

33 Harrison Narcotic Law 1914, Title 26, USC (USA), ss. 4701, 4705; *USA v. Doremus* (1919), 249 US 86; *Webb v. USA* (1919), 249 US 96; *USA v. Behrman* (1922), 258 US 280; *Linder v. USA* (1925), 268 US 5, 18. See also John Helmer, *Drugs and Minority Oppression*, New York: 1975; Alfred Lindesmith, *The Addict and the Law*, New York: 1965; Alfred Lindesmith, 'The Federal Narcotics Bureaucracy and Drug Policy', *Journal of Drug Issues* 8 (1978): 157–72; David Musto, *The American Disease*, London: 1973, 5–132; M. Peyrot, 'Cycles of Social Problem Development: The Case of Drug Abuse', *Sociological Quarterly* 25 (1984): 83–96.

34 Dangerous Drugs Act 1920 (UK) 10 & 11 Geo V c. 46. See Terry Parsinnen, *Secret Passions, Secret Remedies*, Philadelphia: 1983, 183–94; Virginia Berridge and Griffith Edwards, *Opium and the People*, London: 1981, 288–90.

35 Lambert in Helmer, 15, 39. See AA: CA 7; CRS A981 Correspondence Files 1927–1942, League of Nations 46 Old Pt 1; AA: CA 10 Department of Trade and Customs; CRS A425 Correspondence Files, 57/28004 Narcotic Drugs—Annual Report on Traffic 1957; AA: CA 18 Department of External Affairs (II); A1838 Correspondence Files, 933/3/1 Drugs General, Annual Report by Australia; AONSW, Chief Secretary: General Correspondence 1959, A59/927 Annual Report on the Working of Treaties; PROV, VA 860 Chief Secretary's Office, VPRS 4723 Inwards Registered Correspondence, 62/H3586 Narcotic Drugs.

36 Collector of Customs NSW, 13 July 1916, in AA: CA 10; CRS A425 Correspondence Files, 40/5008 Drugs—Control of Habit-Forming and Dangerous Drugs—Morphia, Opium etc.

37 Dr Cumpston, 8 February 1922; other letters and memoranda, 1922–32 in AA: CA 17 Department of Health Central Office; CRS A1928 Correspondence Files, Multiple Number System, 1921–1949, 290/8, Morphine and other Narcotic Drugs, Supplies to Local Medical Practitioners (1921–1935).

38 Dr Cumpston, 14 February 1929, 1 April 1931; in *ibid*.

39 File note, 1 August 1929, in AONSW, Chief Secretary Special Bundle: Police Offences (Drugs Acts) Amendment 1928–34, 5/5413.

40 AA: CA 10; CRS A425 Correspondence Files, 42/2168 Prohibited Drugs—Supply: Dr Q. Ercole—Procedures for Supply.

41 AA: CA 10; CP 723/1 Papers Relating to Narcotic Drugs 1929–1959, Submissions &c on Drugs 1930–41; AA: CA 17; CRS A1928 Correspondence Files, Multiple Number System, 1921–1949, 290/8, Morphine and other Narcotic Drugs.

42 Cumpston, 8 April 1932, 20 March 1935, in *ibid*.

43 Dr Q. Ercole, 29 September 1935; Senior Clerk J.B. Simonds, Department of Trade and Customs, 29 January 1936, in AA: CA 10; CRS A425 Correspondence Files, 42/2168 Prohibited Drugs—Supply: Dr Q. Ercole—

Procedures for Supply.
44 Cases of Gale, Robertson, Madley & Robjent in AA: CA 10; CP 723/1 Papers Relating to Narcotic Drugs 1929–1959, Submissions &c on Drugs 1930–41.
45 *Argus*, Melbourne: 9 July 1938, 3; *SMH*: 6 June 1929, 8; 11 July 1931, 7; 11 May 1928, 6; 7 September 1929, 11.
46 Senior Constable Brown, in PROV, VA 860 Chief Secretary's Office, VPRS 3992 Inwards Registered Correspondence Part III, 37/176; Tasmanian Premier to Prime Minister, 22 January 1937, in AA: CA 7 Department of External Affairs (I); CRS A981 Correspondence Files Alphabetical Series 1927–1942, League of Nations Opium 31; Cumpston, 5 & 27 November 1935, in AA: CA 17; CRS A1928 Correspondence Files, Multiple Number System, 1921–1949, 290/8, Morphine and other Narcotic Drugs, and March 1935, in AA: CA 10; CP 723/1 Papers Relating to Narcotic Drugs 1929–1959, Submissions &c on Drugs 1930–41.
47 McCoy, 42 & 92; *2nd Opium Conference Summary of Information with Regard to the Production and Manufacture of ...Opium Derivatives (Years 1920–3)*, ODC 1 (C. 656 M 234. 1924 XI), in AA: CA 10; CRS A425 Correspondence Files, 40/5008 Drugs—Control of Habit-Forming and Dangerous Drugs—Morphia, Opium etc.; *Report by the Government of the Commonwealth of Australia for the Calendar Year 1930* and ... *1931* in AA: *CA 18*; CRS A981 Correspondence Files, League of Nations 46 Old Pt. 1; *Report of the Federal Health Council of Australia, 7th Session*, Canberra: 1934, in AA: CA 18; CRS A981 Correspondence Files, League of Nations Opium 59; AA: CA 10; CP 723/1, Submissions &c on Drugs 1930–1941; AA: CA 17.
48 Harrison Narcotic Law 1914, Title 26, USC (USA); Narcotic Drugs Import and Export Act 1922–1951, Title 21, USC (USA).
49 Council of the League, 23 December 1923, in AA: CA 18; CRS A981 Correspondence Files, League of Nations Opium 59.
50 *Final Act of the Geneva Conference 1931*, Recommendation 6 in *ibid.*; *Convention for Limiting the Manufacture and Regulating the Distribution of Narcotic Drugs, and Protocol of Signature*, Geneva 13 July 1931; *Report of the Committee of Experts (Experts of the Conference (1931) appointed by the Council of the League on the Proposal of the Health Committee on Diacetylmorphine)*, in AA: CP 723/1, Submissions &c on Drugs 1922–1929.
51 McCoy, 42 & 92; NSW Premier, 7 September 1934, WA Premier, 31 July 1934, Victorian Premier, 25 September 1934, Prime Minister Joe Lyons 4 January 1935; see also *Report of the Federal Health Council of Australia, 7th Session*, Canberra: 1934; all in AA: CA 18; CRS A981 Correspondence Files, League of Nations Opium 59; AA: CA 17; CRS A1928 Correspondence Files, 610/3 League of Nations Consumption of Drugs (1936–8).
52 *Convention of 1936 for the Suppression of the Illicit Traffic in Dangerous Drugs signed at Geneva June 26th 1936*, articles 2 & 6–9.
53 *R. v. Burgess; ex parte Henry* (1936) 55 CLR 608, 669 *per* Dixon J., 658 *per* Starke J., 696 *per* Evatt & McTiernan JJ., 640 *per* Latham J; see also *Commonwealth v. Tasmania* (1983) 46 ALR 625; see also Leslie Zines, *The High Court and the Constitution*, Sydney: 1981, 220–30, esp. 222–3.
54 Opinion of G. Knowles, 30 March 1938, in AA: CA 10; CRS A425, 67/06994.

55　Senator Henty, *CPD, 16 Eliz. II Vol. S. 35*, 352.
56　Comptroller-General Abbott, 28 February 1935; Departmental Summary of Premiers' Replies, 25 January 1938; in AA: CA 18; CRS A981 Correspondence Files 1927–1942, League of Nations Opium 31.
57　Secretary of the Department of External Affairs (see also 2nd Assistant Secretary Costieau, Attorney-General's Department, 18 January 1937); Comptroller-General H. Morris; in AA: CA 5 Attorney-General's Department; CRS A432 Correspondence Files, 34/170 Convention for the Suppression of Illicit Traffic in Dangerous Drugs (1934–1938).

6　Conventional Wisdom

1　AA: CA 42 Department of External Territories (I) Central Office 1941–1951; CRS A518 Correspondence Files, N856/1/5 Conventions. Dangerous Drugs, Illicit Trafficking.
2　Correspondence 1940–41 in AA: CA 18 Department of External Affairs (II); CRS A981 Correspondence Files, League of Nations Opium 52.
3　See T.R. Reese, *Australia, New Zealand and the United States: A Survey of International Relations, 1941–1968*, London: 1969; and Joe Camilleri, *Australian–American relations: The Web of Dependence*, Melbourne: 1980, esp. 1–10.
4　*Opium Convention signed at the Hague, 23 January 1912*, articles 6 & 9; *International Convention Adopted by the Second Opium Conference (League of Nations), and Protocol Relating Thereto, Geneva, 19 February 1925*, article 5; see also *Agreement Concerning the Suppression of the Manufacture of, and Internal Trade in and use of, Prepared Opium signed at Geneva 11 February 1925*.
5　Cabinet briefing for 20 October 1943, in AA: CA 12, Prime Minister's Department; A1608 Correspondence Files 1939–1945, A23/2/13 Opium; AA: CA 18; A1066 Correspondence Files 1945, IC 45/51/1/9 League of Nations Dangerous Drugs Conference.
6　QSA: A/4222, Department of Health and Home Affairs, General Correspondence, 41/6524 Poisons; AONSW, Chief Secretary: General Correspondence 1953, 12/7868, A53/668 Application by Andrew Ungar.
7　Interview with J.G. Starke, Friday, 11 August 1989; AA: CA 12; A461 Correspondence Files, 3rd system 1934–50, J302/1/3 Opium Poppy 1940–48.
8　Medical Equipment Control Committee, 5 February 1946; Director-General of Health A.J. Metcalfe, June 1947; Comptroller-General J.J. Kennedy, 5 July 1945; Drug Houses of Australia; Prime Minister Ben Chifley to State Premiers, 30 July 1947; in AA: CA 12; A461 Correspondence Files, 3rd system 1934–50, J302/1/3 Opium Poppy 1940–48.
9　*Protocol Signed at Lake Success, 11 December 1946*; AA: CA 18; A1838 Correspondence Files, 933/1/3 Pt. 1 Drugs General, UN Narcotic Drugs.
10　*International Convention Adopted by the Second Opium Conference (League of Nations), and Protocol Relating Thereto, Geneva, 19 February 1925*, article 10; UN, ECOSOC, *Economic and Social Council, Official Records Supp. 2, Report of the Commission on Narcotic Drugs*, 1948: E/798, 13.

11 AONSW, Chief Secretary: General Correspondence 1956, 12/7926, A56/712 Control of Pethidine &c; C.L. 6. 1945. XI; *Commonwealth of Australia Gazette*, 1 March 1945; AA: CA 10; CRS A425 Correspondence Files, 58/23167 Narcotic Drugs—Extension of Control to New Drugs 1928–1949.

12 Metcalfe, 19 March 1946; see also Metcalfe, 17 October 1946; in *ibid.*

13 See summary of State opinions, 19 March 1946; Kennedy [no date] 1947; 31 March 1947; Metcalfe, 14 March 1947; in *ibid.*

14 *Victorian Government Gazette*, 16 June 1948; see also *Queensland Government Gazette*, 27 September 1948; *NSW Government Gazette, No. 21*, 27 February 1948; AONSW, Chief Secretary: General Correspondence 1956, 12/7926, A56/712 Control of Pethidine &c.; Ben Chifley, 10 November 1947, in AA: CA 10; CRS A425 Correspondence Files, 58/23167 Narcotic Drugs—Extension of Control to New Drugs 1928–1949.

15 AA: CA 17 Department of Health; CRS A1658 Correspondence Files, 276/1/16 Drugs and Medicines—General Narcotics.

16 PROV, VA 467 Premier's Department, VPRS 1163 Inward Correspondence 1883–1967, P68/2246 Control of Drugs; see also AA: CA 18; A1838 Correspondence Files, 933/3/1 Drugs General, Annual Report by Australia on the Working of International Treaties on Narcotic Drugs.

17 *NSW Government Gazette, No. 83*, 18 May 1951; AONSW, Chief Secretary: General Correspondence 1956, 12/7926, A56/712 Control of Pethidine &c; *Victorian Government Gazette*, 23 November 1949.

18 *Protocol Bringing Under International Control Drugs Outside the Scope of the Convention of 13 July 1931, Paris 19 November 1948*.

19 *Police Offences Amendment (Drugs) Act 1927* (NSW), No. 7, 1927, s. 18(2)(a); see esp. *NSW Government Gazette, No. 18*, 6 February 1959; *Poisons Act 1958* (Vic.), No. 6336 1958, sch. 6.

20 UN, ECOSOC, *Economic and Social Council Resolutions*, 1951: E/1932; UN, ECOSOC, *ESCOR Supp. 13, Report of the CND*, 1951: E/1998, E/CN. 7/227/Rev. 1, 9, 21 & *passim*; *Protocol for Limiting and Regulating the Cultivation of the Poppy Plant, the Production of, International and Wholesale Trade in and use of Opium, New York 23 June 1953*, articles 3–6; AA: CA 18; *A1838 Correspondence Files, 933/2/3 Drugs General, 1953 Opium Protocol*.

21 See debates on the Boggs Act 1951 and the Narcotic Drug Control Act 1956; see also William Eldridge, *Narcotics and the Law*, Chicago: 1962; Alfred Lindesmith, *The Addict and the Law*, New York: 1965, 243–268; Alfred McCoy, *The Politics of Heroin in South–East Asia*, New York: 1972; David Musto, *The American Disease*, London: 1973, 230 *et seq.*; John Helmer, *Drugs and Minority Oppression*, New York: 1975, 99 *et seq.*, 103.

22 UN, ECOSOC, *ESCOR 18th Session Supp. 8; CND, Report of the 9th Session*, 1954: E/2606, E/CN. 7/283, 22–3. See also, for example, *ibid., Report of the CND*, 1952: E/2219, E/CN. 7/240, 5; *ibid., Report of the 11th Session*, 1956: E/2891, E/CN. 7/315, 11.

23 See AA: CA 62 Department of Customs and Excise; CRS A425 Correspondence Files, 58/23167 Narcotic Drugs—Extension of Control to New Drugs 1928–1949.

24 Quoted in Brian Inglis, *The Forbidden Game—A Social History of Drugs*, London: 1975, 183; see also Richard Bonnie & Charles Whitebread, 'The Forbidden Fruit and the Tree of Knowledge—The Legal History of American Marijuana Prohibition', *Virginia Law Review* 56 (1970): 971–1203; Joseph Himmelstein, 'From Killer Weed to Drop-Out Drug: The Changing Ideology of Marijuana', *Contemporary Crises* 7 (1983): 13–38, esp. 19–26; Helmer.

25 *Daily Telegraph*, Sydney: 21 April 1938; AA: CA 10; CP 723/1 Papers Relating to Narcotic Drugs 1929–1959, Illicit Traffic Seizures—Newspaper Reports Thereon; *Smith's Weekly*, Sydney: 23 April 1938, 1; AA: CA 17 Department of Health; CRS A1928 Correspondence Files 1921—1949, 290/36 Drugs and Medicines: Marijuana Obtained from Plants of the Same Name; Nigel Manning, editorial, *Australian Journal of Pharmacy*, Sydney: 30 June 1952; AONSW, Chief Secretary: General Correspondence 1949, B9/951 Sale of Sex Drugs. Press Cuttings re.

26 Customs (Prohibited Import) Regulations (Cwlth) S.R. 1934 No. 152, 2nd Sch. item 7; AA: CA 10; CRS A425 Correspondence Files, 58/6395 Drugs—Narcotic, Control of Indian Hemp; Customs (Prohibited Import) Regulations (Cwlth) S.R. 1956 No. 90, 1st Sch. item 21.

27 See *Courier-Mail*, Brisbane: 11 December 1957, *Daily Telegraph*, Sydney: 11 December 1957 and *Truth*, Sydney: 15 December 1957, all in AA: CA 62, CRS A425, 57/28585 Narcotic Drugs—Cultivation of Marijuana in Queensland.

28 WHO, in AA: CA 17; CRS A1658 Correspondence Files. 564/1/6 World Health Organisation—General. See also resolutions 548G of the XVIIIth session of ECOSOC, 6.14 of the Sixth World Health Assembly and III of the Tenth Session of the CND.

29 *Bulletin on Narcotics* 5(2) (1953): 49.

30 *Ibid.*; UN, ECOSOC, *ESCOR Supp. 8; CND, Report of the 9th Session*, 1953: E/2423, E/CN. 7/262, 4; AONSW, Chief Secretary: General Correspondence 1952, 12/7837, A52/1243 Heroin Consumption; PCOB, 4 January 1949, in AA: CA 17; CRS A1658 Correspondence Files, 564/1/2 Pt. 1 WHO Opium Board (Use of Heroin in Australia).

31 See A.J. Metcalfe, 4 May 1950, in AA: CA 17; CRS A1658 Correspondence Files, 564/1/6 World Health Organisation; see also AA: CA 17; CRS A1658 Correspondence Files, 564/1/2 Pt 1 WHO Opium Board (Use of Heroin in Australia).

32 Pharmacy Board of Victoria, 15 November 1951, and Director-General of Health (NSW), 21 February 1952, in PROV, VA 467; VPRS 1163, Inward Correspondence 1883–1967, 58/2372 Control of Drugs; AONSW, Chief Secretary: General Correspondence 1952, 12/7837, A52/1243 Heroin Consumption; PROV, VA 467; VPRS 1170 Premier's Department Special Files 1880–1960, P52/3180 Premiers' Conference 1952; *Victorian Government Gazette*, 3 March 1953.

33 Director-General of Health, NSW, 28 April 1952, in PROV, VA 467; VPRS 1163, Inward Correspondence 1883–1967, 58/2372 Control of Drugs; Federal Council of the BMA, 17 September 1952, in AA: CA 17; CRS A1658 Correspondence Files, 564/1/33 World Health Organisation—General; A.J. Metcalfe, 4 May 1950, in AA: CA 17; CRS A1658 Correspondence Files, 564/1/6 World Health Organisation—General.

34 Senior Pharmacist R. Cunningham, 'Enquiry into Narcotic Control in Australia', 4 September 1952; memorandum, 27 October 1952, and other correspondence, in AA: CA 17; CRS A1658 Correspondence Files , 276/1/16 Drugs & Medicines—General Narcotics.

35 *Truth*, Sydney: 1 November 1952 (see also 2 November 1952); in *ibid*.

36 Metcalfe, 27 May 1953, Federal Council of the BMA in Australia, 4 March 1953, Metcalfe, 6 March 1953, RACS, 28 July 1953, RACP, 2 April 1953, RCO&G, 11 May 1953, Metcalfe to RACP, 13 April 1953, and other correspondence; all in *ibid*.; Customs (Prohibited Imports) Regulations (Cwlth), S.R. 1953 No. 56, Sch. 1 item 14 in *Commonwealth of Australia Gazette*, 25 June 1953.

37 *SMH*: 30 December 1954.

38 Secretary of the Department of Health, W. Rowe [no date] & other correspondence, in PROV, VA 695 Department of Health; VPRS 6345 Central Administration General Correspondence Files 1920–1981, X804/8 Poisons Act. Heroin; Mr Barry in *VPD, Session 1952–3, Vol. 242*, 1984–5; *Poisons (Heroin) Act 1953* (Vic.), No. 5714, 1953.

39 Metcalfe, 10 October 1953; PROV, VA 695; VPRS 6345 Central Administration General Correspondence Files 1920–1981, X804/8 Poisons Act. Heroin; Wallace, 28 April 1952, in PROV, VA 467; VPRS 1163, Inward Correspondence 1883–1967, 58/2372 Control of Drugs; Director-General of Health, 10 June 1953 and Premier Bob Heffron to Sir Robert Menzies, 18 August 1953; in AONSW, Chief Secretary: General Correspondence 1955, 12/7868, A55/990 Heroin; *Police Offences Amendment (Drugs) Act 1954* (NSW), No 37, 1954, s. 20c; *NSW Government Gazette*, 29 July 1955.

40 *Times*, London: 30 November–14 December 1955; *Medical Journal of Australia, Sydney:* 7 April 1956, 579–81; United Kingdom High Commissioner, 26 January 1956, and other documents, in AONSW, Chief Secretary: General Correspondence 1955, 12/7868, A55/990 Heroin; AA: CA 17; CRS A1658 Correspondence Files, 564/1/2 Pt. 1 WHO Opium Board (Use of Heroin in Australia).

41 See *SMH*: 13 August 1955, 18 August 1955, 5 January 1956; *Daily Mirror*, Sydney: 29 January 1956; *Sun*, Sydney: 30 December 1955.

42 Dr H. Wallace in *SMH*: 13 August 1955 (italics added); Dr D.R.W. Cowan, *Medical Journal of Australia*, Sydney: 7 April 1956, 579–870; Northern Branch of the BMA (NSW) in *Daily Mirror*, Sydney: 6 January 1956; *SMH*: 8 October 1956.

43 Commonwealth Minister of Health, Dr Earle Page, *Herald,* Melbourne: 9 January 1956; see NSW Health Minister, Dr Cameron, in *Daily Mirror*, Sydney: 16 May 1956.

44 *Dangerous Drugs Act Amendment Act 1955* (SA), No. 31 1955, s.6(a); AA: CA 10; CRS A425 Correspondence Files, 59/29252 Narcotic Drugs Annual Report 1955.

45 Interview with Sir William Refshauge, Wednesday, 16 August 1989; Secretary of the Department of Health, L.P. Yeatman, 9 September 1955, in PROV, VA 695; VPRS VPRS 6345 Central Administration General Correspondence Files 1920–1981, X804/8 Poisons Act. Heroin.

46 C. MacKenzie, 18 November 1953, AA: CA 10; CRS A425 Correspondence Files, 52/1244 Narcotic Drugs—Quarterly Returns; AA: CA 10; CRA425 Correspondence Files, 58/6697 Drugs—Narcotic Consumption Statistics 1950–1955.

47 Mr Porter and Mr Doube, *VPD, Session 1955–56*, Vol. 248, 2727, 3733; *Health (Narcotics) Act 1956* (Vic.), No. 5979, 1956.

48 *NSW Government Gazette No. 109*, 7 June 1935; Supplement to *NSW Government Gazette, No. 107*, 6 October 1967.

49 AA: CA 10; A425 Correspondence Files, 58/2090 Prohibited Drugs—Control of, Unification; Senior Pharmacist R. Cunningham, Enquiry into Narcotic Control in Australia, 4 September 1952, in AA: CA 17; CRS A1658 Correspondence Files, 276/1/16 Drugs & Medicines; AA: CA 62; CRS A425 Correspondence Files, Narcotic Drugs 67/06994; AONSW, Department of Health: Poisons Act and Amendments, 1509 Pt. 3, 14/1262; PROV, VA 860, VPRS 4723, Inwards Registered Correspondence Part IV, 62/H3586 Narcotic Drugs; PROV, VA 605, VPRS 6345 Central Administration General Correspondence Files 1920–1981, X804/14 Poisons Act—Re-enactment of Act and Schedules.

50 AA: CA 10; A425 Correspondence Files, 52/834 Seizures of Opium; AONSW, Chief Secretary: General Correspondence 1959, 12/7977, A59/927 Annual Report on the Working of Treaties. See also Eric Rolls, *Sojourners*, St Lucia: 1992, 381.

51 AONSW, Chief Secretary: General Correspondence 1959, 12/7977, A59/927 Annual Report on the Working of Treaties; AA: CA 10 Department of Trade and Customs; CRS A425 Correspondence Files, 57/28004 Narcotic Drugs—Annual Report on Traffic 1957; AA: CA 18; A1838 Correspondence Files, 933/3/1 Drugs General, Annual Report by Australia on the Working of International Treaties on Narcotic Drugs; PROV, VA 860 Chief Secretary's Office, VPRS 4723, Inwards Registered Correspondence Part IV, 62/H356 Narcotic Drugs.

52 Meere, 13 September 1955, in AA: CA 10; CRS A425 Correspondence Files, 55/2477 Drugs and Addiction; PROV, VA 860; VPRS 4723, Inwards Registered Correspondence Part IV, 62/H3586 Narcotic Drugs; AA: CA 18; A1838, 933/3/1 Drugs General, Annual Report by Australia on the Working of International Treaties on Narcotic Drugs; AONSW, Chief Secretary: General Correspondence 1959, 12/7977, A59/927 Annual Report on the Working of Treaties.

53 *Ibid.*; AA: CA 10; CRS A425 Correspondence Files, 57/28004 Narcotic Drugs; PROV, VA 695 Department of Health, VPRS 6345 General Correspondence Files, Z79/II Poisons Act 1962 UN Commission on Narcotics.

54 Model Dangerous Drugs Regulations and Act 1958, r. 24, in AA: CA 17; CRS A1658 Correspondence File; Attorney-General's Department Opinion, 1938, in AA: CA 10; CRS A425 Correspondence Files, 67/06994 Narcotic Drugs.

55 AA: CA 10; CRS A425 Correspondence Files 58/2090 Prohibited Drugs; AA: CA 10; CRS A425 Correspondence Files, 58/23165 Narcotic Drugs—Addiction in Australia.

56 *Queensland Government Gazette No. 118*, 15 November 1940, 1365–1406, r.54.

57 *Health Act 1937* (Qld), 1 Geo.VI No. 31, s.130(1); *Health Act Amendment Act 1941* (Qld), 5 Geo VI No. 8, s.4.; Poisons Regulations 1946 (Qld), r. 51(1).

58 H.G. Wallace, 15 March 1954, in AONSW, Chief Secretary: General Correspondence 1954 12/7884, A54/480 Care and Treatment of Drug Addicts.

59 A. Carter, 13 June 1952, in AA: CA 62; CRS A425 Correspondence Files, 67/06994 Narcotic Drugs.

60 AONSW, Chief Secretary: General Correspondence 1959, 12/7977, A59/927 Annual Report on the Working of Treaties; AA: CA10; CRS A425 Correspondence Files, 58/2090 Prohibited Drugs—Control of, Unification; PROV, VA 860, VPRS 4723, Inwards Registered Correspondence Part IV, 62/H3586 Narcotic Drugs.

61 AONSW, Chief Secretary: General Correspondence 1959, 12/7977, A59/927 Annual Report on the Working of Treaties; R.B. McAllister, 19 February 1965, in Premier's Department (Qld): In-letters—Batch 58: Traffic in Opium and Other Drugs, Part 2.

62 UN, ECOSOC, *ESCOR 18th Session Supp. 8; CND, Report of the 9th Session*, 1954: E/2606, E/CN. 7/283, 18.

63 Mr Cook & Mr Barry, in *VPD, Session 1950–1. Vol. 235*, 3177 & 3179; see also Mr Galvin, in *ibid.*, 3175–7; *Poisons Act 1951* (Vic.), No. 5534.

64 *Single Convention on Narcotic Drugs, Signed at New York 30 March 1961*, articles 19, 20, 21, 31 & 3. For preparatory work, see, for example, UN, ECOSOC, *ESCOR Supp. 9, Report of the CND*, 1949: E/1361, E/CN. 7/186, 32, and the *Report of the CND* in the following years.

65 *Single Convention on Narcotic Drugs*, articles 24, 24(1), 25; UN, ECOSOC, *ESCOR 34th Session, Supp. 9, CND, Report of the 17th Session*, 1962: E/3648, E/CN. 7/432, 35, 33–6.

66 *Single Convention on Narcotic Drugs*, articles 30, 33, 36; see also articles 37 & 38.

67 *Ibid.*, articles 2(5*a*) & (5*b*) and Sch. 4; articles 2(1)–(4) & Sch. I–III.

68 AA: CA 42 Department of External Territories (I) Central office 1941–1951; CRS A518 Correspondence Files, R856/1/5 Proposed Single Convention on Narcotic Drugs; State government comments on Draft Single Convention and Commonwealth Inter-departmental Meeting, 14 August 1959, in PROV, VA 860, VPRS 4723 Inward Registered Correspondence Part IV, 62/H3586 Narcotic Drugs; PROV, VA 467, VPRS 1163 Inward Correspondence 1883–1967, 61/3392 Control of Drugs.

7 The Balance of Power

1 Nigel Manning, 29 July 1959, Victorian Chief Health Officer, Kevin Brennan, 7 September 1959, in PROV, VA 695 Department of Public Health, VPRS 6345 Central Administration General Correspondence Files 1920–1981, X804/14 Poisons Act—Re-enactment of Act and Schedules; memorandum, 31 May 1960, AONSW, Department of Health: 14/1262, Poisons Act and Amendments, 1509 Pt. 3, 14/1262; *Poisons Act 1966* (NSW), Eliz. II No. 31, 1966; W. Sheehan, in *NSWPD, Session 1965–6, 15 Eliz. II Ser. 2, Vol. 61*, 4522.

2   *Poisons Act 1962* (Vic.), No. 6889 1962, ss. 4(1), 31, 32 and *Poisons Act 1966* (NSW), Eliz. II No. 31, 1966, ss. 8(2), 26, 21(1g).

3   *Poisons Act 1962* (Vic.), No. 6889 1962, s.32 & 34(2); *Poisons Act 1966* (NSW), ss. 21(1), 32(1) & 21(2), 26 & 33.

4   PROV, VA 695; VPRS 6345 Central Administration General Correspondence Files 1920–1981, Y84 Poisons Act 1962—UN Commission; *Poisons Act 1966* (NSW), s. 3(1) and schedule.

5   G.R. Fleming and Chairman, Poisons Advisory Committee, 11 May 1962 and 9 November 1962, and Cabinet Submission, 30 August 1962; in AONSW, Department of Health: Poisons Act and Amendments, 1509 Pt 5, 14/1262.

6   Various file notes and correspondence, Cabinet Submission by W.F. Sheehan, 1963, and A.H. Jago, 4 June 1965, in AONSW, Department of Health: Poisons Act and Amendments, 1509 Pts. 5 & 6, 14/1262.

7   *Poisons Act 1962* (Vic.), No. 6889 1962, for example ss. 4(2), 10, 11 & 37; PROV, VA 695; VPRS 6345 Central Administration General Correspondence Files 1920–1981, Z69 Poisons Act 1962, 1959–1975.

8   PROV, VA 695, VPRS 6345 Central Administration General Correspondence Files 1920–1981, Z79/II Poisons Act 1962 UN Commission on Narcotics.

9   PROV, VA 860; VPRS 4723, 62/H3586; PROV, VA 467 Premier's Department, VPRS 1163 Inward Correspondence 1883–1967, P68/2246 Control of Drugs; PROV, VA 695 Department of Health; VPRS 6345 Central Administration General Correspondence Files 1920–1981, Z79/IV Poisons Act 1962 UN Commission on Narcotics.

10 Alfred McCoy, *Drug Traffic*, Sydney: 1980, 261; see generally 256–61.

11 *Ibid.*; PROV, VA 695; VPRS 6345 Central Administration General Correspondence Files 1920–1981, Z79/V Poisons Act 1962 UN Commission on Narcotics.

12 *Poisons Act 1966* (NSW), No. 31, 1966, ss. 27–30, 27; see also *Poisons Act 1962* (Vic.), No. 6889 1962, ss. 21 & 37(d); Drugs of Addiction and Restricted Substances Regulations 1966 (Vic.) S.R. 1966, No. 153, rr. 71–4; *Queensland Government Gazette No. 118*, 15 November 1940, 1365–406, r.54; *Dangerous Drugs Act 1934* (SA), 25 Geo. V No. 2180, s. 7(1)(c).

13 Customs (Prohibited Imports) Regulations (Cwlth), S.R. 1953 No. 56, Sch. 1 item 14; Cwlth S.R. 1956 No. 90, Sch. 1 item 21; *Poisons Act 1966* (NSW), Eliz. II No. 31, 1966, s. 21(1g).

14 PROV, VA 695; VPRS 6345 General Correspondence Files, Z79/IV Poisons Act 1962 UN Commission on Narcotics; Premier's Department (Qld.): In-letters—Batch 58: Traffic in Opium and Other Drugs, Part 2.

15 David Hunter & Clarence Earl, in *NSWPD, Session 1967–8, 16 Eliz. II Vol. 67 & 69*, 327 & 1770.

16 Mr Renshaw, *NSWPD, Session 1967–8, 16 Eliz. II Ser. 3 Vol. 70*, 2562; Askin, *ibid.*, 2765.

17 *Single Convention on Narcotic Drugs, Signed at New York 30 March 1961*, article 2(5) & Schedule IV; H.B. Murphy, 'The Cannabis Habit', *Bulletin on Narcotics* 15 (1963): 15–23; UN, ECOSOC, *ESCOR 28th Session, Supp. 8, CND, Report of the 14th Session*, 1959: E/3254, E/CN. 7/376; UN, ECOSOC,

ESCOR 36th Session, Supp. 9, CND, Report of the 18th Session, 1963: E/3775, E/CN. 7/455, 32 et seq.; UN, ECOSOC, ESCOR 40th Session, Supp. 2, CND, Report of the 20th Session, 1966: E/4140, E/CN. 7/48, 31–8, 38.
18   NSW Government Gazette No. 77, 5 August 1966.
19   Mr Tooth, Proposed Amendments to Health Act 21 October 1966 in Premier's Department (Qld): In-letters—Batch 58: Traffic in Opium and Other Drugs, Part 2; WA Minister for Health MacKinnon, PROV, VA 695, VPRS 6345 Central Administration General Correspondence Files 1920–1981, Z 1350/2 Drugs—Meeting of Commonwealth and State Ministers on Drug Abuse, April 1970, 78. See generally Joseph Himmelstein, 'From Killer Weed to Drop-Out Drug: The Changing Ideology of Marijuana', *Contemporary Crises* 7 (1983): 13–38.
20   See *CPD, Session 1967, Vol. S. 35*, 342–5; *CPD, Session 1967, Vol. H. of R. 54 n.s.*, 726; *CPD, Session 1967, Vol. H. of R. 56 n.s.*; *NSWPD, Session 1966–7, 15 Eliz. II Ser. 3 Vol. 66*, 4479–80; *NSWPD, Session 1967–8, 16 Eliz. II Ser. 3 Vols. 67–70*, 327, 1770, 2436 et seq.
21   CND, 12 September 1966, E/CN.7/AC.6/8; Prohibited Import Regulations (Cwlth), S.R. No. 95, 1966, 4th Schedule; *Supplement to NSW Government Gazette No. 107*, 6 October 1967, r. 52; *Poisons (Amendment) Act 1967* (Vic.), No. 7588 1967, s. 25a; Poisons (Hallucinogenic Drugs) Regulations 1967 (Vic.), S.R. 20 1967; *South Australian Government Gazette*, 18 September 1969, 868.
22   Mr S.D. Tooth in Proceedings of Commonwealth–State Ministers' Meeting on Drugs of Dependence, 14 February 1969, PROV, VA 695, VPRS 6345 Central Administration General Correspondence Files 1920–1981, 1285 Pt. 1.
23   See, for example, *Queensland Government Gazette*, 1 June 1967; Drugs of Addiction and Restricted Substances Regulations 1970 (Vic.) S.R. No. 80, 242–3.
24   Bob Katter, *CPD, Session 1971, Vol. H. of R. 71 n.s.*, 1033.
25   *R. v. Burgess; ex parte Henry* (1936) 55 CLR 608, 669 per Dixon J.
26   Leslie Bury, 13 January 1966; Sir Henry Bolte to Harold Holt, 9 March 1966; Commonwealth–State Conference on Narcotic Drugs Control, 23 March 1966; in PROV, VA 695; VPRS 6345 Central Administration General Correspondence Files 1920–1981, Z79/II Poisons Act 1962 UN Commission on Narcotics.
27   *Narcotic Drugs Act 1967* (Cwlth), Act No. 53, 1967, Preamble, 1st Schedule, ss. 7, 9–11; Sir Henry Bolte, 8 December 1967, in PROV, VA 695; VPRS 6345 Central Administration General Correspondence Files 1920–1981, Z79/II Poisons Act 1962 UN Commission on Narcotics.
28   Commonwealth–State Conference on Narcotic Drugs Control, 23 March 1966; Victorian Senior Pharmacist, R.H. Borowski, 27 October 1966, and Secretary of the Victorian Department of Health, W. Rogan, 2 November 1966, in *ibid*.
29   Commonwealth–State Standing Committee on Control of Drugs of Dependence, 8 December 1966, in *ibid*.
30   John Gorton, 16 October 1968; see also Commonwealth–State Ministers' Meeting on Drugs of Dependence, 14 February 1969; Briefing paper re

Commonwealth–State Ministers' Meeting, 14 February 1969; all in PROV, VA 695; VPRS 6345 Central Administration General Correspondence Files 1920–1981, 1285 Pt. 1 Conferences—Control of Narcotics.

31 Summary Record and Report to Commonwealth–State Ministers' Meeting, in *ibid.*
32 *Ibid.*; Senator Scott in *CPD, 18 Eliz. II Vol. S. 41*, 1632.
33 Interview with Sir William Refshauge, Wednesday, 16 August 1989.
34 Customs (Prohibited Import) Regulations 1974 (Cwlth) and Customs (Prohibited Export) Regulations 1974 (Cwlth); *Narcotic Drugs Amendment Act 1976* (Cwlth), No. 176 of 1976; Senator Scott and Health Minister, A.J. Forbes, July 1969 in Commonwealth–State Ministers' Meeting on Drugs of Dependence, PROV, VA 695; VPRS 6345 Central Administration General Correspondence Files 1920–1981, 1285 Pt. 1 Conferences—Control of Narcotics.
35 Mr Viney in *NSWPD, Session 1976–77–78, 25–26–27 Eliz. II Ser. 3 Vol. 133*, 7871.
36 Interview with Sir William Refshauge, Wednesday, 16 August 1989.

8 Shadows of the Past

1 *Convention on Psychotropic Substances 1971, Signed at Vienna, 21 February 1971*, articles 20(1) & 22; *Protocol Amending the Single Convention on Narcotic Drugs, 1961, Signed at Geneva 25 March 1972*, article 14 amending article 36 & article 15 amending article 38; *Commentary on the Protocol Amending the Single Convention on Narcotic Drugs*, New York, 1976: E/CN.7/588, 83.
2 *Convention on Psychotropic Substances 1971, Signed at Vienna, 21 February 1971*, article 19.
3 *Protocol Amending the Single Convention on Narcotic Drugs, 1961*, article 5 amending *Single Convention on Narcotic Drugs*, article 12(5); article 11 enacting new article 21 *bis*.
4 *Ibid.*, article 6 amending article 14; article 7 enacting new article 14 *bis*.
5 *Psychotropic Substances Act 1976* (Cwlth), Act No. 87 1976; Lionel Bowen, *CPD, Session 1976, Vol. H. of R. 99 n.s.*, 215.
6 Prime Minister, William McMahon, to Victorian Premier, Henry Bolte, 9 December 1971, PROV, VA 695 Department of Health, VPRS 6345 Central Administration General Correspondence Files 1920–1981, Z1421 Drugs—Psychotropic Substances.
7 *Dangerous Drugs Act Amendment Act (No. 2) 1970* (SA), No. 65 of 1970, s. 9 amending *Dangerous Drugs Act* 1934 (SA), No. 2180 of 1934, s.11; *Health Act Amendment Act 1971* (Qld), No. 20, 1971, s. 13 inserting *Health Act 1934–1971* (Qld), s. 130M; see also Poisons Regulations 1967 (Qld), r. R2.01.; *Poisons (Amendment) Act 1967* (Vic.), No. 7588 1967, s. 62a.
8 Don Chipp in *CPD, Session 1970, Vol. H. of R. 69*, 141; *ibid., Vol. H. of R. 70*, 2460; *CPD, Session 1972, Vol. H. of R. 8*, 3269; *CPD, Session 1973, Vol. H. of R. 83*, 1356; *ibid., Vol. H. of R. 86*, 2826.
9 Mr Jago in *NSWPD, Session 1969–70, 19 Eliz. II Ser. 3 Vol. 86*, 5340.

10 *Poisons (Amendment) Act 1970* (NSW), No. 53, 1970, ss. 21(2a) & 45a; PROV, VA 695; VPRS 6345 Central Administration General Correspondence Files 1920–1981, Z 1350/2 Drugs—Meeting of Cwlth & State Ministers on Drug Abuse—Canberra, April 1970; *Dangerous Drugs Amendment Act (No. 2) 1970* (SA), No. 65 of 1970, s. 5 substituting new Dangerous Drugs Act 1934–1970 (SA), s. 5(2) & (4); *Health Act Amendment Act 1971* (Qld), No. 20 1971, ss.7 & 12 substituting new *Health Act 1934–1971* (Qld) ss. 130(2) & 130J; *Customs Amendment Act No. 2 1971* (Cwlth), No. 134 1971, s. 8 inserting *Customs Act 1901–1971* (Cwlth), s. 235 (1)(c) & (4).

11 *Customs Amendment Act No. 2 1971* (Cwlth), No. 134 1971; *Customs Act 1901–1971* (Cwlth), s. 233B (c), (ca); Don Chipp, *CPD, Session 1971, Vol. H. of R. 74*, 3421.

12 *Customs Amendment Act No. 2 1971* (Cwlth), No. 134 1971, s. 7 inserting *Customs Act 1901–1971* (Cwlth), s. 233B (1)(c), (1)(ca) & (1B).

13 *CPD, Session 1971, Vol. H. of R. 74*, 4282, 4287.

14 Australia, Parliament, *Report from the Senate Select Committee on Drug Trafficking and Drug Abuse*, Parl. Paper 1971 vol. 8, Canberra: 1975, 135–257, 135, 155, 200, 212–18.

15 *CPD, Session 1972, Vol. S. 53*, 163.

16 Don Chipp, in *CPD, Session 1973, Vol. H. of R. 86*, 2826–7.

17 Cameron, Maugher, Barraclough, Jensen & Deane, in *NSWPD, Session 1969–70, 19 Eliz II Ser. 3 Vol. 86*, 5421, 5438–45, 5482–7.

18 Joseph Himmelstein, 'From Killer Weed to Drop-Out Drug: the Changing Ideology of Marijuana', *Contemporary Crises* 7 (1983): 13–38, 32.

19 Quoted in *NSWPD, Session 1976–77–78, 25–26–27 Eliz. II Ser. 3 Vol. 133*, 7779–80.

20 *Progress Report from the Joint Committee of the Legislative Council and Legislative Assembly Upon Drugs*, Sydney: 1978, in Parliament of NSW, *Joint Volumes of Papers, 2nd Session 1976-77-78, Vol. III*, 165–7.

21 *Single Convention on Narcotic Drugs, Signed at New York 30 March 1961*, article 2(5) & Schedule IV.

22 Dr Klugman in *CPD, Session 1970, Vol. H. of R. 66*, 254, *CPD, Session 1970, Vol. H. of R. 69*, 1560–3; Dr Cass in *CPD, Session 1971, Vol. H. of R. 71*, 668–9, *CPD, Session 1971, Vol. H. of R. 74*, 2099–2101; Senator Cavanagh in *CPD, Session 1971, Vol. S. 50 n.s.*, 2725; Dr Everingham in *CPD, Session 1971, Vol. H. of R. 73*, 972; *CPD, Session 1971, Vol. S. 48 n.s.*, 1790–5.

23 *Poisons Act 1966 (NSW)*, No. 31, 1966, s. 20; *Poisons (Amendment) Act 1970* (NSW), No. 53, 1970; *Dangerous Drugs Act 1934* (SA), No. 2180 of 1934, s. 3; *Narcotic and Psychotropic Drugs Act Amendment Act 1974* (SA), No. 112 of 1974, s. 2(a); *Poisons Act 1962* (Vic.), No. 6889 1962, s. 26(1); *Poisons (Drugs of Addiction) Act 1976* (Vic.), No. 8961, 1976, s. 5. See *Advertiser*, Adelaide: 31 May 1974, 1, 21 June, 8, and 25 June, 7.

24 *Customs Amendment Act No. 2 1971* (Cwlth), No. 134 1971, s. 2; *Yager v. Queen* (1977) 139 CLR 28, see 45 *per* Mason J., 34 *per* Barwick J., 36 *per* Gibbs J. Only Murphy J. (dissenting), 50, appears to have attempted to give meaning to every word in the section.

25 *Public Health (Prohibited Drugs) Ordinance 1957* (ACT), No. 9 of 1957; Public Health (Prohibited Drugs) Regulations, No. 4 1965 (ACT), r. 3 & Schedule in *Commonwealth of Australia Gazette*, 3 June 1965.

26 Don Chipp (quoting Attorney-General Kep Enderby), in *CPD, Session 1975, Vol. H. of R. 94*, 1859–1861.

27 *Australian*, Sydney: 12 August 1975, 1–2; 13 August 1975, 1.

28 *Public Health (Prohibited Drugs) Ordinance 1975* (ACT), No. 37 of 1975, s. 2 & 4; see also *CPD, Session 1975, Vol. H. of R. 96*, 1186; *CPD, Session 1975, Vol. S. 63 n.s.*, 1125.

29 Correspondence 12 August–12 September 1975; PROV, VA 695; VPRS 6345 Central Administration General Correspondence Files 1920–1981, Z1420.

30 Malcolm Fraser to all State Premiers, 15 July 1976; in Premier's Department (Qld): In-letters—Batch 58: Traffic in Opium and Other Drugs, Part 5.

31 *Customs Amendment Act 1977* (Cwlth), No. 154, 1977, s.10 substituting new *Customs Act 1901–1977* (Cwlth), s.235(2)(c); *Poisons (Drugs of Addiction) Act 1976* (Vic.), No. 9861 1976, s.6, substituting *Poisons Act 1962* (Vic.) No. 6889 1962, s.32(1), (2) & (5), & Sch. 11; Mr Roper, *VPD, Session 1976, Vol. 330*, 5889.

32 Restricted Cabinet Minute, 4 May 1976; Restricted Cabinet Minute, 6 September 1976; Cabinet Decision No. 25104; Queensland Minister for Health, Dr Llew Edwards, to Queensland Premier, Joh Bjelke-Petersen, 21 September 1976; Cabinet Papers, 25 November 1976; in Premier's Department (Qld): In-letters—Batch 58: Traffic in Opium and Other Drugs, Part 5. See *Health Act Amendment Act 1976* (Qld), amending *Health Act 1934–1976* (Qld), s.130(2).

33 See various correspondence in Premier's Department (Qld): In-letters—Batch 58: Traffic in Opium and Other Drugs, Part 4–8; *Courier-Mail*, Brisbane: 20 February 1971 & 12 October 1971.

34 See correspondence with constitutents in Premier's Department (Qld): In-letters—Batch 58: Traffic in Opium and Other Drugs, Part 3.

35 *CPD, Session 1976, Vol. S. 69 n.s.*, 435–6, 614–15, 1510–11; T. Newbery in *QPD, Session 1976–77, 25 & 26 Eliz. II Vol. 271*, 296–7.

36 Statutory declarations by Peter Dimitriou and G.E. Smith; see also other statements quoted in *CPD, Session 1976, Vol. S. 69 n.s.*, 436–40, 1266–7; 1389–90; T. Newbery, in *QPD, Session 1976–77, 25 & 26 Eliz. II Vol. 271*, 297.

37 See statements by P. Dimitriou, G. Smith, G. Carr and D. Dillon, quoted in *CPD, Session 1976, Vol. S. 69 n.s.*, 437–9.

38 Russ Hinze, in *QPD, Session 1976–77, 25 & 26 Eliz. II Vol. 271*, 305; Joh Bjelke-Petersen, quoted in *CPD, Session 1976, Vol. S. 69 n.s.*, 1266; see also T. Newbery, in *QPD, Session 1976–77, 25 & 26 Eliz. II Vol. 271*, 296–7.

39 D. Dillon, quoted in *CPD, Session 1976, Vol. S. 69 n.s.*, 439; Newbery, in *QPD, Session 1976–77, 25 & 26 Eliz. II Vol. 271*, 296.

40 Premier's Department (Qld): In-letters—Batch 58: Traffic in Opium and Other Drugs, Part 7.

41 *QPD, Session 1982–3, Vol. 289*, 2689; K. Stewart, in *NSWPD, Session*

1969–70, 19 Eliz II Ser. 3 Vol. 86, 5346; Mr Roper, in *VPD, Session Comm. 1976,* Vol. 330, 5891.

42 NSW, Parliament, *Memorandum from the Joint Committee of the Legislative Council and Legislative Assembly Upon Drugs, Joint Volumes of Papers,* 2nd Session 1976–77–78, vol. III, Sydney: 1977, 10; Neville Wran in *NSWPD, Session 1976–77–78, 25–26–27 Eliz. II Ser. 3 Vol. 132–3,* 6518, 6518–19, 8836–7.

43 *Poisons (Further Amendment) Act 1977* (NSW), No. 110, 1977; see *NSWPD, Session 1976–77–78, 25–26–27 Eliz. II Ser. 3 Vol. 133,* 7749 *et seq.*

44 Coleman, Whalan and Wran, in *ibid.*, 7775, 7869, 8833 & 8836; Neville Wran quoted in *ibid.*, 7763, 7797, 9962–3, *NSWPD, Session 1976–77–78, 25–26–27 Eliz. II Ser. 3 Vol. 132,* 6518.

45 Australia, Parliament, *Drug Problems in Australia—An Intoxicated Society?* (Report of the Senate Standing Committee on Social Welfare, Senator Peter Baume, Chairman), Parl. Paper 228, Canberra: 1977, 15, 1, 1–17; Recommendations 65–7, 9.

46 Dr Tonkin and Premier Don Dunstan, *SAPD, Session 1976–77,* Vols. 1–2, 1065, 2156.

47 SARC, *Final Report,* see for example 4–38.

48 *Ibid.*, 217 *et seq.* (see also SARC, *The Social Control of Drug Use* (discussion paper), 92–7).

49 *Ibid.*, 300–11, Recommendation 59, 374–5 (see also SARC, *Cannabis* (discussion paper)).

50 For example, see *CPD, Session 1980, Vol. S. 86,* 282–90.

51 See *SAPD, Session 1978–79,* Vols 1–3 and *Session 1979, passim,* for example, *Session 1979,* 216 (14 969 petitioners), 473 (2548 petitioners); Mr Wilson, *SAPD, Session 1978–79,* Vols 1–2, 1411; see also 689, 1545.

52 Des Corcoran in *SAPD, Session 1979,* 25–6.

53 NSW, Parliament, *Progress Report from the Joint Committee of the Legislative Council and Legislative Assembly upon Drugs, Joint Volumes of Papers,* 2nd Session 1976–77–78, Vol. III, Sydney: 1978, 43–4, 105.

54 NSWRC, Vol. 1, 1–2; see also *NSWPD, Session 1976–77–78, 25–26–27 Eliz. II Ser. 3 Vol. 132,* 7114–20.

55 Alfred McCoy, *Drug Traffic,* Sydney: 1980, 299–309; NSWRC, Vols 1–3, and *Further Report, Joint Volumes of Papers,* 3rd Session 1980–1, Vol. II, Sydney: 1980.

56 NSWRC, Vol. 3, 1592, 1576–92, 1672–1977, 1605, 283 *et seq.* The only change Mr Justice Woodward was prepared to recommend was that first offenders should have their criminal records expunged after a certain time: 308.

57 *NSWPD, Session 1979–80, 28–29 Eliz. II Ser. 3, Vol. 150,* 2665.

58 Interview with Senator Peter Baume, 5 September 1989.

59 ARCID, *Book A,* A7; see also Ministerial Statement by Prime Minister Malcolm Fraser in *CPD, Session 1977, Vol. H. of R. 106,* 1659–60.

60 *Ibid.*, 16 colour plates following xx.

61 ARCID, *Book B,* B51–B165 (Narcotics Bureau), B353–B444 (coastal surveillance); *Book C,* C270 *et seq.* (various law enforcement techniques); *Book D* ('A

National Strategy'), D29 *et seq.* (uniform Acts), and Recommendations; *Book F* ('Outlines of Recommended Uniform Legislation').

62 *Ibid., Book C*, C218–C269, C269; *Book D*, Recommendation 159; *Australian*, Sydney: 22 June 1981, in Premier's Department (Qld): In-letters—Batch 58: Traffic in Opium and Other Drugs, Part 8.
63 *CPD, Session 1980, Vol. S. 84*, 757, 758–9, 827.
64 Ministerial Statement, in *CPD, Session 1980, Vol. H. of R. 117*, 865–8; Leader of the Opposition, Bill Hayden, in *ibid.*, 868–73; Leader of the opposition in the Senate, John Button, in *CPD, Session 1980, Vol. S. 84*, 750–4; but see also Dr Neal Blewett, in *CPD, Session 1980, Vol. H. of R. 118*, 1748–51.
65 See *CPD, Session 1979, Vol. H. of R. 114*, 2890, 2902–10.
66 ARCID, *Book B*, Canberra: 1980, B51–B165, B72, B96–7, B93, B162 & B164.
67 Senator Don Chipp, *CPD, Session 1980, Vol. S. 83 n.s.*, 2827 and *CPD, Session 1980, Vol. S. 84 n.s.*, 757; NSWRC, *Vol. 1*, 19–20; NSWRC, *Further Report*, 2171–4; *CPD, Session 1979, Vol. S. 82 n.s.*, 872; Senator Don Chipp, *CPD, Session 1979, Vol. S. 83 n.s.*, 2314.
68 Ralph Hunt, and Victorian Minister of Health, W. Houghton, 8th Meeting of Commonwealth & State Ministers on Drug Abuse, Canberra, 9 June 1978, 23–4, in PROV, VA 695; VPRS 6345 Central Administration General Correspondence Files 1920–1981, Z1350, Meeting of Commonwealth & State Ministers on Drug Abuse; interview with ex-Director, Drugs of Dependence Section, Jean Nolan, Wednesday, 16 August 1989.
69 Interviews with ex-Director-General of Health, Sir William Refshauge, ex-Director, Drugs of Dependence Section, Jean Nolan, ex-Senior Medical Adviser on Drugs of Dependence, and First Assistant Secretary, Medical Services Division, Dr Les Drew; Wednesday, 16 August 1989.
70 *Ibid.*; 'Richard Hill', 'Drugs: Time for Honest Debate', *Medical Journal of Australia* (1980): 188–9, 213–4; see also Les Drew, 'Why are We Concerned About Illegal Narcotic Use?', *Australian and New Zealand Journal of Psychiatry* 13 (1979): 157–8.

9 A Thoroughly Modern Melee

1 NSWRC, *Vol. 1*, 334; *Report of the Inter-Departmental Working Party on the Drug Problem in Victoria, Vol. 1*, Parl. Paper 69, Melbourne: 1980, 23.
2 NSWRC, *Vol. 3*, 1579; ARCID, *Book D*, D31; *Book F* ('Outlines of Recommended Uniform Legislation').
3 NSWRC, *Further Report, Joint Volumes of Papers, 3rd Session 1980–1, Vol. II*, Sydney: 1980, 1865–2198; ARCID, *Book A*, A347–A348.
4 *Customs Amendment Act 1979* (Cwlth), No. 92 of 1979, ss.6, 8, 12 & 16 inserting new *Customs Act 1901–1979* (Cwlth), ss.196A–B (body searches), Division 1a, ss.219A–K (listening devices), amending s.235 (penalties) and inserting new Schedule VIII (commercial quantity).
5 *Customs Amendment Act 1979* (Cwlth), No. 92 of 1979, s.13 inserting new *Customs Act 1901–1979* (Cwlth), ss.243A–S, esp. ss.243A(3), B, D. Compare ss.229 & 229A.

6   Sir William McMahon, Wal Fife & Michael Hodgman in *CPD, Session 1979, Vol. H. of R. 114*, 2610, 2611, 1591 & 2600.
7   Alfred McCoy, *Drug Traffic*, Sydney: 1980.
8   Mr Williams in *VPD, Session 1982–3, Vol. 369 Assembly*, 3531–2, *VPD, Session 1983–4, Vol. 372 Assembly*, 2113, 2115 (italics added); T.W. Roper in *VPD, Session 1983–4, Assembly*, 5294.
9   Royal Commission of Inquiry into Drug Trafficking (Mr Justice Donald Stewart, Commissioner), Canberra: 1983; Minister for Administrative Services, Kevin Newman, *CPD, Session 1981, Vol. H. of R. 122 n.s.*, 2579; *CPD, Session 1982, Vol. H. of R. 127 n.s.*, 1566; see *CPD, Session 1984, Vol. H. of R. 137 n.s.*, 2883–93, *CPD, Session 1984, Vol. H. of R. 139 n.s.*, 1326–35.
10 *Drugs, Poisons and Controlled Substances Act 1981* (Vic.), No. 9719, 1981, ss. 73, 77; see also Drugs, Poisons and Controlled Substances Regulations 1985 (Vic.), S.R. 61, 1985; W. Borthwick, *VPD, Spring Session 1981, Vol. 359*, 925, 926.
11 *Drugs, Poisons and Controlled Substances Act 1981* (Vic.), No. 9719, 1981, Part X, ss.124–8, 125, 86, 87, 94, 78–9, 73–4.
12 *Drugs Poisons and Controlled Substances (Amendment) Act 1983* (Vic.), No. 10002, 1983, s.7 substituting new *Drugs, Poisons and Controlled Substances Act 1981–1983* (Vic.), ss.71–5, 86.
13 *Customs Act 1901–1979* (Cwlth), s.235—maximum penalty life imprisonment; *Drugs Poisons and Controlled Substances Act 1981–1983* (Vic.), No. 9719, 1981, s.71—maximum penalty twenty-five years and in addition 2500 penalty units; *Controlled Substances Act 1984* (SA), No. 52 of 1984, s.32(5)—maximum penalty both twenty-five years and $250 000; *Drug Misuse and Trafficking Act 1985* (NSW), Act No. 226, 1985, ss.23(2), 24(2), 25(2) & 33—maximum penalty life imprisonment or $500 000 or both; *Drugs Misuse Act 1986* (Qld), No. 36 of 1986, s.8—life imprisonment with hard labour 'which cannot be mitigated or varied by a court'; *Drugs of Dependence Ordinance 1989* (ACT), No. 11 of 1989, s.164—maximum penalty life imprisonment.
14 *Drugs Poisons and Controlled Substances (Amendment) Act 1983* (Vic.), No. 10002, 1983, s.7 inserting new *Drugs Poisons and Controlled Substances Act 1981–1983* (Vic.), No. 9719, 1981, ss.85–6; *Controlled Substances Act 1984* (SA), No. 52 of 1984, ss.46, 47(1); *Crime (Confiscation of Profits) Act 1986* (SA), No. 17 1986, s.4(1) & (2); *Drugs Misuse Act 1986* (Qld), No. 36 of 1986, s.33(1) & (2).
15 *National Crime Authority Act 1984* (Cwlth), No. 41 of 1984 as amended; *Telecommunications (Interception) Amendment Act 1984* (Cwlth), No. 6 of 1984 as amended; *Proceeds of Crime Act 1987* (Cwlth), No. 87 of 1987 as amended; *Crimes Legislation Amendment Act 1988* (Cwlth), No. 65 & 66 of 1988.
16 Re internal searches: *Customs Amendment Act 1979* (Cwlth), No. 92 of 1979, s.6; *Drugs Misuse Act 1986* (Qld), No.36 of 1986, s.17. Re listening devices: *Customs Amendment Act 1979* (Cwlth), No. 92 of 1979, s.8; *Telecommunications (Interception) Act* 1979 (Cwlth), No. 114 of 1979 as amended; *Drugs Misuse Act 1986* (Qld), No. 36 of 1986, ss. 24–9. Re warrantless searches: *Drugs Poisons and Controlled Substances (Amendment) Act 1983* (Vic.), No. 10002, 1983, s.7; *Controlled Substances Act 1984* (SA), No. 52 of 1984, s.52; *Drug Misuse and Trafficking Act 1985* (NSW), Act No. 226, 1985, s.37(4); *Drugs Misuse Act 1986* (Qld), No. 36 of 1986, ss.14–15; *Drugs of Dependence Ordinance 1989* (ACT),

No. 11 of 1989, s.184. Re warrantless search of premises: *Drugs Misuse Act 1986* (Qld), No. 36 of 1986, s.18.

17 *Drugs of Dependence Ordinance 1989* (ACT), No. 11, 1989, ss.121–3; *Controlled Substances Act 1984* (SA), No. 52 of 1984, ss.34–40.

18 *Drugs Poisons and Controlled Substances (Amendment) Act 1983* (Vic.), No. 10002, 1983, s.7, substituting new *Drugs, Poisons and Controlled Substances Act 1981–1983* (Vic.), ss.73(1)(*a*), 75(*a*), 76; *Controlled Substances Act 1984* (SA), No. 52, 1984, ss.31, 32(6); *Public Health (Prohibited Drugs) Ordinance 1975* (ACT), No. 37, 1975, s.4; *Drugs of Dependence Ordinance 1989* (ACT), No 11 of 1989, ss.162(2), 171(1).

19 T. Sheahan, in *NSWPD, Session 1984–85–86, 33–34 Eliz. II Ser. 3 Vol. 188*, 10615–17.

20 *Drug Misuse and Trafficking Act 1985* (NSW), Act No. 226, 1985, ss.30–3. A separate penalty ($5000/two years) is provided by s.31, where the amount supplied was in between an 'indictable quantity' and a 'small quantity'. Under s.29, possession of a 'traffickable quantity' (typically ten times a 'small quantity' and half an 'indictable quantity') is deemed to be possession for the purpose of supply. I have described this in-between penalty established by s.31 as relating to 'traffickable' quantities, although a person could be penalised under it for the possession of a much smaller quantity of a prohibited drug or plant, if cultivation, manufacture or supply could actually be proven.

21 Interview with Commonwealth Minister for Community Services and Health, Dr Neal Blewett, 25 October 1989; *CPD, Session 1983, Vol. H. of R. 131 n.s.*, 78.

22 *CPD, Session 1984, Vol. H. of R. 137 n.s.*, 2733; *National Crime Authority Act 1984* (Cwlth), No. 41 of 1984.

23 Interview with Dr Neal Blewett, 25 October 1989; Interview with Dr Les Drew, 16 August 1989; Mick Young in *CPD, Session 1985, Vol. H. of R. 142*, 2775; Official Release from the Special Premiers' Conference on Drugs, Canberra: 2 April 1985, in Val Brown, Desmond Manderson *et al.*, *Our Daily Fix*, Canberra: 1986, 210–14.

24 *Ibid.*, 213, 210.

25 Bray, C.J. quoted in *SAPD, Session 1983–4, Vol. 3*, 2516; *Controlled Substances Act 1984* (SA), No. 52 of 1984, ss.32, 47, 31(2) & 32(6); Mr Oswald in *South Australia Parliamentary Debates, Session 1983–4, Vol. 3*, 3534–5; Dr J.R. Cornwall, *SAPD, Session 1983–4 Vol. 2–3* 1315, 2819; see also *Advertiser*, Adelaide: 10 June 1983, 14 June 1983.

26 *Controlled Substances Act 1984* (SA), No. 52 of 1984, ss.4, ss.34–40.

27 *Ibid.*; J.C. Burdett and Mr Oswald in *SAPD, Session 1983–4, Vol. 3*, 2653, 3535.

28 *SAPD, Session 1983–4 Vol. 1–2*, 449–51, 1314–15.

29 *Controlled Substances Act Amendment Act 1986* (SA), No. 64 of 1986, ss.5 & 8 amending *Controlled Substances Act 1984* (SA), No. 52 of 1984, s.32 and inserting new s.45a.

30 Hon. R.I. Lucas, S.G. Evans & E. Goldsworthy, in *SAPD, Session 1986*, 1139–40, 1533 & 1539.

31 See J. Cornwall and K. Griffin, in *ibid.*, 1144, 1050.
32 Chairman of Committees, *ibid.*, 1632, 1632–5.
33 See Leader of the Opposition, John Olsen, and Speaker of the South Australian House of Assembly, in *ibid.*, 1923, 2180. See also J. Slater, R. Ritson, L. Arnold & J. Olsen, 2177, 1053, 1538 & 1925.
34 *Controlled Substances Act Amendment Act 1986* (SA), No. 64 of 1986, s.5 amending *Controlled Substances Act 1984* (SA), No. 52 of 1984, s.32; Dr Cornwall in *SAPD, Session 1986* (unbound), 1142.
35 Mr Ingerson, in *ibid.*, 2178.
36 Lynn Arnold, in *ibid.*, 1536.
37 *Liquor Acts and Other Acts Amendment Acts 1985* (Qld), No. 81 of 1985, s.16 amending *Liquor Act 1912–1985* (Qld), 3 Geo. V No. 29, s.47A.
38 Bill Gunn in *QPD, Session 1986, 35 Eliz. II Vol. 303,* 277–280; *Drugs Misuse Act 1986* (Qld), No. 36 of 1986, ss.14–18 (searches), 17 (internal searches), 25 (listening devices), 33(1), 33(2) & 34(2) (forfeiture).
39 *Ibid.*, sch. 2.
40 *Ibid.*, ss.5–9.
41 *Ibid.*, ss.5(a), 6(a), 8(a), 8(b), 9(a) & 9(b).
42 *Ibid.*, ss.5(b), 6, 8, 9, 11.
43 *Health Act 1937–1971* (Qld), 1 Geo. VI No. 31, s.130b(1) & (5); *Drugs Misuse Act 1986* (Qld), No. 36 of 1986, s.60 & sch. 6 amending *Health Act 1937–1986* (Qld), 1 Geo. VI No. 31, s.130B(1) and deleting s.130B(5).
44 Mr Cahill, in *QPD, Session 1986, 35 Eliz. II Vol. 303,* 361–2.
45 Angus Innes, *ibid.*, 381, 382.
46 Mr Mackenroth and Mr Vaughan, *ibid.*, 351–4, 374; 439–44 *passim.*

Conclusion: Voices in the Wilderness?

1 *Single Convention on Narcotic Drugs, Signed at New York 30 March 1961,* articles 2(5a) & (5b) and sch. 4; Customs (Prohibited Imports) Regulations (Cwlth), S.R. 1953 No. 56, sch. 1 item 14 in *Commonwealth of Australia Gazette,* 25 June 1953.
2 *Drugs, Poisons and Controlled Substances Act 1981–1992* (Vic.), s.56; *Drug Misuse and Trafficking Act 1985–1992* (NSW), ss.10, 25, 30–2; *Drugs of Dependence Act 1989–1992* (ACT), ss. 59 (methadone), ss. 161(2), 164 (3)& 171 (offences), Part IV, Div. 1 (research or education).
3 *Liquor Act 1992* (Qld), No. 21, 1992, ss.134(b), 136(1g), 251; *Drugs Misuse Act Amendment Act 1990* (Qld), No. 9, 1990.
4 *Drugs of Dependence (Amendment) Act (No. 2) 1992* (ACT), inserting *Drugs of Dependence Act 1989–92* (ACT), s. 171a; see Michael Moore, *ACT Hansard.*
5 *Bulletin,* Sydney: 6 December 1988, 66–74; *ibid.*, 21 August, 1886: 11–14; Chris Eaton in the journal of the Australian Federal Police Association; Ex–Victorian Assistant Police Commissioner Paul Delianis, *Daily Telegraph,* Sydney: February 1989; Law Council of NSW and NSW Bar Association, *Sunday Telegraph,* 26

March 1989; Brian Donovan, Law Council of Australia, Criminal Law Section, in *ibid*; Australia, Parliament, *Drugs, Crime and Society* (Report of the Parliamentary Joint Committee on the National Crime Authority, Peter Cleeland, MHR, Chairman), Parl. Paper 116, Canberra: 1989; interview with Peter Cleeland, 4 September 1989.

6   Senator Peter Baume, Senate speech [no date] 1989; interview with Senator Peter Baume, 5 September 1989.

7   See NSCCDD, 26 March 1971 in PROV, VA 695 Department of Public Health; VPRS 6345 Central Administration General Correspondence Files 1920–1981, Z80 Poisons Act 1962—'Opium'; INCB, *Statistics on Narcotic Drugs for 1979*, New York: 1980; *Report of the INCB for 1982*, New York: E/INCB/61; *Single Convention on Narcotic Drugs*, articles 24 (opium), 25 (poppy straw), 31 (import–export system) & 20(1*d*) (import and export statistics); *Protocol Amending the Single Convention on Narcotic Drugs 1972*, article 9 amending *Single Convention 1961*, article 19; article 10 amending article 20; *Report of the INCB for 1980: Demand and Supply of Opiates for Medical and Scientific Needs*, New York: E/INCB/ 52/Supp., 144–6, 159–62; *Report of the INCB for 1981*, New York: E/INCB/56, 29; *Report of the INCB for 1985: Demand and Supply of Opiates for Medical and Scientific Needs*, New York: E/INCB/1985/1/Supp., 10, 19–21.

8   *UN Convention Against Illicit Traffic in Narcotic Drugs and Psychotropic Substances*, articles 3(5), 5–7, adopted by the *United Nations Conference for the Adoption of a Convention Against Illicit Traffic in Narcotic Drugs and Psychotropic Substances*, Vienna, 19 December 1988; see UN, ECOSOC, E/CONF.82 and related documents.

9   See *ibid*.; reports in *Canberra Times:* 27 June 1989, 3, and 27 September 1989, 9; various conversations with Mr Justice Russell Fox, QC, and Ian Mathews; Ian Mathews and Russell Fox, *Drugs Policy—Fact, Fiction, and the Future*, Sydney: 1992, 69–94.

10 See, for example, early Ministerial Statements on the issue by Dr Neal Blewett, in *CPD, Session 1985, Vol. H. of R. 142 n.s.*, 3083–6, and *ibid., Vol. 154 n.s.*, 1929–37.

11 *Drugs of Dependence Act 1989–1992* (ACT), s.93(1); *Drugs Misuse Act Amendment Act 1987* (Qld), No. 53, 1989, s. 5.

12 Interviews with Peter Cleeland, MHR, 4 September 1989 and Senator Peter Baume, 5 September 1989.

BIBLIOGRAPHY

Acts and Regulations

Only major 'drug' laws which have been used in this book to indicate the broad trends in Australian drug policy are included below. Other Acts and amendments are fully referenced in the text where appropriate. The ordering is chronological by jurisdiction. Although the way in which Acts of Parliament are cited varies slightly between jurisdictions and over time, I have, for the sake of clarity, cited all Acts consistently according to AGPS recommended style.

ACT

Public Health (Prohibited Drugs) Ordinance 1957
Public Health (Prohibited Drugs) Ordinance 1975
Poisons and Dangerous Drugs Act 1978
Drugs of Dependence Ordinance 1989
Drugs of Dependence (Amendment) Act (No. 2) 1992

COMMONWEALTH

Customs Act 1901
Narcotic Drugs Act 1967
Customs Amendment Act 1971
Psychotropic Substances Act 1976
Customs Amendment Act 1979

INTERNATIONAL

Commonwealth of Australia Constitution Act 1901 (UK)
Harrison Narcotic Law 1914, Title 26, USC (USA)
Dangerous Drugs Act 1920 (UK)
Marijuana Tax Act 1937, Title 26, USC (USA)

NEW SOUTH WALES

Opium Duty Act 1857
Sale and Use of Poisons Act 1876
Poisons Act 1902
Police Offences (Amendment) Act 1908
Police Offences Amendment (Drugs) Act 1927
Police Offences Amendment (Drugs) Act 1934
Police Offences Amendment (Drugs) Act 1954
Poisons Act 1966

Poisons (Amendment) Act 1970
Drug Misuse and Trafficking Act 1985

QUEENSLAND
Aboriginals Protection and Restriction of the Sale of Opium Act 1897
Health Act 1937
Health Act Amendment Act 1941
Drugs Misuse Act 1986
Drugs Misuse Act Amendment Act 1990

SOUTH AUSTRALIA
Opium Act 1895
Dangerous Drugs Act 1934
Narcotic and Psychotropic Drugs Act Amendment Act 1974
Controlled Substances Act 1984
Controlled Substances Amendment Act 1986

VICTORIA
Opium Duty Act 1857
Sale and Use of Poisons Act 1876
Opium Smoking Prohibition Act 1905
Poisons Act 1915
Poisons Act 1920
Poisons Act 1927
Poisons (Heroin) Act 1953
Poisons Act 1962
Poisons (Drugs of Addiction) Act 1976
Drugs, Poisons and Controlled Substances Act 1981
Drugs, Poisons and Controlled Substances (Amendment) Act 1983

International Agreements

Agreement Concerning the Suppression of the Manufacture of, Internal Trade in and Use of, Prepared Opium, Geneva, 11 February 1925

Agreement for the Control of Opium Smoking in the Far East, Bangkok, 27 November 1931

Convention for Limiting the Manufacture of and Regulating the Distribution of Narcotic Drugs, and Protocol of Signature, Geneva, 13 July 1931

Convention of 1936 for the Suppression of the Illicit Traffic in Dangerous Drugs, Geneva, 26 June 1936

Convention on Psychotropic Substances, Vienna, 21 February 1971

Convention against Illicit Traffic in Narcotic Drugs and Psychotropic Substances, Vienna, 20 December 1988
International Convention Adopted by the Second Opium Conference (League of Nations) and Protocol Relating Thereto, Geneva, 19 February 1925
Opium Convention, The Hague, 23 January 1912
Protocol signed at Lake Success, 11 December 1946
Protocol Bringing Under International Control Drugs Outside the Convention of 13 July 1931...As Amended by the Protocol Signed at Lake Success on 11 December 1946, Paris, 19 November 1948
Protocol for Limiting and Regulating the Cultivation of the Poppy Plant, the Production of, International and Wholesale Trade in and Use of Opium, New York, 23 June 1953
Protocol Amending the Single Convention on Narcotic Drugs, Geneva, 25 March 1972
Single Convention on Narcotic Drugs, New York, 1961
Treaty of Peace, Versailles, 28 June 1919

Law Reports

Baxter v. Ah Way (1909) 8 CLR 626
Beckwith v. Queen (1976) 135 CLR 569
Bile Bean v. Davidson (1905) 22 Rep. PD & TM Cases 553; (1906) 23 Rep.
DPP v. Brooks [1974] AC 862
Forbes v. Traders' Finance Corp. (1972) 126 CLR 429
He Kaw Teh v. Commonwealth (1985) 157 CLR 523
Hill v. Donohoe (1911) 13 CLR 224
King v. Ah Lin (1909) 8 CLR 325
Kingswell v. Queen (1985) 159 CLR 264
Linder v. USA (1925) 268 US 5
R. v. Bull (1974) 131 CLR 203
R. v. Meaton (1986) 160 CLR 359
Shillinglaw v. Taffs (1897) 23 VLR 525
Sweet v. Parsley (1969) 53 Crim. App. Reps. 221
USA v. Behrman (1922) 258 US 280
USA v. Doremus (1919) 249 US 86
Webb v. USA (1919) 249 96
Williams v. Queen (1978) 140 CLR 591
Yager v. Queen (1977) 139 CLR 28

Parliamentary Papers

In addition to the sources listed below, I have made extensive use of Commonwealth and State *Parliamentary Debates* from 1870 to 1990, as well as various *Votes & Proceedings* and *Gazettes*. References to specific volumes are to be found, where appropriate, in the notes.

COMMONWEALTH

Australia, Parliament, *Another Side to the Drug Debate ... A Medicated Society?* (Further report of the Senate Standing Committee on Social Welfare), Parl. Paper 98, Canberra: 1981

Australia, Parliament, *Drug Problems in Australia—An Intoxicated Society?* (Report of the Senate Standing Committee on Social Welfare, Senator Peter Baume, Chairman), Parl. Paper 228, Canberra: 1977

Australia, Parliament, *Drugs, Crime and Society* (Report of the Parliamentary Joint Committee on the National Crime Authority, Peter Cleeland, MHR, Chairman), Parl. Paper 116, Canberra: 1989

Australia, Parliament, *Opium: Report by the Comptroller-General of Customs*, Parl. Paper 1907-8 vol. 2, Sydney: 1908

Australia, Parliament, *Report from the Senate Select Committee on Drug Trafficking and Drug Abuse*, Parl. Paper 1971 vol. 8, Canberra: 1975

Australian Royal Commission of Inquiry into Drugs (Hon. Justice E.S. Williams, Commissioner), *Report, Books A–F*, Canberra: 1980

Commonwealth & States of Australia, *Conference on Uniform Standards for Food & Drugs*, Sydney: 1910

Commonwealth & States of Australia, *Second Conference on Uniform Standards for Food & Drugs*, Sydney: 1913

Commonwealth & States of Australia, *Third Conference on Uniform Standards for Food & Drugs*, Sydney: 1923

Commonwealth & States of Australia, *Fourth Conference on Uniform Standards for Food & Drugs*, Sydney: 1927

Royal Commission into Customs, & Excise Tariffs, *Report*, Sydney: 1906

Royal Commission of Inquiry into Drug Trafficking (Mr Justice Donald Stewart, Commissioner), Canberra: 1983

Royal Commission on Secret Drugs, Cures & Foods (Octavius Beale, Commissioner), *Report, Vol. 1*, Melbourne: 1907

Royal Commission on Uniform Standards for Foods and Drugs in the States of the Commonwealth of Australia (Dr J. Ashburton Thompson, Commissioner), *Report*, Sydney: 1913

NEW SOUTH WALES

NSW Legislative Assembly, *Report upon Chinese Camps*, Sydney: 1884

NSW Legislative Assembly, *Sydney City & Suburban Sewage and Health Board Eleventh Progress Report*, Votes & Proceedings vol. V, 1875–6

NSW Legislative Council, *Conference on Chinese Question*, Sydney: 1888

NSW Legislative Council, *Report from the Select Committee on Law*

Respecting Practice of Medicine, in *Journal* 1887–8, vol. 43 pt. 4
NSW Parliament, *Memorandum from the Joint Committee of the Legislative Council and Legislative Assembly Upon Drugs,* Joint Volumes of Papers, 2nd Session 1976-77-78, vol. III, Sydney: 1977
NSW, Parliament, *Progress Report from the Joint Committee of the Legislative Council and Legislative Assembly Upon Drugs,* Joint Volumes of Papers, 2nd Session 1976-77-78, vol. III, Sydney: 1978
NSW, Parliament, *Report of the Industrial Commission of NSW on ... Pharmacy Chain Stores* (Mr Justice Browne, Commissioner), Parl. Paper vol. VIII, 1938–40
NSW, Parliament, *Report of the NSW Committee of Inquiry into the Legal Provision of Heroin,* Joint Volumes of Papers, 3rd Session 1980–1, vol. II, Sydney: 1981
Royal Commission into Drug Trafficking (Mr Justice Woodward, Commissioner), *Further Report,* Joint Volumes of Papers, 3rd Session 1980–1, vol. II, Sydney: 1980
Royal Commission into Drug Trafficking (Mr Justice Woodward, Commissioner), *Report, Vols 1–3,* Joint Volumes of Papers, 2nd Session 1979–80, vol. III, Sydney: 1981
Royal Commission on Alleged Chinese Gambling and Immorality (Mayor Manning, Chairman), *Report,* Sydney: 1892

SOUTH AUSTRALIA

Royal Commission into the Non-Medical Use of Drugs (Prof. Ronald Sackville, Chairman), *Cannabis* (discussion paper 2), Adelaide: 1978
Royal Commission into the Non-Medical Use of Drugs (Prof. Ronald Sackville, Chairman), *Final Report,* Adelaide: 1979
Royal Commission into the Non-Medical Use of Drugs (Prof. Ronald Sackville, Chairman), *The Social Control of Drug Use* (discussion paper 3), Adelaide: 1978

UNITED KINGDOM

British Parliamentary Papers, Food & Drugs 1 (1852–5), Irish University Press (facsimile edition), Shannon: 1968
British Parliamentary Papers, Food & Drugs 2 (1857–?), Irish University Press (facsimile edition), Shannon: 1968
British Parliamentary Papers, Health—Medical Profession 1 (1828–34), Irish University Press (facsimile edition), Shannon: 1968
British Parliamentary Papers, Health—Medical Profession 3 (1847–8), Irish University Press (facsimile edition), Shannon: 1968
British Parliamentary Papers, Health—Medical Profession 5 (1882), Irish University Press (facsimile edition), Shannon: 1968
United Kingdom, Parliament, *Report from the Select Committee on Patent Medicines,* Parl. Paper, vol. IX, London: 1914

VICTORIA

Australian Royal Commission of Inquiry into Drugs (Hon. Justice E.S. Williams, Commissioner), *On Matters of Particular Relevance to the State of Victoria*, Melbourne: 1980

Victoria, Parliament, *Report of the Interdepartmental Working Party on the Drug Problem in Victoria vol. 1*, Parl. Paper 69, Melbourne: 1980

Government Archives

COMMONWEALTH (AUSTRALIAN ARCHIVES)

AA (ACT): Attorney-General's Department CA 5; CRS A432 Correspondence Files
——; CRS A456 Correspondence Files
——; CRS A2863 Bill Files 1901–
AA (ACT): Cabinet Secretariat (I) CA 3; CRS A2700 Curtin, Forde & Chifley Ministries 1941–49
——; CRS A4906 4th Menzies Ministry 1954–55
——; CRS A4933 4th & 5th Menzies Ministry 1950–55
AA (ACT): Department of Customs and Excise CA 62; CRS A425 Correspondence Files 1956–75
AA (ACT): Department of External Affairs (I) CA 7; CRS A1 Correspondence Files
AA (ACT): Department of External Affairs (II) CA 18; CRS A981 Correspondence Files 1929–42
——; CRS A989 Correspondence Files 1943–44
——; CRS A1066 Correspondence Files 1945
——; CRS A1838 Correspondence Files
AA (ACT): Department of Health CA 17; CRS A1928 Correspondence Files 1921–49
——; CRS A1658 Correspondence Files (second series)
AA (ACT): Department of Trade and Customs CA 10; CP 46/3 Papers Relating to Opium Traffic 1925–33
——; CP 723/1 Papers Relating to Narcotic Drugs 1929–59
——; CRS A425 Correspondence Files 1935–56
AA (ACT): Prime Minister's Department CA 12; CRS A2 Correspondence Files 1904–20
——; CRS A461 Correspondence Files 1934–50
——; CRS A1608 Correspondence Files 1939–45

NEW SOUTH WALES (ARCHIVE OFFICE OF NEW SOUTH WALES)

AONSW, Attorney-General Special Bundle: Proposed Amendments to Police Offences Act 1904–7, 5/7745.2

——: Working of Inebriates Act 1901–9, 5/7751.1–2
AONSW, Chief Secretary: General Correspondence 1950–59, 12/7816–7977
AONSW, Chief Secretary Special Bundle: Police Offences Amendment (Drugs) Bill 1924–34, 3/2376.2
——: Police Offences (Drugs Acts) Amendment 1928–34, 5/5413–5
AONSW, Colonial Secretary Special Bundle: Chinese 1888, 4/884.1
——: Chinese Immigration 1880–1, 4/829.1
——: Re Sale of Patent Medicines by Grocers 1901, 4/955.4
——: Poisons Bill 1916–30, 5/5397–8
AONSW, Confidential Printed Papers 1870–1901, 2/8095.3
AONSW, Department of Health: Poisons Act and Amendments Parts 1–19, 14/1262–5
AONSW, Pharmacy Board, 7/5189–92
AONSW, Premier's Department: Correspondence Files 1941, 9/3190
AONSW, Premier's Department Special Bundle: Prohibition 1914–22, 7/5929

QUEENSLAND (QUEENSLAND STATE ARCHIVES)

Premier's Department, Queensland, In-letters, Batch 58—Traffic in Opium and Other Drugs 1920–present
QSA, Colonial Secretary's Office, Special Batches—Aborigines COL/140–5
——; Special Batches—Chinese COL/13
QSA, Department of Health and Home Affairs, General Correspondence
——; Special Batches—Health Acts A/27292
QSA, Home Office, General Correspondence
——; Special Batches—Health A/31739–40
QSA, Home Secretary, Special Batches—Food, Drugs and Poisons A/31729–32
——; Special Batches—Health A/31738
QSA, Home Secretary's Department, General Correspondence
QSA, Premier's Department, In-letters 1898–1940
——; Special Batches—Health A/6615–6

UNITED NATIONS

United Nations, Commission on Narcotic Drugs, E/NR. /SUMM. Summary of Annual Reports of Governments
United Nations, ECOSOC, E/CONF. 82, Documents relating to UN Conference for the Adoption of a Convention Against Illicit Traffic
——; E/SR., Economic and Social Council Official Records, Summary Records
——; E/RES., Economic and Social Council Official Records, Resolutions

——; E/CN.7, Economic and Social Council Official Records, Supplement
United Nations, International Narcotic Control Board, E/INCB/? Report of the INCB for [annual publication]
United Nations, International Narcotic Control Board, E/INCB/? Statistics on Estimates for [annual publication]
United Nations, International Narcotic Control Board, E/INCB/? Statistics on Narcotic Drugs for [annual publication]
United Nations, International Narcotic Control Board, E/INCB/? Statistics on Psychotropic Drugs for [annual publication]
United Nations, Permanent Central Narcotics Board, E/INCB/? Statistics on Narcotic Drugs for [annual publication]

VICTORIA (PUBLIC RECORD OFFICE OF VICTORIA)
PROV, VA 860 Chief Secretary's Office, VPRS 3992 Inwards Registered Correspondence Part III
——; VPRS 4723 Inwards Registered Correspondence Part IV
PROV, VA 695 Department of Public Health, VPRS 6345 Central Administration General Correspondence Files 1920–1981
PROV, VA 1349 Pharmacy Board Victoria, VPRS 1774 Correspondence Files 1880–1965
——; VPRS 1867 Legal Opinions 1877–1959
——; VPRS 3620 Annual Reports 1880–1977
PROV, VA 467 Premier's Department, VPRS 1163 Inward Correspondence 1883–1967
——; VPRS 1170 Special Files 1880–1960

Other Primary Sources

In addition to the sources listed below, I have made use of various newspapers including the *Age*, *Argus*, *Bulletin*, *Courier-Mail*, *Daily Mirror* and *Sydney Morning Herald*. References to specific issues are to be found, where appropriate, in the notes.

PUBLISHED

Cheong C., *Chinese Remonstrance to the Parliament and People of Victoria*, Marshall & Co., Melbourne: 1888
Clarke M., 'Cannabis Indica', *Colonial Monthly* 1 [new series] (1868): 454–68
Cole E., *The Pound Pamphlet Word for Word*, Cole's, Melbourne: [no date]
Comptroller-General of Customs, 'Importation of Opium into Australia', *Health 3* (1925): 113–16
Henderson J., *The Opium Slave and Other Verses*, Gordon & Gotch, Brisbane: 1913
'Humanity', *Sketches of Chinese Character*, Beacham, Castlemaine: 1878

Knaggs S., *Common Complaints and Simple Remedies*, Horden, Sydney: 1906
Knaggs S., *Tea Poisoning*, Gibbs, Shallard & Co., Sydney: 1874
Kong Meng L. et al. (eds), *The Chinese Question in Australia*, Bailliere, Melbourne: 1879
Official Report of Anti-Opium Demonstration, Houghton & Co., Sydney: 1894
Rosenberg D., 'The Referendum and Patent Medicines', *Australasian Medical Gazette* (1913): 487–88, 527–8
Rowell E., *Battling the Wolves of Society: The Narcotics Evil*, Signs, Warburton, Vic. 1929
Scarlett M., *The Life of Quong Tart*, Maclardy, Sydney: 1911
Short W., *NSW Pure Food Act 1908*, Turner & Henderson, Sydney: 1910
Speech of Mr Samuel Smith Relative to the Opium Trade with China, Robert Barr, Fitzroy: 1890
Temperance in Australia, Temperance Book Depot, Melbourne: 1889
'The Drugs Act and the Medical Practitioner', *Sydney University Medical Journal* (1929): 85–7
Tart Q., *A Plea for the Abolition of the Importation of Opium*, HT Dunn, Sydney: 1897
Vale J., *Why Dry?*, Temperance Book Depot, Melbourne: 1918?
Victorian Alliance Annual, Barton, Dunn & Wilkinson, Melbourne: 1885–89; Griffith & Co., Melbourne: 1890–94; Modern, Melbourne: 1895–1909
Woodward C., *Peeps into Gaols, Police Courts, Opium Dens*, Australian Baptist Publishing, Sydney: 1933

UNPUBLISHED

Dawson W., Annals of Psychiatry in NSW 1850–1900, Mitchell Lib. MSS. 1418
Hilder E., 120 years of Medical Registration in NSW, Mitchell Lib. Q 610.3/3AI
Langwell's Pharmacy, Pharmaceutical Records 1906–51, Mitchell Lib. MSS. 1563
Lea-Scarlett E., Quong Tart—A Study in Assimilation, Mitchell Lib. MSS. 1669
MacArthur Brown K., Medical Practice in Old Parramatta, Mitchell Lib. A/2684
Morrison G., Correspondence and Papers, Mitchell Lib. MSS. 312
Parkes Sir Henry, Correspondence, Mitchell Lib. A 870-A 910
Tart Q., Petitions and Addresses from the Chinese Community of NSW, Mitchell Lib. Q 325.251/2
G.W., The Humble Plea of the Poor Chinee!!, Mitchell Lib. Q 301.451/23

Secondary Sources

Only selected Australian sources are listed here. Further references can be found, where appropriate, in the notes.

Bell P., *Headlining Drugs*, NSW Drug & Alcohol Education & Information Centre, Surry Hills: 1982
Boreham P. et al. (eds), *The Professions in Australia*, UQP, St. Lucia: 1976
Brown V., Manderson D. et al., *Our Daily Fix*, Pergamon, Canberra: 1986
Carney T., *Drug Users and the Law*, Law Book, Sydney: 1987
——, 'The History of Australian Drug Laws: Commercialism to Confusion?', *Monash University Law Review* 7 (1981): 165–204
Centennial History of the Pharmaceutical Society of Queensland, [no details]: 1980
Commonwealth Department of Health, *Cannabis*, AGPS, Canberra: 1984
Cummins C., *A History of Medical Administration in NSW*, Health Commission of NSW, Sydney: 1979
Davis S., *Shooting Up*, Hale & Iremonger, Sydney: 1986
Drew L. (ed.), *Man, Drugs & Society*, ADFA, Canberra: 1981
Elliott I., 'Heroin: Mythologies for Law Enforcers', *Criminal Law Journal* 6 (1982): 6–43
——, 'Heroin Myths Revisited: The Stewart Report', *Criminal Law Journal* 7 (1983): 333–46
Feehan H., 'Personalities, Professions, and Poisons', *Victorian Historical Journal* 48 (1977): 161–78
——, 'Joseph Bosisto', *Victorian Historical Journal* 50 (1979): 221–36
Fox R. & Mathews I., *Drugs Policy—Fact Fiction and the Future*, Federation Press, Sydney: 1992
Grimwade J., *A Short History of Drug Houses of Australia Ltd*, Hutchinson, Richmond: 1974
Haines G., *The Grains and Threepenn'orth of Pharmacy*, Lowden, Kilmore: 1976
Hicks N., *This Sin and Scandal*, ANU Press, Canberra: 1978
Hirst D., *Heroin in Australia*, Quartet, Melbourne: 1979
Journal of Drug Issues 22 (1992) (3)
Krivanek J., *Heroin—Myths and Reality*, Allen & Unwin, Sydney: 1988
Lonie J., *A Social History of Drug Control in Australia* (Royal Commission into the Non-Medical Use of Drugs South Australia (Prof. R. Sackville, Chairman), Research Paper 8), Gillingham Printers, Adelaide: 1978
Manderson D., 'The First Loss of Freedom: Early Opium Laws in Australia', *Australian Drug and Alcohol Review* 7 (1988): 439–53

——, 'Iatrogenesis? Medical Power and Drug Laws 1900–1930', *Australian Drug and Alcohol Review* 7 (1988): 455–65
——, *Proscription and Prescription* (National Campaign Against Drug Abuse Monograph Series No. 2), AGPS, Canberra: 1987
——, 'Rules and Practices: the "British system" in Australia', *Journal of Drug Issues* 22 (1992): 521–33
——, 'Trends and Influences in the History of Australian Drug Legislation', *Journal of Drug Issues* 22 (1992): 507–20
McLaren I., *The Chinese in Victoria: Official Reports and Documents*, Red Rooster, Melbourne: 1985
McCoy A., *Drug Traffic*, Harper & Row, Sydney: 1980
——, *The Politics of Heroin in South-East Asia*, Harper & Row, New York: 1972
McWhinney A., *A History of Pharmacy in WA*, Pharmaceutical Council of WA, Perth: 1975
Marks R., 'A Freer Market for Heroin in Australia', *Journal of Drug Issues* 20 (1990): 129–74
Pensabene T., *The Rise of the Medical Practitioner in Victoria*, ANU Press, Canberra: 1980
Poynter J., *Alfred Fenton*, Oxford University Press, Melbourne: 1974
Rinaldi F. & Gillies P., *Narcotic Offences*, Law Book Co., Sydney: 1991
Roe M., 'The Establishment of the Australian Department of Health', *Historical Studies* 17 (1976–77): 176–92
Rolls E., *Sojourners: Flowers and the Wide Sea*, University of Queensland Press, St Lucia: 1992
Sekuless P., *The First 50 Years*, Pharmacy Guild, Canberra: 1978
Smith F., *The People's Health 1830-1910*, ANU Press, Canberra: 1979
Starke J., 'The Convention of 1936 for the Suppression of the Illicit Traffic in Dangerous Drugs', *American Journal of International Law* 31 (1937): 31–43
Travers R., *Australian Mandarin*, Kangaroo Press, Netley: 1981
Walker D., 'Continence for a Nation', *Labour History* 48 (1985): 1–14
Wardlaw G. (ed.), *Drug Trade and Drug Use*, ADFA, Canberra: 1982
——, *Drug Use and Crime*, Australian Institute of Criminology, Canberra: 1978
Whitlock, F., *Drugs, Morality and the Law*, University of Queensland Press, St Lucia: 1975
Willis E., *Medical Dominance*, Allen & Unwin, Sydney: 1983
Willis J., 'New Victorian Drug Legislation', *Legal Services Bulletin* 6 (1981): 270–3
Woltring H., 'Examining Existing Drug Policies: The 1988 UN Convention', *Criminology Australia*, April/May 1990: 19–20
Yarwood A. & Knowling M., *Race Relations in Australia*, North Ryde: 1982

INDEX

Abbott, Edward   76, 113
Aboriginals Protection and the Sale of Opium Act 1897 (Qld)   33–4
Aborigines
 opium and   32–6: Chinese and 33–6; legislation in Queensland and South Australia   32–4; segregation   34–5
Ackerman, Jessie   30
addiction
 images of   102, 104–5, 159
 maintenance of by medical prescription   103, 105–9, 133–5: amongst Chinese   135; amongst doctors   108, 133, 144; end of   144–5
 rise and fall of disease model   24, 44, 50, 101–4, 106, 146, 154
 treatment of   144–5, 187, 191, 197; *see also* addiction, maintenance of
 see also medical profession; public health; *and specific substances*
Afghan   17–18
Age, Melbourne   5, 8, 32, 50
AIDS   11, 206
alcoholism and alcohol prohibition   101
 see also temperance movement
amphetamines   144, 148, 157–8, 195
Anslinger, Harry   65, 123
 see also United States, Federal Bureau of Narcotics
APC tablets   136
Argus, Melbourne   80–1
Argyle, Dr Stanley   70, 95–6
Arnold, Lynn   193, 194
Askin, Robin   146
Australian   165
Australian Bureau of Criminal Intelligence   189
Australian Journal of Pharmacy   124
Australian Labor Party   149, 163–5, 168–70, 188–90

Australian Royal Commission of Inquiry into Drugs   174–6, 181

barbiturates   144, 157–8, 195
Barry, W. P.   128
Bates, Harvey   153, 176
Baume, Peter   170, 173, 174, 204–5, 207
Beale, Octavius   52–3, 82, 101
Beckett, W.   75
Bjelke-Petersen, Joh   168, 195
Blewett, Professor Neal   188–9
Bolte, Henry   149–50
Borowski, R. H.   143
Borthwick, W. A.   185
Bosisto, Joseph   56, 57, 85
Bray, Chief Justice Sir John   191
Brennan, Kevin   141
British Medical Association, Federal Council of (Australian branch)   111, 126–7, 129–30
'British system'   *see* addiction, maintenance of
Browne, Justice   91
Bruce, Stanley   71, 74
Bruntnell, Albert   100
Bulletin
 articles: 'The Chinese in Australia' 19–20, 24, 25; 'Mr and Mrs Sin Fat'   26–7
 subjects mentioned: alcohol 51–2; heroin 204; Quong Tart   46, 49
bureaucracy
 general approach of: and early power   65–6, 97, 106, 113, 141; changing role   154, 165–6, 177, 201
 increasing Commonwealth influence   150–2
 see also Customs; Health; Commonwealth–State division of powers
Butchers, C. L.   63

Cairns Drug Action Committee   167
Campden-Main, Anita   167
cane toads   196

Index

cannabis
  patterns of use: in nineteenth century 3; from 1960s 144, 147, 163, 181
  myths and fears about 72–3, 124–5, 146–8, 162–3, 167–8, 192–3; *see also* Australian Labor Party, sexuality and drugs, young people and drugs
  control of 62, 64, 72–3, 104, 125, 142, 147, 160, 164, 168, 196–7
  status under Single Convention 138, 146, 194
  recommendations of commissions of inquiry 169, 170, 171, 174, 175
  law reform 164–6, 168, 186–7, 188–9, 191, 192–4, 204
  see also 'illegal drugs'
Carruthers, Joseph 40
Carter, Godfrey 7
Cedar Bay 166–8
Chaffey, Captain Frank 100
Chemist and Druggist of Australasia 53, 83
chemists *see* pharmacy
Chifley, Ben 121
Chinese
  hostility to 17–20
  opium suitable for smoking *see* Chinese, prepared opium and prepared opium and 20–7 (*see also* opium, prepared): Aborigines and 34–6 (*see also* Aborigines); connections with racism 22–7; discussion of in debates on prohibition 56–8; history of use 45–6; incidence and prevalence 20, 22; sexual mythology 24–6, 27, 27–9, 34; stance of Chinese on prohibition 44–50 (*see also* Quong Tart) after prohibition: and communism 123–4; legally maintained 135 (*see also* addiction); as traffickers 61, 104; as users 68–9, 75–6, 132
Chinese Restriction and Regulation Act 1888 (NSW) 17–18, 22, 46
Chipp, Don 159, 161, 164–5, 175–6, 177
Clarke, Marcus 3
Cleeland, Peter 207
cocaine 102, 109, 132
  use in nineteenth century 5, 8

control of 62, 63–4, 67, 86, 88, 90, 100, 104, 196–7
'crisis' 95–8, 100
Cole, E. W. 50
Commonwealth–State division of powers 11, 39, 66, 67–8, 74, 107, 112–13, 128
  development of Cwlth–State consultative structures 131–2, 141, 149–50, 151–2, 175
  increasing Cwlth encroachment 143, 149–50, 160, 165
  see also bureaucracy; Customs; Health
communism and drugs 123–4
confiscation of assets *see* meta-law provisions
Conroy, Alfred 43, 56
Controlled Substances Act 1984 (SA) 190–1; *Amendment Act 1986* 192–4
Convention Against Illicit Traffic in Narcotic Drugs and Psychotropic Substances 1988 205
Convention on Psychotropic Substances 1971 157–8
Cook, Dr 76
Corcoran, Des 172
Cornwall, Dr John 191, 192–4
Costigan, Frank 184
Courier-Mail 167
CS & IR (CSIRO) 118–19
Cumpston, Dr John 43, 66, 67, 76, 107–8
Cunningham, R. 127, 132
Curtin, John 117
Customs Amendment Act 1979 (Cwlth) 182–3
Customs Amendment Act No. 2 1971 (Cwlth) 160–1, 164
Customs, Commonwealth Department of
  enforcement activities 61, 132, 152, 153, 167, 176
  approach and expanding influence of 65–6, 67–9, 109, 119, 120–1, 134, 150–3
  distrust and decline 151–4, 176–7
  Federal Narcotics Bureau 153, 175, 176–7
  see also Commonwealth–State division of powers; Health

Daily Mirror 129

257

Daily Telegraph 30, 55, 125
dangerous drugs *see* 'illegal drugs';
    and specific substances
Deakin, Alfred 40, 52, 54
Delevingne, Malcolm 71
Devine, Tilly 96
diacetylmorphine *see* heroin
Dibbs, George 17, 18, 31
Dick, Dr 88, 96
Dickie, V. O. 151
doctors *see* medical profession
Drew, Dr Les 178
*Drug Misuse and Trafficking
    Act 1985* (NSW) 188,
    242 n20
drugs of dependence *see* ' illegal
    drugs'; *and specific substances*
Drugs Misuse Act 1986 (Qld)
    195–8; amended 204
*Drugs, Poisons and Controlled
    Substances Act 1981* (Vic.) 185–6;
    Amendment Act 1983 184, 188
Dunstan, Don 171, 172, 192

Earl, Clarence 146
Edwards, Llew 166
Elkington, John 44
Enderby, Kep 165
Ercole, Dr Q. 108
Evatt, Justice Herbert 112

Federal Narcotics Bureau *see*
    Customs
Fife, Wal 183
Fisher, Andrew 63
Fitzgerald, John 87
Fosbery, Edmund 22
Fox, Justice Russell 205
Fraser, Malcolm 166
Fysh, Philip 19

Garran, Sir Robert 63
Gates, S. M. 90
Geneva Convention 1925 71–3, 88,
    97, 117, 119
Geneva Convention 1931 73–4,
    110–11, 122
Geneva Convention 1936 111–13
Germany 62, 118
Gorton, John 151
Great Britain *see* UK
Griffin, K. T. 192
grocers, as drug distributors 81,
    84–5, 90–1
    see also patent medicines
Gunn, Bill 195

Hague Convention 1912 62–3, 117
Hall, Ernest 73
Hamer, Rupert 165
Harrison Act 1914 (USA) 62, 70,
    105
Hawke, Bob 189
Hayden, Bill 160
Health Act 1937 (Qld) 134
Health, Commonwealth Department
    of
    approach of 65, 107–9, 118–19,
        120–1, 178
    changing role and approach of
        153–4, 177–8, 195, 201
    resentment of Customs department
        see Customs
Health (Narcotics) Act 1956 (Vic.)
    131
Henderson, J. Fordel 4
Hensman, Justice 85
heptalgin 122
Herald, Melbourne 95
heroin 209 n6
    control of 62, 63–4, 74, 86, 88,
        107–9, 160, 196–7, 203
    use of, in Australia 110, 111,
        125–6; from the 1960s 144,
        181
    prohibition of: Australian and UK
        opposition to 111, 125–6, 129;
        Commonwealth and State action
        for 126–9; criticism of
        129–31; position in Victoria
        130, 205; UN and US pressures
        110–11, 125, 127
    status under Single Convention
        138
    proposals for law reform 203–6
    see also 'illegal drugs'; AIDS
Hinze, Russ 168
Hodges, Charles Powell 27
Hodgman, Michael 183
Holman, William 43, 55
Holt, Harold 149
Hughes, Billy 69
Hunt, Ralph 177

'illegal drugs'
    cultivation of: illegal 131, 169,
        186, 187; legal *see* morphine
    language dealing with 10–11,
        97–8, 103–4, 104–5, 136, 195,
        201–2, 225–6 n31
    possession of (*see also* cannabis
        law reform): specific offence
        55, 64, 95, 99–100; penalties

Index

64, 95, 99–100, 186–7, 188, 196–7; attitudes to   105, 165, 171, 185; law reform   187, 191–2
proposals for law reform   203–6
schedules dealing with   122, 132, 141–3, 185, 195
social policy issues concerning   10–11, 12–13, 135–6, 163, 184–5, 194, 202, 207
trafficking in: structure of provisions   159–60, 166, 171, 182–3; penalties   142, 160, 166, 169, 182, 185–7, 188, 191, 194, 196–8, 204, 241 n13; attitudes to   98, 159, 161, 169, 174–5, 181, 188; organised crime and   163, 173, 181–2, 183–4, 189, 190, 198, 205–6; *see also* Mr Big, meta-law provisions
see also specific substances
Illustrated Sydney News   6
Innes, Angus   197
Intercolonial Medical Journal of Australia   5
international agreements   *see specific Conventions*
International Narcotics Control Board   137, 157, 203, 205

Jago, A. H.   143, 159
Johnson, William   45, 56
Joint Committee Upon Drugs (NSW)   169, 172
Jones, Professor Hardin   162–3

Katter, Bob   149
Knaggs, Dr Samuel   50

Lambert, Alexander   106
Latham, Chief Justice Sir John   112
laudanum   9–10, 21, 68–9, 86, 135
law, faith in, and assumptions   12–13, 41–3, 53, 66, 99, 147, 192–3, 196, 202–3, 207
see also specific Acts and Regulations
Lazzarini, Carlo   97, 103
League of Nations
  Australian reports to   61, 109, 117
  Health Committee of   73, 119–22, 125
  influence of   70–4
  opposition to heroin   110–11

Leigh, Kate   96
Liquor Acts and Other Acts Amendment Act 1985 (Qld)   195, 204
LSD   144, 148, 157, 195
Lyons, Joseph   74, 76, 111
lysergic acid   *see* LSD

Mackay, Donald   173
Mackay, Inspector   96, 97
Mackenroth, Terry   198
maintenance   *see* addiction
Manning, Nigel   141
marijuana   *see* cannabis
McCormack, William   75
McCoy, Alfred   173, 183
McGirr, Gregory   88
McGirr, James   72, 90, 91, 103, 121
McMahon, William   158, 183
McTiernan, Ernest   95, 112
Medical Journal of Australia   178
medical profession
  authority over 'drugs'   63–4, 81, 86, 91–2, 102–3, 154
  changing status of   5–7, 42, 80–4, 92, 154, 201
  heroin and 126–30; *see also* heroin
  see also addiction
Meere, F. A.   133
Menzies, Robert   117, 149
Meston, Archibald   33, 34–5
meta-law provisions   158–9, 173, 175–6, 181, 182–3, 186–7, 190, 195, 205, 241–2 n16
Metcalfe, A. J.   120–1, 126–7, 126–8
methadone   118, 122, 203
Mills, Stephen   66–7
Mitchell, Commissioner James   105
Moore, Michael   204
morphine   62, 63–4, 66, 86
  legal manufacture in Australia   118–19, 138, 205, 213 n52
  prescribed for addicts   107–9; *see also* addiction
Morris, H.   113
Mr Big   183–4, 187–8, 194, 197–8
Mr Sin   26–7, 101, 184
Munro, James   31

Narcotic Drugs Act 1967 (Cwlth)   150
Narcotic and Psychotropic Drugs Act 1934 (SA)   191
narcotics   *see* 'illegal drugs'; *and specific substances*

259

National Campaign Against Drug
  Abuse   190
National Crime Authority   189, 190
National Health & Medical Research
  Council   127, 131, 133, 141, 145,
  148
National Standing Control
  Committee on Drugs of
  Dependence   151, 152, 160, 166,
  182
Neitenstein, Captain F. W.   101
Newbery, Tom   167–8

O'Connell, Police Constable   95–6
O'Loghlen, Sir Bryan   31
Oakley, R.   75
Ogilvie, Albert   109
opiates
  medical uses and development of
    4–5, 126
  demography of use (*see also*
    specific substances)   4–5, 7–8,
    106–7, 121, 132–3, 143–4, 181
  alleged dangers of   24, 29, 102
  prescribed for addicts
    (maintenance)   *see* addiction
  international control of   73–4,
    122–3, 137, 157–8, 205–6; *see
    also specific Conventions*
  oversupply of, and Australia   205
  see also specific substances
opium
  use in nineteenth century   4–5, 7
  monopolies   21–2, 75–6, 117–18
  control of   63–4, 86, 88, 142
  prepared: Aborigines; and   *see*
    Aborigines; and British colonies
    117–18; campaign against
    40–1; Chinese and   *see* Chinese;
    conference on   40; duty on
    20–1, 30–1, 39; prohibition of
    41, 48, 54–8; proposals for
    prohibition in Victoria   30–2,
    42; White women and   25–6,
    27–30, 40
  suitable for smoking   *see* opium,
    prepared
Opium Act 1895 (SA)   32, 41
Opium Jack   104
Opium Proclamation (Cwlth)
  introduction of   43, 54–5, 57
  changes to   64, 73, 100, 120, 122,
    125, 128
  General Order 1020,   66–8, 108
Opium Protocol 1953   122, 137
Opium Smoking Prohibition

Act 1905 (Vic.)   55–7, 68
organised crime   *see* 'illegal drugs'

Paris Protocol 1948   122
Parkes, Sir Henry   17–18, 21, 45
Parliamentary Joint Committee on
  the National Crime Authority
  204
patent medicines   6, 7, 52–4, 81–2,
  82–4, 86, 90–1
  see also grocers
Pensabene, T. S.   6
Permanent Central Opium Board
  71, 73–4, 117, 119, 125, 131, 137
pethidine   119–21
Pharmaceutical Benefits Act 1951
  (Cwlth)   121
Pharmaceutical Chemists Act 1920
  (Vic.)   86–7
pharmacy
  changing status and role of   6, 83,
    84–7, 90–2
  economics of   86, 90–1
  Pharmacy Boards: behaviour of
    84, 87–90; decline   90, 142–3;
    power of   6, 68, 84–5, 134, 210
    n15
  resistance to legislation   71–2, 88,
    95
Poisons Act 1962 (Vic.)   141–3
Poisons Act 1966 (NSW)   141–3
Poisons Acts 1915–1958 (Vic.)
  63–4, 73, 95, 99–100, 104, 122
Poisons (Amendment) Act 1970
  (NSW)   159–60, 162
*Poisons and Dangerous Drug
  Ordinance 1933* (ACT)   104
*Poisons (Drugs of Addiction) Act
  1976* (Vic.)   166, 169
*Poisons (Further Amendment) Act
  1977* (NSW)   162, 168–9
Poisons (Heroin) Act 1953 (Vic.)
  128
*Police Offences (Amendment) Act
  1908* (NSW)   55–7, 217 n55
*Police Offences Amendment (Drugs)
  Act 1927* (NSW)
  introduction of   64, 72–3, 84,
    88–9, 97
  expansion of   108, 121, 122, 131
*Police Offences Amendment (Drugs)
  Act 1934* (NSW)   90, 100
*Police Offences Amendment (Drugs)
  Act 1954* (NSW)   129
police powers   *see* meta-law
  provisions

Index

poppy straw *see* morphine, legal manufacture
possession *see* 'illegal drugs'
Pratten, Herbert 100
Protocol Amending the Single Convention 1972 157–8
Psychotropic Substances Act 1976 (Cwlth) 158
public health 42, 43–4
  see also disease model
Pure Food Acts (NSW & Vic.) 42, 53–4, 82, 86

Quong Tart 27, 29, 44–50, 57, 61, 215 n23

Refshauge, Sir William 130, 152, 154
Renshaw, Jack 146
Report upon Chinese Camps (NSW) 27–8, 44, 47
Retail Trades Association (NSW) 85
Review of Reviews 47–8
Richardson, H. F. 54
Robinson, Inspector 89–90
Rolleston Report *see* UK
Roper, Tom 184
Roth, Dr Walter 34, 35–6
Rowell, Earle 102, 104
Royal Australian Colleges 127–8
Royal Commission on the Activities of the Federated Ship Painters and Dockers Union (Cwlth) 184
Royal Commission on Alleged Chinese Gambling and Immorality (NSW) 28–30, 45, 47
Royal Commission into Customs, and Excise Tariffs (Cwlth) 34, 48
Royal Commission into Drug Trafficking (NSW) 173–4, 177, 239 n56
Royal Commission of Inquiry into Drug Trafficking (Cwlth) 184
Royal Commission into the Non-Medical Use of Drugs (SA) 171–2, 192
Royal Commission into Secret Drugs, Cures, and Foods (Cwlth) 52–3, 82
Royal Commission on Uniform Standards for Foods and Drugs (Cwlth) 83, 85
Rushton, M. 83

Sackville, Ronald 171, 173

Sale and Use of Poisons Act 1891 (Qld) 32
Sale and Use of Poisons Acts 1876 (NSW & Vic.) 6, 9
Salomons, Sir John 46
Scanlan, Alan 165
Scott, Dr Thomas 24
Scott, Senator 152, 153
Select Committee on the Poisons Bill (UK) 9–10
Senate Select Committee on Drug Trafficking and Drug Abuse 160–1
Senate Standing Committee on Social Welfare 170, 171
sexuality and drugs 24–6, 27, 27–9, 34, 43, 52, 56, 72, 124–5, 148, 162, 195
  see also Chinese
Seymour, Richard 26, 29
Sheahan, Terry 188
Sheehan, William 141, 143
Short, William 101
Single Convention on Narcotic Drugs 1961 137–8, 141, 143, 149–50, 157–8
Smith, L. L. 31–2, 54
Smith's Weekly 72
Special Premiers' Conference on Drugs 190, 192
Starke, J. G. 118, 205
State Drug Crime Commission (NSW) 189
Stewart, Justice Donald 184, 189
Storey, John 51
Sun, Sydney 129
Sunday Times, Sydney 98
Sydney City & Suburban Sewage & Health Board (NSW) 22–3
Sydney Morning Herald 43, 51, 98, 100, 128, 129, 130

Taylor, A. S. 7
temperance movement 8, 50–2
Thompson, Detective-Inspector 88–9
Thompson, Dr J. Ashburton 23, 40, 83, 85
Times, London 129
Tooth, S. D. 147, 148
trafficking *see* 'illegal drugs'
Trainer, John 193
Truth, Sydney 125

United Kingdom
  influence on Australia 70, 70–1,

261

United Kingdom
　influence on Australia (cont.)
　　74, 117
　policies of　62, 117
　Rolleston Report　106, 109
　see also heroin; League of Nations;
　　United Nations
United Nations　119
　Australia: relationship with　138,
　　201, 205–6; reports to　121,
　　131, 132–3
　Commission on Narcotic Drugs
　　119, 122, 123, 125, 136, 137,
　　147, 148
　Division of Narcotic Drugs　119
　Expert Committee on Addiction-
　　Producing Drugs　119, 125–6
　see also heroin; League of Nations;
　　United States of America
United States of America
　Federal Bureau of Narcotics
　　65–6, 70, 105–6, 120, 123–5,
　　152
　influence on Australia　124–5,
　　127–30, 201
　policies of　62, 70, 71, 117–18,
　　122–4, 137–8

　see also heroin; League of Nations;
　　United Nations

Viney, Arthur　153

Wade, Charles　82
Wallace, H. J.　126, 129, 134
war, effect on drug use and policy
　95, 117–18, 144
Whitlam, Gough　164
Whitton, Percy　69, 71
Wickham, Detective-Inspector
　88–9, 98
Williams, M. T.　183–4
Williams, Sir Edward　174–6
Willis, Evan　81, 86
Wollaston, H. N. P.　61
Woodward, Charlie　104
Woodward, Mr Justice　173, 181,
　239 n56
Wran, Neville　169–70, 174

Yee Hing　47–8
young people and drugs　144, 145,
　146–8, 162–3, 167–8
　see also cannabis, LSD